THE LIBERATOR

DANIEL O'CONNELL

THE LIBERATOR

DANIEL O'CONNELL

AND THE

IRISH PARTY

1830-1847

by Angus Macintyre

THE MACMILLAN COMPANY

NEW YORK

The Macmillan Company, New York
Printed in the United States of America

For
J. M. M.

Acknowledgements

FOR USE of a letter in the Melbourne Papers at Windsor Castle, I acknowledge the gracious permission of Her Majesty the Queen.

I wish to thank the Trustees of the National Library of Ireland and the authorities of University College, Dublin, for permission to publish material in their archives. I am also grateful to the staffs of those institutions and of the Public Record Office, Northern Ireland, the Public Record Office, London, and the British Museum.

Quotations from the Melbourne Papers, the Ellice MSS in the National Library of Scotland, the Graham MSS at Netherby, the Hughenden MSS, the Diary of E. J. Littleton, first Lord Hatherton, and material at Hatfield relating to the second Marchioness of Salisbury, I owe in the first instance to Michael Brock Esq., of Corpus Christi College, Oxford. It is a pleasure to record here my debt to his generosity and encouragement. I am indebted to Russell Ellice Esq., Sir Fergus Graham Bt., the National Trust, Lord Hatherton and the Marquess of Salisbury for their kind permission to publish quotations from the other sources listed above, and to the Marquess of Anglesey for allowing me to quote extracts from his book, *One-Leg: The Life and Letters of Henry William Paget, First Marquess of Anglesey* (Jonathan Cape).

I wish to thank Dr. Bruce Graham, Mrs. C. R. Dick and Dr. Theodore Zeldin for their valuable help at different stages in the preparation of this book. I am also most grateful to Mr. Christopher Dorling for his work on the maps.

Magdalen College, Oxford   A.D.M.
October 1964

Contents

ix

Abbreviations

Add. MSS.	Additional Manuscripts, British Museum.
D.E.M.	*Dublin Evening Mail.*
D.E.P.	*Dublin Evening Post.*
D.N.B.	*Dictionary of National Biography.*
F.J.	*Freeman's Journal.*
Hansard	Hansard's Parliamentary Debates, Third Series.
H.O.	Home Office.
N.L.I.	National Library of Ireland, Dublin.
N.L.S.	National Library of Scotland, Edinburgh.
P.P.	Parliamentary Papers.
P.R.O.	Public Record Office, London.
U.C.D.	University College, Dublin.

For the author, full title, date and place of publication of those works cited, after the first instance, in shortened form, see Bibliography.

Introduction

IRELAND and its problems profoundly influenced the political history of Great Britain in the nineteenth century. The Act of Union of 1800, by conferring legislative and governmental responsibility for Ireland on the Parliament of the United Kingdom in which Ireland was granted its own, not ungenerous share of representation, was an attempt at a final settlement of the old problem of Anglo-Irish relations. In reality the Union created what nineteenth-century Englishmen called 'the Irish Question', confronting the English people, Parliament and Government with complex and inescapable issues of a kind largely foreign to English experience and scarcely calculated to enlist English sympathies. In 1843, the economist Nassau William Senior wrote gloomily and presciently that when 'the Irish Question . . . has been forced on our attention we have felt like a dreamer in a nightmare, oppressed by the consciousness that some great evil was rapidly advancing—that mere exertion on our part would avert it, but we had not the power to will that exertion'.[1] On a more mundane level, the diarist Charles Greville saw the impact of Ireland on the structure of politics as confusing and disruptive, 'a vast babel of conflicting opinions and hostile passions and prejudices' which created 'innumerable sub-divisions upon all Irish matters' inside the main party divisions.[2]

The Catholic question provided the first great test of the Union settlement. The grant of Catholic Emancipation in 1829, conferring on Daniel O'Connell the title of 'the Liberator' and giving him the most spectacular political triumph of his career, also opened the way for the formation under his leadership of the first Irish nationalist party in the House of Commons. In Irish history, the period

[1] Nassau William Senior, *Journals, Conversations and Essays relating to Ireland* (1868), I, 18.

[2] *The Greville Memoirs: A Journal of the Reigns of King George IV, King William IV and Queen Victoria*, by Charles Greville, ed. Henry Reeve (1913): *Journal*, 26 January 1844, V, 225–6.

which saw the rise and fall of this party, the period from Emancipation to the Famine, seems to possess a definite organic unity. The country's problems between 1830 and 1847 differed in urgency, degree and even in kind from those confronting her when she finally emerged from the terrible catastrophe of the Famine. Indeed the failure of successive Governments in this period to find adequate solutions to the main and inter-related problems of the population and the land system undoubtedly condemned Ireland to that brutal remedy and its consequences. Yet this failure was not the result of mere indifference. The age of O'Connell witnessed a series of important reforms in Ireland, undertaken by Governments partly in obedience to current ideas about economics and society but also, in a more tangible and immediate fashion, in response to the presence and activity of the O'Connellite party in Parliament. It might indeed be said that by these measures Ireland was hauled into nineteenth-century Great Britain and left there ill-equipped to withstand its powerful and destructive pressures.

There exists no study devoted principally to the history of the Irish party under O'Connell. Even the best general surveys of the period, such as R. B. McDowell's *Public Opinion and Government Policy in Ireland, 1801-46* (1952) or George O'Brien's *The Economic History of Ireland from the Union to the Famine* (1921), cannot supply the focus and detail required, while the numerous biographies of O'Connell himself necessarily treat the period and the party too exclusively in terms of their subject's own remarkable career and personality.[1] While the great extra-parliamentary movements for Catholic Emancipation and Repeal of the Act of Union have been studied and O'Connell's original and important contributions to the techniques of mass political organization are now well enough known,[2] this interest in O'Connell as an agitator and popular leader

---

[1] The most useful biographies are William Fagan, *The Life and Times of Daniel O'Connell* (1848), near-contemporary, uncompleted but accurate; Michael MacDonagh, *Daniel O'Connell and the Story of Catholic Emancipation* (1929); Denis Gwynn, *Daniel O'Connell* (1929); and Seán Ó Faoláin, *King of the Beggars* (1938), an eloquent and provocative portrait. There is also a symposium, *Daniel O'Connell: Nine Centenary Essays*, ed. Michael Tierney (1947).

[2] See, in particular, James Reynolds, *The Catholic Emancipation Crisis in Ireland, 1823-1829* (1954); John F. Broderick, S. J., 'The Holy See and the Irish Movement for the Repeal of the Act of Union with England, 1829-47', *Analecta Gregoriana*, LV (1951); and Denis Gwynn, *Young Ireland and 1848* (1947), 1-97.

has tended to obscure the long middle section of his career and to distract attention from his leadership of the first Irish party in Parliament.

Why was Daniel O'Connell the leader of this party? The question cannot be answered without some knowledge both of O'Connell's early life and career and of the revival of Irish political consciousness during the struggle for Catholic Emancipation. Chapter One thus provides an indispensable prelude to the account, in Chapter Two, of the rise of the Irish party between 1830 and 1833, the first of the main themes of this book. The role of the O'Connellite party in the Irish political system and in the wider sphere of British politics form the themes respectively of Chapters Three and Four. In Chapters Five, Six and Seven, which deal with the three most important Irish issues confronting Parliament between 1835 and 1841, I have tried to set the party against the economic and social background of Ireland, to establish the attitudes of the party, its leader and Irish opinion to these issues and to show how these problems and the attempts to solve them influenced English parties and politicians. The final theme (in Chapter Eight) is the decline, disintegration and eventual collapse of the O'Connellite party and movement in the years which saw the revival of mass nationalist agitation in Ireland, the great political crisis over the repeal of the Corn Laws and the coming of the Famine.

Whatever the final judgement on O'Connell's party, there can be no doubt of its success as a political pressure group. From the conclusion in 1832 of the struggle for Parliamentary Reform until the effective rise of Chartism and the Anti-Corn Law League in the early 1840's, the Irish Question formed a central theme of British politics. An Irish policy first divided and finally disrupted the Whig Government of Earl Grey, largely caused the dismissal of its successor under Lord Melbourne and destroyed Sir Robert Peel's Conservative Government in 1835. Melbourne's long second Administration was dominated and bedevilled by its relationship to the Irish party and by its programme of Irish legislation. After 1841, the noticeable decline in the preoccupation of Parliament with Irish issues was partly the consequence of the decline of the Irish parliamentary party. With the Repeal movement, rising to its climax in 1843, the centre of gravity in Irish politics shifted decisively from Parliament to Ireland; and although Ireland provided the pretext for the repeal of the Corn Laws as well as the occasion for the destruction of Peel's Government, Peel's Irish policies owed little directly to the pressure of a strong or united Irish party in the House of Commons.

Although this book is not intended as another biography of O'Connell, it is impossible to dissociate the first Irish party from the personality and reputation of its leader. For over thirty years O'Connell dominated Irish politics, commanding a support and wielding an authority which was scarcely questioned until the last years of his life, and for most of this period he played a leading and highly controversial part in British politics. Like Charles Stewart Parnell, O'Connell ended his career in the corrosive and, in Irish politics, all too-familiar atmosphere of bitterness and failure, but unlike Parnell, he left behind no lasting romantic image. The hideous tragedy of the Famine, which swept away so much of the old populous Ireland, seemed also to obliterate the memory of a great reputation, and few Irish people today would regard O'Connell, unreservedly, as the most remarkable political leader ever produced by Catholic Ireland. Men may agree with the judgement of the historian Sir Llewellyn Woodward (and of Charles Greville) that the Liberator's 'best work for Ireland was done before 1830'.[1] If this verdict is not necessarily to be reversed, it will at least be valuable to understand the grounds for it.

[1] E. L. Woodward, *The Age of Reform, 1815–1870* (1962), 341; Greville, *Journal*, 7 June 1847, VI, 88–9.

CHAPTER I

The Making of the Liberator

DANIEL O'CONNELL was born on 6 August 1775 at Carhen House, a mile north of the small town of Cahirciveen in County Kerry. His father, Morgan O'Connell, had established himself at Carhen after his marriage to Catherine O'Mullane of Whitechurch, County Cork, whose family owned a freehold estate of £300 a year near Mallow; but the O'Connell family itself had long been settled in south-west Kerry, notably in the peninsula which included the baronies of Iveragh and the two Dunkerrons and formed one of the most westerly points of Europe. This beautiful but inhospitable land between Dingle Bay and the mouth of the Kenmare River was 'the O'Connell country'; and it is important, for any understanding of Daniel O'Connell's character and career, to determine at the outset the nature of his family and class background.

He was certainly not, as is sometimes supposed, either a peasant or of peasant stock.[1] The O'Connells were an old Catholic gentry family which had produced High Sheriffs of Kerry from the time of Edward VI until the reign of James I, when Maurice O'Connell of Bally Carbery held the office. The family's history during the later seventeenth century was chequered, the head of the sept being transplanted under the Cromwellian settlement to County Clare where he founded a Catholic landed family, but in the generation before O'Connell himself, the O'Connells of Kerry produced two quite distinguished figures. One of O'Connell's uncles, Daniel Charles, Count O'Connell, rose to the rank of General in the French army, had also been a Colonel in the English service and as a devoted

[1] Cf. E. J. Hobsbawm, *The Age of Revolution* (1962), 138.

servant of the Bourbons, refused to take the oath of allegiance to Louis Philippe in 1830. Another uncle, Moritz, Baron O'Connell was for nearly sixty years until his death in 1830 Chamberlain to three Emperors of Austria.[1]

Locked away in their remote county, the family had contrived, despite the Penal Laws against Catholics, to retain part of their lands, in particular the mountain estate of Glencara with its house of Darrynane near the shores of Cahirdonnel Bay. Even before Catholics were legally allowed in 1782 to buy freehold land, Maurice O'Connell, the head of the family, was enlarging his estate through the trusteeship of a conforming Protestant kinsman. Little is known of Daniel's father, a landowner in a small way who also kept a store in Cahirciveen, the most profitable purpose of which was the handling of contraband silks, laces and wines smuggled in from the coast. The most important figure in Daniel's early life was certainly his uncle Maurice, 'Old Hunting Cap', who combined in one person the characters of tribal patriarch, hard-headed landlord and grazier, and successful smuggler. Once Deputy Lieutenant of the county and a fervent loyalist, Maurice O'Connell personified the transition from an old Gaelic, tribal society to the new, harsher and Anglo-Irish world of landlords and tenantry. He adopted the young O'Connell as his heir, paid for his education abroad at the English Colleges of St. Omer and Douai between 1791 and 1793, supported him during his preparation for the Bar at Lincoln's Inn and finally left his nephew the house and estate of Darrynane, worth then about £1,000 a year, in 1825.

The political conservatism instilled into the young O'Connell by his family background and by an education under priests of the *ancien régime* was temporarily reinforced by some direct experience of the French Revolution.[2] But two years as a law student in London

---

[1] For the family's history, see Mrs. Morgan John O'Connell, *The Last Colonel of the Irish Brigade, Count O'Connell, and Old Irish Life at Home and Abroad* (1892); articles in *D.N.B.* on Count Daniel and Baron Moritz O'Connell; MacDonagh, *O'Connell*, 2 ff.; Edward MacLysaght, *Irish Families: Their Names, Arms and Origins* (1957), 85–6; John Burke, *A Genealogical and Heraldic History of the Commoners of Great Britain and Ireland* (1835), II, 565–9.

[2] The revolutionaries, who suppressed the English colleges, subjected O'Connell and his brother to some rough treatment on their departure from France, which they left on the day of Louis XVI's execution. O'Connell always retained vestiges of his continental education, pronouncing the word Empire, for instance, as 'Empeer'.

between 1794 and 1796 proved an effective antidote. Under the influence of the works of Voltaire, Rousseau, Gibbon and Paine, he passed through a period of religious scepticism and deism which left him, even after he recovered his faith, with a lasting concern for toleration. Libertarian doctrines were provided by William Godwin's works, notably *An Enquiry Concerning Political Justice* and *Caleb Williams, laissez-faire* economics by Adam Smith; and the trial of Thomas Hardy and the members of the Corresponding Society in 1794 played an important part in his conversion to liberalism.[1] O'Connell was a true heir of the Enlightenment and the Revolution. After his years in London, the principles of civil and religious equality, freedom of conscience and speech and economic individualism had sunk deeply into his mind. In no sense an intellectual and with almost no interest in art or literature (though he apparently enjoyed the novels of Dickens and sometimes indulged a taste for theological disputation), he never analysed in any detail his views on politics and society.[2] All the stock liberal doctrines, in their most optimistic and sometimes in their crudest forms, were for him self-evident truths, and it needed only the later influence of Benthamite utilitarianism to turn him, in Gladstone's words, into 'as thorough an English Liberal, as if he had had no Ireland to think of'.[3]

O'Connell's nationalism was grounded in the political experiences of Ireland during his early manhood. He was called to the Irish Bar in May 1798, on the day when Lord Edward Fitzgerald was arrested in Dublin; less than two years later, the Irish Parliament whose legislative independence had been won in 1782 voted away its own existence. If O'Connell was too young to play any part in the events of 1798–1800, he was the right age to be decisively influenced by them. Although he sympathized strongly with the United Irishmen's programme of Parliamentary Reform and Catholic Emancipation and was probably a member of that body, he was horrified by the effects of the Rebellion of 1798 and, then and later, regarded any attempt at armed rebellion as a disastrous mistake.[4] On the other

[1] See *Daniel O'Connell: His Early Life and Journal, 1795–1802*, ed. Arthur Houston (1906), a fascinating case-history of the making of a Radical.

[2] His single attempt at history, *A Memoir of Ireland, Native and Saxon* (1843), was a failure, and is indeed almost unreadable.

[3] W. E. Gladstone, in *The Nineteenth Century*, XXV, No. 143 (1889), 156.

[4] He was a Freemason until 1801, and at the time of Emmet's Rebellion in 1803 joined the loyalist Lawyers Artillery Corps.

hand, he strongly opposed the passing of the Union in his first public speech outside the law courts; and in doing so, on the grounds that the Irish Parliament despite its exclusively Protestant character would pass Catholic Emanicipation, he was also opposing the politics of his uncle and family who believed, like many other Catholics, that Pitt would keep his promise to carry Emancipation through the United Kingdom Parliament.[1]

Patriotic and Catholic politics were in these early years quite secondary to the pressing claims of a legal career and a rapidly growing family. In 1802, he made what his uncle regarded as an improvident love-match with his cousin Mary, the daughter of Edward O'Connell, a doctor in Tralee; a first child Maurice was born in 1803, followed by Morgan in 1804 and later by three daughters and two more sons. O'Connell's remarkable legal career, based on practice in the Four Courts in Dublin and at the assizes of the Province of Munster in both equity and at common law, was the reward of prodigious energy, native wit and knowledge of peasant character, and of great skill (and unscrupulousness) in cross-examination. It was also a tribute to good health and formidable powers of work. For twenty-five years, until he was over fifty, he rose at 4 a.m., did three and a half hours' work before breakfast and put in over eleven hours' legal and political work during the day on an average of six hours of sleep.[2] His professional income rose steadily from £60 in 1799 to £420 in 1800, £775 in 1804, £1,077 in 1806, £2,598 in 1808 and £3,808 in 1814, until by 1828 he was earning the spectacular sum of between £6,000 and £7,000 a year.[3]

The Bar occupied a peculiarly important position in Irish society. Closely connected by long tradition with politics, particularly with radical and nationalist politics, it was one of the few professions in which an able and ambitious Catholic could compete on level terms

[1] The family's view was the better Catholic politics at the time, O'Connell's the better nationalist doctrine. His speech in 1800 to a Catholic meeting in Dublin, though of no importance at the time, proved decidedly useful later. 'It was the Union', he used to say, 'which first stirred me up to come forward in politics.'

[2] MacDonagh, O'Connell, 126.

[3] MacDonagh, op. cit., 46–7, 198. Figures for 1822–8 are given by Reynolds, Catholic Emancipation Crisis, 38, n. 16, which show that O'Connell earned £34,715 in fees in these seven years. The figures for 1828 are taken from O'Connell to Bentham, 3 August 1828, O'Connell MSS, N.L.I. 5759.

with Protestants, even if before 1829 he could not expect final recognition of success in the shape of promotion to the Bench. The Bar offered a career open to the talents in conditions of full publicity, in a country and among a people for whom law courts and litigation were objects of the most passionate interest. Moreover from 1801 until at least 1829, the law courts to some extent filled the gap left in Irish political life by the disappearance of the Irish Parliament, which had been, for all its exclusive character, the one great national institution in the country; and in one vital respect, the Bar, in admitting members of the rising Catholic middle class, was more representative of the country than Grattan's Parliament had ever been.

O'Connell's careers in law and in politics were therefore closely related. Fame and popularity as an advocate were vital factors in his rise to the political leadership of the Irish Catholics, while political importance greatly increased the scope of his legal practice. It was not coincidental that his professional income first mounted rapidly between 1806 and 1809, with the first serious revival of the Catholic movement since the Union and with his own rise to prominence in it. Barristers like Denis Scully, Richard Lalor Sheil and O'Connell himself were now beginning to challenge the highly conservative and largely aristocratic monopoly in Catholic leadership. Plausible, self-confident and ingenious, trained in a hard oratorical school, barristers formed a professional group inside the Catholic body whose influence was generally thrown on the side of radicalism and action and who were well placed to publicize the Catholic cause in the course of their profession. On several occasions, notably in the case of *Rex v. John Magee*, the editor of the liberal *Dublin Evening Post* charged in 1813–14 with seditious libels on the Viceroy (the Duke of Richmond) O'Connell used a defending brief to publicize the Catholic movement in the most dramatic way, uttering in his savage assault on the Government much worse libels than those under complaint.[1] 'The Counsellor' was the first and not the least deserved of O'Connell's popular titles.

The whole issue of Catholic Emancipation, for more than twenty years the most controversial problem in British politics, turned on the exclusion of Catholics from what has been aptly called 'the state in its institutional aspect'.[2] The victory of 1829 marked in one sense simply the end of a long process by which, from the mid-

---

[1] So violent was O'Connell's speech in 1814 that Magee repudiated his own counsel. [2] Norman Gash, *Mr. Secretary Peel* (1961), 138.

eighteenth century onwards, the social and political structure of the Penal Laws was slowly but surely dismantled.[1] After 1793, when the great Act of the Irish Parliament admitted Catholics to both the municipal and parliamentary franchises, Catholics were legally barred only from membership of Parliament and the Privy Council and from those higher legal and political posts (such as judge and sheriff) whose holders were required to take the oath of supremacy and to make a declaration against transubstantiation, although they would also have been required to assert that the invocation of Saints and the sacrifice of the Mass were idolatrous. It was of course a question not merely of legal eligibility but of political power and administrative practice, of breaking the grip of the Protestant Ascendancy on the state in Ireland.

The crucial event in the history of the Irish Catholic movement was the founding of the Catholic Association in 1823. Previous Catholic bodies had been small, middle class affairs composed of gentry, merchants, barristers and journalists, often unable or unwilling to evade the rigorous laws (such as the Irish Convention Act of 1793) concerning elective, representative organizations, and for the most part confining their activities to the decorous presentation of annual petitions for relief to Parliament. In 1813 and 1814, divisions in the movement came to a head on the question of the Veto, the most important of the religious securities with which Henry Grattan in his Bill of 1813 planned to accompany Emancipation. O'Connell, with the support of the Irish hierarchy and clergy, strongly opposed any attempt to control the Church by giving the State a veto on the appointment of bishops, while many laymen, including aristocratic leaders of the Catholic community like the Earl of Fingall and Lord Gormanstown as well as lawyers like Sheil, were ready to take the Veto as the price of settlement. This deep split, masking a struggle for power within the movement, was not healed until O'Connell's emergence as undisputed leader and the adoption, on 10 May 1823, of a scheme worked out by O'Connell and Sheil for a new Catholic organization.

The Catholic Association at first differed from earlier bodies only in the legal ingenuity displayed in its constitution. But in February 1824 O'Connell sponsored a plan for the creation of a large and

[1] Reynolds, *Catholic Emancipation Crisis*, 7–8, gives a convenient summary of the legislation affecting landownership and inheritance, education and the Catholic clergy after 1750.

permanent fighting fund, in theory as much as £50,000 a year, to be organized nationally and used to further the Association's political demands as well as for religious and educational purposes. The 'Catholic Rent' was an immediate and astonishing success, transforming a middle-class club in a few months into a national mass movement. Members of the Association paid annual subscriptions of £1 or more, associates as little as a penny a month. By the autumn of 1824, over £300 was being collected weekly; by March 1825 £13,000 was already invested in government funds; and in 1828, with the Rent bringing in a total of £22,700, the Association contained 15,000 members and some three million associates.[1] O'Connell was now the undisputed leader of a great political *levée en masse*. The Association with its headquarters at the Corn Exchange in Dublin represented a triple alliance of the Catholic middle class, priesthood and peasantry, with some support from sections of the Protestant gentry and intelligentsia; and if its immediate aim was Emancipation, it was also a vehicle for all the country's discontents and grievances, from the conditions of land tenure and rents to tithes and church rates, education and the administration of justice. It could not be snuffed out by legal action. The first Association, suppressed in March 1825 by the Government, was re-formed in July as the New Catholic Association.

This formidable movement confronted a vulnerable political system. Most of the Irish borough constituencies, where the franchise was confined to small, oligarchical corporations, were securely in the hands of private patrons who, by one calculation, returned 21 of the 35 borough M.P.s before 1832;[2] but the counties with their large freeholder electorates offered a most promising field for intervention. Most of the 64 county M.P.s were returned by or were members of the predominant, local landed families, but the power of these electoral interests depended on their control of the forty-shilling freeholders, the overwhelming majority of whom were Catholics. If this control were challenged, if the freeholders revolted against their Protestant landlords, the most important part of the electoral system would at once collapse. There was no power to which the landlords could appeal for support. They could not conceivably evict and thus disfranchise freeholders on the scale which would be required; even on a small scale, such a policy was fraught

[1] Reynolds, op. cit., 28, 30, 61–2; Gash, *Peel*, 385.
[2] McDowell, *Public Opinion*, 44–5.

with disagreeable social consequences. Nor could the landlords look to the Irish Government, which possessed only a limited quantity of electoral influence even in normal times and would certainly be as powerless as the landlords.

The General Election of 1826 provided the first unmistakable proof that Tory and anti-Catholic landed influence was no match for organized Catholic numbers. Notably in Waterford and Louth but also in County Dublin, Roscommon, Westmeath and Monaghan, the freeholders, whipped up by agitators from Dublin and led to the polls by their priests, threw over their landlords and returned emancipationist candidates. Yet these successes were not the result of a deliberate policy on the part of O'Connell and the Association. Thomas Wyse, the chief architect of victory in Waterford against the powerful Beresford interest, had little or no initial encouragement from the central organization, although O'Connell did come down to campaign for Villiers Stuart, the emancipationist candidate. The success in Louth of Alexander Dawson, a small landowner and barrister, was a still more independent effort, although priests and individual agitators like Sheil were once again prominent. In the other counties, emancipationist successes owed far more to the activity of local priests and to the support of friendly local interests than to the policy of the Association or its leaders in Dublin.[1]

Peel in London, recognizing at once the potential significance of these isolated victories, saw the possibility of a revolution 'if one of the remaining bonds of society, the friendly connection between landlord and tenant, is dissolved'.[2] O'Connell was quite as impressed and probably more surprised. In 1825, he had actually agreed in London to the disfranchisement of the forty-shilling freeholders as one of the 'wings' (the other being state payment of the Catholic clergy) attached to Sir Francis Burdett's Emancipation Bill, which passed the Commons by 248 votes to 227 before being thrown out by the Lords. After Waterford and Louth, O'Connell hurriedly and publicly recanted his opinion of the political servility of the freeholders and used part of the Association's funds to compensate voters who had been evicted by their landlords.

[1] For these elections, see Reynolds, *Catholic Emancipation Crisis*, 94–6; J. J. Auchmuty, *Sir Thomas Wyse, 1791–1862* (1939), 81–96; Richard Lalor Sheil, *Sketches Legal and Political*, ed. M. W. Savage (1855), I, 167–82; McDowell, *Public Opinion*, 104–5.

[2] Peel to Sir George Hill, 18 July 1826, Peel Papers, Add. MSS 40388, 66.

During the period of extreme political uncertainty following the retirement of Lord Liverpool in March 1827, the break-up of his Government and its replacement by the short Canning and Goderich Ministries, both favourable to Emancipation, O'Connell's policy was one of cautious restraint. But the formation in January 1828 of the Duke of Wellington's Government, with Peel, hitherto the leading opponent of the Catholic claims, as Home Secretary, was the signal for an impressive display of the power of the Catholic Association, when simultaneous protest meetings were held under its aegis in two-thirds of the Irish parishes. In the same month of January, the Association resolved to oppose all supporters of the Wellington Government, whether or not such men were also opposed to Emancipation; and in May the Association, in a rare fit of independence, refused to accept O'Connell's suggestion that this resolution be revoked as a gesture of gratitude for the Government's acceptance of the repeal of the Test and Corporation Acts. The incident was not unimportant. When in June 1828 William Vesey Fitzgerald was appointed President of the Board of Trade and thus obliged to stand for re-election in his County Clare seat, the Association was committed to opposing him.

O'Connell's decision to stand for Clare was reached only after considerable and justified hestitation. There was certainly no legal bar to a Catholic's candidature, but equally there were no precedents for centuries. Vesey Fitzgerald was on paper a powerful candidate, an experienced politician who had held the seat since 1818, an emancipationist, a kind and popular landlord who was certain to be supported by the main landed interests and the son of a former M.P. for Clare who had been a follower of Henry Grattan.[1] In reality, once O'Connell had taken the field Fitzgerald's defeat was certain. Under the leadership of priests and agitators, disciplined voting squads of forty-shilling freeholders swamped the gentry and £50 voters and after a five-day poll remarkable for its orderliness and sobriety, swept O'Connell to victory by 2,057 votes to 982. 'All the great interests broke down', the appalled Fitzgerald wrote to Peel, 'and the desertion has been universal. Such a scene as we have had! Such a tremendous prospect as it opens to us . . . The organization

[1] Vesey Fitzgerald had been M.P. for Ennis (1808-12, 1813-18), Co. Clare (1818-28), a Lord of the Treasury (1809-12, 1812-17), Chancellor of the Exchequer in Ireland (1812-16) and Postmaster-General (1826-8). He was created a peer in 1835 and was later President of the Board of Control (1841-3).

exhibited is so complete and so formidable that no man can contemplate without alarm what is to follow in this wretched country.'[1]

For Wellington and Peel, O'Connell's victory was decisive. Clare showed that Waterford and Louth had not been exceptional. The Irish landlords, Whig and Tory, seemed rapidly to be losing all political control over their tenantry to O'Connell and the Association, who would at the first opportunity go on to attack the whole Irish county representation. Not only would many Catholics be elected who could not legally take their seats but also, even more serious, it seemed to the Government that the end of the political influence of property would mark the beginning of social revolution. Public order and the structure of society itself could only be maintained by the immediate concession of Emancipation.

The final settlement was a strange blend of generosity, calculation and pessimism. It completely satisfied the Catholics' demand for civil equality, throwing open to them all public offices except those of Regent, Lord Chancellor of England and Ireland, and Lord Lieutenant in Ireland. None of the fundamental ecclesiastical securities, which had clogged all earlier proposals, were demanded. New or revised oaths for public office satisfied Catholic scruples. But two political securities, only one of which could be regarded as permanent, were exacted. A separate Act disfranchised the forty-shilling freeholders by raising the Irish county franchise to £10 freehold. A further Act suppressed the Catholic Association.[2]

Catholic Emancipation brought about a fundamental and revolutionary change in the Constitution, passing 'a sentence of death on the Anglican settlement made at the 1688 Revolution'.[3] Yet the means by which it was obtained were quite as revolutionary as the settlement itself. The Catholic Association under O'Connell, the most powerful political machine British history had ever witnessed, had wrested the initiative from Parliament, where a Commons majority in favour of some form of Emancipation had existed for many years, and had forced a reluctant Government to carry through a major constitutional reform. All along, Ireland had prevented a relatively calm and parliamentary solution of the problem, and she

[1] Fitzgerald to Peel, 5 July 1828, *Memoirs by the Rt. Hon. Sir Robert Peel*, I, 114–15, quoted by Gash, *Peel*, 522.

[2] See Gash, *Peel*, esp. Ch. 16; and G. I. T. Machin, *The Catholic Question in English Politics, 1820 to 1830* (1964).

[3] Gash, *Peel*, 582.

precipitated the final crisis. For Wellington and Peel, the existence in Ireland of a militant and organized public opinion, nationalist in origin and potentially separatist in aim, endangered the unity of the Kingdom. Neither man was confident that concession would appease the forces of Irish discontent. Perhaps they would not have resented being branded as the fools in Lord Melbourne's well-known estimate of the results of Emancipation, that 'What all the wise men promised has not happened, and what all the damned fools said would happen has come to pass.' At great political and personal cost, they had shored up the Union and given its future defenders a far stronger position from which to conduct its defence.

CHAPTER II

The Advent of the Irish Party

Origins : the O'Connell 'connexion'

THE success of the Irish movement before 1829 concealed fundamental differences between the aims of the Association's leaders and
of the mass of their followers in the country. Emancipation was
essentially the interest of a rising Catholic middle class, of gentry
owning or holding land, lawyers and journalists, merchants, shopkeepers, small and large tenant farmers, a broad and growing class
which demanded a full share in local and central government and of
which O'Connell himself, with his interests in land, the legal profession, banking and brewing, was a perfectly representative
member.[1] This class, with the open support of the Catholic Church
authorities, had no wish to see a revolution in the system of land
tenure and ownership brought about by the peasantry as a result of
their involvement in the representative system; and the disfranchisement of the forty-shilling freeholders, by which Peel and Wellington
hoped to forestall an electoral landslide, was in one sense a positive
advantage to the Irish leaders. The voting support of a relatively
small proportion of a violent and potentially revolutionary peasantry

[1] For his interests in land, see below p. 225. He was a founder-director and
in 1841 Governor of the National Bank of Ireland, and one of the chief investors
in a concern acquired by his fourth son Daniel in 1831 and known as the O'Connell Brewery, which suffered from the competition of Guinness's, the unsale-
ability of its porter and the unbusinesslike methods of its owners. See Patrick
Lynch and John Vaizey, *Guinness's Brewery in the Irish Economy, 1759–1876*
(1960), 91, 144–5; *Correspondence of Daniel O'Connell, the Liberator*, ed. W. J.
Fitzpatrick (1888), I, 421, n. 5. He also had, after 1836, a proprietorial share in
the *Dublin Review*, a quarterly magazine.

was a distinctly double-edged weapon, and peasant electors, though certainly amenable to clerical influence, were also most exposed to the reprisals of their landlords. While O'Connell could be certain of the peasantry's general support, the problem of controlling them was perhaps made easier by their being unenfranchised, a position which could indeed be exploited by O'Connell to add weight and urgency to his political demands.

In February 1830, O'Connell finally took his seat as M.P. for Clare; a month earlier, he had begun his first campaign for the Repeal of the Act of Union.[1] As the architect of a great if (for most Irishmen) largely symbolic act of liberation, his hold on the admiration of the mass of his countrymen was both complete and deserved, while his masterful confidence in his own political judgement was increased by the absence of any rival. The Tory Government's narrow-minded decision not to make him a King's Counsel, while promoting other much less distinguished Catholic barristers, and the tactless and over-legalistic refusal of Peel, supported by the House of Commons, to allow him to take his seat without another election under the Relief Act, insulted his pride and sapped any confidence he may have had in the intentions of England towards Ireland.

The struggle for Emancipation had confirmed him in his opposition to the Union. In theory at least, Repeal was a cause in which all sections of the Irish people, Catholic and Protestant, could unite, since an Irish legislature would confer economic, social and political benefits on all classes; and O'Connell certainly believed that Repeal would be conceded, as Emancipation had been, to an overwhelming show of strength from Ireland. This calculation, which took little account of the very different attitudes of English opinion to the separate issues of Catholic disabilities and the Legislative Union, was undoubtedly over-optimistic. But the Repeal movement itself, after an unpromising beginning, soon gathered strength and momentum under the stimuli of government prescription and the Liberal revolutions in France and Belgium.[2] By October 1830, the Irish

[1] See his Letters to the Protestants and People of Ireland, 1, 7, January 1830, in Fagan, *O'Connell*, II, 23, 24–30.

[2] The revived Irish nationalist movement thus preceded and finally formed part of the great wave of Liberal and nationalist revolutions in Europe in 1830. Although there is no evidence of direct co-operation between the Irish and any European movements, O'Connell made the fullest possible use of the religious and political analogies between Belgium, where the Catholics were struggling successfully to break the Union of 1814 with Protestant Holland, and Ireland.

Government was acting as if it had to deal with a potentially revolutionary situation. At the Home Office in London, Peel, anxiously watching for trouble in the industrial districts in England, sanctioned military precautions taken in Ireland by Sir Henry Hardinge, the Chief Secretary: 'Let us take them as quietly as we can ... *but let us take them.*'[1] Hardinge, though he believed that the 'Mania for the Repeal is spreading in the Provinces amongst the lower orders', concluded that 'We shall have no crisis here ... unless it first breaks out in England, or Belgium is protected by France in either of which cases, a convulsion may be attempted here to occupy our hands at Home'.[2] But despite the official view that O'Connell was 'too wary and too timid to risk himself in any illegal enterprise',[3] Peel, Hardinge and the Lord Lieutenant, the Duke of Northumberland, would not tolerate the existence of O'Connell's political organizations. On at least three occasions between April and the fall of the Tory Government in November 1830, they made use of a convenient Act to crush these bodies as a danger to the public peace and as part of 'a plan on an enlarged scale to subvert the Government as established by Law', by organizing 'associations for dissolving the connection with England by intimidation' and by usurping 'an extensive series of measures, more especially those belonging to the Legislature'.[4]

O'Connell's programme now covered, in addition to Repeal, a wide range of economic and political demands including parliamentary reform with manhood suffrage and the ballot, reforms in county and municipal government, the abolition of tithes, reform and codification of the law, the repeal of the Sub-letting Act of 1826, a tax of 20 per cent on absentees' incomes (as an alternative to a Poor Law) and changes in the law, as it affected the Catholic Church, governing charitable bequests.[5] This programme, radical, Catholic and

---

[1] Peel to Hardinge, 14 October 1830, H.O. Papers, 79/9, 53–8.
[2] Hardinge to Peel, 21, 12 October 1830, Peel Papers, Add. MSS 40313, 129, 52.
[3] Hardinge to Peel, 12 October 1830, Peel Papers, Add. MSS 40313, 56–8.
[4] Hardinge to Peel, 12 October 1830, Peel Papers, Add. MSS 40313, 53–5. For use of the Act (10 Geo. IV, c. 1), which had earlier suppressed the Catholic Association, see Peel to Northumberland, 22 April 1830; to Hardinge, 14 October 1830; Northumberland to Peel, 30 October 1830, H.O. Papers, 79/9, 17–28, 59–65; 100/234, 338–9.
[5] O'Connell to the People of Ireland, 7 January 1830, in Fagan, *O'Connell*, II, 24–30; to Edward Dwyer, 27 September 1830, a public letter in Peel Papers, Add. MSS 40313, 61.

nationalist, appealed strongly to middle-class interests and aspira-
tions, while it drew attention in a distinctly more cautious fashion
to the economic grievances of the peasantry; and on this basis,
O'Connell largely succeeded in retaining the support of the triple
alliance of the Emancipationist movement and in providing the
essential ideological foundations of his parliamentary party.

But it was a notable feature of O'Connell's tactics that the main
nationalist issue did not impinge on the General Elections of July–
August 1830 and April–May 1831, which were fought by him on a
broad anti-Tory front. There was as yet no question of an independent assault on the representation. Indeed in 1830 O'Connell himself, for the first and last occasion in his career, actually took part in
an electoral compromise with a Tory, Lord George Beresford, to
share the representation of County Waterford. In 1831, following
his policy of supporting the Whig Ministry on the Reform Bill, he
backed the candidatures of two Ministers, Sir Henry Parnell in
Queen's County and Viscount Duncannon in County Kilkenny, and
kept in close touch with the latter, who seems to have been the
Whigs' unofficial representative in Irish election matters.[1]

These Elections destroyed the long-standing Tory majority in the
Irish representation.[2] In 1830 it was estimated, admittedly by a
Whig, that the opposition to the Tories made a net gain of 14 Irish
seats; in 1831, at least 10 more seats were captured by Whigs, more
or less radical Reformers and O'Connellites, all of whom could be
relied upon to support the Whig Government on the vital question
of parliamentary reform.[3] The Irish representation now included
Catholic gentry and squires like Lord Killeen, Richard More
O'Ferrall, Sir John Burke, Henry Lambert, The O'Conor Don,
Walter Blackney and Sir John Miley Doyle, leading Catholic
members of the old Association like Richard Lalor Sheil, Thomas
Wyse, O'Gorman Mahon and O'Connell's eldest son, Maurice,

[1] Fagan, *O'Connell*, II, 51–2; *Pilot*, 7 March; 2 May 1831; *O'Connell Corr.*, I,
253–60.

[2] According to Wellington in 1834, the Government had always been able to rely
on 70 Irish Members 'before the Reform Bill'. This was strictly true only for the
period before 1830; Lady Salisbury, 16 November 1834, Salisbury MSS.

[3] Lord Brougham, *Life and Times*, III, 55, as cited by A. Aspinall, *Three Early
Nineteenth Century Diaries* (1952), xxi, n. 1; E. Halévy, *A History of the English
People in the Nineteenth Century* (1950), III, 33. For a general description of the
1831 Election in Ireland, which indicates a Liberal gain of 12 seats, see Sheil,
Sketches, II, 329–53.

together with liberal Protestants, nearly all of them landowners, such as Major William Macnamara, Charles Walker, Sir Richard Musgrave, the Hon. F. W. Mullins, E. S. Ruthven and M. L. Chapman.

It was not immediately apparent to contemporaries, aware of the imprecise political affiliations of many Irish Members, particularly of the new Catholic M.P.s, that the Tory grip had been so rudely shaken. After the 1830 Election, an informant of Peel gave the Tory Government no less than 74 Irish supporters, including 29 of the 35 borough Members; nine certain opponents included O'Connell and eight firm Whigs such as Thomas Spring Rice, Sir John Newport, Duncannon and James Grattan. Seventeen Members, ranging from aggrieved, anti-Catholic Ultra Tories like the two Lefroys through Whigs like Viscount Brabazon, Sir Henry Parnell, Fitzstephen French and Dominick Browne to future Repealers such as The O'Conor Don and Macnamara were thought to be neutral. Of so-called Government supporters, E. S. Ruthven and Daniel Callaghan shortly became Repealers, while Viscount Acheson, the Earl of Belfast, the Hon. Richard Fitzgibbon and the Hon. Standish O'Grady were plainly Whig Unionists in 1832.[1]

The magnetic attraction for independent M.P.s of the claims of the Government of the day, charged with carrying on 'the King's business', and the reliance of many successful anti-Tory candidates on their own electoral influence or on good local organizations rather than on the publicity and funds of the current O'Connellite organization, were considerable initial obstacles to the establishment of an independent Irish party under O'Connell's leadership. Moreover, several of his most prominent associates refused to support the Repeal agitation. Thomas Wyse was and remained a Unionist on principle.[2] The O'Gorman Mahon, who began his long and adven-

[1] Pierce Mahony to Peel, 27 August 1830, H.O. Papers, 100/235, 97–106. Cf. Hardinge to Peel, 18 August 1830, Peel Papers, Add. MSS 40313, 19–20, who did not expect more than five successful Catholic candidates, '& excepting O'Connel (sic), men of property & old family connexion on the spot'. Hardinge's extreme dislike of O'Connell, who had refused to answer in the approved gentlemanly fashion for violent personal attacks, led Hardinge to down-grade O'Connell socially and, incidentally, to mis-spell his name consistently.

[2] See below p. 56 for Wyse's attitude in 1832. Fagan, O'Connell, II, 63–5, gives details of the Declaration against Repeal of 1830, officially sponsored by the Whig Duke of Leinster but organized by Pierce Mahony, a rich Catholic solicitor and former Emancipationist politician, and signed by a medley of Whig and Tory Unionists, including at least one future Repeal M.P., F. W. Mullins of Kerry.

turous career on the Clare hustings in 1828 and ended it as a highly respected member of Parnell's Home Rule party, when T. P. O'Connor described him as 'the last survivor of the once multitudinous race of the Irish gentlemen', proved distinctly troublesome to O'Connell, failing to follow his lead in Parliament, quarrelling with the O'Connells over his seat for Clare and almost certainly playing some part in an obscure and unsuccessful attempt in 1832 to damage O'Connell's moral reputation.[1]

The position of Richard Sheil, after O'Connell the most conspicuous Irish orator, was typical. In October 1830, Hardinge reported after an interview with him that Sheil 'is disposed to support the Government in opposing O'Connel on the repeal of the Union . . . [and] thought that many Catholics would follow his example'. The Chief Secretary was eager to pay Sheil's price (help from the Government in obtaining a constituency) because he believed that Sheil was 'most important at the present moment—not so much for his own individual value, as the advantage of separating him from O'C., and affording the Irish R.C. Members a leader under whom they can support the Govt. ag^t the Repeal of the Union & O'C'.[2] Peel and Wellington saw the force of this argument, but Peel emphasized that

> We dread a parliamentary connexion with Sheil—that is, we dread being instrumental in effecting his Return, and thereby assuming the Responsibility of whatever Vagaries he may hereafter commit. We have no confidence in the discretion of Irish orators and (between ourselves) the communication made to you by Sheil does not encourage much confidence in his political honesty. He makes a reservation on the score of Reform, which he calls Moderate Reform—but this very question of Reform may be the all-important, vital Question . . .[3]

[1] Denis Gwynn, *The O'Gorman Mahon: Duellist, Adventurer and Politician* (1934), 110–32, 135–7, 241. Mahon's spurious title was generally accepted by contemporaries. For the attempt to blackmail O'Connell as a heartless seducer, see Denis Gwynn, *Daniel O'Connell and Ellen Courtenay* (1930), who with John H. Horgan, 'O'Connell: The Man', in *Daniel O'Connell, Nine Centenary Essays*, ed. Michael Tierney (1949), 274–9, defends O'Connell against all charges of immorality brought in his own day by *The Times*, later by Sir James O'Connor, *History of Ireland* (1925), I, 251, and by W. B. Yeats in the Irish Senate. See further below p. 277.

[2] Hardinge to Peel, 13, 22 October 1830, Peel Papers, Add. MSS 40313, 67–71, 136–7.

[3] Peel to Hardinge, 16 October 1830, Peel Papers, Add. MSS 40313, 100–1, wrongly dated in Charles Stuart Parker, *Sir Robert Peel from his Private Papers* (1891), II, 161.

Where the Tories hesitated, fobbing Sheil off with promotion to King's Counsel and viceregal dinners, their opponents plunged. In March 1831 the Marquess of Anglesey, the new Whig Lord Lieutenant, placed at Sheil's disposal the vacant rotten borough of Milborne Port in Dorset and thus tied him to a general support of the Government.[1] After the General Election of 1831, Sheil achieved some independence as one of the Members for Louth, but he was not officially in O'Connell's party until his speech in November 1832 in support of Repeal at the National Political Union and his unopposed return for Tipperary as a Repealer in December 1832.[2]

O'Connell's following in the Commons before 1832 might best be described as an eighteenth-century 'connexion' grouped loosely around an important political figure, rather than as a distinct parliamentary party. Many of its members were the direct heirs and beneficiaries of Emancipation, others had successfully capitalized on the popularity with the Irish county electorate of the cause of parliamentary reform, which to some extent cut across traditional party divisions in Ireland and largely benefited O'Connell, who had supported it long before the Whigs came to power. Complacent expectations that the great popular leader, the Catholic squire-demagogue with his long experience of enthusiastic Irish audiences and unquestioning subordinates, would fail in the highly critical, intensely English and club-like atmosphere of the Commons were soon disappointed. John Cam Hobhouse, the veteran Radical, noting that O'Connell 'had spoken almost every night since taking his seat, and had spoken sensibly', thought that his 'Parliamentary value was, at that time, under-rated'.[3] It says much for O'Connell's vitality and adaptability that at the age of 55, with one career already behind him, he was able at once to impress his personality on an assembly most of whose members were strongly prejudiced against him on personal as well as on political grounds.

---

[1] The Marquess of Anglesey; *One-Leg: The Life and Letters of Henry William Paget, First Marquess of Anglesey* (1961), 200, 201, 376, n. (a). Anglesey frankly believed that Irish demagogues could be emasculated by the spoils system.

[2] W. McCullagh Torrens, *Memoirs of the Right Honourable Richard Lalor Sheil* (1855), II, 108–10, 130–4; Sheil, *Sketches*, II, 344–5.

[3] Lord Broughton, *Recollections of Long Life* (1910), 11 February 1830, IV, 8; see also Greville, *Journal*, 5 February 1830, I, 281, for O'Connell's successful maiden speech. But cf. Ellenborough's account of O'Connell's hostile reception at Brooks's in November 1830, in Earl of Ellenborough, *A Political Diary, 1828–30*, ed. Lord Colchester (1881), I, 409.

Even in the unreformed House of Commons, radical political views were no bar to acceptance. In O'Connell's case they gave him the entreé into a small but active group of English Radicals including Joseph Hume, Daniel Whittle Harvey, Henry Hunt and Sir Francis Burdett, most of whom had been influenced, like O'Connell himself, by the teachings of the doyen of English radicalism, the aged but still vigorous Jeremy Bentham. O'Connell's debt to Bentham, 'my most revered master', 'the Newton of the Law,'[1] was direct and lasting. Their correspondence from 1828 until the year before Bentham's death in 1832 shows clearly that O'Connell's powerful but simplifying mind, already prepared by his early admiration for Godwin and Adam Smith, was strongly attracted by the seemingly simple certainties of utilitarianism.[2] Whole-heartedly endorsing the formula of 'the greatest possible good to the greatest possible number',[3] O'Connell fully adopted the Benthamite programme of political and legal reform, and if he added nothing new to the general stock of radical ideas, his contribution to the popularization of these ideas and to the practice of radical politics was immense. In his cast of mind and use of language, O'Connell remained a true pupil of Bentham, to whom he owed his faith in the reforming power of legislation, his *laissez-faire* economic views, his unwillingness to interfere drastically with existing property relations, his horror of social revolution and his consistent refusal to use force to achieve political ends. His religious beliefs offered in practice no ground for disagreement since he stood, like Bentham, for a complete separation of Church and State.

In practical terms, O'Connell's radical views, which he was ready

[1] O'Connell to Bentham, 26 October 1828; 22 April 1829, O'Connell Papers N.L.I., 5759. See further, *The Works of Jeremy Bentham*, ed. J. Bowring (Edinburgh, 1843–59), X, 594–605; XI, 12, 21–3, 24–30, 32–3, 37–9, 60–1, 63–4, for the relations, personal and political, between Bentham, O'Connell and other Radicals.

[2] An important collection of the Bentham-O'Connell correspondence, some of which was used by John Bowring, is preserved at University College, Dublin, though there are a few notable letters among the O'Connell Papers, catalogued and uncatalogued, in the National Library. Bentham's letters, which reveal his affection and admiration for O'Connell, are largely concerned with his attempts to further his schemes of law reform and codification through the Radical pressure group in Parliament, John Bowring and the *Westminster Review* and by a national publicity campaign.

[3] O'Connell to Bentham, 3 August 1828, O'Connell Papers, N.L.I., 5759, in which he supports codification, parliamentary reform and the ballot.

to support by parliamentary speeches and votes,[1] ensured him the sympathy and frequently the support of the English Radicals on most Irish questions, with the significant exception of Repeal itself; and as the acknowledged leader of the nucleus of an Irish party, he was always able to exert a powerful influence on uncommitted Irish Whig and Liberal M.P.s, who were ready on issues outside Repeal to accept his leadership in Parliament.

O'Connell and the Whigs

Earl Grey's Government was confronted, soon after its accession to power in November 1830, by the urgent necessity to define its official attitude towards O'Connell. In theory, three policies were possible. The Whigs might buy off O'Connell with place or office; they might attempt to stamp out an increasingly formidable agitation in Ireland by prosecuting its leader and outlawing his movement; or they might try to settle Irish discontents at their source by pushing through a programme of reforms. In practice, several factors confused the choice between appeasement and coercion. Where Peel and Wellington had been able to regard O'Connell as an irreconcilable opponent, Grey and his colleagues had to deal with a nominal ally whose vote and influence in the Commons had helped them into office and whose support, vital in March and April 1831 on the first Reform Bill, remained of some importance for their existence as a Government. These embarrassing obligations exposed the Government to external pressure in the matter of Irish reforms, but while the Whigs were prepared to go some way towards meeting Irish demands, they were Unionists before they were reformers.[2] Even the suspicion of an understanding with Irish nationalists might have seriously damaged the Government in England; an open alliance was impossible on personal as well as political grounds; and when leading Ministers regarded O'Connell as a personal enemy, they were not slow in 1831 and again in 1833 to act on their view that his

---

[1] See McDowell, *Public Opinion*, 127–8, for a list of his early speeches. He opposed West Indian slavery, the monopoly of the East India Company, Jewish disabilities, the blasphemy laws and flogging in the Army and supported free trade, the reduction of the National Debt, manhood suffrage and the Liberal cause in Europe, particularly in Belgium, Poland and Spain.

[2] Indeed according to the Whig Solicitor-General many Liberals thought by 1832 that Ireland, 'wholly incapable of laws or liberty', could only be ruled by force: *Life of John, Lord Campbell*, ed. The Hon. Mrs. Hardcastle (1881), II, 7.

political agitation represented a permanent threat to the unity of the Kingdom and to public law and order in Ireland.

The Government's policies reflected the difficulties and inconsistencies of its position. In December 1830, consistent with the generally accepted view of O'Connell as a political mercenary, the Whigs made an extremely clumsy attempt to settle him with high judicial office.[1] Anglesey, before leaving for Ireland, saw him in London and at one interview, according to O'Connell, 'talked . . . for two hours . . . [and] went so far as to discuss my private affairs in order to prevail on me to repair my fortunes!'[2] Giving O'Connell no credit for sincerity and completely failing to understand his relationship to Irish opinion, the Government succeeded only in insulting him. O'Connell, wrote Anglesey, *'is not to be had.* He is flying at higher game than a judgeship, and he is secure of a better income from the deluded people than *any Government* can venture to give to *any Person* whatever.'[3]

Any confidence which O'Connell might have had in the Whigs had already been destroyed by their Irish law appointments. They began by retaining both the law officers of Wellington's Government, one of whom, John Doherty, the Solicitor-General, was a bitter enemy of O'Connell and almost at once virtually called him a liar in the Commons. O'Connell protested angrily to Anglesey against this 'most wanton *assault'* and declared that nothing which he had said 'in our last conversation . . . could be construed into any pledge' to support the Government 'or to accept any kind of favour'.[4] Although both Doherty and Henry Joy, the Attorney-General, were rapidly transferred to the Bench, O'Connell disapproved almost as strongly of their successors. Both were Protestants and the new Attorney-

---

[1] Melbourne to Anglesey, 18 December 1830, *Lord Melbourne's Papers*, ed. Lloyd C. Sanders (1889), 167–9. Possible offices were the Mastership of the Irish Rolls or a Chief Justiceship in Calcutta: Ellenborough, *Diary*, 11 December 1830, in Aspinall, *Three Diaries*, 33; Auchmuty, *Wyse*, 139.

[2] O'Connell to W. Bennett, 31 December 1830, *O'Connell Corr.*, I, 237.

[3] Anglesey to Melbourne, 21 December 1830, Plas Newydd Papers, quoted by Anglesey, *One-Leg*, 378.

[4] O'Connell to Anglesey, 20 November 1830, Plas Newydd Papers, quoted by Anglesey, *One-Leg*, 377. For Doherty's career and quarrels with O'Connell, see Madden, *Ireland and Its Rulers*, I, 59–60, 64–90, 91–101. Attempts by Anglesey, Duncannon and Lord Brougham to pacify O'Connell met with little real success; Anglesey, op. cit., 245, 377; Brougham to Sir Francis Burdett [n.d. December 1830], quoted by M. W. Patterson, *Sir Francis Burdett and His Times, 1770–1844* (1931), II, 588.

General, Francis Blackburne, a successful lawyer of strictly conservative views, had actually opposed Emancipation. On their legal
advice would depend the Government's official attitude to O'Connell's political organization, and O'Connell saw their appointments
as a declaration of war as well as a refusal to implement the terms of
Emancipation.[1]

Anglesey's instructions from Viscount Melbourne, the Home
Secretary, show clearly that the Government was from the first prepared for drastic action. If O'Connell's

> meetings should attempt to assume a more permanent character—if
> they should adjourn from time to time, and fix periods for their re-
> assembling—if they should form Committees, and in any manner raise
> money . . . if in short, they should betray or manifest a desire to renew
> under another name the Roman Catholic Association, I then equally
> see no course . . . but that of exercising the Power vested in you by
> Law, of prohibiting by Proclamation any such Assembly.[2]

The Whigs, seriously envisaging a future of 'perpetual disquietude,
increased political violence, and ultimately revolt and civil war',
were uneasily aware of the limits of their power against an opponent
of O'Connell's ingenuity, who could certainly obtain enough of the
requisite local support to defeat any attempt to apply the Seditious
Meetings Act. The Insurrection Act, directed principally against
outrages committed at night, could not be used to suppress political
meetings, and suspension of Habeas Corpus, the most extreme
course, could only be temporary. Besides, the Whigs, as representatives of the party of civil and religious liberty, found it hard to devise
any law to suppress O'Connell's agitation without destroying 'the
constitutional right of discussion and petition, a right', as Melbourne
put it, 'which none of us wish to infringe upon or restrict'.[3]

But the Government was ready and indeed eager to proceed
against O'Connell himself.[4] Anglesey's campaign of proclamations

[1] For O'Connell's views on Blackburne and on Philip Crampton, whom he
regarded as incompetent, see *O'Connell Corr.*, I, 470-2, 474-5. For Blackburne's
politics, see E. Blackburne, *Life of the Rt. Hon. Francis Blackburne* (1874), 62;
Stanley to Melbourne, 30 December 1830, H.O. Papers, 100/234, 380.

[2] Melbourne to Anglesey, 18 December 1830, H.O. Papers, 100/235, 146-7;
to Anglesey [n.d. December 1830], *Melbourne Papers*, 166-7.

[3] Melbourne to Anglesey, 2, 13 January; 26 February 1831, H.O. Papers,
79/9, 81-3, 84-8, 107-12.

[4] Melbourne to Stanley, 13 January 1831; Stanley to Melbourne, 14 January
1831, H.O. Papers, 79/9, 84-6; 100-236, 71/3; Anglesey to Lady Anglesey
[n.d. January 1831], quoted by Greville, *Journal*, 22 January 1831, II, 110.

against his organizations, to which he replied by improvising new associations, holding 'private' breakfasts and calling for a run on the banks, culminated in his arrest on 18 January 1831 with seven of his closest associates, on thirty-one charges of conspiracy, seditious libel and unlawful assembly 'to excite discontent and disaffection' against the laws and the Government.[1] In London the Cabinet was at first uneasy, and Viscount Althorp, the leader of the Commons, who had little confidence in the Irish law officers, seriously doubted the legality of the Irish Government's action.[2] But Edward Stanley, the Chief Secretary, was jubilant, writing to Melbourne that 'the Attorney General said to me yesterday, "I now give him bound hand and foot, into your custody—don't let him go", . . . I think he may be dealt with—*and transported*—and if he were, I really hope Ireland would be tranquil'.[3]

O'Connell now proceeded to outwit and outmanoeuvre his opponents. Respectable Liberals like Lord Rossmore were sent to lobby Anglesey; others, like Lord Cloncurry and the Earl of Meath, were asked to join in a non-Repeal, Reform agitation. Sir William Gossett, the Under-Secretary in Ireland, believed 'that an appeal has been made to Lord Althorp by O'Connell, and that his Friends have greater hopes from the other side of the Water, than from this'.[4] Every advantage was taken of legal technicalities and of the evident lack of sympathy between the Court of King's Bench, with its Ascendancy affiliations, and the Whig Government. To the shocked surprise of Anglesey and the more philosophical disappointment of Melbourne, Chief Justice Charles Kendal Bushe allowed O'Connell and his friends to withdraw their first pleas of demurrer, by which they admitted the offences but objected to the relevance of the prosecution, and to plead not guilty to all the charges.[5]

[1] Stanley to Melbourne, 1, 16, 18, 25 January 1831; Indictment drawn up by Blackburne, [n.d. January 1831], H.O. Papers, 100/236, 9–11, 40, 57–8, 89–91, 34–5. This official correspondence gives a complete picture of the Government's actions, of O'Connell's counter-measures and of the circumstances of his arrest.

[2] Althorp to Earl Spencer, 22 January 1831, quoted in W. M. Torrens, *Memoirs of Viscount Melbourne* (1878), I, 359; Melbourne to Stanley, 20 January 1831, H.O. Papers, 79/9, 93.

[3] Stanley to Melbourne, 26 January 1831, H.O. Papers, 100/236, 23–5.

[4] Gossett to Stanley, 29 January 1831, H.O. Papers, 100/236, 36; O'Connell to T. O'Mara, 22 January 1831, *O'Connell Corr.*, I, 243–5.

[5] Anglesey to Stanley, 5 February 1831; Melbourne to William IV, 8 February 1831, H.O. Papers, 100/236, 113–14; 79/9, 97–101.

The Government was now much less sure of eventual success. In February 1831 Lord Duncannon, standing for re-election in his ancestral county of Kilkenny on his appointment as First Commissioner of Woods and Forests, scraped home by only 61 votes against opposition which had been inspired by O'Connell and organized by his agents.[1] This threatening move against a popular and liberal politician who was personally on good terms with O'Connell had been made after the Government, now desperately in need of Irish support on the Reform Bill, had agreed to postpone the trial in exchange for O'Connell's willing plea of guilty.[2] In the Commons, Stanley and O'Connell vehemently denied strong rumours of negotiations and the Government kept up stern appearances through March and April, but in May the law officers conveniently decided that O'Connell's offences were punishable only under a statute which had then expired.[3]

The Government's campaign against nationalist and radical newspapers in Ireland was equally unsuccessful. Prosecutions in January 1831 of the editors of the *Freeman's Journal* and the *Morning Register*, for publishing one of O'Connell's letters on his own case while it was *sub judice*, did not succeed in their main purpose of forcing O'Connell to choose between acknowledging his authorship or allowing others to suffer on his behalf.[4] Even when the Government won a case, as against the *Pilot*, O'Connell's official newspaper, in 1833, it did so only by the most dubious methods, including the packing of juries, which provided O'Connell and his followers with excellent material for their denunciations in the Commons of the Government's savage treatment of the Irish press. The Whigs went much further than their Tory predecessors, who had relied on gentle persuasion and discreet support. Between 1831 and 1834 they initiated thirteen newspaper prosecutions, set up two Government

---

[1] Edward Dwyer to O'Connell, 23 February 1831, O'Connell MSS, U.C.D.; O'Connell to W. Bennett, [n.d. January 1831], *O'Connell Corr.*, I, 246; *Pilot*, 16 February 1831.

[2] Anglesey to Melbourne, 12 February 1831, H.O. Papers, 100/236, 123–4; O'Connell to Blackburne, 11 February 1831, *O'Connell Corr.*, I, 247.

[3] Melbourne to Anglesey, 31 March; 4 April 1831, *Melbourne Papers*, 179–81; Grey to Burdett, 3 April 1831, Patterson, *Burdett*, II, 586–7; Opinions of English and Irish law officers, 25 May 1831, H.O. Papers, 100/238, 27.

[4] Brian Inglis, *The Freedom of the Press in Ireland, 1784–1841* (1954), 194–204, provides a good general account of these cases and of Whig policy towards the Irish press.

newspapers, the *Dublin Times* and the *Empire*, neither of which, despite substantial subsidies from the secret service money, was commercially successful, and tried to use their control of the issue of newspaper stamps to gag the troublesome *Pilot*.[1]

The Whigs' high-handed treatment of O'Connell undoubtedly increased the strength and justification of the Repeal movement. O'Connell was now deeply suspicious of the Government's intentions. Impervious to most forms of criticism, he felt that they had treated him, a Catholic gentleman of good, old family, like a common criminal; and in June 1832 when he was officially supporting the Government, he angrily warned Stanley to remember 'that he was Secretary for Ireland when common thief-takers were sent to his [O'Connell's] house, to drag him from the bosom of his family'.[2] The unfortunate Anglesey was treated with abusive contempt. 'He is just like a woman', O'Connell told E. J. Littleton, Anglesey's own Chief Secretary, in 1833, 'who will hate her most intimate & amiable friend the moment she discovers that men think her prettier than herself.'[3] But the real enemy was 'the Saxon' Stanley, 'snappish, impertinent, overbearing high Church Mr. Stanley' whom O'Connell believed with some justice to have planned his arrest and to have blocked every radical reform in Ireland.[4]

Stanley, thirty-one in 1830 when O'Connell was fifty-five, was a resourceful administrator and a brilliant debater, a master of sarcasm and invective. Totally lacking in sympathy for Irish methods and susceptibilities, somewhat authoritarian in spirit and arrogant in manner, he had a profound contempt and dislike (which he never concealed) for O'Connell and for most of the Irish Members. The bitter feud between the two men found frequent expression in debates on Irish issues between 1831 and 1833. In August 1831,

---

[1] A. Aspinall, *Politics and the Press* (1949), 124–5, 145–7; Inglis, *Freedom of the Press*, 207; Peel to Hardinge, 20 October 1830; Hardinge to Peel, 22 October 1830, Peel Papers, Add. MSS. 40313, 127, 136. See below pp. 83–6, for O'Connell's own use of the press.

[2] Hansard, XIII, 805, 18 June 1832, O'Connell.

[3] Littleton, *Diary*, 24 July 1833, Aspinall, *Three Diaries*, 351–2; *O'Connell Corr.*, I, 243, 268, 278–9, 284, 318.

[4] O'Connell to Duncannon, 4 December 1831, *O'Connell Corr.*, I, 282; Hansard, XIII, 780, 18 June 1832, Stanley, complaining that O'Connell always referred to him as 'The Saxon'. Not all Irish Members shared O'Connell's feelings about Stanley. For Sheil's not unfriendly article, 'Mr. Stanley in Ireland', in *New Monthly Magazine* (August 1831), see Sheil, *Sketches*, II, 355–74.

Stanley protested 'against the course which the hon. and learned gentleman had thought proper to adopt, in coming down there night after night and without proper notice charging the Irish Government with having acted unfairly in this case, in that case, or in the other case'. O'Connell replied that Stanley's self-satisfaction and haughtiness totally unfitted him to govern Ireland. In June 1832 during a debate on the Irish Reform Bill, O'Connell lashed out at Stanley 'who sat there sneering and laughing at him', or at least he was 'laughing at something else when the Irish Bill was under discussion. That was just what he expected.'[1] While Stanley remained a Whig Minister, even unconnected with Ireland, there could be no real *rapprochement* between O'Connell and the Whigs and little chance of buying O'Connell off with office or place.

In October 1831 Dr. John Doyle, the Catholic Bishop of Kildare and Leighlin and the most outstanding figure in the hierarchy, was engaged by the Secretary-at-War, the Irish Whig Sir Henry Parnell, to approach O'Connell again. The moment was well-chosen, for O'Connell, prompted by Anglesey's diplomat brother Arthur Paget and by the veteran Radical Sir Francis Burdett, had strongly supported the Government after the House of Lords' rejection of the Reform Bill on 10 October.[2] Brougham and Holland of the Cabinet were particularly anxious to come to some permanent arrangement with him.[3] Even Grey, despite his intense dislike of O'Connell's character and methods, hoped that O'Connell's promotion to King's Counsel and a promise to find a post for his son-in-law were 'only preliminaries to a more useful connexion with him'. Grey thought that O'Connell, 'With the greatest opportunities & the most powerful means that almost any man ever possessed of raising his own character, & serving the Publick, . . . has unfortunately used them in a way that has proved most injurious to both.' But he was quite ready to admit O'Connell's 'good service' on Reform and 'on many previous occasions' and he may possibly have sanctioned Parnell's indirect approach.[4]

---

[1] Hansard, V, 1122–4, 1129–30; XIII, 563, 10 August 1831, 13 June 1832, Stanley, O'Connell.

[2] W. J. Fitzpatrick, *The Life, Times and Correspondence of the Right Rev. Dr. Doyle* (1880), II, 328; McDowell, *Public Opinion*, 154.

[3] Le Marchant, *Diary*, 18 August 1831, Aspinall, *Three Diaries*, 117; Holland to Anglesey, 27 August 1831, Plas Newydd Papers, quoted by McDowell, *Public Opinion*, 155.

[4] Grey to Burdett, 3 April; 22 October 1831, Patterson, *Burdett*, II, 586–7,

The Bishop did his best with a difficult assignment. A first feeler was, he told Parnell, 'more successful than I anticipated'; the *Pilot* made gallant efforts to justify a possible acceptance of office; but when Dr. Doyle saw O'Connell again in December, he did not inform him of the precise terms of the offer and indeed, thought him right to reject such an isolated and indefinite proposal without a guarantee that any of his demands, including the removal of Stanley, a more radical approach to Irish questions and the appointment of Liberals in posts under government and in local administration, would be met.[1] According to Doyle, O'Connell was under the strongest pressure from the 'agitators and the public press' and suspected that the Government 'intended only to delude him'. The Bishop urged the Whigs 'to come to an understanding with Mr. O'Connell on his going to London . . . , for without him you cannot in his lifetime govern this country,' but, he added, 'I can no longer serve you in any negotiation with him.'[2]

The Whigs and Ireland

If the Irish Question had been solely or even largely a matter of political adjustments and personalities, as Lord Holland and others in their estimates of O'Connell seem occasionally to have imagined, the Whigs would doubtless and gladly have settled it on a basis of political concessions and rewards.[3] But no Government, least of all one dedicated to the principles and practice of Reform, could have ignored for long the grave social, economic and religious problems of Ireland; and between 1831 and 1833, the Whigs attempted to carry through a programme of Irish reforms, the nature of which illustrates not only Whig legislative priorities and preoccupations but also shows the extent and limits of the influence of the Irish party, in its early years, on legislation.

596; Sir William Gossett to O'Connell, 26 October 1831, O'Connell Papers, N.L.I., uncatalogued, conferring precedence on O'Connell next after H.M.'s Second Sergeants, the only direct favour he received from any Government.

[1] Doyle to Parnell, 17 October 1831, *O'Connell Corr.*, I, 286; *Pilot* 19 October 1831; O'Connell to Duncannon, 19 October; 4 December 1831, *O'Connell Corr.*, I, 277-9, 280-4.

[2] Doyle to Parnell, 23 December 1831, Fitzpatrick, *Doyle*, II, 335-6. Dr. Doyle's relations with O'Connell rapidly deteriorated after this episode.

[3] Holland to Anglesey, 3 January 1831, Plas Newydd Papers, quoted by McDowell, *Public Opinion*, 142-3.

Thus, the Whigs did not tackle the basic problems of the land system and postponed the questions of a Poor Law and a reform of municipal government.[1] Stanley's attempt in 1833 to carry out a much-needed reform of the Irish grand juries, the chief civil and judicial authorities in the counties and the strongholds of the landed interest, received little support from O'Connell and his followers, who as Catholic and liberal Protestant landowners seem to have suffered no burning sense of exclusion from county government, whatever its real inequities and abuses.[2] Grand jury reform was a convenient election issue, but Stanley's unsuccessful proposal to throw the whole burden of county cess, then borne largely by occupying tenants, on to the landlords raised a vigorous and obstructive protest from O'Connell himself.[3]

On the other hand, while Stanley's creation of a new Board of Works which advanced money for public works to grand juries and landowners found general if critical support, the Whigs' attempt in 1831 to provide Ireland with an undenominational system of primary education was strongly supported and staunchly defended by O'Connell and his followers.[4] The concept of the State as a neutral but broadly Christian educational agent could perhaps never have succeeded in Ireland even with the goodwill of moderates on both sides. Yet despite the attacks of the aggressively ultramontane Archbishop of Tuam, Dr. John MacHale, the opposition of educational interests connected with the Established Church and the scruples of the Ulster Presbyterians, which together forced the Board of National Education to allow denominational education in

---

[1] Melbourne to Stanley, 2, 22 January 1831, H.O. Papers, 122/15, 59; 79/9, 94–5; *Melbourne Papers*, 176–7. See also R. D. Collison Black, *Economic Thought and the Irish Question* (1960), 20–1, 100–1.

[2] Hansard, XV, 955–63, 19 February 1833, Stanley. All parties pungently criticized the system; see Peel to F. Leveson Gower, 23 November 1829, H.O. Papers, 100/245, 77–86; and T. Spring Rice, *Inquiry into the Effects of the Irish Grand Jury Laws* (1815). For an excellent account of the attempts at reform, see, Black, *Economic Thought*, 168–75, who says that an Act of 1836, giving some representation to cess-payers, proved 'inadequate and ineffectual'.

[3] Hansard, XV, 963–4, 19 February 1833, O'Connell. Stanley's Bill died on the way to a Select Committee.

[4] For the education scheme, which was successfully pressed on the Government by Thomas Wyse, Bishop Doyle and Lord Cloncurry, see Auchmuty, *Wyse*, 78–84; Fitzpatrick, *Doyle*, II, 253–8, 328–9; *Personal Recollections of Lord Cloncurry* (1849), 389–90; Cabinet Minute by Stanley, 9 August 1831, H.O. Papers, 100/239, 50–3; Hansard, VI, 1249–61, 9 September 1831, Stanley.

many of its schools, the system itself survived and flourished.[1] The number of children (most of them Catholic) in its schools rose from 107,000 in 1833 to 355,000 in 1843 and to over half a million by 1853. In 1851 41 per cent of the Irish male population were literate, 58 per cent could at least read. Whatever its shortcomings, the system played a vital part in the education of peasant Ireland.[2]

The Whigs could not exclude Ireland from their plans for parliamentary reform. The representative system had suffered drastic disfranchisement of its constituencies by the Act of Union and of electors in 1829, when from figures produced in 1832 by Nicholas Philpot Leader, M.P. for Kilkenny, 191,000 forty-shilling freeholders out of a county electorate of 216,000 had been affected.[3] But a small total electorate (between 20,000 and 30,000 before 1832)[4] and a highly defective system of registration had not prevented Whig and O'Connellite successes, for the whole representation was heavily weighted in favour of the 32 counties returning 64 of the 100 Irish Members. In these constituencies, the £10 freeholders showed themselves Whig if not nationalist in opinion. But no less than 18 of the 33 borough constituencies were completely immune to contests of any kind, while many of the so-called 'open' boroughs were controlled by local, usually Tory magnates.[5] Even in the counties, the swing towards the left before 1832 had benefited the traditional sources of political power, for in 1830 at least 41 of the 64 county M.P.s belonged to landed families which had had

[1] See R. Barry O'Brien, *Fifty Years of Concessions to Ireland* (1883), I, 126–215; T. O'Raifeartaigh, 'Mixed Education and the Synod of Ulster, 1831–40', *Irish Historical Studies*, IX, No. 35 (March 1955), 281–99; and the life of the system's most persistent English opponent, G. C. B. Davies, *Henry Phillpotts, Bishop of Exeter, 1778–1869* (1954), 128, 334–5.

[2] Commissioners of National Education to Lord Ebrington, 26 April 1839, H.O. Papers, 100/257, 87–92; O'Brien, *Fifty Years*, I, 206. Literacy figures from J. M. Wilson, 'Statistics of Crime in Ireland, 1842 to 1856', *Journal of the Dublin Statistical Society* (November 1857), Appendix, Tables G. and H., 115–16. See also James Johnston Auchmuty, *Irish Education* (1937); David Kennedy, 'Education and the People', in *Social Life in Ireland, 1800–45*, ed R. B. McDowell (1957), 57–70.

[3] Hansard, XIII, 580–5, 13 June 1832, N. P. Leader.

[4] Reynolds, *Catholic Emancipation Crisis*, 168, gives a figure of 'about 16,000' in 1830. Leader's figures point to a larger electorate, at least in 1831–2.

[5] Hansard, XIII, 583, 13 June 1832, Leader, whose classification of 10 close corporation and 8 nomination boroughs was never challenged.

representatives in eighteenth-century Parliaments.[1] O'Connell had everything to gain from any measure of reform which might throw open the boroughs and allow him either to break the grip of landed interests in the counties or to use them for his own purposes.

The Whig plan proposed to add five Members to the representation, one additional Member each for the cities of Belfast, Limerick and Waterford and for the town of Galway, with one extra Member for Dublin University. In all boroughs, there was to be a uniform £10 household franchise; in the counties, the £10 freeholders were to be joined by those holding 21-year leases of a value of £50; in eight so-called 'counties' of cities and towns, the franchise would be an amalgam of the county and borough franchises.[2] There was to be no disfranchisement since all the Irish parliamentary boroughs, whatever the size of their present electorates, were thought to be places with large populations and commercial importance. The whole plan was ingeniously contrived to reconcile general Whig principles, particularly with regard to borough representation, with an obvious anxiety to prevent a revolutionary transfer of power in Ireland. The Whigs believed that some reforms, even if their tendency was to replace Catholic for Protestant influence in Irish politics, were inevitable. After Emancipation, reform could not conceivably be denied on religious grounds, and to deny it for political reasons would be to play into the hands of the nationalists. The Government, aware that the Opposition might regard this Bill as the most revolutionary of the three Reform Bills, therefore kept all changes to a minimum. A £10 borough franchise would give boroughs the reform they had hitherto escaped; 'the great and important interests' of four boroughs would be recognized by an additional Member each; and the Protestant interest would itself be strengthened by the additional University Member.[3]

The Government's central position between the extremes of Tory reaction and O'Connellite radicalism had definite tactical advantages. In April 1831 the Tory Member for Liverpool, General Gascoyne,

[1] McDowell, *Public Opinion*, 43.

[2] Hansard, III, 862–7, 24 March 1831, Stanley.

[3] See esp. Stanley's speeches, Hansard, IX, 595–606; XIII, 119–25, 19 January; 25 May 1832; Norman Gash, *Politics in the Age of Peel* (1953), 50–64, the best account of the framing and passing of the Irish Bill; and *Annual Register* (1832), 200–15.

successfully called on the House to vote against any decrease in the English representation. Somewhat disingenuously, he denied any hostility towards the Irish representation, but it was obvious that the original Whig plan (a House of 596, with 105 Irish Members) would have given Ireland greater weight in the parliamentary system than she was to enjoy with 105 Members in a House of 658. O'Connell had every interest in defeating Gascoyne's motion, and in a passionate and excited speech he warned the Commons of the possible effects on Irish opinion. The majority for the motion was only eight votes, 55 Irish Members following O'Connell in support of the Government (an interesting indication of the state of the unreformed Irish representation), 36 supporting Gascoyne.[1] The motion, perhaps decisive in the long run for the whole question of Irish representation at Westminster, conveniently excused the Whigs in 1832 from increasing Irish representation by more than a few seats and allowed them to resist Irish pressure on this crucial point. Lord Grey would never have agreed to any increase in the Irish county representation; as for the additions to the Irish boroughs, these would remain few since he personally sympathized with many of the Opposition's objections; but because it was 'absolutely necessary to make an addition to Scotland, . . . a corresponding addition to Ireland could not be avoided'.[2]

Defeat on Gascoyne's motion, followed by a General Election and the long crisis on the English Reform Bills, upset the Government's plan to pass the Irish measure quietly under the shadow of the English Bill. Delayed and isolated, reaching its committee stage only after the English Bill had passed, the Irish measure became the subject of bitter and contentious debate. In March 1831, giving his support to the first English Bill as a 'Radical Reformer' who favoured universal manhood suffrage, shorter parliaments and the ballot, O'Connell laid down the policy which he and his party were consistently to follow on Irish reform. Essentially, this was to demand increased representation and a low franchise. But his first reaction to the details of the Irish Bill was to express the 'great satisfaction'

[1] Hansard, III, 1528, 1659–65, 1690–1700, 18, 19 April 1831, Gascoyne, O'Connell, Division. The Opposition expected a majority of 16 or 17: Ellenborough, *Diary*, 20 April 1831, Aspinall, op. cit., 81–2.

[2] Gash, *Politics*, 62; Littleton, *Diary*, 21 January 1832, Aspinall, op. cit., 182, for the Government's agreement on this point with the proposal of the Tory 'waverer', Lord Wharncliffe.

of himself and the Irish people; carried away by his own enthusiasm for reform and forced quickly to decide on his tactics, he had committed a tactical blunder.[1] When he tried later to lower the franchises he was accused by Crampton, the Irish Solicitor-General, of having earlier supported the Government's plan and attacked by Stanley for flagrant inconsistency in supporting the Whigs in the Commons and opposing them in Ireland.[2]

The Whigs kept the most rigid control over their measure, which had been prepared entirely without consultation with O'Connell; and Irish Members remained ignorant of its details until Stanley's introductory speech in March 1831. Grateful for valuable Irish support on the English Bill and hoping to obtain O'Connell's general acquiescence in their Irish plan, Ministers dropped this imperious attitude. In July 1831 Althorp and O'Connell met to discuss what O'Connell privately called Stanley's 'humbug "improvements"' in the Bill; and in September O'Connell and Sir John Newport, the aged doyen of the Irish Whigs, went as a deputation from Irish Members to meet Althorp, Lord John Russell and Stanley.[3] O'Connell later claimed that he had made some impression on the first two and on Thomas Spring Rice, but that Stanley had been adamant against any concessions.[4]

The Irish case for increased representation rested primarily on arguments from population. At least seven Irish counties had populations of well over 200,000 each. Antrim, Down and Tipperary were all larger than most of those English counties which were each to gain two more seats, while only Yorkshire and Lancashire had a larger population than County Cork. O'Connell compared the treatment of Scotland, which with a population of two millions was to receive eight more Members and a representation of 53, with that of Ireland, which despite a population of over seven millions was to gain only five new Members above her present total of 100.[5] The Irish party's demands rose progressively throughout the debates, from O'Connell's request for 11 more seats in March 1831 to 25 in

[1] Hansard, III, 181–209, 708, 868–72, 8, 22, 24 March 1831, O'Connell; *Pilot*, 7 March 1831.

[2] Hansard, XIII, 778–86, 792–6, 18 June 1832, Crampton, Stanley.

[3] O'Connell to R. Barrett, 2 July 1831; to P. V. Fitzpatrick, 21 September 1831, *O'Connell Corr.*, I, 267, 272.

[4] Fagan, *O'Connell*, II, 167–8; Hansard, XIII, 571–2, 13 June 1832, O'Connell; *Pilot*, 23 January 1833.

[5] Hansard, III, 196–9, 868–72, 8, 24 March 1831, O'Connell.

January and 47 in June 1832.[1] Although O'Connell argued cogently against the Whig doctrine of the representation of 'interests' by pointing out that it was impossible to distinguish between the manufacturing and agricultural interests in Ireland, where the former virtually did not exist, his arguments had no effect on the Government.[2]

Similarly, the Whigs stuck in essentials to their plan of Irish franchises, comfortably defeating attempts to restore the forty-shilling vote and to introduce a £5 freehold franchise. Irish M.P.s argued that the disfranchisement of 1829 had not formed part of a solemn unalterable compact, that an Irish £10 franchise, after all costs, charges and expenses, would be the equivalent of £20 in England and would produce a county electorate of only 26,000 and that a £5 standard would at least give the counties 60,000 to 90,000 electors. But Stanley caustically described the forty-shilling freeholders as mostly land squatters, with no title except long possession, 'the lowest and most venal' class of elector; and Russell, though more conciliatory, could not conscientiously go back on his support of their disfranchisement in 1829.[3] The Government's sole concession, the reduction of the county leasehold qualification from £50 to £10, promised more than it performed; in 1847, there were only about 5,000 electors of this class in a total county electorate of nearly 60,000.[4]

O'Connell, who believed that the Bill would open up 17 or 19 boroughs, took less interest in the £10 household franchise. But other Irish Members, notably Leader and Dominick Browne, the Whig M.P. for Mayo, tried to show that this franchise would leave at least a third of the boroughs with less than 300 electors, the standard used in dealing with the smallest English boroughs. Stanley readily admitted that 'there were towns . . . which it might

[1] *Pilot*, 12 January 1832; Hansard, XIII, 463–5, 6 June 1832, O'Connell. *The Times*, 20 January 1832, conceded that on population alone Ireland should have 225 members, or over a third of the House; N. P. Leader, comparing Ireland with England on the basis of acreage, population, revenue, imports and exports, estimated Ireland's rightful representation at 161 Members, Hansard, IX, 607–9, 19 January 1832.

[2] Hansard, XIII, 775, 18 June 1832, O'Connell.

[3] Hansard, XIII, 589–90, 584, 570–7, 769–78, 579, 590, 13, 18 June 1832, Sheil, Leader, O'Connell, Stanley, Russell.

[4] Hansard, XIII, 1010–15, 25 June 1832, Stanley, O'Connell; C. R. Dod, *Electoral Facts* (1852), 151. For technical reasons, O'Connell was able to lower the length of lease required from 21 to 20 years.

be expedient to disfranchise', but he quickly added that the Bill had
been framed on the principle of no disfranchisement and thus disposed of Browne's plan to redistribute the seats of five of the smallest
boroughs.[1] The Whigs showed great tenderness for the electoral
rights of freemen in the borough corporations. Their original plan
had confined these rights only to existing freemen and their children
but they were finally prepared, under Tory pressure and after surprising representations from O'Connell himself, to continue all
resident freemen in perpetual possession of their franchise and even
to allow non-resident freemen, provided that they had been admitted
before 30 March 1831, to retain this right for their own lives.[2]

The additional University seat ran the Government into worse
difficulties. Irish Members continuously attacked the Whigs for
adding one seat to an institution which Sheil, himself a Trinity man,
unfairly called 'the silent sister in the family of science' and which
would have had, on the limited franchise originally proposed, a constituency of only 200, all necessarily Protestants. Grey, intensely
irritated by sniping Irish criticism, admitted that many English
Whigs disliked the plan and that it would have been better to give
the seat to Kilkenny.[3] The Cabinet first decided to stand by the
original proposal and only at the last moment surrendered to continuous pressure by throwing open the franchise to all M.A.s, a proportion of whom were Catholics. For Irish Liberals, this concession
proved valueless, a large University constituency (over 2,000 in
1832) returning two Conservatives throughout O'Connell's lifetime.[4]

A Boundary Act, which passed both Houses virtually without
debate, accompanied the main Bill. In England, reform of boundaries was used deliberately to increase many borough constituencies, but in Ireland, where boundaries had been rationalized at
the time of the Union, the purpose in 1832 seems to have been
the largely negative one of preventing any swamping of borough

[1] Hansard, XIV, 187–90, 527–9, 9, 18 July 1832, Browne, Stanley, O'Connell,
Leader. O'Connell, who opposed Browne, would not hear of any disfranchisement.

[2] Hansard, XIII, 1259–64, 2 July 1832, F. Shaw, O'Connell; see further
below, pp. 108–9, for the electoral significance of the freemen.

[3] Hansard, IX, 623–5; XIII, 596–8, 19 January; 13 June 1832, Sheil, Sir R.
Heron; Gash, *Politics*, 59, quoting *Correspondence of William IV and Earl Grey*,
ed. Earl Grey (1867), II, 451, 456.

[4] The University representation was always solidly Unionist. See James
Johnston Auchmuty, *Lecky: A Biographical and Critical Essay* (1945), 85–99.

constituencies by county voters. Boundaries were thus either left unchanged or drawn closely round the respective boroughs, and the Boundary Commissioners, working to the plan of enlarging only to secure a minimum of 200 electors, scarcely succeeded in this modest aim.[1] After 1832, five boroughs had less than 200 electors, ten less than 300. Although O'Connell twice complained of the vague and unsatisfactory information in the Commissioners' Reports, it is hard to see why he and his followers did not press this important point further, for fixed borough boundaries were the main factors, after the high £10 franchise, in limiting the size of many borough constituencies between 1832 and 1847.[2]

The registration clauses of the Act essentially renewed the old system. O'Connell particularly objected to two features which differed materially from the system adopted in England. The English registration was 'to be effected by a person responsible to a jury for any wilful misconduct'; in Ireland, the assistant barrister was 'totally irresponsible'. In England no claimant could be called on to show his title without notice, while in Ireland no such notice was required. Stanley admitted that the existing system needed alteration, but he was not prepared to apply the English system to Ireland beyond lowering the fee for the certification of voters from 2s. 6d. to parity with England at 1s.[3] Registration in Ireland soon proved open to much abuse and was unpopular with all parties. The Whigs' failure to tackle it in 1832 recoiled on their own heads in 1840-1, when Stanley himself, then a Conservative, used the issue to damage his old colleagues; and the system itself remained unchanged in O'Connell's lifetime, probably benefiting his movement more than the cause of his opponents.[4]

In 1832, O'Connell called the Irish Reform Bill 'conservative', 'the new-fangled phrase now used in polite society to designate the Tory ascendency', and he continued in later years to denounce it as an 'insulting injustice', 'the exclusive production of Mr. Stanley confirmed by the anti-Irish party which he commanded in the

[1] Boundary Reports (Ireland), P.P. 1831-2, XLIII, i-ii, Instructions from E. G. Stanley to Captain Gipps, 29 October 1831. There are almost no traces of discussion of the Bill in Hansard.

[2] Hansard, XIII, 564-8, 769-78, 13, 18 June 1832, O'Connell. Dod, *Electoral Facts* (1852), 151, has figures which show an actual decline in the total borough electorate in the period 1832 to 1851; but see below Appendix A, No. 6.

[3] *F.J.*, 16 June 1832.

[4] See further below pp. 88-93, 165-6.

Cabinet'.[1] Tories saw the Bill as a revolutionary measure likely to 'undermine British connexion, destroy the Established Church and ruin the security of property', and certainly a breach of what Peel called 'a great experiment in government', the settlement of 1829.[2] Yet of all the important Irish measures in Parliament in this period, none passed so easily through that bastion of Toryism, the House of Lords. Tory rhetoric, doing service for effective opposition, doubtless represented a real fear that the Bill would destroy the Irish Tory party. But if it effectively prevented the Conservatives from obtaining a majority in the Irish representation, the Bill was in reality a fundamentally conservative measure. It more than trebled the electorate (to about 92,000 in 1832), but ensured that each Irish Member of Parliament represented an average of nearly 74,000 persons as compared with one to 27,000 in England. The ratio of borough electors to borough populations was much the same in the two countries, but in the Irish counties, the most vulnerable part of the electoral system, only one person in every 115 was enfranchised as against one in 24 in England.[3] The Whigs had not deliberately designed the Irish Bill to further their own electoral fortunes, scarcely a feasible aim against O'Connell's commanding position in Irish politics. But the Bill was designed to prevent the nationalists from absorbing the entire representation, and in this limited aim it was successful. It was an important factor in limiting the size of an independent Irish party, creating in effect a three-party balance in the electoral system; and when after 1835 the system reverted temporarily to a two-party dichotomy, the Whig architects of the Bill reaped their reward in a large Liberal majority in Ireland.

If the Irish Reform Act was the work of a united Cabinet, the reform of the Established Church in Ireland proved, in Sir James Graham's words, 'the fatal subject of difference' for Grey's Government.[4] For its large establishment of four archbishops, eighteen bishops and some 2,000 clergymen, the Church enjoyed before 1833 a gross annual income of between £800,000 and £1,000,000. Its wealth, privileges and comparatively small membership (800,000

[1] Hansard, XIII, 150, 25 May 1832, O'Connell; O'Connell to Lord Durham, 21 October 1834, O'Connell Papers, N.L.I., 423; Fagan, *O'Connell*, II, 159–67.

[2] Hansard, XIII, 125–32, 142, 165–74, 25 May 1832, Shaw, Peel, Lefroy. Peel was ready to drop the nomination boroughs, but for the Irish Tories borough reform was the most objectionable part of the Bill.

[3] Dod, *Electoral Facts* [xii]; below, Appendix A, No. 6.

[4] C. S. Parker, *The Life and Letters of Sir James Graham* (1907), I, 169–70.

among over 6,000,000 Catholics)[1] placed the Church in an extraordinary and anomalous position, comparable, in Sydney Smith's
devastating analogy, to the butchers' shops established by the
British in Hindu India. There was, he wrote of the Church, 'no
abuse like it in Europe, in all Asia, in all the discovered parts of
Africa, and in all we have heard of Timbuctoo!'[2] But the Act of
Union had solemnly built this relic of past English policy into the
constitution of the Kingdom and united it with the Established
Church in England, thus guaranteeing it a large measure of English
support and sympathy. The simple argument of 'No Church, No
Union' could be used against all the enemies of the Irish Church
(who were generally the enemies of Church Establishments everywhere), against the Utilitarian Radicals, William Cobbett, the
increasingly powerful Dissenter interest in England and the Irish
Catholics, even against those like the Whigs and the Evangelical
party in the Church who wished to reform the Church for its own
future welfare, all of whom could be held up as accomplices or
unconscious tools in O'Connell's conspiracy against the integrity
of the United Kingdom.[3]

The Irish Church became a leading issue in a great contemporary
debate on the relations between Church and State. Indeed for men
as different as John Wilson Croker, the Tory publicist, and the young
John Henry Newman it raised even greater issues. To Croker, 'The
question of the Irish Church serious enough in itself becomes a
thousand times more so (in extent though not in principle) by its
being the field of battle in which we are to fight for all property & all
our institutions.'[4] The Oxford Movement rose directly from the
urgent political necessity to defend the Church against liberalism,
against any further development of the principles assumed to lie

---

[1] Census of Commissioners of Public Instruction, 1834, quoted by W. D.
Killen, *Ecclesiastical History of Ireland* (1875), II, 462–3. For Church income,
see Richard Burn, *The Ecclesiastical Law* (9th edn. 1842), ed. Robert Phillimore,
I, 415, xx; John D'Alton, *The History of Tithes, Church Lands and other Ecclesiastical Benefices* (1832), 49–54. See also Returns in P.P. 1835, XLVII, (81) 1–3;
(388), 1–29, which show that well over one-third of the 2,045 parishes contained
less than 50 Protestants and that a third of the benefices were held by non-
resident clergymen.

[2] Sydney Smith, *Works* (1850), III, 687.

[3] See, for instance, the arguments in Madden, *Ireland and Its Rulers*, II,
162–77.

[4] Croker to Burdett, 29 March 1835, Patterson, *Burdett*, II, 635.

behind the Irish Church Temporalities Act of 1833, which John Keble called an 'act of national apostasy' and a 'direct disavowal of the sovereignty of God'; and from the religious necessity, as laid down by Newman, to assert 'the real ground on which our authority is built—OUR APOSTOLICAL DESCENT', in case the Church should be disestablished and disendowed.[1]

Contemporaries like Lord Grey were right to regard O'Connell's aim as 'the total subversion of the Protestant Establishment',[2] yet it did not follow, as O'Connell's opponents (notably the Whigs) also believed, that he and his fellow-Catholics would gladly replace it with a Catholic Establishment. From the Veto controversy until the end of his life, O'Connell consistently opposed all schemes for a direct connection between the State and the Catholic Church.[3] His plan in 1832 for a concurrent endowment of all denominations envisaged the abolition of tithes, with compensation, and the raising of a land income-tax to pay all clergymen; since the Government would have no control of this fund, there would be no connection between the clergy, Catholic or Protestant, and the State. This ingenious plan was considerably in advance of Irish Catholic opinion and, significantly, was never raised by him in Parliament.[4]

Irish disestablishment, even in the reforming 1830's, was a bold programme, and O'Connell's occasionally moderate attitude and willingness to accept somewhat unsatisfactory instalments were caused by his anxiety to find English allies and to disarm English hostility. He had to contend with the traditional Protestant beliefs, quite as strong among anti-State Church Nonconformists as among Anglicans, in the wickedness of the Church of Rome and in the doubtful political allegiance of its adherents in the United Kingdom, as well as with a public opinion which judged its Catholics by continental examples and could not understand how the Irish could be both Catholic and liberal. It made little difference that O'Connell

---

[1] R. W. Church, *The Oxford Movement, Twelve Years 1833–1845* (1891), 82–3; *Newman's Apologia pro vita sua* (1931), 134 ff.; Tract I, 'Ad Clerum', in *Tracts for The Times*, by Members of the University of Oxford (London, 1840), I, 1–2; Halévy, *History*, III, 130–82, the classic account of the whole religious debate.

[2] Grey to Sir John Newport, 2 October 1832, Newport Papers, N.L.I., 796.

[3] See esp. O'Connell to Peel, 18 May 1838, Peel Papers, Add. MSS 40425, 86–94.

[4] O'Connell to National Political Union, 14 July 1832, in Fagan, *O'Connell*, II, 142–4. A. de Tocqueville, *Journeys to England and Ireland (1958)*, 132–3, 136, 145, 171–2, throws much light on Catholic opinion on the subject of Establishment.

always maintained a very considerable measure of political independence both of the Papacy and, at least until towards the end of his
life, of the Catholic Church authorities in Ireland, who were his
allies but not his masters.[1]

By the end of October 1832, when the Cabinet settled on a plan of
Irish Church reform which was 'quite as large', according to Grey,
'as we could hope to carry' considering both English public opinion
and the overwhelmingly Tory House of Lords, the Whigs had passed
through their first major internal crisis.[2] The crucial issue had been,
as it was to remain, the right of Parliament to appropriate surplus
Church revenues for secular purposes; and the liberal section of the
Government, including Russell, Althorp, Durham and Anglesey,
had failed to carry this point outright against Stanley, Graham, the
Duke of Richmond and Grey himself.[3] The Irish Church Temporalities Bill, introduced by Althorp on 12 February 1833, proposed to
abolish church cess, yielding annually £60,000 to £70,000 and raised
from Catholics as well as Protestants, and to replace it by a graduated
tax of 5 per cent to 15 per cent on all clerical incomes over £200,
the proceeds to go to Church purposes. Ten of the twenty-two
bishoprics were to be abolished; a Board of lay and ecclesiastical
Commissioners was to be empowered to suspend appointments to
parishes where no religious service had been performed for three
years; and finally, by the 147th clause, it was proposed to create a
fund of between £2,000,000 and £3,000,000 by allowing the tenants
on the bishops' extensive estates to buy their land outright in place
of the present short-term leases. From this fund the State would pay

---

[1] W. E. H. Lecky, *Leaders of Public Opinion in Ireland* (1912), II, 230–3, was
the first historian (in 1861) to do justice to O'Connell as a Catholic democrat.
But see also McDowell, *Public Opinion*, 122–5; Broderick, 'The Holy See',
Analecta Gregoriana, LV, 22–5, 192 ff. O'Faoláin, *King of the Beggars*, 74–95, is
interesting on O'Connell's personal religion; and Canon O'Rourke, *The Centenary
Life of O'Connell* (1900), 283–7, gives O'Connell's own heterodox view express-
ed to Gladstone in 1834, that Protestants were 'internally' united to the true
Church.

[2] Grey to Russell, 25 October 1832, Spencer Walpole, *Life of Lord John
Russell* (1889), I, 190.

[3] For Russell's threat to resign and the Cabinet crisis, see Walpole, *Russell*, I,
188–92; Parker, *Graham*, I, 175–7, 179–80. Stanley's conservative position is
well illustrated by his private correspondence on Church reform with the Primate, Lord John George Beresford, Archbishop of Armagh; Stanley to Armagh,
30 September 1832; Armagh to Stanley, 4 October 1832, Beresford–Leslie
MSS, N.L.I., 4838.

the bishops the equivalent of their former rents and any surplus, since it would be the result of legislative action, would be at Parliament's disposal.[1]

The liberal Whigs seemed to have saved their faces. Despite the fears of Whig party managers, the Bill was a great initial triumph for the Government in and out of the House, bringing it the support of Whigs and moderate Radicals, Dissenters and moderate Churchmen, and of the Irish under O'Connell, who expressed his 'great satisfaction and delight' at a plan which 'recognized the right of Government to look into the state of ecclesiastical property thereafter' and who even joined in the ovation, 'the most tumultuous cheering' Le Marchant had ever heard in the Commons, given to Stanley's closing speech.[2] Furthermore, the Bill caused a serious division within the Opposition, for while Peel objected strongly to clause 147 as an application of Ricardo's theory that every increase of the net produce of an estate which was the creation of society could be justly confiscated, he was prepared to concede the reduction of bishoprics, the abolition of certain taxes which brought the Catholic peasant into collision with the Establishment and the re-distribution, inside the Church, of Church revenues. The gulf was unbridgeable between these views and the arguments of High Church Tories like Sir Robert Inglis, who thought the Bill contrary to the Coronation Oath, the Act of Union, the Relief Act of 1829 and the oath taken by M.P.s, and who opposed the re-distribution of revenues as well as the abolition of bishoprics, these vital links in the Church's claim to apostolic succession and authority.[3]

On 21 June, after the rest of the Bill had passed with massive majorities, clause 147 was reached. The Cabinet had settled on the vague formula of 'religious and charitable purposes', a term under-

---

[1] Hansard, XV, 561–77, 12 February 1833, Althorp; William Law Mathieson, *English Church Reform, 1815–40* (1923), 76–7.

[2] Le Marchant, *Diary* [February 1833]; Littleton, *Diary*, 12 February 1833, Aspinall, op. cit., 299–301, 303; Greville, *Journal*, 14 February 1833, II, 362; Hansard, XV, 577–8, 12 February 1833, O'Connell.

[3] Hansard, XV, 589–607, 12 February 1833, Peel; Peel to Henry Goulburn, 26 April 1833, Parker, *Peel*, II, 218–20; Hansard, XV, 578–85; XVI, 1393–7; XVII, 986–92, 1386–7, 12 February, 1 April, 6, 20 May 1833, Inglis; see also Killen, *Ecclesiastical History*, II, 461–2, n. 1, for a typical Irish High Church view. The crisis in the Tory party can be followed in Greville, *Journal*, 14, 22, 27 February 1833, II, 363, 369, 371; and in Ellenborough, *Diary*, 12 March 1833, Aspinall, op. cit., 315–16.

stood to include the payment of the Catholic clergy, some assistance to education and possibly poor relief; but just before the debate on the clause, a Cabinet majority surrendered to Stanley and to its own anxiety to avoid collision with the Lords by deciding to drop the whole clause.[1] The attempts of Liberal Ministers like Althorp and Russell to minimize the importance of the clause were highly disingenuous as well as ineffective.[2] While Stanley was announcing the Government's decision, O'Connell, Cobbett and some Irish Members loudly protested, and O'Connell immediately delivered a savage attack on men who had asked Parliament to pass the Irish Coercion Bill in return for 'a great and important principle of relief', but who now 'sacrificed their principles in order to keep their places'. He repudiated a Bill which, though the Irish people had no interest in the number of bishops, simply treated these churchmen like ninepins.[3]

Their sudden surrender undoubtedly damaged the Whigs, shocking their 'independent' Liberal supporters, infuriating the Irish and advertising their own divisions. Stanley was indeed 'half a Tory',[4] but he had conclusively won the first round in the struggle which ended with his own resignation in May 1834. With Tory support and by a majority of 131 the clause was cut out of the Bill, but a minority of 149, including nearly 100 English and Scottish Radicals and liberal Whigs, nearly all the Repealers and a few Irish Whigs, was an ominous sign for the future. To a barrage of Irish protests and amendments, including Sheil's attempt to write the substance of clause 147 into the Bill's preamble, the Bill finally passed easily in the Commons against an incongruous opposition of English Radicals, Irish and English Tories and O'Connell, who was more intransigent than most of his party.[5]

[1] Le Marchant, *Diary* [21, 22 June], 1833; Ellenborough, *Diary*, 22 June 1833, Aspinall, op. cit., 338-40; Peel to Goulburn, 19 June 1833, Parker, *Peel*, II, 221-2. There was no question, as Creevey thought, of a compromise with Peel; *The Creevey Papers*, ed. Sir H. Maxwell (1903), II, 255-6.

[2] See Le Marchant, *Diary* [22 June], 1833, Aspinall, op. cit., 339; and Hansard, XVIII, 1096, 21 June 1833, for Russell's declaration that 'this country could not stand a revolution once a year'.

[3] Hansard, XVIII, 1075-7, 21 June 1833, O'Connell; see below pp. 44ff. for the Coercion Bill of 1833.

[4] Greville, *Journal*, 26 June 1833, II, 390-1.

[5] Hansard, XIX, 282-3, 301, 8 July 1833, Divisions; Goulburn to Peel, 25 June 1833, Peel Papers, Add. MSS 40333, 162-5, which shows that the Tories expected and could not avoid these Radical 'allies'.

The overwhelmingly Tory House of Lords, still smarting from its defeat on the Reform Bill and containing a powerful minority of nearly 80 Ultra Tory diehards under the Duke of Cumberland's leadership, might well have killed the Bill out of hand.[1] That the Lords did not do so (and indeed passed it with only one important alteration, by which the funds of a suspended benefice were to be used first to build a church and glebe-house in the parish in question),[2] was due largely to Wellington, who after some alarming hesitation produced by his own strong dislike of the Bill preferred to enrage the diehards rather than to break with Peel and perhaps plunge the country into another constitutional crisis.[3] But by this time O'Connell had not unjustifiably lost all interest in a measure which, without Appropriation, merely carried out a mild though doubtless necessary reorganization of the Irish Church.

The independent party

The Whigs' Irish programme of 1831–3, whatever its shortcomings, was not only a tribute to O'Connell's success in maintaining constant pressure on the Government, but also represented the payment of a political debt of honour. From November 1830 and throughout the long Reform crisis of 1831–2, Irish support was always valuable and at times even vital for the Whigs; without it, to take the most important instance, they would not have obtained their majority of one on the crucial Second Reading of the first Reform Bill in March 1831. O'Connell's personal contribution to the victory of Reform was considerable. Even after the large English reforming majority of the 1831 Election had powerfully strengthened the Whigs' position, they took some pains to obtain the support of

[1] See David Large, 'The House of Lords and Ireland in the Age of Peel, 1832–50', *Irish Historical Studies*, IX, No. 36 (September 1955), 375–9; E. Hughes, 'The Bishops and Reform, 1831–3: Some Fresh Correspondence', *English Historical Review*, LVI, No. CCXXIII (July 1941), 459–90, for the opposition of a majority of the Bishops; and A. S. Turberville, *The House of Lords in the Age of Reform, 1784–1837* (1958), 345–6.

[2] For the minor political crisis caused by this amendment, see Le Marchant, *Diary*, 21 July 1833; Littleton, *Diary*, 12, 25, 26 July 1833, Aspinall, op. cit., 347, 352, 354, 361–3.

[3] See esp. Wellington to Peel, 23 July 1833, Peel Papers, Add. MSS. 40309, 264–5, quoted in part by Parker, *Peel*, II, 218; Large, 'House of Lords', loc. cit., 377–8.

O'Connell and his followers and were duly grateful when, as in the crisis of May 1832, it was forthcoming.[1] In the early nineteenth-century Commons, where party discipline was inchoate and customarily informal and where Members' personal interests often obscured their party allegiance, the Irish party, by far the largest group under the control of a politician unconnected with Government or the official Opposition, represented a formidable concentration of political power. Before 1833 the control of between 20 and 30 followers, 'a stout little phalanx, sitting below the Treasury Benches next the Bar',[2] allowed O'Connell to save the Government from defeat on the important issue of the Russo-Dutch Loan in January 1832 by arranging for the abstention of seven or eight Irish Members, and to threaten, on another occasion, that 'There are 37 (sic) of us, & if they do *not* carry the [Reform] Bill we will destroy them, & if they *do*, we shall destroy them'.[3] The Whig managers found great difficulty in controlling a party most of whose members could not always be kept in line by Whig hospitality and who occasionally held their own meetings. Obedience to the pressure of Irish public opinion, which offended against all traditional notions of the 'independence' of Members, made the Irish embarrassing and unrespectable allies, 'perfect swindlers', according to one observer, who were 'the warmest admirers of the Government' in private and 'open mouthed against it' in the House.[4]

The General Election of 1832 saw the emergence of the Repeal party as an independent political force. In addition to its 39 members, O'Connell could generally rely on the support of at least half of the 36 Irish Whig-Liberals and on the co-operation of the increased number of English and Scottish Radicals. Most contemporaries, exaggerating the strength and cohesion of the Radical contingent in

---

[1] Duncannon to O'Connell, 28 November 1831, *O'Connell Corr.*, I, 279–80; Broughton, *Recollections*, 10, 14, 18 May 1832, IV, 222, 226, 233.

[2] Littleton, *Diary*, 8 March 1832; Ellenborough, *Diary*, 15 July 1831, Aspinall, op. cit., 206, 107. Ellenborough estimated the party at 29.

[3] Hansard, IX, 940–1, 26 January 1832, O'Connell; Ellenborough, *Diary*, 15 July 1831; 26 January 1832, Aspinall, op. cit., 106–7, 184–5.

[4] Le Marchant, *Diary* [n.d. March 1832], 1 August 1832, Aspinall, op. cit., 211, 279; cf. the Radical Henry Hunt's description of 'the wily lawyer' and his 'gang of impostors' in August 1831, in Gwynn, *O'Gorman Mahon*, 146–7. Sir John Campbell was one of the few Ministers to remain on good terms with O'Connell, whom he considered 'a very extraordinary fellow' of vast powers and resources; Campbell to Sir G. Campbell, 23 March 1833, *Campbell*, II, 33–4.

the reformed House, included the Irish in it. Lord Mahon, for instance, saw a House of 150 Conservatives, 320 Whigs and Ministerialists and 190 'thick-and-thin Radicals, Repealers from Ireland, members or friends of the political Unions, . . . Cobbettites and Humeites and Irish blackguards'.[1] In reality the new House, although it contained many new Members and a huge, heterogeneous majority on paper for the Government, was not strikingly different in terms of class and economic interest from its unreformed predecessors. But there were distinct and (for conservatives) alarming differences in terms of atmosphere and political alignment. One of the most remarkable of these was singled out by Greville, who recognized in 'the swagger of O'Connell, walking about incessantly, and making signs to, or talking with his followers' the existence of a new party.[2]

Peel saw the Radicals and the Irish as the real opposition to the Government, and the struggle over the Irish Coercion Bill, the most important issue immediately confronting the new Parliament in 1833, seemed to prove him right.[3] Disorder and lawlessness in the Irish countryside, that other Ireland where, as George Cornewall Lewis wrote in 1836, there was 'less security of person and property than in any other part of Europe, except perhaps in the wildest parts of Calabria or Greece', was in no sense a new problem.[4] Since the mid-eighteenth century, the Irish peasantry had been in intermittent but continuous revolt against its social and economic position. Degraded for centuries on the score of race and religion, dispossessed of their tribal lands by an alien landlord class to whom they had little cause for gratitude, the peasants formed a virtually autonomous community cut off by its differences of language, customs, lack of education and above all by its economic position from the rest of Irish society. The evolution by the peasantry of a defensive network

[1] Mahon to Peel, 8 January 1833, Parker, *Peel*, II, 209–11. Littleton, *Diary*, 28 January 1833, Aspinall, op. cit., 290, put the Radicals at 130; Halévy, *History*, III, 65, thinks they were not above 50 or 60.

[2] Greville, *Journal*, 10, 22 February 1833, II, 361, 369; see also Halévy, *History*, III, 62–3. For an official Whig view of the Repeal party in 1833, see below, App. B, 2, pp. 307–8, Charles Wood to Sir John Hobhouse, 9 April 1833, Hobhouse Papers, Add. MSS 36467, 38–43.

[3] Peel to Goulburn, 3 January 1833; to Croker, 5 March 1833, Parker, *Peel*, II, 212–13, 215–16.

[4] George Cornewall Lewis, *On Local Disturbances in Ireland and on the Irish Church Question* (1836), 1, 3–44.

of secret societies, administering a law of opinion on a strict code of retributive justice and constituting 'a vast trades' union for the protection of the Irish peasantry: the object being . . . to keep the actual occupant in possession of his land, and in general to regulate the relation of landlord and tenant for the benefit of the latter',[1] was the direct consequence of land hunger; and this land hunger was itself a consequence of the dramatic rise in the Irish rural population, which had more than doubled since 1770 and was still increasing up to the Famine. The peasants were indeed struggling for existence, passively by sub-dividing their holdings, by squatting illegally on bog and mountainsides or by taking land at extremely high, quite uneconomic rents, actively by waging war on those, like improving landlords or the collectors of rents, tithes and taxes, who threatened their hold on the land.

The Irish Government, confronted from the end of 1830 with a great wave of agrarian disorder sparked off principally by attempts to collect tithes, relied for over two years on its power to proclaim disturbed districts under the Peace Preservation Act and on a large army of 25,000 troops organized in flying columns and supported by a somewhat inadequate constabulary force. By the beginning of 1833 the Government had become convinced that the forces of law and order, never particularly efficient, had collapsed in many districts of Ireland. The official crime figures for 1832—over 9,000 in all, including 242 murders and 568 cases of arson—presented a terrible picture of lawlessness and disorganization. The authorities were frequently unable to secure convictions or even to arrest offenders; victims and witnesses were often intimidated; and the whole rural population showed its passive sympathy with culprits by refusing to come forward with information.[2]

Stanley and Melbourne had always believed that only the sternest measures could meet the situation. Indeed their whole approach to Ireland differed so radically from Anglesey's, who was horrified by the conditions of Irish rural life and wanted simple and radical solutions for Irish problems, that Grey had to use all his tact to prevent a complete break-up of the Irish administration.[3] In April 1831,

[1] Lewis, *Disturbances*, 99.
[2] Hansard, XV, 733, 15 February 1833, Grey; see also Lewis, *Disturbances*, Chs. III, IV.
[3] McDowell, *Public Opinion*, 147–52; Anglesey, *One-Leg*, 251, 261, 272–5; Parker, *Graham*, I, 171; *Creevey Papers*, ed. Maxwell, II, 265.

Stanley and Melbourne had failed to force a particularly repressive measure through the Cabinet, by including in a new Bill for the registration of firearms a clause rendering any person found with arms in a proclaimed district liable to transportation—a proposal far too strong for their colleagues and vehemently attacked by O'Connell in the Commons.[1] But in 1833 the Whigs were at least unanimous that the emergency required a great extension of powers, which would enable them to suppress political agitation as well as agrarian disorder.

The Government, far from seeing peasant outrages as the product of a special agrarian situation, insisted that these were directly connected with O'Connell's nationalist movement. 'We have to deal', Anglesey wrote, 'with a widespread conspiracy . . . The prevailing topics of excitement are Tithes and the repeal of the Union. . . . I apprehend the greatest possible danger must result, from allowing the People of Ireland to labour under the delusion that the Repeal of the Union, is an object which it is within *their* power, or that of *their Leaders and Representatives* in Parliament to accomplish.'[2] But even if political propaganda against the tithe system together with the Repeal campaign in the 1832 Election had increased popular excitement, the evidence proves conclusively that Irish disturbances, whatever the Whigs thought, were not fundamentally political in origin. O'Connell as well as the Catholic Church authorities had always strongly condemned direct action by the peasantry, and by January 1833 he was horrified by the state of the country, recommending immediate military reinforcements and promising that he and his movement would do all in their power to prevent 'insurrectionary outrages'.[3] His constitutional movement seemed about to be swallowed up by the social revolution which, as an Irish landlord, he had always feared. On another front, faced by perhaps the most repressive Irish measure ever proposed by an English Government, he was now involved in Parliament in a struggle for political existence.

His opposition to the Coercion Bill of 1833 was certainly his most

[1] Althorp to Earl Spencer, 2 July 1831, Torrens, *Melbourne*, I, 371; Anglesey, *One-Leg*, 262–3; O'Connell to Fitzpatrick, 9 July 1831, *O'Connell Corr.*, I, 268.

[2] Anglesey: Memo on Illegal Confederacies, 6 January 1833, H.O. Papers, 100/241, 79–81; Melbourne to Anglesey, 16 January 1833, Ibid., 100/244, 502–5, seeing a parallel between O'Connell's organizations and the Volunteers of 1782.

[3] Lewis, *Disturbances*, 100, 174–8, and passim; Fitzpatrick, *Doyle*, II, 413–14; O'Connell to Duncannon, 14 January 1833, *O'Connell Corr.*, I, 317.

sustained and impressive parliamentary performance. The House of Commons was confronted by the greatest popular leader of the day at the height of his intellectual and physical powers. Tall, broad-shouldered and burly, with his black wig, green frock-coat and black, broad-brimmed hat, O'Connell dominated the Commons' debates, 'that huge massive figure staggering with rage—the face darkened with all the feelings of scorn and rancour'.[1] His magnificent voice and violent, unrestrained eloquence compelled the attention and even the unwilling admiration of his English audience. The struggle began with the debate on the King's Speech, which asked for additional powers to put down disturbances and to preserve and strengthen the Union and which O'Connell immediately described as 'the most bloody and brutal speech ever delivered by a King—and it's Stanley's writing'![2] He replied with a passionate indictment of Whig policy in 'one of the most furious speeches' which the experienced Hobhouse had ever heard. He denounced the Whigs' partial administration of justice, their numerous newspaper prosecutions and their failure to reform Irish institutions, protesting bitterly against any infringement of Irish liberties and insisting that past and present misgovernment was the real cause of Irish disturbances. Indeed if Ministers suppressed political activity, which acted, he claimed, as a brake on these outrages, he prophesied that 'there would be, not a moral revolution or a political revolution, but a revolution of the sword in Ireland'.[3]

This speech made a deep impression, but the initial sympathy of many new English Members was lost and, according to Le Marchant, a good case was ruined by a series of speeches from Repealers, whose long complaints and accusations 'at length heartily wearied the House' and turned several Members overnight from friends into 'violent adversaries'.[4] O'Connell could perhaps have silenced his supporters, but the temptation to show the strength of his party might have proved irresistible even to a less angry and passionate man. Huge majorities of over 300 against his own amendment calling for a committee of the whole House to consider the King's Speech

---

[1] Madden, *Ireland and Its Rulers*, I, 225–6.
[2] Littleton, *Diary*, 5 February 1833, Aspinall, op. cit., 296.
[3] Hansard, XV, 148–77, 5 February 1833, O'Connell; Broughton, *Recollections*, 5 February 1833, IV, 281: '. . . the great Irish agitator, not the Member of the Imperial Parliament.'
[4] Le Marchant, *Diary* [n.d. February 1833], Aspinall, op. cit., 295.

and against a less sweeping amendment sponsored by the English Radicals showed clearly not only that the Radicals' strength had been much exaggerated but also that O'Connell's struggle would be a long and uphill one, in which he could expect no substantial support from the great body of ministerialist Whigs.[1]

The Bill, introduced in the Lords by the Prime Minister himself in a speech in which he put forward the official thesis on the effects of political agitation and referred to O'Connell's organization as extending over the whole country and obtaining possession of the whole power of the state, was, according to one astonished Tory, 'a compound of the Proclamation Act, the Insurrection Act, the Gagging Bill, the Suspension of the Habeas Corpus Act & Martial Law!'[2] It empowered the Lord Lieutenant for a year to proclaim disturbed areas where no meetings of any kind could be held, to suspend Habeas Corpus, to substitute courts martial for the ordinary courts and to ban all meetings to petition Parliament unless ten days notice had been given and his own permission obtained.[3]

O'Connell fought the Bill at every stage and by all conventional means, dividing at every opportunity, prolonging debates, initiating general discussions on Irish affairs and appealing outside Parliament for the support of Radical organizations in the provinces, notably in Nottingham and Birmingham.[4] In Parliament he was supported by between 80 and 90 Irish Members and English Radicals, but while the latter, including Cobbett, Hume, John Arthur Roebuck, Henry and Edward Lytton Bulwer, George Grote, Henry Warburton and Thomas Attwood proved staunch allies, the Irish Liberals were less dependable. A meeting of 56 Repealers and Liberals refused to agree to O'Connell's proposal to use openly obstructive tactics. Some Liberals such as Henry Lambert, William O'Reilly, Sir Richard Keane, Richard More O'Ferrall and George Evans actually voted for the Bill,[5] and even some Repealers, violent enough against the

---

[1] Hansard, XV, 455, 458–62, 8 February 1833, Divisions.

[2] Ellenborough, *Diary*, 15 February 1833, Aspinall, op. cit., 302.

[3] The Bill, which passed the Lords almost unopposed, was accompanied by a Change of Venue Bill allowing trials to be removed to adjoining counties or to Dublin.

[4] Le Marchant, *Diary* [n.d. March 1833]; Littleton, *Diary*, 27 February 1833, Aspinall, op. cit., 314–15, 308. For his attempt to secure Irish Tory support, see *O'Connell Corr.*, I, 324–7. At Dudley, the Solicitor-General ran into some trouble from his constituents over Irish coercion; *Campbell*, II, 33.

[5] McDowell, *Public Opinion*, 158; O'Connell to Fitzpatrick, 11 March 1833,

Government in the House, used distinctly odd language in private:
'I wish to heaven', Henry Grattan told Hobhouse, 'you would hang
or shoot O'Connell and pass some Algerine Act if you like, but not
this Bill.'[1]

The Government might have been in serious difficulties with the
Bill which in its full extent had, according to Le Marchant, very
few '*real* supporters', but for Stanley, who redeemed Althorp's
weak and obviously reluctant introduction of the measure in the
Commons with one of his most brilliant speeches. One old Member,
George Byng, who had been forty-three years in the Commons,
told Lady Holland that 'neither Pitt nor Fox ever produced such an
effect',[2] and it was generally agreed that O'Connell, who was accused of having described the House as 'six hundred scoundrels' at a
meeting in the City, had been at least temporarily defeated. He was
seen next day sitting 'downcast upon one of the high benches, and
when reproaches were levelled at him . . ., [pretending] to be asleep
instead of cheering or returning them glances of defiance as before'.[3]

The Government was never in danger of defeat, but O'Connell's
delaying tactics and the lack of genuine support for the Bill caused its
majorities to fall steadily from 377 on the First Reading to 259 on
Cobbett's motion to postpone the Bill, and without Tory support,
to 141 in a House where the Government's majority on paper, even
without the entire Radical-Irish contingent of 80 or 90, was at least
400.[4] Ministers were forced to modify the courts-martial clauses

---

O'Connell Corr., I, 329–30. Lambert and More O'Ferrall doubtless shared the
view of their friend Bishop Doyle, who by 1833 preferred 'the despotism of
gentlemen' to that of 'the brutal *canaille* of the Trades' Unions and Blackfeet
confederacies'; Doyle to Lambert, 1 March 1833, Fitzpatrick, *Doyle*, II, 458–9.

[1] Broughton, *Recollections*, 1 March 1833, IV, 292–3. Le Marchant, *Diary*
[n.d. March 1833], Aspinall, op. cit., 313–14, has a version slightly more dis-
creditable to Grattan.

[2] Le Marchant, *Diary* [n.d. March 1833], Aspinall, op. cit., 313–14; Lady
Holland to Henry Fox, 1 March 1833, *Elizabeth, Lady Holland to Her Son,
1821–1845*, ed. Earl of Ilchester (1946), 140–1.

[3] Littleton, *Diary*, 26 February 1833; Le Marchant, *Diary* [n.d. March 1833],
Aspinall, 307–8, 312–13; Broughton, *Recollections*, 27 February 1833, IV, 292.
But cf. Ellenborough's description of O'Connell's 'great speech' a week later to
an ungenerous House, *Diary*, 5 March 1833, Aspinall, op. cit., 312.

[4] For a pessimistic Tory's view of the aims of the Irish and Radicals, who
would 'stop the Business of the Country till their views and ends are secured',
see Sir Edward Knatchbull to his wife, 1 March 1833, Sir H. Knatchbull-
Hugessen, *A Kentish Family* (1960), 212.

which nearly all their supporters condemned; more important they conceded under Irish pressure that no district would be proclaimed for refusal to pay tithes. O'Connell and his party had always insisted that coercion was aimed partly to enforce tithe payment, and Stanley's obvious anger at the concession seemed to prove them right.[1]

The Government succeeded after a month of protracted and bitter debates in obtaining its Coercion Bill. The whole episode undoubtedly cost the Ministry some of its popularity with its English supporters in the Commons, who resented being forced to support so extreme a measure only to see it modified at 'the dictation of O'Connell', and in its final form, O'Connell and his party believed that it was 'now a more foolish than an infernal Bill'. 'As O'Connell says', wrote Sheil, ' "the fangs have been plucked out of it".'[2] The Bill no doubt helped the Government to contain Irish agrarian disorder, though it could do little more. It had no effect on O'Connell's political position in Ireland even if, perhaps wisely, he did not attempt to test its efficiency. The real importance of the Coercion Bill was that it clearly marked the end of one distinct phase in the history both of the Irish party and of the Grey Government. After it, no reconciliation seemed possible between the two, and in opposition to it the party had demonstrated its independence, unity and effectiveness under determined leadership. In reality, the episode showed that unless Ireland was to be treated in future as a rebellious colony and governed as such, the Whigs had no choice but to retreat sooner or later from their uncompromising position and to come to terms with a new and potentially disrupting force in politics.

[1] Hansard, XVI, 589–90, 758–60, 767–8, 13, 18 March 1833, Althorp, Stanley.
[2] Le Marchant, *Diary* [n.d. April 1833], Aspinall, op. cit., 318; O'Connell to Fitzpatrick, 21 March 1833, *O'Connell Corr.*, I, 340; Sheil to E. Dwyer, 1 April 1833, O'Connell Papers, N.L.I., 5242.

CHAPTER III

The Irish Political System in the Age of O'Connell

General Elections, 1832–41

THE General Election of December–January 1832–3, the first under the Irish Reform Act, was of fundamental importance in the history both of the Irish party and of the Irish political system. For the first time in British political history, a strong and well-organized third party intervened successfully on a national basis in the traditional conflict between Whigs and Tories. In marked contrast with the leaderless and individualistic English Radicals, the Repeal party was united in its political opinions and under O'Connell's undisputed leadership. Supported by a formidable political machine geared to influence public opinion, to raise funds and to fight elections, the party in 1832 made a large-scale assault on the hitherto almost unchallenged electoral influence of the landowning class, and its impact, falling on the Irish political structure at its most sensitive point, disrupted an existing two-party system.

The Election produced contests in 45 out of the 66 Irish constituencies, a proportion which was much the highest of any Election in O'Connell's lifetime, with Repealers standing in all 19 contested counties and in 18 of the 25 contested boroughs.[1] If these figures were not higher, it was because Repeal found little or no support in the 15 constituencies of Ulster (returning 22 M.P.s) where landed Conservatism was almost unchallenged except in some centres of urban Liberalism like Belfast, Armagh and Londonderry. For the rest of Ireland the results showed that the Repealers, less powerful in landed influence than either of the other two parties, had largely

[1] See Appendix A, No. 5.

51

depended for success on popular enthusiasm and on effective electoral organization both in Dublin and in the provinces. O'Connell's party emerged even after losing three of its members by election petitions, as the largest single Irish party with 39 Members, most of them firmly pledged to support Repeal.[1] For Irish Toryism, the Election was little short of a disaster. With only 29 Members (their successful candidate at Carrickfergus was unseated in 1833 and the House decided not to issue any new writ for that corrupt borough), the Irish Conservatives had fallen very low from the years before 1830 when they had held a majority of the Irish representation. The optimistic calculations of these English Conservative managers who had expected somewhere between 41 and 52 seats were very wide of the mark.[2]

The 36 Whigs and Liberals had little cause for congratulation. They might reasonably have expected to capitalize on the past achievements and future possibilities of Reform and to repeat in Ireland the great ministerialist landslide which characterized the English elections. Instead, two Ministers, Thomas Spring Rice and Lord Duncannon, found themselves excluded from the seats of Limerick and County Kilkenny which they had held respectively since 1820 and 1826; and in many other constituencies, the Repeal intervention with its strong Radical bias completely outbid the more cautiously reformist programmes of Irish Liberals. Nearly every Repeal candidate, following O'Connell's lead, called for the abolition of tithes, church rates and vestry cess, a reform of the grand jury laws, the ballot, triennial parliaments and in some cases for an Irish Poor Law in addition to Repeal of the Union. The tithe agitation, in full swing in many parts of the country, was an important factor in

---

[1] See Appendix B. McDowell, *Public Opinion*, 134, and Charles Gavan Duffy, *Young Ireland* (1896), I, 4, estimate the party's strength at 'at least thirty-eight' and 40 respectively. J. H. Whyte, 'Daniel O'Connell and the repeal party', *Irish Historical Studies*, XI, No. 44 (September 1959), Appendix, 316, arrives at a total of 35. His list cannot be considered complete because it includes three Repealers, L. Maclachlan (Galway Borough), W. J. O'Neill Daunt (Mallow) and James Rorke (Co. Longford), who were shortly declared not duly elected and were unseated, and because it does not include several M.P.s who, if they were not actually pledged Repealers in 1832, certainly voted for O'Connell's Repeal motion in April 1834. They were M. J. Blake, R. M. Bellew, Sir Richard Nagle, W. Roche and Charles Walker.

[2] Arbuthnot to Bonham, 8 October 1832; Hardinge to Peel, 24 November 1832, Peel Papers, Add. MSS 40617, 5; 40313, 169.

the Repeal party's success. Durham told Hobhouse that the tithe policy of Stanley, 'the fortunate youth', 'had managed to lose every election in Ireland';[1] and certainly in the case of Repeal candidates like Sheil in Tipperary, Feargus O'Connor (later the Chartist leader) in County Cork, Sir Richard Nagle in Westmeath and the Ruthvens in Dublin City and County Kildare respectively, their active participation in the tithe agitation virtually ensured their success. Disturbances, outrages and riots proved an effective form of intimidation at election time, deterring voters in many county constituencies from openly expressing unpopular opinions at the polls. With generally superior local organizations and with the only central organization worthy of the name behind them, no less than 14 of the 39 Repealers were returned without a contest in 1832, as against 16 Conservatives (4 from northern boroughs, 12 from northern counties) and only 4 Liberals.

One remarkable feature of the Election, which was never to be repeated in O'Connell's lifetime, was the highly successful use of the Repeal pledge. This electoral device, usually associated with the attempts of English Radicals 'to transform parliament from a debating club of the upper ruling classes to an assembly of delegates automatically recording the will of their constituents',[2] was not new in Irish politics. But where the scheme of pledges devised by the Catholic Association after the Clare election of 1828 does not seem in practice to have been very successful, the Repeal pledge was taken by the great majority of successful Repeal candidates in 1832.[3]

In the large, two-member constituency of Cork City, for example, the pledge was used in a dramatic way to unite the Repeal interest behind its two candidates, Dr. Herbert Baldwin and Daniel Callaghan. Baldwin, a doctor for many years in the city, a man of considerable reputation and property and a cousin of O'Connell, was an ideal candidate, an out-and-out Repealer and the 'Leviathan of Munster Radicals'.[4] But Callaghan, a government contractor and the son of an immensely successful Cork merchant, had had a chequered career as M.P. for Cork. First elected in 1830 apparently with Tory

[1] Broughton, *Recollections*, 13 November 1832, IV, 258–9.
[2] Gash, *Politics*, 29.
[3] For earlier use of the pledge, see Reynolds, *Catholic Emancipation Crisis*, 102.
[4] Madden, *Ireland and Its Rulers* (1844), I, 164; Dod, *Parliamentary Pocket Companion*, 1833.

support, he began by supporting Wellington's Government; by 1831 he was liberal enough to vote for the Reform Bill; and in 1832, under the influence of Feargus O'Connor's campaign in the county and under pressure from the Cork Trades' Association, he declared himself a Repealer, a remarkable example of the effect of the Repeal campaign on Irish politics and politicians.[1] But it was feared that his failure to give a distinct Repeal pledge in his election address might split the nationalist interest,[2] and on the hustings he and Baldwin were put through a regular political catechism by the secretary of the Cork Political Union, answering 'I will' to the Repeal and various Radical pledges. Thereafter, their joint victory, despite some personal rivalry, was never in doubt.[3]

So strong was the pressure of the pledge on Whig and Liberal candidates in 1832 that some like Sir Richard Keane in County Waterford, Henry Lambert in County Wexford and William O'Reilly in Dundalk made conditional declarations in favour of Repeal.[4] Keane, for instance, dependent on the interest of the Whig Duke of Devonshire as well as on the second votes of electors who would certainly vote first for J. M. Galwey, an unequivocally pledged nationalist, scraped through a trying position by announcing that he would resign if he voted against Repeal, which he regarded as 'an imposing weapon to get justice for Ireland'.[5] Refusal to pledge themselves cost several prominent Liberals their seats, among them the Catholic Lord Killeen, eldest son of the Earl of Fingall and M.P.

---

[1] Madden, op. cit., I, 191–2, 195–201, who gives a vivid description of the solidly nationalist, democratic and working-class character of the Trades' Association. See Treasury List [1830], Peel Papers, Add. MSS 40401, 181 ff., where Callaghan is classed with some justice as 'doubtful', though he supported the Tory Government on the crucial vote of 15 November 1830, Hansard, I, 551.

[2] D.E.P., 8 December 1832.

[3] D.E.P., 13 December; Pilot, F.J., 24 December 1832. They defeated their nearest Tory opponent by over 800 votes in a constituency of over 4,000.

[4] Lambert was not opposed in 1832, his conditional declaration satisfying the well-organized 'Liberal' interest in Wexford; Times, 21 November; Pilot, 19 December 1832. But he lost his seat in 1835 after O'Connell had attacked him for supporting Coercion; Pilot, 23 March 1834; O'Connell to Fitzpatrick, 11 March 1833, O'Connell Corr., I, 329–30. For O'Reilly's election, see F.J., 21 September; 22 October; 5, 29 December 1832. His vote against the Repeal motion in 1834, belying his carefully-phrased approval of Repeal in 1832, was probably the main reason for the loss of his seat in 1835.

[5] Times, 20 November; D.E.P., 27 December 1832. His abstention on the Repeal motion in 1834 was thus highly politic.

for County Meath since 1830,[1] Nicholas Philpot Leader at Kilkenny[2] and Sir Henry Parnell, M.P. for Queen's County for 27 years, an expert on economic problems and Secretary-at-War from 1831 to 1832, who had been supported by O'Connell in 1831 but now found himself attacked by the *Pilot* as 'the Whig Judas' and deserted by his former supporters.[3]

The defeat of Thomas Wyse in Waterford City was even more remarkable. A wealthy Catholic landowner in Waterford and with a family tradition of representation behind him, Wyse had been a leading member and the official historian of the Catholic Association. As M.P. for Tipperary since 1830 and a strong supporter of parliamentary reform, the National Education system and an Irish Poor Law, Wyse was one of the most distinguished Irish Members, a possible rival to O'Connell and certainly a candidate of formidable qualifications.[4] The nationalist candidates in Waterford were Henry Winston Barron, a local Catholic landowner who had performed important services for the Emancipationist cause in the Waterford County election of 1826 and for O'Connell personally in 1830, and Roger Hayes, a partner in the O'Connell Brewery.[5] Both received support from O'Connell, both were adopted as candidates in the National Political Union in Dublin, but Hayes was not put forward officially until a deputation of the Waterford Political Union, acting on O'Connell's suggestion, had failed to extract an unqualified pledge from Wyse.[6] In Waterford, 1,241 registered electors were

---

[1] *Pilot*, 3 December; *D.E.P.*, 18 December 1832, which unfavourably compared the dubious qualifications of a young soldier of fortune (Morgan, O'Connell's second son, who had been an officer in the Irish South American Legion under Bolivar and also served in the Austrian Army) with Killeen's past services.

[2] *F.J.*, 4, 7 December 1832.

[3] *Times*, 17 December; *Pilot*, 14 December 1832. Parnell (later 1st Baron Congleton), who had been dismissed for refusing to support the Government on the Russo-Dutch Loan in January 1832, found a seat at Dundee. His Whiggism apart, Parnell's main offence in 1832 was that he had helped to draw up the Irish Reform Bill.

[4] Auchmuty, *Wyse*, passim; Dod, *P.P.C.*, 1838. A product, like Sheil, of Stonyhurst and Trinity College, Dublin, where he had a brilliant career, Wyse married (1821) Laetitia, daughter of Lucien Bonaparte, Prince of Canino, from whom he was separated in 1828. For his character and later relations with O'Connell, see below p. 152.

[5] *F.J.*, 8 December; *D.E.P.*, 13 December 1832; Auchmuty, *Wyse*, 81–96, 115. The Barron family owned the *Waterford Chronicle*.

[6] *F.J.*, 24, 27 September; 7 November; 8 December; *Times*, 16 November 1832.

fairly evenly divided between 641 £10 householders, as in most boroughs the basis of nationalist and Liberal strength, and 548 freemen, most of them solid in support of the Tory candidate, William Christmas of Tramore, a young local landowner. Barron, with the promise of 500 votes including those of the Beresford tenantry, whose landlord, the Marquis of Waterford, was taking no part in the election, was safe enough; but Hayes and Wyse effectively split the rest of the 'Liberal' interest and in an election distinguished by a good deal of rioting and recrimination, Christmas was returned as the second Member by over 100 votes.[1]

O'Connell used the weapon of the pledge with brutality and some disregard for consistency. With Wyse, whose characteristic and not unreasonable attempts to discuss the exact details of Repeal and future legislative arrangements aroused considerable and inconvenient debate inside the Repeal party organization, O'Connell insisted on the simple, unqualified pledge to support total Repeal; but he would also allow no general exemption for the 32 M.P.s who had opposed Stanley's Tithe Bill.[2] On the other hand, he was ready to make an exception for an old and valuable friend, William Roche, a Catholic banker who had contributed 'immense' sums towards the struggle for Emancipation.[3] O'Connell not only sponsored him in Dublin as the second Repeal candidate for Limerick City together with the pledged David Roche, a Protestant landowner with estates in Clare and Limerick, but also came down in person for the election and recommended William Roche as 'the only man he knew after thirty years acquaintance, of whom he could say that no pledge need be demanded'. With the powerful Limerick Political Union behind them, the Roches successfully disposed of Whig and Tory opposition.[4]

---

[1] *F.J.*, 22 December 1832. Wyse was unsuccessful despite the support of the Catholic Bishop Dr. Abrahams and of the retiring M.P., Sir John Newport, P.C., then 76, who had been one of the City's Members since 1803 and Chancellor of the Irish Exchequer in the 1806 Whig Government.

[2] *F.J.*, 17, 24 August; 24, 27 September; 7 November 1832.

[3] *Pilot*, 3 December 1832.

[4] *F.J.*, 2 November; 3, 5 December; *D.E.P.*, 6 December; *Times*, 3, 7 December 1832. For this friendly act, O'Connell had to face criticism in his own organization. For the Roche cousins, who held both Limerick seats without serious opposition until 1841, when Sir David Roche was joined by a Liberal, John O'Brien, see Dod, *P.P.C.*, 1833; Dod, *Electoral Facts*, under Limerick City. O'Connell's confidence in William Roche was not misplaced. He voted for the Repeal motion in 1834.

The 1832 Election in Ireland thus provides an example of the use of the electoral pledge on a scale and with a success for which there is no parallel in England. For the Repeal party, the pledge was the weapon of its electoral independence and a guarantee of solidarity against the subtly corrosive pressures of British political life. In this respect it was more effective than the National Council, held in January 1833 after the elections and before the meeting of Parliament, which was not indeed designed on exclusive party lines.[1] All Irish M.P.s and peers were either invited or were at liberty to attend it, and O'Connell hoped somewhat ingenuously to attract opponents and uncommitted Members just as he had hoped to find Conservative allies before the Election itself.[2] But of the 30 to 35 M.P.s who attended the Council's two sessions in a hotel opposite the old Irish Parliament on College Green, only three were not Repealers.[3] The Council heard a report on Irish revenue, taxes and funded debts from Michael Staunton, the editor of the *Morning Register*; it discussed the soap and paper trades, grand jury reform, the abolition of tithes and various measures of franchise reform, but there was no discussion of Repeal itself, and in general the results of the Council disappointed those like Henry Grattan and John O'Connell who hoped that it would lead to unity of purpose and action and that it would act as the working model of an Irish legislature.[4]

The Conservative *Dublin Evening Mail*, in prophetic doggerel, neatly summarized the problem facing O'Connell and his party in 1833:

[1] See Reynolds, *Catholic Emancipation Crisis*, 102, for a precedent from 1828; *Pilot*, 10, 12 January 1832, for a Council held in January 1832 but attended by only 14 M.P.s.

[2] *Times*, 23, 24, 31 January; 5, 18 March; 6, 29 October 1832, for the strange flirtation of some Dublin Tories with Repeal. These moves, essentially a product of Tory resentment, were confined to Dublin Corporation; and O'Connell's readiness to co-operate was caused by his eagerness to find a Tory Repeal candidate for Dublin City, a plan which failed because he could not swing his party into supporting it; *O'Connell Corr.*, I, 301-12; *Times*, 29 November; 1, 8 December 1832.

[3] These M.P.s were Sir Richard Keane (Co. Waterford), M. L. Chapman (Westmeath) and Garret Standish Barry (Co. Cork), all Liberals with 'popular' constituencies. A number of Repealers like Andrew Lynch, W. N. Macnamara and F. L. Macnamara, while approving of the Council, were unable to attend it.

[4] *Times*, 4, 21-4 January 1833. John O'Connell, *Recollections of a Parliamentary Career* (1894), I, 28-9, thought that it served only one useful purpose, in making Members mutually acquainted; it could not do more because so many Members were new to business.

Place—or Repeal

That is the question. Whether Hurlothrumbo
Free from the Trades', the Tail, the Volunteers,
The loud huzzas of mobs, from Slevin's taunts
And Thomas Steele's astounding eloquence—
Shall clutch at place, and on the winds bestow
His vow in Heaven, and doom Repeal to hell?
Or whether, with a desperate fidelity
He'll cling to Erin Green, 'till he achieves
The one thing needful—the Repeal?[1]

Certainly the General Election of 1835, held almost exactly two years after that of 1832 and following the abrupt dismissal of the Whigs in November 1834, found O'Connell and his party in a markedly changed position. The Conservatives were confronted in Ireland by a Whig-Repeal front ready to fight the elections on a platform of 'No Tories, No Tithes'. An informant in London advised O'Connell 'to prepare & that instantly, for an election. You should strain every nerve to encrease your parliamentary force in Ireland, for depend upon it you are *personally* more interested in the issue of the pending struggle than any other man in the empire. No matter at what risk, an effort will be made to crush *you* . . .'[2]

During the Election, the bolder spirits among the Irish liberals like William Sharman Crawford and William Smith O'Brien joined O'Connell's Anti-Tory Association, his electoral organization in Dublin, but there were also numerous instances of O'Connell's support for Whig and Liberal candidates. Morgan O'Connell offered his seat for County Meath to his father, 'to make way for such a man as Sharman Crawford or any person whom you deem fitted for the trust' while Morgan himself tried his hand at Athlone, where 'there would be a severe contest as Lord Castlemaine is understood to have expressed his determination of fighting it to the last'.[3] Crawford was in fact returned at Dundalk without opposition. For County Carlow, O'Connell was prepared to sponsor a Whig,

[1] *D.E.M.*, 29 January 1833. Slevin was a leading member of the Dublin Trades' Union, Steele a Protestant landowner from Clare and one of O'Connell's most faithful personal followers.

[2] Charles Phillips to O'Connell, 25 November 1834, O'Connell Papers, N.L.I., uncatalogued; *O'Connell Corr.*, I, 506–7.

[3] Morgan O'Connell to O'Connell [n.d. December 1834], O'Connell Papers, N.L.I., uncatalogued.

the Hon. John Ponsonby and an English Liberal, Alexander Raphael, while his agent in Waterford supported Wyse for the city and was ready to support Captain Villiers Stuart, 'a thoroughgoing Anti-Tory', for the county.[1] The Whig Lord Rossmore wrote most amicably to O'Connell from Rome, stressing the importance of supporting Protestant candidates in order to refute the allegation that O'Connell depended almost entirely on Catholic support, and reporting that '2 of my sons will be returned for Monaghan and the King's County—on them Ireland may depend to the last spark—as she may on my friend Sharman Crawford—why not return him? The times require the assistance of Leader and Wyse—you would gain great credit . . . by getting the latter returned and English members have an opinion of Leader's integrity.'[2]

From England, the Radical Henry Warburton acted as intermediary for various Whig interests, notably those of the Marquess of Lansdowne and Earl Fitzwilliam, in dealings with O'Connell. Warburton wrote in December 1834:

A.B. writes me word: 'Who are the candidates for Kerry and Wicklow that Mr. O'Connell wishes to have supported? I may do harm to their cause, if I ask such and such a peer to aid them, as Mr. O'Connell's friends. But name the candidates and I can ask his Lordship to support the individuals.'

Now the way in which I put the case was this. That if they would name their Whig candidates, and such Whig candidates would pledge themselves to oppose the Tories, your friends would co-operate with them at the Elections for Kerry and Wicklow . . . I conceive it is for them, not for you, to name their candidates.[3]

[1] O'Connell to N. A. Vigors, M.P. [n.d. December 1834], *O'Connell Corr.*, I, 512; Rev. John Sheehan to O'Connell, 8 December 1834, O'Connell Papers, N.L.I., uncatalogued. Villiers Stuart was not adopted in this election, but was returned unopposed at a bye-election in September 1835 and sat until 1847.

[2] Rossmore to O'Connell, 17 December 1834, O'Connell MSS, U.C.D. The Hon. Henry Westenra sat for Monaghan (1835-42), when he succeeded his father in the peerage; the Hon. John Craven Westenra was M.P. for King's County (1835-47). For Rossmore's public support of O'Connell in 1835, see *Times*, 23 December 1835.

[3] Henry Warburton to O'Connell, 20 December 1834, O'Connell MSS, U.C.D. In Wicklow, the two Whig sitting Members were unopposed. In Kerry the Catholic Whig Lord Kenmare, despite pressure from the official Whig leaders, supported Maurice Fitzgerald, the Knight of Kerry (a Lord of the Admiralty in Peel's Government) against O'Connell's nephew, Morgan John O'Connell, and F. W. Mullins. The Knight was handsomely defeated. For a vivid running account of the election, see O'Connell to John O'Connell [n.d.

In January, Warburton wrote regretting that a delay in forwarding
one of O'Connell's letters made it 'too late to apply to the Duke of
Devonshire' about Dungarvan where a Liberal finally defeated a
dissident Repealer, but he was able to assure O'Connell that the
Whig ex-Chief Secretary E. J. Littleton, James Abercromby, the
influential Liberal backbencher and Sir John Hobhouse had all
exerted themselves over the Wicklow and Kerry elections.[1] The
Whigs were ready enough to make common cause with O'Connell,
even if some had misgivings. Thomas Spring Rice, who had been
excluded in 1832 from the seat for Limerick City which he had held
since 1820, wrote to his political patron, Lord Lansdowne: 'You
perceive what an artful game O'Connell is playing in Ireland. He
wishes to induce men of our opinions to place themselves in positions where he may hereafter reproach them with ingratitude if they
do not to some extent make themselves joints of his tail.'[2] But the
electoral alliance affected Repealers as well as Whigs. At Youghal
where the Whig Devonshire interest was important, John O'Connell
was careful to describe himself simply as a 'reformer'; and the
election address of Christopher Fitzsimon, M.P. for County Dublin
in 1832 and successful again in 1835, stressed his support for the
abolition of tithes, 'the blood-stained impost', for corporation reform, ballot, shorter parliaments and franchise reform, and announced that he would 'combine in every constitutional effort to
drive from power the present Orange administration'. Like his
leader, however, he did not omit some mention of Repeal.[3]

The Election was altogether less hard fought than its predeces-
sor. The Conservatives enjoyed the slight advantage that a Conservative Government was in power, but a more important factor in their
gain of nine seats was that the Whigs' co-operation with O'Connell
could be held up as 'a partnership with rebellion',[4] while much

---

January], 15 January; to his wife, 21 January; to Fitzpatrick, 21, 22 January
1835, *O'Connell Corr.*, I, 515-16, 517-19.

[1] Warburton to O'Connell, 20 January 1835, O'Connell MSS., U.C.D.

[2] Spring Rice to Lansdowne, 7 December 1834. Monteagle Papers, N.L.I.
See also McDowell, *Public Opinion*, 162, for the suspicions of the Liberal Louis
Perrin, M.P. for Monaghan (1832-5), for Cashel (1835) and Irish Attorney-
General from April to September 1835.

[3] John O'Connell to E. J. Littleton, 20 December 1834, Teddesley MSS.,
quoted by McDowell, *Public Opinion*, 162; C. Fitzsimon, Address to Co. Dublin
Electors, 1 January 1835, O'Connell Papers, N.L.I. uncatalogued; *D.E.P.*,
4 January; *Times*, 16 January 1835.   [4] *Times*, 16 January 1835.

political capital could be made out of the alleged increase in the interference of the Catholic priesthood in elections and in vivid denunciations of O'Connell's declared policies of 'exclusive dealing' and intimidation.[1] Hardinge, the Chief Secretary, reported to Peel that 'The State of the Country in the midst of a General Election was never more free from actual riot & disturbance, altho' the excitement by the interference of the Priests is very great . . . O'Connell finds that his atrocious threats have enlisted many neutral parties into active opposition against him (as in the case of Lord Kenmare & the Whigs of Kerry), & is now very tame in his language & evidently dispirited.'[2] No doubt also the overwhelming defeat of the Repeal motion in April 1834 had robbed the cause of some of its momentum, while the electoral alliance prevented O'Connell from whipping up enthusiasm by a policy of pledges.

The Irish representation appeared in 1835 to be fairly evenly divided between the three parties. Of the Whig-Liberal contingent of 33 Members, 16 (or 12 more than in 1832) had been returned without opposition, largely by county constituencies, though Whig landed influence which had secured the return of 25 county Members in 1832 now returned only 21. Of 34 Repealers, 20 were county Members, but the number of their M.P.s who were elected unopposed had dropped slightly from 14 to 11. In 1832 the borough representation had been divided between 10 Conservative seats, 11 Whig and 19 Repeal; in 1835, the figures were 15, 12 and 14 respectively. In round terms, the Conservatives, now with 38 Members, had gained from the Whigs in the counties and from the Repealers in the boroughs; successes in Carlow, Athlone and in one of the Belfast seats were brilliantly capped by the greatly reduced majorities of O'Connell and E. S. Ruthven in Dublin and by the unseating of these two on a petition in 1836.[3] But while these gains were encouraging for Irish Conservatives, the results confirmed the

[1] *Times*, 29 December 1834; 28 January 1835; *Annual Register* (1835), 14–15; see also P.P. 1835 (197), XLV, 433 ff., Communications relative to the marching of people during the late Kerry election.

[2] Hardinge to Peel, 12 January 1835, Peel Papers, Add. MSS 40314, 7–8.

[3] Hardinge to Peel, 12 January 1835, [n.d. January 1835], Peel Papers, Add. MSS. 40314, 7–10; 40421, 161–2, expecting gains of '10 or 12 seats' from 28 to 'about 40'; a second estimate of 6 gains was too low. Two Repealers, Andrew Carew O'Dwyer, M.P. for Drogheda (1832–5) and Feargus O'Connor, M.P. for Co. Cork (1832–5), were later unseated for lack of the necessary property qualifications.

pronounced 'left-wing' orientation of the Irish representation, giving the Whig Government between 1835 and 1837 the support of 67 Irish Members and pleasing Lord Holland, who thought that he 'perceived certain symptoms, in the late elections, of a decline of the supremacy of O'Connell over public opinion in Ireland. If so, is it owing to a reaction in favour of Tories or Orangemen, or to an increase of an intermediate and temperate party, who are earnest for redress of grievances, but not disposed to swear allegiance to the "great liberator" ?'[1]

The Whigs, who had been in power for over two years when the General Election of 1837 was held in July and August on the accession of Queen Victoria, thus possessed the advantage which had worked slightly in the Conservatives' favour in 1835; but following O'Connell's lead, the Government's supporters in Ireland, including Repealers and orthodox Whigs and Liberals, improved on the occasion and made effective propagandist use of the Queen's name during the Election.[2] The General Association, O'Connell's party organization, was firmly ministerialist and included many Whigs and Liberals. In July it was exhorted by O'Connell to 'rally, one and all, in every county, city and town returning members to Parliament, and secure the return of the Queen's friends'; the Association's central election committee was called 'The Friends to the Queen', and the Repeal placard in the Corn Exchange was changed to 'The Queen and Liberty, the Queen and the Constitution, the Queen and Reform'.[3] The *Annual Register*, though disapproving of this use of the Queen's name by O'Connell and the Whigs, thought that it came within 'the chartered licence of a general election' and commented that 'If O'Connell . . . could influence the Whigs, they were fully as much enabled to control O'Connell; nor, under these circumstances, can we see anything degrading to either party in their co-operation for a common and paramount object.'[4]

O'Connell's electoral slogan of 'Justice for Ireland' implied confidence in the promised legislation of the Whig Government. With-

[1] Holland to Lord Cloncurry, 12 February 1835, Cloncurry, *Personal Recollections*, 361.

[2] So also, in a less direct way, did the Whig Ministers; see Russell to Mulgrave [n.d. July 1837], *Annual Register* (1837), 239.

[3] *Pilot*, 5 April; *F.J.* 1, 15 July; O'Connell to Arthur French, secretary of the Association, 15 July 1837. For use of the Queen's name in England, see M. G. Brock, 'Politics at the Accession of Queen Victoria', *History Today*, III, No. 5 (May 1953), 329–38.   [4] *Annual Register* (1837), 6, 28, 239.

out such a Government, tithe and municipal reform, which had been for several years the subjects of long parliamentary battles against an increasingly powerful opposition, would never be achieved. Further, for the first and only time in O'Connell's life an Irish administration (under Lord Mulgrave, Lord Morpeth and Thomas Drummond) had secured a large measure of popular support. With these advantages the Whig-Repeal alliance made up most of the ground it had lost in 1835, and with reference to 71 Whigs and O'Connellites the *Dublin Evening Post* could well speak of 'the great and irresistible demonstration of strength' by the Liberal party in Ireland.[1] Discomfited Tories pointed to the increased number of Catholic Members and to their alleged lack of rank and property as well as to the fact that the number of O'Connell's own followers, exclusive of Irish Whigs and Liberals, corresponded more or less exactly to the Ministry's overall majority in the Commons, and *The Times* was horrified that an English Protestant Government would henceforth depend for its existence on the votes of Irish Catholics.[2] The Government's serious losses in England were to a considerable extent counterbalanced by the combined Whig and Repeal contingent from Ireland, and the Election clearly demonstrated that the alliance with O'Connell was not a generous luxury but a political necessity for the Whig Government.

As the senior partners, the Whigs gained most from the alliance. Their Members for the first time comprised a majority of the representation; their six gains were made equally in counties and boroughs; and although it is possible that they could not have made these gains without the help of previously O'Connellite organizations in the constituencies, their new Members owed little or nothing to O'Connell personally. As for the Repeal party, many of them were now indistinguishable from their Whig allies, as William Sharman Crawford acidly pointed out in his general attack on O'Connell's policy of uncritical and unquestioning support of the Government.[3]

[1] *D.E.P.*, 22 August 1837, which claimed a clear gain of 10 seats to the Ministry. More accurate figures were given by Mulgrave and Russell: a majority of 37 'on a rather unfavourable estimate' and figures of 70 Ministerialists (41 County, 29 Borough M.P.s) to 35 Conservatives; Mulgrave to Russell, Russell to Melbourne, 9, 13 August 1837, Russell Papers, P.R.O. 30/22/2F.

[2] *Times*, 21, 28 August 1837, which placed the Ministry's overall majority at 41 and gave O'Connell control of about half of the 72 Irish Liberals.

[3] Crawford began his attack soon after the Election with a series of public letters; *F.J.*, 26 August; 2, 11, 15, 19, 21 September 1837.

O'Connell only once referred to the cause to which he and his followers were pledged when he said after the elections that although the Whigs were trying to make Repeal unnecessary, 'Remember that I am a REPEALER . . . remember I tell you it is my belief that justice will never be done to you until you have once again a parliament in College-green.'[1] A few new followers of O'Connell like Edmund Boyle Roche in County Cork, Robert Dillon Browne in County Mayo and Patrick Somers at Sligo were elected, but these accessions were balanced by defeats, deaths and resignations, and to put the strength of O'Connell's personal following at 32 Members may well be to exaggerate it.[2] One great triumph had been the recapture of Dublin from the Conservatives, when O'Connell and his Liberal ally, Robert Hutton, defeated two strong opponents by less than 100 votes in an election in which over 7,000 electors were polled.

If the Election marked a recession for the Conservatives, this was not for want of organization and activity. A total of 445 Conservative candidates was expected in the three Kingdoms, with a further 10 or 12 likely to appear in Ireland. £2,400 was raised by the party in London for Dublin City where two organizations, a committee to superintend the registry and the Metropolitan Conservative Society, were already in flourishing existence, and after the Election, London Conservatives raised another fund to petition against the elections of O'Connell and his followers.[3] The dissolution of the Orange Order in 1836 probably had little effect on the Conservatives' electoral fortunes in 1837, since Orangeism was concentrated in the North where the Conservatives were practically unassailable and where in 1837 well over half of their Members (19 out of 34) were returned without opposition of any kind. The party's leaders and electoral experts had expected losses of between five and eight seats. F. R. Bonham doubted the word of Sir Frederick Shaw, the Tories' unofficial leader in Ireland, that he could guarantee 36 Members; he himself thought that Ministers did not expect to gain more than five seats

[1] O'Connell to the People of Ireland, *F.J.*, 7 September 1837.

[2] F. W. Mullins lost his Kerry seat, Dominick Ronayne, M.P. for Clonmel since 1832, died early in 1836 and Edward Ruthven was not re-elected for Co. Kildare as a result of some quarrel with O'Connell (*F.J.*, 26 August 1837). Sheil is included as a Repealer almost out of courtesy. In February 1838, he accepted an official appointment (Commissioner of Greenwich Hospital) from the Government as the prelude to political office.

[3] Lord Granville Somerset to Peel [n.d. July 1837], Peel Papers, Add. MSS 40423, 346, quoted by Gash, *Politics*, 415.

but wisely added that he could 'give no opinion or attempt to reason on anything that may happen in that eccentric land'.[1] But both Bonham and Hardinge, who expected that the Government's majority of between 40 and 45 in Ireland would give it an overall majority in the House of 20 or 25, were unduly pessimistic; after election petitions, the Ministry had gained four Irish seats and a majority in the Irish representation of 34.[2]

O'Connell had already launched in April 1840 the second and most important of his Repeal campaigns by the time of the General Election of July 1841. But whereas in 1832 the Repeal cause had achieved spectacular successes, in 1841 the party suffered a crippling electoral defeat. In part this was a consequence of the initial weaknesses of the Repeal movement, which was designed more for extra-parliamentary agitation than for the winning of parliamentary elections, but it was also the result of the long alliance with the Whig Government which had disrupted the original party of 1832, only 12 of whom survived as M.P.s after 1841. Place and patronage proved irresistible temptations to over a quarter of the party, while a lack of the necessary property qualifications or disagreements with O'Connell had accounted for others.[3]

O'Connell's parliamentary support of the Government had indeed continued uninterruptedly until the elections even while he was organizing the new nationalist agitation, so that after six years of close co-operation it was not easy for the Irish electorate to make distinctions between candidates where such distinctions hardly existed. Repeal and the Repeal pledge played only a minor part in the Election. In Dublin City, for instance, O'Connell was quite ready to ally with 'an excellent Government candidate', the Marquess of Kildare, the eldest son of the Whig Duke of Leinster, despite the fact that O'Connell's Dublin supporters would certainly have preferred 'an out-and-out Repealer'.[4] In the end, O'Connell stood in coalition with the sitting Liberal M.P., Robert Hutton, and despite a vigorous canvass they were defeated by the Conservatives, John

[1] Bonham to Peel, 5, 9 August 1837, Peel Papers, Add. MSS 40424, 10–11, 42–3.
[2] Hardinge to Graham, 13 August 1837, Graham MSS. Two Liberals elected for Belfast were unseated in favour of two Conservatives. Shaw's estimate of 32 before the hearing of petitions was thus an exact one; Shaw to Peel, 19 August 1837, Peel Papers, Add. MSS 40424, 102–3.
[3] See below pp. 159–63.
[4] O'Connell to John O'Connell, 28 May 1841, *O'Connell Corr.*, II, 267–70.

Beattie West and Edward Grogan. There seems to have been only one case where refusal to take a Repeal pledge cost a sitting M.P. his seat. Andrew Lynch, Repeal M.P. for the borough of Galway since 1832, retired in 1841 because he would not pledge himself. He could scarcely have reconciled this with his appointment in 1838 to a Mastership in Chancery in England, and certainly not in a constituency where the two Repeal candidates were supported by the powerful Catholic Archbishop of Tuam, Dr. John MacHale, who had been one of the few members of the hierarchy to support O'Connell and the new Repeal campaign almost from the beginning.[1]

It was noticed during the Election that O'Connell, then aged nearly 66, seemed tired and dispirited. He had looked forward to it with gloomy foreboding and had pressed the Whigs at least to dissolve Parliament and to go to the country as a Government.[2] John O'Connell, his third and favourite son, who was largely responsible for the day-to-day management of the elections, was instructed from London by his father to moderate the Repeal agitation and to tell Thomas Davis, at this time co-editor with John Blake Dillon of the *Morning Register* and a recent recruit to the Repeal Association, that 'the want of funds is a decisive reason for not urging the Repeal as we otherwise would. This is really the secret of our weakness.'[3]

Certainly the Election campaign as a whole, with its uncertain handling of the Repeal issue and its attempts, which helped the Irish Liberals as much as O'Connell's own party, to whip up popular feeling against the Corn Laws, bears all the marks of listlessness and declining vigour.[4] Lack of clear direction from their leader was reflected in inefficiency, dissatisfaction and difficulties within local constituency organizations and with their leading members. From Limerick Sir David Roche wrote to O'Connell that 'we are in sad mess in the county. General Bourke won't stand, [Smith]

---

[1] *Pilot*, 7 July 1841; Broderick, 'The Holy See', *Analecta Gregoriana*, LV (1951) 112–15.

[2] *Times*, 5, 6 July 1841; O'Connell to Fitzpatrick, 19 February; 12 May 1841, *O'Connell Corr.*, II, 260–1, 265.

[3] O'Connell to John O'Connell, 29 May 1841, *O'Connell Corr.*, II, 270–1; same to same, 21, 26, 28, 29 May 1841, John O'Connell, *Recollections*, II, 10–21.

[4] For O'Connell's speeches and manifestos on Repeal, see *Pilot*, 28 June; *D.E.P.* 27 July 1841. He talked much of 'Monopolists and Anti-Monopolists' and supported the Whig plan of a fixed corn duty, although believing that complete abolition would be best for Irish agriculture; *Pilot*, 28 June; 12 July 1841.

O'Brien the present member won't pay a shilling even of his own expences, we this day as a last resort have set up Caleb Powell, he takes the place sooner than we should be disgraced by submitting to F[itz]Gibbon . . .' Roche himself, after nine years of holding one of the city seats, wanted now to retire, though he was eventually returned without opposition, and he was anxious for O'Connell to take Powell's place for the county so that he could come down and put an end to serious divisions in the city.[1] Yet both Limerick constituencies were impregnable Liberal strongholds in the sense that no Conservative could conceivably have succeeded in either; in 1832, two Repeal candidates had run the Whig sitting Members in the county quite close, while the city returned two Repealers until 1841.

From County Clare, a solidly Repeal constituency, O'Connell was informed that

> We have as yet only one Tory candidate [C. M. Vandeleur] & your friends MacNamara & O'Brien. MacNamara's Election I think safe— & Vandeleur cannot beat O'Brien but by Bribery—& his money is flying *freely* & *heavily* in all directions. I FEAR FOR THE RESULT as we are without money even for the ordinary Expences of the Election, as we have no Liberal Club, or Bond of Union amongst us.[2]

MacNamara and O'Brien, Repeal Members since 1832, were in fact in no danger, but if Repealers were worried in the county which had seen the revolutionary election of 1828 there could not be a clearer indication of their generally defensive and uncertain state of mind in

[1] Sir David Roche to O'Connell, 23 June 1841, O'Connell Papers, N.L.I. uncatalogued. Caleb Powell became Smith O'Brien's co-Member in 1841 and with him joined the Repeal Association in 1843. The Hon. Richard Fitzgibbon, brother of the second Earl of Clare and a powerful local figure, Lord-Lieutenant of the county and Colonel of its Militia, represented the county as a Whig from 1818 to 1841. The electoral interest built up in the county by the first Earl was shared from 1820 to 1832 with another legal family, that of Lord Guillamore (O'Grady). The election of Fitzgibbon and the Hon. Standish O'Grady in 1832 was said to have cost the former £11,000 and was fought in 'the real old Irish election style', with insults, counter-insults and challenges flying between Fitzgibbon and his nationalist opponent, Godfrey Massey, a Protestant landowner, whose lineage in his own view was much nobler than Fitzgibbon's, 'a man', according to Massey, 'whose prosperity is built upon the ruins of his country'. This was a reference to the first Earl's part in the passing of the Union. See *Times*, 2, 8 December; *F.J.*, 22, 27 December 1832; *O'Connell Corr.*, I, 534-5; McDowell, *Public Opinion*, 43-4.

[2] Richard Scott to O'Connell, 9 July 1841, O'Connell Papers, N.L.I. uncatalogued.

1841. In Mallow, County Cork, where in 1832 W. J. O'Neill Daunt, later O'Connell's secretary, had temporarily upset the entrenched interest of the Whig Sir Charles Denham Jephson-Norreys, O'Connell was told that 'a movement is in progress against Sir Denham Norreys, originating not with the Repealers . . . but with the aristocratic party . . . Although the repealers value the existence of the Melbourne administration as they do the blood in their veins, they cannot be brought to support [Norreys]'. He had done nothing to prevent the persecution of tenants who had voted for Daunt nine years earlier.[1] In Dublin and in the larger constituencies, Repeal supporters may have realized that their cause was in opposition to Whiggism, but in Mallow and probably in many other small boroughs or remote counties, the memory of local grievances or of the Whig-O'Connellite alliance played a much greater part in the elections than the cause of Repeal. It was indeed believed in England, not without some justification, that nationalist agitation in Ireland was simply a device for embarrassing a future Conservative Government in the Whigs' interest.[2]

Of the nationalist contingent, some, like The O'Conor Don, were Repealers only in name and might more accurately be described as old personal followers of O'Connell who had undoubtedly been Repealers in 1832, and more recent recruits like Sir Valentine Blake, Patrick Somers and Robert Dillon Browne brought the party no great credit. O'Connell's own prestige and popularity in Ireland had survived a series of damaging episodes, including the Raphael affair of 1836 when he was charged with having virtually sold a seat in Parliament, the revelation in 1839 that the finances of the Precursor Society were entirely under his control and the attacks made upon him and his alliance with the Whigs by Sharman Crawford.[3]

[1] D. M. Collins to O'Connell, 2 June 1841, O'Connell Papers, N.L.I. uncatalogued. Jephson-Norreys was M.P. for Mallow (1826–59), with a short interruption in 1833 until he regained his seat on petition. As Lord of the Manor of Mallow and owner of much of the town, he found no great difficulty in defeating a Tory opponent in 1841.

[2] *Times*, 7 July 1841, which continued to see an alliance based on 'a bargain to betray the Irish state'; the Whigs would fight under the Repeal slogan in order to obtain the Irish Members they so desperately needed to offset the Conservative majority in England. See also Duffy, *Young Ireland*, I, 4–5; O'Connell to Fitzpatrick, 26, 28 January 1841, *O'Connell Corr.*, II, 256–8.

[3] For the Raphael affair, see below p. 123; for the Precursor Society, see below pp. 120, 163. Duffy, *Young Ireland*, I, 6–7, believed that the allegations about Precursor finances alienated many supporters, but Sir James Graham, thinking

The results in 1841 proved conclusively that in electoral terms this alliance was as disastrous for the Repeal party as it was beneficial to the Whigs and Liberals, who emerged as easily the largest Irish party. With at least 47 Members (and probably more, since some of the Repealers might be added to this total) as against 40 Conservatives and only 18 Repealers, they reaped the harvest of their Government's legislative and administrative record and of the widespread fear and mistrust of the intentions of the Conservatives towards Ireland. In an Election in which there were only 20 contests, no less than 60 M.P.s, 31 Whig-Liberals and 29 Conservatives, were returned without opposition, a convincing demonstration both of the strength of Whig and Tory landed and personal influence and of the absolute necessity for O'Connell's movement of electoral organization and popular enthusiasm. The two leading parties were fairly evenly balanced in their sources of support, since the slight advantage enjoyed by Conservatives in counties was more than balanced by the Liberals' hold on the borough constituencies. As for the Repealers, they had lost since 1832 13 borough and 8 county seats; but for their firm hold on several counties and on a handful of boroughs, the party might have been almost eliminated.[1]

This survey of electoral history allows some conclusions to be reached about the nature of the Irish party system. One historian has argued that from 1832 to 1847 Ireland possessed a simple two-party system, formed by opposition to or support for Catholic Emancipation and Parliamentary Reform.[2] Yet it could also be argued that it was precisely this system which fell apart in 1832 with the intervention of an independent and nationalist third party, and that between 1832 and 1834 O'Connell made a determined effort to present his party and its programme as the only alternative to Toryism, the politics of the Protestant Ascendancy. 'There is no longer', he wrote in a manifesto of October 1833, 'a Catholic party opposed to a Protestant party', as there had been before 1829. 'The Catholics have got all they wanted as a particular body . . . The fading remnant of the Ascendancy is at one side, the universal

---

the 'disclosure of O'Connell's "appropriation" . . . well-timed and quite delightful', was also sure that 'the Catholics will not admit that he is a convicted knave'; to Bonham, 2 January 1839, Peel Papers, Add. MSS 40616, 54.

[1] See below Appendix A, 4.

[2] J. H. Whyte, 'Daniel O'Connell and the repeal party', *Irish Historical Studies*, XI, 304–8.

People at the other. The Government can not stand neutral without deserting its every duty.'[1] This claim was certainly bold and premature, and the Whig alliance of 1835 and 1841, while apparently reconstituting a two-party system in Ireland, also put a stop temporarily to the nationalists' attempt to supplant Liberal Unionism in Irish politics. But with the rise of the Repeal movement in the 1840's, Ireland reverted again to the three-party system of 1832-4. The judgement of the great historian Elie Halévy that the Election of 1847, held after O'Connell's death, showed that 'a new Irish party was in process of formation, implacably hostile to England' and independent of the two main parties, might perhaps be modified in the light of the actual results in 1847.[2] But if later Irish nationalists learnt the lessons of O'Connell's ultimate failure, they tended also to forget that the real ancestor of the independent party of Isaac Butt, Charles Stewart Parnell and John Redmond was the Repeal party as it emerged from the 1832 Election.

A party system in the process of slow transition from the old Whig-Tory to a new Nationalist-Unionist dichotomy presents special problems in analysis and interpretation. Thus while between 1835 and 1841 the O'Connellite party in some sense retained its separate identity, contemporaries tended to make no distinction between its members and more orthodox ministerialists. For both *The Times* and the *Annual Register* all Irish M.P.s supporting the Whig Ministry were 'joints' of 'O'Connell's tail'.[3] His party was thus held to include Repealers elected in 1832 or earlier, men who owed their seats to O'Connell's influence or to local nationalist organizations and Whigs or Liberals who owed their positions to family influence, individual status or to Liberal constituency organizations, many of which had been nationalist in 1832. This view, useful enough for the Whigs' opponents in that it emphasized O'Connell's power and degraded the Government for its reliance on him, was only half-true. O'Connell undoubtedly exercised a powerful influence on Irish Whigs and Liberals, particularly on those with large and 'popular' constituencies. Lacking a leader of O'Connell's stature, they

[1] O'Connell to his Constituents, 8 October 1833, O'Connell Papers, N.L.I., 422.
[2] Halévy, *History*, IV, 181; see also below, p. 294.
[3] *Times*, 6 February 1835; 21 August 1837, referring to the 'Whig-Radical' majority in Ireland; *Annual Register* (1837), 241, calling Whig and O'Connellite successes 'a mere elongation of Mr. O'Connell's *tail*'.

naturally tended to follow his lead in Parliament in support of Whig measures, and when after 1837 the Government's existence depended on O'Connell's continuing support, this alone was a powerful incentive to accept his leadership. It is therefore possible to regard O'Connell as the leader between 1837 and 1841 of an Irish Liberal party of some 70 members, an informal coalition of Repealers, Whigs and Liberals, in which Liberals like Wyse and William Smith O'Brien as well as more conservative Whigs like Lord Acheson and Sir Charles Jephson-Norreys combined a considerable degree of personal independence with an attitude of general co-operation with O'Connell.

It is possible, using maps based on electoral results, to construct a general picture of the political geography of Ireland.[1] There was a clear and striking division between the Conservatism of the north, based on the Province of Ulster but including also the counties of Donegal and Sligo, and the rest of Ireland, where Repeal and Liberalism, the left wing and centre parties of Irish politics, were on the whole evenly balanced at least until 1841 and were certainly far stronger than Conservatism. Ireland was indeed effectively partitioned before the middle of the nineteenth century. In the north, 20 seats remained constantly in Conservative hands, as against only four in Liberal possession. In the other three Provinces, there were 11 Repeal, 14 Liberal and only six Conservative-dominated seats, two of these from the University.[2]

The territorial area under the direct influence of the politics of Dublin consisted of the counties neighbouring on the city—Dublin, Kildare, Meath, Wicklow, Carlow and perhaps Louth—in which contested elections were the rule and not, as in the north-east, the exception.[3] No doubt there were important economic and religious

[1] Appendix D, Figs. 1–6, which are based largely on the information given by Dod in his *Parliamentary Pocket Companion*, published annually, and in his useful compendium, *Electoral Facts, 1832–52*. But Dod, while invaluable for information on constituencies, electorates, results and personal details of M.P.s, including their clubs, residences and often their occupations, is not infallible on specific electoral influences, at least in Ireland; more important, a Member's religion and the exact shade of his politics, particularly as between Repeal and Liberal, not infrequently escapes him. In these cases and wherever possible, Dod's information has been corrected by the evidence of newspapers and stray references in Hansard or in private correspondence.

[2] Appendix D, Fig. 6.

[3] Appendix D, Figs. 2–5 for this and subsequent conclusions on the political geography of Ireland.

factors at work in this Dublin area, the consequence of past Catholic and Protestant settlements and of contemporary agrarian conditions. But at a time when the political influence of property, making ideally for quiet compromises between landed interests, tended constantly to assert itself, the remarkable political activity of this area is directly attributable to the influence of Dublin itself. In 1832, not a single Conservative was returned in the whole area except in the special case of the University; in 1835, when Conservatives were eventually successful in Dublin, Conservatives were also returned in Carlow county and borough, but in 1837, with the return of O'Connell and a Liberal in Dublin, Conservatives were ousted in both Carlow constituencies. In 1841 the Conservative triumph in Dublin was reflected in successes in the counties of Dublin, Carlow and in one of the Wicklow seats. These results, partly explicable in terms of the overall electoral situation, show that the Dublin area was the most sensitive, perhaps the most politically conscious part of Ireland, a direct consequence of the area's proximity to the capital whose numerous and politically committed newspapers reported its politics with an accuracy which was never bestowed on the politically stable northern area or on the often confused situations in western constituencies. There is also no doubt that at least as far as the nationalist cause was concerned, the Dublin area was most open to the intervention of O'Connell's central organization.

Indeed, partly as a result of improved communications, partly because of its position as the capital and as the centre of O'Connell's movement, Dublin and its politics exercised a powerful influence on the whole electoral system. But this influence was neither uniform nor always direct, its tendency being rather to break in upon the strong regionalism of Irish life and to give to the obscure struggles of local politics a flavour of national importance. Some areas, for different reasons, were less open to this influence than others. Liberalism in Belfast and the north, fighting a losing battle against great odds, owed little or nothing to the inspiration of Dublin. Cork and Limerick, yielding little in the radicalism of their politics to Dublin, were important commercial and political centres in their own right and with their own provincial spheres of influence. In some western constituencies, eccentricities abounded, and politics were so confused by old family feuds and personal loyalties as often to lose pattern and even significance. In County Galway the families of Burkes, Blakes and Bodkins, D'Arcys, Dalys and Martins competed for supremacy, and a Repealer, on retiring from an election, might well give his support to a Conservative rather than to a Liberal because of an old feud between the latter's family and his own. To a lesser extent in Mayo and Clare, intricate family and personal rivalries complicated electoral politics, which were very different in character from the clear-cut struggles in Dublin and in most other constituencies in southern Ireland.

In 1832, there were few areas outside Ulster where Repealers were not successful. In the eastern sea-board counties, only Wexford and Wicklow remained Whig or Liberal. In the south and west, from Waterford to Cork and Kerry and up to Limerick, Clare and Galway, in the inland counties from Carlow, Kilkenny and Tipperary up to the midland areas of Queen's and King's Counties, Kildare and Westmeath, Repealers outnumbered the combined Liberals and Conservatives. The limits of nationalist support seem only to be reached with the more northerly midland counties of Cavan and Longford. The Elections of 1835 and 1837 did little to change this general picture, if Repealers and Liberals are thought of as one party. But for the future of the Repeal party, isolated Conservative gains in 1835 at Dublin in the east, Carlow and Queen's County inland and in Cork in the south, were ominous signs; graver still was the steady encroachment of Liberalism in areas where Repeal had been very strong in 1832, notably in the east and south. In 1841 both Conservatives and Liberals consolidated their positions in those areas where they had made gains in 1835 and 1837, the former in the eastern and inland counties, the latter particularly in the south and south-west. Repeal, which in 1832 had been strong in every area of Ireland outside Ulster, was now scattered and disrupted. Only the south and west, parts of the Provinces of Munster and Connaught, remained in any way comparable to what they had been in 1832, and the Province of Leinster, the political heartland of Ireland, had been almost completely lost.

The membership of the party

The composition of the Repeal party in Parliament was largely dictated by the property qualifications for M.P.s: a freehold estate yielding £600 a year for county M.P.s, an estate of £300 for borough Members. In Ireland, where to a much greater extent than in England property was synonymous with land, these requirements ensured that the great majority of Irish M.P.s of all parties would be drawn from the landed gentry and aristocracy. In England it may have been relatively easy to evade these identical standards, but in Ireland the requirements were stringently enforced, at least for Repealers, by opponents who constantly impugned their qualifications at election time and who had at hand a powerful weapon in the election petition to substantiate their allegations.[1]

Thus in 1832 over three-quarters of the members of the Repeal party, 31 out of 39, were either landowners or men who derived their incomes in whole or in part from the ownership of land; furthermore, thirteen were Protestants, a tribute to the tradition of Protestant nationalism as it had been consecrated in the Irish Parliament as well as the result of the property qualifications.[2] Only six Repealers, most of whom like Daniel Callaghan, William Roche, Dominick Ronayne and Richard Sullivan sat for city or borough constituencies, are identifiable as having had exclusively or primarily commercial interests, but it is noticeable that a fair proportion of the party combined landed with commercial commitments. O'Connell, his eldest son Maurice and Cornelius O'Brien were directors of the National Bank of Ireland (founded in 1834), while O'Connell also had a financial interest in brewing. Thomas Fitzgerald had West Indian interests; J. M. Galwey was a wine-merchant as well as a large land-agent, while Henry Barron and Henry Grattan had newspaper interests and William Roche was a landowner as well as a private banker. Again, at least eleven members of the party were also members of the legal profession, but only two, Andrew Lynch and A. C. O'Dwyer, seem either to have practised seriously as barristers or to have been dependent on the profession for their livelihood. For instance, W. F. Finn's commercial activities were certainly far more important to him than his having been called in his youth to the Irish Bar; and Sheil, who had earlier depended on his practice at the Bar as well as on writing high-flown dramas for the London stage, scarcely practised and fortunately did not write plays again after his marriage to a landed heiress in 1831.[3]

[1] See Gash, *Politics*, 105–6, for English practices in evading the qualifications.

[2] Appendix B, 2, gives notes on each member of the party in 1832, on which these and other statements and calculations are based.

[3] Sheil thus joined the ranks of the landed interest if he was not, by virtue of his father's estate, there already. Neither John nor Maurice O'Connell practised successfully, and their father did not practise after 1829. Cornelius O'Brien, the only solicitor in the party, was also a landowner and bank director.

In comparison with the other Irish parties the Repeal party did contain a small proportion of 'new men' whom it would not be easy to classify as belonging to the gentry class. But 28 members or nearly two-thirds of the party came from well-established and well-known gentry families, both Catholic and Protestant. They included Catholics like Richard Bellew, younger brother of Sir Patrick Bellew, 7th Bt., The O'Conor Don, who was an important Roscommon landowner, J. H. Talbot, H. W. Barron, Sir Richard Nagle, 2nd Bt., and Walter Blackney, all four of whom were or became Justices of the Peace and Deputy-Lieutenants in their respective counties; and Protestants like Colonel the Hon. Pierce Butler, son of the 11th Viscount Mountgarret, F. W. Mullins, eldest son of the Hon. and Rev. Frederick Mullins, Henry Grattan, the second son of the great Anglo-Irish leader, the Macnamaras, father and son, with their 15,000 acres in Clare and a claim of descent from the ancient Admirals of Munster, and N. A. Vigors, Charles Walker, David Roche and the Ruthvens, all substantial landowners in Carlow, Wexford, Waterford and Kildare respectively.

The Conservative party, while it undoubtedly contained a larger proportion of the sons or relations of peers than either of the other two parties, certainly could not boast a monopoly either of the aristocracy or gentry or even of its Protestant, Anglo-Irish elements. In terms of social background, there was essentially no difference between *most* Repealers and Irish Whigs or Liberals, whether Protestant like Sharman Crawford, Smith O'Brien, the Hon. Richard Fitzgibbon and Viscount Clements, or Catholic like Thomas Wyse, Richard More O'Ferrall and Henry Lambert. If the social status of the Repeal party *as a whole* was slightly lower than that of the other parties, the difference was clearly one of degree rather than of kind. The standard adopted by one historian (the holding of local office) shows clearly that many Repealers, as magistrates, Deputy-Lieutenants and Sheriffs, had considerable local status and importance; if a few were 'status-seekers', whose local office followed on their being for one reason or another Members of Parliament, most had long-standing and undeniable family claims on these positions.[1]

But the debate between historians on the social status of the

[1] See Sir Henry Blackall and J. H. Whyte, 'Correspondence on O'Connell and the repeal party', *Irish Historical Studies*, XII, No. 46 (September 1960), 139–43.

Repeal party will remain inconclusive unless the argument is carried somewhat further. First and most important was the overwhelmingly landed character of the party. The great majority of its members were closely connected, as landowners and landlords, with the existing land system, and their economic interests and social background vitally affected the party's general outlook and activity in Parliament. No doubt the party was less powerful in terms of sheer landed influence than its rivals, since even its landed members owed their seats more to their political opinions and to popular support than to their own electoral influence as landlords. A few such as James Roe and Patrick Lalor were definitely small landowners or leaseholding middlemen. Feargus O'Connor was a member of an old but impoverished and declining gentry family. The available evidence strongly suggests that as a whole the Repealers' landed commitments were smaller than those of most Whigs and Liberals and a great deal smaller than those of the Conservatives.[1] It still remains true that O'Connell's party was a party of landlords, that land continued to predominate over commerce or the professions as its vital interest and indeed that this landed interest actually increased throughout the party's existence as men like the White brothers, Luke and Henry, Sir William Brabazon, Sir Valentine Blake, E. B. Roche and later Smith O'Brien and Caleb Powell replaced representatives of the commercial interest like Finn, Galwey and Sullivan and lesser landowners like Roe, Lalor and O'Connor.

Secondly, it is important to account for the high proportion of Repealers who were at once Catholic, landowners and the representatives of old gentry families. These were the products of that remarkably resilient and adaptable class, the Irish Catholic gentry, who now demanded the political power from which they had long been debarred. By a curious historical accident, the Penal Laws, by depriving Catholics of much though not necessarily all of their lands, had forced many representatives of gentry families into the occupations of trade and commerce and had thus directly brought about the rise of a small but prosperous Catholic middle class during the eighteenth century. This hybrid class, a fusion of gentry, their younger sons and men of humbler origin, had risen largely on the profits of the provision and linen trades and of banking; and after 1782, with the equalization of property rights between Catholics and

---

[1] See Appendix C.

Protestants in Ireland, these profits must have been used on a considerable scale to acquire land or to increase family holdings.[1]

The family history and background of many Repealers strikingly conformed to this general pattern. William and David Roche were descended from one of the richest Catholic merchant families in Limerick, which had married into landed families in the second half of the eighteenth century; R. M. Bellew, a member of an old landed family in Louth, was related to the Bellews of Mount Bellew in Galway, landowners and merchants on a large scale in the third quarter of the century.[2] Barron, Blackney, Nagle, Talbot and The O'Conor Don were all plainly of gentry stock. Sheil was the son of an Irish Cadiz merchant who bought an estate in Waterford, and J. M. Galwey has been shown to have been of a respectable gentry family. The O'Connells, as we have seen, were perfect archetypes of their class.[3]

Finally, the party was remarkable for its interlocking family relationships. No less than eight of its members, three sons, two sons-in-law, a brother-in-law, and two cousins were closely related to O'Connell himself, while Nicholas Fitzsimon was the brother of one of O'Connell's sons-in-law and Morgan John O'Connell, who entered Parliament in 1835, was his nephew. The Roches were cousins and Cornelius O'Brien married a niece of William Roche, as did Galwey a cousin of Barron. Sheil and Bellew were brothers-in-law, and Sheil's stepson, John Power, was M.P. for County Waterford after 1837. J. H. Talbot was the father-in-law of James Power, M.P. for County Wexford from 1835, and Power's brother-in-law was Nicholas Fitzsimon. In addition there were three pairs of fathers and sons, the Butlers, the Ruthvens and the Macnamaras.

Electoral organization in Ireland

The success of any third party intervention in the Irish electoral system plainly depended on a central party organization. In 1832 such an organization, the National Political Union, was already in

[1] See esp. Maureen Wall, 'The rise of a Catholic middle class in eighteenth-century Ireland', *Irish Historical Studies*, XI, No. 42 (September 1958), 91–115.

[2] Wall, op. cit., 102, n. 37; 106–7, has notes on the Roches, Bellews and the Wyse family in the eighteenth century. Catholic Liberal M.P.s fit into the same general pattern.

[3] See Blackall, 'Corr.', *Irish Historical Studies*, XII, 139–43, under GALWEY, SHEIL; for the O'Connell family, above pp. 1–2.

existence. It had been formed in November 1831 to support Parliamentary Reform as a continuation of the many O'Connellite organizations banned by Governments since 1829, and resembled both its model, the Catholic Association, and its contemporary English counterparts like the Birmingham Political Union under Thomas Attwood, in that it was principally designed to influence public opinion and to bring pressure to bear on Parliament by meetings, petitions and press publicity in support of a particular cause. With the Election of 1832, the National Political Union became for the first time an electoral machine and party headquarters, and in subsequent Elections its successors were put to the same uses. This achievement, as original in its way as O'Connell's earlier exploitation of the power of organized public opinion, has certainly been less widely recognized by historians.

Each O'Connellite organization floated between 1832 and 1841 was largely middle class in composition. Its members, who were elected and paid annual subscriptions of at least £1, met weekly at the Corn Exchange in Dublin, though more often during an Election. The organization was, in theory at least, run by a standing committee. In practice it was entirely under O'Connell's control, exercised either personally or through trusted agents of whom the most important was Patrick Vincent Fitzpatrick, the son of Hugh Fitzpatrick, a successful Catholic bookseller in Dublin. O'Connell had every reason to be grateful to Fitzpatrick, who was finally rewarded when at O'Connell's request Lord John Russell appointed him in 1847 to the lucrative sinecure of Assistant Registrar of Deeds in Dublin. His relationship to O'Connell resembled that of F. R. Bonham to Peel, in that Fitzpatrick's wide knowledge of Irish constituencies and political personalities was constantly at O'Connell's disposal; he occasionally involved himself at O'Connell's request in electoral politics and kept in close touch with supporting newspapers and their editors, particularly with Richard Barrett of the *Pilot*.[1]

But here the resemblance ends. For Fitzpatrick was at the same time O'Connell's private banker, organizer of the O'Connell Annuity Fund or Tribute (of which he received a percentage) and frequently treasurer of the central party organization. Through his

---

[1] See, for instance, O'Connell to Fitzpatrick, 27 May 1833; 10, 19 May; 24 June 1834; 4 January 1835; 8 December 1840, *O'Connell Corr.*, I, 351, 435-7, 511-12; II, 253-4, 403-4.

hands passed all the funds subscribed to indemnify O'Connell for
the loss of his practice as a barrister and to pay for the expenses of
his organization, and part of this money was undoubtedly used as an
election fund. In O'Connell's political machine, the discreet, efficient and charming Fitzpatrick, 'your Chancellor of the Exchequer',[1]
as he once described himself to O'Connell—played an unobtrusive
but vital part, the full significance of which is missed if he is described simply as O'Connell's faithful supporter or as his financial
agent.[2] He was also the only one of his contemporaries with whom
O'Connell, who had little time or inclination for writing letters, kept
up a regular and confidential correspondence.[3]

The composition of O'Connell's organizations varied with the
changes in his political strategy. The National Political Union, which
had contained Whigs and Liberals in April 1832, was exclusively
nationalist by December. The Anti-Tory Association of November
1834 was still too closely identified with O'Connell's policies to
attract any but advanced Liberals,[4] but of the General Association
of Ireland, formed in September 1836 and dissolved after it had
served its turn in the 1837 Election, Lord Mulgrave wrote from
Dublin stressing

> . . . the importance it is likely to derive from its great success and its
> extraordinary growth . . . It has now been not three months in exis-
> tence . . . comprising the dead time of the year in Dublin, with no
> immediate positive grievance because no complaint to find with the
> Government, . . . yet because it represents national and not sectarian
> interests, it has already attained an influence much beyond that of the
> Catholic Association at the commencement of 1829 . . . It is a very
> remarkable fact that nearer one fourth than one fifth of the Members
> are *Protestants*, being a larger proportion than they bear to the whole
> population of the country.

[1] Fitzpatrick to O'Connell, 21 February 1831, O'Connell Papers, N.L.I.,
uncatalogued: 'Cash continues to come in steadily & satisfactorily & I am working the uncollected districts with gratifying prospects of success. I have no doubt
of making the operation permanently productive . . . The splendid *coup* that has
been made . . . [by] your Chancellor of the Exchequer.'

[2] McDowell, *Public Opinion*, 156; Gwynn, *Young Ireland and 1848*, 69.

[3] Few of Fitzpatrick's own letters survive, but it is one of the great merits of
O'Connell's *Correspondence*, edited by W. J. Fitzpatrick, that it prints so many
of O'Connell's letters to Fitzpatrick.

[4] *Times*, 2, 9 April 1832; M. J. Blake, M.P. to Edward Dwyer, 1 December
1834, O'Connell Papers, N.L.I. 5242; *Northern Whig*, 8 December 1834, for
Sharman Crawford's membership.

With seven peers, seven sons or brothers of peers, 'several large Protestant landed Proprietors, some of the richest Merchants in Dublin, Cork, etc.—some of the most leading lawyers and most of the rising talent of the Bar', the Association's respectability was unimpeachable, and most important of all, it included 46 M.P.s or almost half of the Irish representatives. Mulgrave thought that it was to the Irish feeling of inequality with England,

> . . . this feeling national in its character and comprehensive in its application that the General Association owes its Birth . . . Its objects are limited and proclaimed—its proceedings are open . . . and the fact was they guarded themselves on all those points [of law, especially questions of maintenance and barratry in the defence of tithe defendants] even more studiously than all these Conservative Associations recently so widely established in England or than these new Protestant Associations in this country . . .[1]

The General Association, 'the Catholic Association in a new name and somewhat broader basis',[2] was certainly the most imposing of all O'Connell's organizations before the Repeal Association, at least from the Whigs' viewpoint, and it played an important part in the Liberal successes in 1837.

The Repeal Association of the 1840's, with its educative and propagandist slant, its Repeal wardens, arbitration courts and reading rooms, its sponsorship of mass demonstrations and its large peasant membership under middle class leadership, was not primarily an electoral organization but rather the old Catholic Association improved and modernized. Indeed there are indications that O'Connell came to regard the organizations of the 1830's, with their emphasis on electoral needs, as comparative failures, diversions from the true basis of political action and useful only under a Whig Government. After 1841, the situation seemed designed for a repetition of the *coup* of 1829.[3] Nonetheless the earlier organizations had considerable electoral importance and merit some detailed examination.

[1] Mulgrave to Russell, 26 November 1836, Russell Papers, P.R.O. 30/22/2D.

[2] O'Connell to Archbishop MacHale, 2 July 1836, *O'Connell Corr.*, II, 69–70; to D. R. Pigot, 2 July 1836, O'Connell Papers, N.L.I. 423. For the Association's aims, which included household suffrage, ballot, triennial parliaments, one-member electoral districts, the abolition of the property qualification for M.P.s and free trade, see O'Connell, Memo [n.d. 1836], O'Connell Papers, N.L.I. 423.

[3] O'Connell to Fitzpatrick, 17 July 1841, *O'Connell Corr.*, II, 278–9. The Repeal Association proved ineffective as an electoral organization in 1841, though it was more successful in 1847 under John O'Connell.

As the official, national centre of O'Connell's movement, each central body acted as a clearing house for information on constituencies and candidates, and at each Election O'Connell and his principal lieutenants submitted long and detailed reports on the electoral situation in the constituencies, either as reports to a standing election committee, as in 1834–5, or as reports based on personal investigation by O'Connell himself, given in speeches to a general meeting.[1] The publicity given in the organization's proceedings to the details of local politics not only gave provincial supporters an added sense of importance and confidence but also acted as a deterrent against the use of all those kinds of private influence, landed or personal, legal or illegal, on which opponents might rely, while it almost certainly deterred some opponents from contesting expensive marginal seats. Although direct evidence on this latter point is not easy to produce, the constant criticisms of opponents that the organization constituted an unwarrantable and unconstitutional interference between electors and candidates is indirect proof of its effectiveness.

At each Election the slogans and watchwords of the party were provided by O'Connell's speeches at party meetings in Dublin, to be adopted by the local clubs in their election campaigns. The immediate electoral influence of the central body was most evident in Dublin and in the Dublin area, but this was of the utmost importance because of the powerful influence of the politics of the metropolis on Irish politics in general. In Dublin, where the two extremes of Irish politics carried on a fierce and evenly balanced struggle for supremacy, the central party organization acted as a local election club, superintending the registration of voters, whipping up enthusiasm and bringing electors to the polls. In 1832 a committee of the National Political Union was set up to supervise the first registry under the Reform Act in collaboration with the Dublin Trades' Political Union, a body whose membership of traders, shopkeepers, artisans and labourers gave it an aura of genuine radicalism which contrasted and conflicted with the more aristocratic and gentlemanly atmosphere of the National Political Union.[2] This committee suc-

---

[1] Cf. *Times*, 1 December 1832; *D.E.P.*, 2 December and throughout December 1834; *F.J.*, 12 July 1837; *Pilot*, 28 June; 12 July 1841.

[2] *D.E.P.*, 23 August 1832. Its legal advisers were the Repealer A. C. O'Dwyer and David Richard Pigot, Liberal M.P. for Clonmel (1839–41), Irish Solicitor and Attorney-General and finally, in 1846, Chief Baron of the Exchequer. Only

ceeded in producing 7,000 notices of registry. Although many of these were either rejected or not taken up, the nationalists were said before the election to be 'triumphant in the registry',[1] and there is no doubt that the great victory of O'Connell and E. S. Ruthven in 1832 was the direct result of superior organization. In Dublin, the largest constituency in Ireland with 7,000 registered electors in 1832 and over 12,000 in 1841, with its exclusively Protestant Corporation and some 1,500 Conservative freemen, its important mercantile interests (whose politics, Liberal if not nationalist in 1832, became increasingly Conservative) and its well-organized working-class elements, victory at election time went to the efficient and the unscrupulous. Conservative successes in 1836 on a petition and in 1841 by the narrow margin of less than 200 votes were a tribute to the growing strength of their organization.

The selection of candidates was generally the preserve of O'Connell himself or of the local constituency clubs, but several examples have already been produced from the 1832 Election which show the importance of the central body in this respect.[2] In later Elections, candidates were often formally adopted in Dublin, but this was in nearly all cases a recognition of what had already been decided by O'Connell or a local club. Direct intervention from Dublin would have been virtually impossible in 1835 and 1837, when O'Connell supported various candidates who might well have been objectionable to many members of the central organization, and O'Connell would scarcely have tolerated much open discussion of his choices or allowed a body which he strictly controlled to interfere with the flexibility of his electoral policy. Besides, such interference would have been resented by the local constituency organizations, who were

after much negotiation were some of the Trades Unionists admitted to meetings of the N.P.U. in 1832. See *D.E.P.*, 24 November; 17 December 1831; 5, 7 April 1832. O'Connell tried to muzzle the Trades Union by amalgamating it with his own organization, and his experience of its independent radicalism helped to form his well-known opposition to all trade union activities. See Rachel O'Higgins, 'Irish Trade Unions and Politics, 1830–50', *The Historical Review*, IV, No. 2 (1961), 208–17.

[1] *Times*, 8, 24 September; 14 November; *D.E.P.*, 24 November 1832.

[2] See above pp. 55–6. The N.P.U. also intervened decisively in Co. Dublin behind Christopher Fitzsimon, in Co. Clare against O'Gorman Mahon and with less success at Dungarvan, where a great effort was made to dislodge the Hon. George Lamb, Melbourne's brother, Under-Secretary of State at the Home Office and M.P. for Dungarvan since 1820; *F.J.*, 3, 10, 19, 22 December; *Times*, 7, 8, 12 December; *D.E.P.*, 15, 18 December 1832; 10 January 1833.

ready in many cases to accept O'Connell's nominees but who jealously preserved their own formal independence. After 1833, the main party centre was perhaps more important as a symbol of organization and power, providing the mystique on which the party greatly depended for its popular appeal, than as a national electoral machine, with the important exceptions of Dublin and its neighbouring constituencies.

The press played a vital role in O'Connell's political system. It would indeed be difficult to exaggerate the contribution made by the Dublin press and even more perhaps by the provincial newspapers to the party's electoral successes. The country was flooded by newspapers. In Dublin alone in this period there were at least ten, and of the thirteen main provincial newspapers, five or six were nationalist or strongly radical, five were Conservative and only two were Whig or moderately Liberal.[1] O'Connell effectively controlled three of the four 'left-wing' Dublin newspapers. The *Pilot* was entirely under his control, its owner-editor Richard Barrett receiving a constant stream of manifestos, policy-directives and private letters from O'Connell in London or at Darrynane, and the *Freeman's Journal* and the *Morning Register*, while retaining formal editorial independence, both generally supported O'Connell's movement.[2]

O'Connell's manipulation of the press was undoubtedly crude and authoritarian, stemming, as Dr. Inglis suggests, from his early political experience when 'newspapers were cowed and malleable'.[3] He insisted on editorial obedience to the party line laid down by

[1] Nationalist-radical: *Mayo Telegraph, Tipperary Free Press, Southern Reporter, Carlow Morning Post, Castlebar Telegraph* and (?) *Kilkenny Moderator*; Conservative: *Roscommon Gazette, Carlow Sentinel, Mayo Constitution, Cork Constitution* and *Belfast News-Letter*; Whig-Liberal: *Northern Whig* and *Newry Examiner*.

[2] The one exception in Dublin was the Whig *Dublin Evening Post* whose editor, F. W. Conway, was described by Charles Gavan Duffy, who knew the world of Dublin journalism intimately, as 'a stipendiary writer for the Castle'. E. J. Littleton certainly gave the paper preferential treatment over news; Inglis, *Freedom of the Press*, 207; Aspinall, *Politics and the Press*, 122, 255–6. For O'Connell and the *Pilot*, see O'Connell to Barrett, 12 April; 11 September; 8 October 1833; drafts of open letters to Duncannon, Durham, People of Ireland, 12, 20, 27 September; 11, 12 October 1834, O'Connell Papers, N.L.I., 422, 423, and numerous letters in *O'Connell Corr*. O'Connell himself owned no daily or weekly newspaper, though he had a proprietorial interest in the *Dublin Review*, a monthly magazine.

[3] Inglis, *Freedom of the Press*, 224.

himself whatever the risk to consistency, and on the constant reiteration of clear and simple political slogans. Literary style, intellectual content and journalistic ethics were secondary considerations. Newspaper owners and editors were ready to take the consequences for printing his potentially libellous material because they were paid to suffer in silence. When in January 1834 Barrett was fined and sent to prison for six months for seditious libel, O'Connell paid him a total of £656, a sum which included his £100 fine, £150 in American subscriptions and weekly sums during his imprisonment amounting to £406.[1]

The financial dependence of Liberal newspapers on the favour of O'Connell's political organizations in the matter of notices of meetings, lists of subscriptions and advertisements, was well demonstrated in 1839, when the liberal press, which had at first given little support to O'Connell's new agitation, was brought sharply into line by threats to withdraw the favour of the Precursor Society.[2] O'Connell's movement was indeed well served by press support and publicity. Although the official circulations of O'Connellite newspapers were perhaps not impressive, their actual circulations were certainly much greater. For every Irishman who could afford personally to subscribe to a newspaper (at an annual cost of some £5 even after the Whig Government's reduction of the Irish stamp duty from 2d. to 1d. in 1836), at least ten, probably twenty people would have read a newspaper or had it read to them in public houses, in the many political or social clubs and later in the two hundred reading-rooms provided throughout the country by the Repeal Association. The fact that O'Connellite newspapers were in competition with each other tended to limit their individual circulations, but the combined circulation of the *Pilot*, the *Freeman's Journal* and the *Register* between 1831

[1] O'Connell to Barrett, 7 June 1833, *O'Connell Corr.*, I, 357–60; Payments by D. O'Connell for Repeal and Public Purposes, O'Connell MSS, U.C.D. In 1831, Michael Staunton of the *Register*, a man of greater integrity and independence than Barrett, was guaranteed all his expenses at the time of his prosecution; *O'Connell Corr.*, I, 248, n. 7. For the theory and practice of buying newspapers outright, see O'Connell to John O'Connell, 19 September 1840, John O'Connell, *Recollections*, I, 327–9; to Fitzpatrick, 26 January 1841, *O'Connell Corr.*, II, 257.

[2] Brian Inglis, 'O'Connell and the Irish Press, 1800–42', *Irish Historical Studies*, VIII, No. 29 (March 1952), 24–6. In September 1845, the Repeal Association paid £60, £80, £46 and £22 respectively to the *Nation*, *Freeman's Journal*, *Pilot* and *Register*; T. M. Ray to O'Connell, 9 September 1845, O'Connell MSS, U.C.D.

and 1841 was not far below that of the leading Conservative newspaper, the *Dublin Evening Mail*. If the Whig *Dublin Evening Post* is included, together with the preponderance of radical newspapers in the provinces, then it is clear that even before the founding in 1842 of the *Nation*, whose extraordinary success and originality revolutionized Irish journalism, the 'left-wing' Irish press considerably outweighed its Conservative counterpart.[1]

O'Connell's autocratic treatment of supporting newspapers, no doubt deplorable in one who proclaimed his belief in a free and independent press, certainly reflected a fear that government might follow the old practice of 'buying' newspapers. The Proclamation Fund, open to periodical investigation by the Commons, steadily decreased in amount throughout the early nineteenth century; a large part went towards the official *Gazette*, and there were no complaints from Irish Members about its use before it ceased altogether in 1846. The Irish secret service money, although officially limited to £5,000 a year, was a different matter. O'Connell's allegations in July 1831 that pensions were being paid out of it to Irish journalists were never denied. Indeed in 1852 Lord John Russell positively declared that all Chief Secretaries had used the fund to buy newspaper support, and his colleagues of 1830–4, Stanley and E. J. Littleton, were probably less scrupulous and more active in manipulating the press than most Chief Secretaries.[2] In O'Connell's defence, it must be said that he was confronted with bribable journalists and bribing officials. But his whole attitude to the press had extremely unfortunate effects. As Dr. Inglis has suggested, it stifled the growth of genuinely independent Irish newspapers and made for inevitable conflict after the emergence of the *Nation*.[3] Finally, it was partly responsible for the bitter and disastrous quarrel with *The Times*, which refused, unlike the Irish newspapers, to be browbeaten into submission, and which pursued O'Connell, his party and his

[1] Inglis, *Freedom of the Press*, Appendix C, 233, for a chart of circulations. Doubts about these figures as being too low are expressed by Whyte, 'O'Connell and the repeal party', *Irish Historical Studies*, XI, 307. The calculation of £5 p.a. (4d. a copy) is confirmed by Lord Brougham's experience in 1833, when he was presented with a bill for £15 9s. 7d., 3½ years' unwitting subscription to the Government's *Dublin Times*: Aspinall, *Politics and the Press*, 149.

[2] See A. Aspinall, 'The Irish "Proclamation" Fund, 1800–1846'; 'The Use of Irish Secret Service Money in subsidizing the Irish Press', *English Historical Review*, LVI (April 1941), 279–80, LVI (October 1941), 639–46.

[3] Inglis, 'O'Connell and the Press', *Irish Historical Studies*, VIII, 1 ff.

movement with the most abusive, relentless and unscrupulous hostility.

O'Connell's own contribution to the electoral fortunes of his party was of course enormous. In 1832, having sat previously for Clare, County Waterford and Kerry, O'Connell after some genuine hesitation and in response to Fitzpatrick's urgent advice exchanged his safe Kerry seat for a candidature in Dublin.[1] This move, successful in 1832, had important consequences. It increased the electoral and political importance of Dublin and helped to restore to the city some of those qualities as a capital which it had possessed under the Irish Parliament, but which it came dangerously near to losing altogether after the Union. It meant that at every Election the Conservative party concentrated much of its energies in defeating him in what was certainly the most expensive constituency in the country. Again, the need to return to Dublin probably limited the extent of O'Connell's election tours in the provinces. He generally visited the main centres of the south and west—Waterford, Cork, Limerick, Kerry and the constituencies of his immediate family, holding meetings, rallying support for candidates and often personally directing an election; but in the leisurely conditions of nineteenth-century electioneering, when the dates of polling varied widely in the different constituencies, it was still possible for him to be present at several provincial elections before returning to face his own contest in Dublin.

The extent of his personal influence is shown by the large 'Household Brigade', most of whom had relatively safe seats. In Kerry the O'Connell name and interest carried on a long and evenly matched battle with the far stronger territorial interest of the Catholic but unfriendly Whig Lord Kenmare, winning both seats in 1832 and 1835; but in 1837 O'Connell was 'greatly mortified' by the defeat of one of his nominees, and in 1841 the two interests shared the representation.[2] From Meath, one of the safest nationalist county strong-

[1] O'Connell to Fitzpatrick, 22, 29 September; 25 October; 20 December 1832, *O'Connell Corr.*, I, 304–12, 315; Fitzpatrick to O'Connell, 28 August 1832, O'Connell Papers, N.L.I. uncatalogued: The Whigs 'say that if you do not stand for Dublin the fate of the question [Repeal] is sealed for the next Parliament . . . the Metropolis must give the example to the country at large'.

[2] See *F.J.*, 11, 12 December 1832; *Pilot*, 3 January 1833; *O'Connell Corr.*, I, 508–10, 516–19; II, 106–8, 112; John O'Connell to O'Connell, 8 December 1834, O'Connell MSS, U.C.D., for the ins and outs of Kerry electoral politics. M. J. O'Connell, Daniel's nephew, held one seat from 1835 to 1852, when he

holds, O'Connell heard in 1841 from three local priests that 'in consideration of the doubtful issue of the pending contests for Dublin you have been this day unanimously elected to represent the Co. of Meath in Parliament. Mr. Corbally . . . removed every obstacle to that great national object by withdrawing himself as a candidate.'[1] Kilkenny, the safest nationalist borough seat and uncontested throughout the period, was so much in O'Connell's gift that Joseph Hume, the English Radical, was offered and accepted it after his defeat in Middlesex in 1837.[2] The independent Sharman Crawford was so disgusted by his constituents' servility to O'Connell's wishes that he resigned as M.P. for Dundalk in 1837, while of Cashel, it was said that 'We never yet elected an M.P. . . . without the consent of the Liberator', a fact which worked considerably in the Whigs' favour, for a borough which had elected a Repealer without a contest in 1832 became a safe seat for Whig Ministers.[3]

Only one northern constituency felt the power of O'Connell's influence. At Londonderry George Dawson, Robert Peel's brother-in-law, made unsuccessful efforts to unseat the Whig Sir Robert Ferguson in 1832 and 1837. On the second occasion, he was beaten, according to his own account, by 'the fraud and treachery of the R. Catholic voters', eighty of whom had promised to support him, but O'Connell had 'sent down orders from the association to vote against me' and these electors had obeyed him. Dawson was most upset by the 'bare-faced and shameful conduct' of the Catholics, and he was particularly aggrieved because O'Connell had said to him in London that he hoped Dawson would be an M.P., that he would indeed go to Derry to canvass for him if he could spare the time, 'out of gratitude' perhaps for Dawson's small contribution to the

retired apparently through lack of the necessary financial qualifications: J. H. Whyte, *The Independent Irish Party, 1850–9* (1958), 47.

[1] Messrs. Boylan, Burke and Leonard to O'Connell, 9 July 1841, O'Connell MSS, U.C.D. For the delicate restoration of Matthew Corbally to his seat when O'Connell chose Co. Cork instead, see O'Connell to Fitzpatrick, 11, 17 July 1841, *O'Connell Corr.*, II, 276, 278.

[2] It was John O'Connell's seat from 1841–7. See Edmund Smithwick to Daniel O'Connell, 21 May 1841, O'Connell Papers, N.L.I. uncatalogued: '[that] the Electors of Kilkenny will be honoured either by yourself or your son John, is the anxious wish of the honest portion and they are the greater number and [I] am happy to say the most influential.'

[3] B. A. Kennedy, 'Sharman Crawford's Federal Scheme for Ireland', in *Essays in British and Irish History*, eds. H. A. Cronne et al. (1949), 241; *O'Connell Corr.*, II, 268, n. 8.

passing of Catholic Emancipation.[1] Dawson's honourable though naïve character did him credit, but he was far too scrupulous to succeed in an Irish election.

Under the Irish Reform Act, the registration of voters took place at a special session in each constituency, at which claims were examined and decided upon by the chairman of the sessions or by an assistant barrister. This process was not new in Ireland, but largely because of doubts as to the legality of superintending the registration by means of a central committee and subordinate local bodies, it was an exceptional county which had its own club in operation before the Reform Act. The *Morning Register* referred specifically to Louth, Meath and Waterford when it noticed in 1832 that in places 'in which a club . . . had achieved on a former occasion the independence of a county, opposition has been deemed so hopeless *now*, that there has either been no contest at all, or one so brief and decisive as only to attest the utter folly of attempting to control popular power once thoroughly awakened'.[2] The rapid increase in the number of these local election clubs was partly due to the Reform Act, by which every Irish voter was disfranchised until he registered under its provisions. O'Connell realized apparently somewhat earlier than Peel that in the registration clauses of the Act lay electoral success or failure, and Ireland showed, at a slightly earlier date than England, that these clauses 'unexpectedly provided the greatest single stimulus to the organization of the electorate for party purposes that had so far been created by law'.[3]

As early as August 1832, in a series of public letters printed in supporting newspapers and read out in the National Political Union, O'Connell called for 'a parochial committee in each parish [and] a County Independent Club in each county', and went on to explain in clear and simple language the technicalities of the franchises and the methods of registration. Finally, these local organizations, of which the county clubs were much the most important, were to collect the National Rent which O'Connell hoped would be 'amply sufficient, after indemnifying all those who are unjustly

[1] Dawson to Peel, 16 August 1837, Peel Papers, Add. MSS 40424, 71–2; Dawson's Election Diary, P.R.O. Northern Ireland. See Gash, *Peel*, 533–4, for Dawson's speech in 1828 announcing his sudden conversion to the necessity of Emancipation. Peel was infuriated and embarrassed by this badly-timed action.

[2] *Pilot*, 2 January 1833, quoting *Morning Register*.

[3] Gash, *Politics*, xiii; cf. Peel to Arbuthnot, 8 November 1838, Parker, *Peel*, II, 368.

prosecuted or persecuted in person or in property [as a result of refusal to pay tithes], to assist the repeal candidates in the coming elections'.[1]

O'Connell's appeal was remarkably successful. At least 24 constituencies in 1832 possessed clubs working in the Repeal interest, as against 9 Conservative and 11 Whig-Liberal organizations. While these Repeal centres often called themselves 'Liberal' or 'Independent' Clubs, it is impossible to see in this the reflection of a two-party system. The 'independence' of a constituency meant usually the overturning of some established electoral interest, whether of a person or a family, and the designation 'Liberal' was perhaps deliberately chosen to attract Whig support for Repealers.[2] The Meath Independent Club, the Reform Registry Political Union of Longford and the Liberal Club in Limerick were all staunchly nationalist organizations. But these local clubs, although formed in many places in response to O'Connell's initiative, were nearly always formally independent of his central organization. O'Connell made several attempts, at least on the level of registration, to unify the local and central parts of his movement. In 1833 he stressed the importance of the activity of individuals in 'attending to the franchise', who were to keep in close touch with Edward Dwyer, one of his Dublin agents, and in 1834 the Anti-Tory Association sent out detailed lithograph questionnaires from its central election committee, requesting information on the prospects of candidates, the standing and conduct of present M.P.s, the state of the registry, the position of the different interests and their attitudes in particular to the tithe question, so 'that there should be a perfect unity of opinion between them [the central committee] and the provinces'.[3] The General Association of 1836 was planned with a central finance committee with Fitzpatrick as treasurer, to supervise the collection of 'the Irish rent' in collaboration with committees for each Province and with

[1] *Times*, 27 August 1832; *F.J.*, 13 September 1832; Daniel O'Connell, *Seven Letters on the Reform Bill and the Law of Elections in Ireland* (Dublin, 1835), reprinting letters to the *Pilot* in 1832.

[2] Perhaps also in Ireland the adjective 'Liberal' retained something of its originally revolutionary and continental flavour. See Halévy, *History*, II, 81–2, n. 3; III, 180, n. 1, for the arrival of the term in English politics, and below, pp. 96–7, for its more exact connotations in Irish politics.

[3] O'Connell to the People of Ireland, 12 April 1833; 25 August 1834; Anti-Tory Association lithograph circular, [dated 1834], O'Connell Papers, N.L.I. 422, 423, 5243.

persons responsible for each county; and local affiliated committees would attend to the registration outside Dublin. In 1838 the Central Board of Registration was formed, though it does not seem to have been very effective; and registration problems formed an important part of the *raison d'être* of the Precursor Society.[1]

The constituency clubs remained at least formally independent, a tribute to the strength of Irish regional feeling. But as the main links between unofficial parish bodies and O'Connell's central organization, they played a crucial part in his electoral system and generally followed the line laid down by O'Connell himself. Indeed this obedience to the party leader meant that clubs which had been dominated by Repealers in 1832 became increasingly Whig or ministeralist in tone and composition, and that by 1841 many of them were working in the Liberal-Unionist interest.[2]

The electoral success of most O'Connellite candidates depended primarily on these voluntary local organizations, admirably suited as these were for the supervision of the registry, the basic task of any early nineteenth-century electoral organization. This activity, requiring detailed local knowledge, involved making lists of potential electors, bringing the claimants to register in person, often paying their expenses of certification and objecting whenever possible to the claims of opponents. The first registry under the Reform Act determined the representation of many constituencies from 1832 to 1847 and even beyond; and the Act's registration clauses, containing no provisions as in England for an annual revision of the registry, seem generally to have favoured O'Connell's party and his Liberal allies. Certainly the Conservatives continually complained about the system. Joseph Devonsher Jackson, the party's electoral expert in Ireland, who had seen the system at first hand as chairman of the registry sessions in County Londonderry, told Peel in 1837 that

[1] O'Connell to D. R. Pigot [through Fitzpatrick], 2 July 1836; O'Connell, Memos, 17, 19 April 1838; Objects and Principles . . . of the Precursor Society, 18 August 1838; O'Connell to his Constituents, 29 September 1838, O'Connell Papers, N.L.I. 423.

[2] This was the case, for example, in Co. Louth, where the Independent Club which ran two Repealers in 1832 successfully sponsored two Liberals in 1841 (one of whom, R. M. Bellew, had admittedly been a Repealer), and in Co. Limerick, where two nationalists had come close to defeating the sitting Whig Members in 1832 but which returned Smith O'Brien in 1837 and 1841 despite O'Connell's attempts to unseat him; see *O'Connell Corr.*, II, 183–4; *Pilot*, 11, 12 January 1837.

... the present monstrous state of the Irish representation, fully one half of the Members sent from Ireland being literally returned by Mr. O'Connell & the Roman Catholic Clergy, [is caused by] the present state of the Registries in Ireland, occasioned by the departures from the principles & regulations of the English Reform Bill, which were permitted by the Legislature when passing the Reform Bill for Ireland . . .

Jackson thought that 'gross perjury' was 'frequently resorted to by the candidates for Registration as to the question of Value', while the omission in the Act of any machinery for appeals against the decisions of assistant barristers was a further grievance.[1]

James Emerson Tennent, beaten at Belfast in 1837, explained to his leader that

... what chiefly defeated us was the accursed System of imperfect registration involved in the Irish reform bill. Although there are not more than 1800 voters entitled to poll [in Belfast] nearly 4000 remain upon the face of the registry since 1832, affording the most facile materials for the manufacture of faggot votes . . . If we cannot get an amended Registration Act for Ireland immediately, no man in his senses will be found to contest a borough against a popish constituency. But with a *bona fide* constituency annually registered no radical would presume to contest Belfast.[2]

But partial revenge was not far off for the Irish Conservatives. During the first statutory re-registry of all electors in 1838, thanks partly to the growth and activity of local Tory clubs and partly to a judicial ruling of 1837 which stringently defined the franchise requirement of £10 'clear annual value', there occurred a definite swing on the registries towards the Conservatives. Jackson reported this to Peel with much pride, and it played a considerable part in the Conservative gains of 1841.[3]

Two examples might be given of the activity of these local organizations. In County Longford, whose constituency of about 4,000

[1] Jackson to Peel, 28 September 1837; 31 August 1836, Peel Papers, Add. MSS 40424, 173–8, 113–16.
[2] Tennent to Peel, 9 August 1837, Peel Papers, Add. MSS 40424, 51–3. In March 1838, he regained his seat on petition. Colonel Chatterton, the unsuccessful Tory candidate at Cork City, was less lucky and equally aggrieved; ibid., 40424, 63–4.
[3] Jackson to Peel, 9 January 1841, Peel Papers, Add. MSS 40429, 6–7; *Times*, 30 June 1841. After 1837, a potential elector had to swear, on oath, and be prepared to prove that he could pay an additional rent of £10 over and above all existing charges.

before the Relief Act dropped to 600 in 1829 and rose again to nearly 1,900 after the Reform Act, the local Repealers and Conservatives assiduously attended to the registry in 1832. A Reform Registry Political Union in the town of Longford with three sub-centres in the county was founded, largely Catholic in membership but also containing Anglicans and Presbyterians. Its registration expenses were mostly defrayed by a fund amounting to £435, and if the registry of 1832 was not so much in favour of the 'independent' interest as had been expected, this was ascribed (a common Irish complaint) to the partiality of a revising barrister, and the fault was corrected in 1836 when the Tories were very incensed at the decisions of a Mr. George French, a relation of the Liberal M.P. for Roscommon, who was said not only to hold radical views but to have refused to listen to objections by Conservative agents. These men showed great ingenuity in 1832, obtaining duplicate certificates (which were technically illegal), bringing up one man to register as a £20 freeholder, and when his claim was rejected, producing the same man with a new £10 claim but in a different suit of clothes. Some dead men were registered when the agents produced their old certificates and had them renewed.[1] It is therefore no surprise to find that in Longford two Conservatives were seated on a petition in 1833 against the successful Repeal and Liberal candidates, or that in 1837, following their favourable registry of 1836, a Repealer and a Liberal were triumphant.

At the first registry in Cork City, the second largest constituency in Ireland with 4,322 electors in 1832, the assistant barristers refused to accept the evidence of a paid agent, a heavy blow to the Conservatives whose local association, with a view to the great registry expected for both the city and the county, had hired 12 agents; the nationalists in 1832 had only volunteers of whom a Mr. Henry Barry, a shipping agent and farmer, was the most active. A Tory complaint that many unqualified persons were registered was balanced by a legal opinion of Baron Pennefather's on section 9 of the Reform Act, arrived at 'after considerable doubt and difficulty' but in harmony with his Conservative politics, that 368 non-resident freemen were entitled to vote. The Tories' reliance on their freemen (a disciplined force in all of some 1,200 voters) told against

[1] Third Report of Select Committee on Fictitious Votes, P.P. 1837-8, XIII, Qs. 6435-57, 10364-71, 10870-2, 6646, 8199-231, 10906-40; *F.J.*, 3 December 1832.

them badly in 1835 when their opponents accused them of 'running bucks', or polling freemen and other voters by right of houses which they had left or did not reside in at the time of the election. On petition the Tories were unseated and Cork City remained a safe Repeal-Liberal seat, the £10 freeholders consistently outvoting the Tory freemen, who were indeed also described as 'a marketable commodity'.[1]

In a few places, the candidate himself supervised the registry. In Kilkenny, the Repealer Colonel Butler managed this operation so successfully in 1832 that 900 of the 1,250 freeholders were said to support him, and he certainly never faced a contest throughout the period.[2] But an inefficient supervision of the registry could be disastrous, as O'Connell discovered in 1836 when he lost his Dublin seat because despite all his warnings a sizeable proportion of his voters had failed to pay all their municipal taxes to qualify as £10 householders. This disaster to his prestige and to his pocket came about, as he complained, 'principally by the non-payment of the pipe-water for the year 1834. So that all this calamity comes upon us by the neglect of payment of the miserable pipe-water rent for which everybody gets value'.[3]

At election time, the constituency clubs were responsible for the adoption of candidates and for the general management of an election, calling meetings, using their funds for all the incidental electoral expenses, including the payment of agents and messengers, the hiring of space in newspapers for election addresses, organizing carriages for distant voters, providing refreshments and every kind of gratification up to direct bribery, rallying support and ensuring

[1] First and Second Reports of Select Committee on Fictitious Votes, P.P. 1837–8, XIII, Pt. I, Qs. 5616–20, 5974–81, 6029–35, 2832–7, 3787–9, 3823. By 1838, the Liberals were properly organized, with a registration fund and a treasurer. *Times*, 6 November 1832, for Pennefather's decision, which applied only to Cork.

[2] *F.J.*, 17 September; 5 December; *Times*, 19 November 1832. In Co. Wicklow James Grattan, the Liberal representative of the powerful Fitzwilliam interest, was equally successful in 1832; *F.J.*, 19, 21 December 1832.

[3] O'Connell to Fitzpatrick [n.d. March 1835]; 5, 8 January 1835, *O'Connell Corr.*, I, 531–2, 513–14. The business of guarding the Dublin registry did not run smoothly. A Mr. Seton undertook the task in January 1835 on the motion of the Anti-Tory Association; in 1836 the Central Independent Club took over from him, and he bombarded O'Connell with angry letters claiming that his expenses for 1835 had not been paid; see esp. A. Seton to O'Connell, 17 November 1836, O'Connell Papers, N.L.I. uncatalogued.

electoral discipline. In 1832 it was vital, especially in two-member constituencies or in places involved in a three-cornered contest, to agree on official Repeal candidates. For doubtful constituencies in later years, devoted O'Connellites like Father Sheehan of Waterford often made considerable sacrifices so that 'the Liberal interest' should not be divided. Again, the 1832 Election was remarkable in that it produced in contested constituencies the highest proportion of valid votes to registered electorate (in many cases over 90 per cent, rarely below 80 per cent) in any of the Elections of the period[1]. Indeed in two-member constituencies with two Repeal candidates, ticket-voting for these candidates was almost the rule in 1832, partly the result of popular enthusiasm, partly the consequence of good organization.

In the hotly-disputed constituency of County Carlow, both sides carried the practice of exact ticket-voting to the point of artistry. Efficient electoral organization was provided for nationalist candidates by a vigorous Independent Club, and their Tory opponents, based on the landed interests of the Kavanagh and Bruen families, were just as well if not so formally organized. In 1832 the local club put up two candidates in coalition, a Repealer Walter Blackney and a Liberal, Thomas Wallace, K.C., a Protestant and M.P. for Drogheda in 1831–2, an unusual arrangement which received the sanction of the National Political Union. The Conservative candidates, Colonel Henry Bruen and his father-in-law Thomas Kavanagh, were supported by their own family interests and by a string of local noblemen.[2] For the first few days of the election, in 'a fierce neck and neck contest',[3] the Tories maintained a precarious lead; but the £10 freeholders and superior organization finally sent Blackney and Wallace to the top of the poll with these remarkable figures:

Blackney: 657
Wallace: 657

[1] In Waterford City, 1,140 voters out of 1,241; Cork City, 3,696 out of 4,322; Monaghan, 2,128 out of 2,139; Longford, 1,255 out of 1,294; Queen's County, 1,379 out of 1,470; King's County, 1,196 out of 1,310. These are the larger constituencies. In smaller places, like Mallow (450 out of 458), the proportions could be even higher. Return . . . Electors: P.P. 1833, XXVII, 289–310. Cf. proportions in 1835: Waterford, 970: 1,473; Cork, 3,359: 4,461; Monaghan, 1,026: 2,472; Longford, 983: 1,581; Return . . . Electors: P.P. 1836, XLIII, 469–78.

[2] *F.J.*, 9 October; 5, 7 December; *Times*, 11, 17 October; 24 December 1832.

[3] *D.E.P.*, 15 December 1832.

Bruen: 483
Kavanagh: 470

The practice of ticket-voting laid down in 1832 persisted in later Carlow elections, and 'sweeping the countryside' for electors, who were then 'cooped' until needed, was freely practised by Conservative landlords. In 1842 John O'Connell, based nearby on the impregnable nationalist seat of Kilkenny City, replied in kind. For three weeks, 120 Carlow freeholders were kept comfortably under guard in Kilkenny until nomination day, when they were brought in a great ceremonial procession to Carlow. If this force had numbered only 9 more, the Conservatives would have been defeated.[1] But even in Ireland 'cooping' on this heroic scale was unusual.

The Irish Conservative party, including most of the Irish peerage and at least half the landowning gentry, naturally relied largely for electoral success on local, territorial influence. But with strong organizations in Dublin and in the larger provincial centres like Cork and Waterford, a plentiful supply of candidates and a strong supporting press, untroubled by shortages of money and with overwhelming strength in the north, the Conservatives formed in 1832 and in a sense throughout the period the real opposition to O'Connell in Ireland.[2] Yet while they were ready to organize themselves locally, the Conservatives produced no outstanding leader and little in the way of a constructive political programme. Staunchly Unionist and fiercely Protestant, unable to forget the 'betrayal' of 1829 and unwilling to absorb the reformist lessons of Peel's Tamworth Manifesto of 1834, they took their tone from great magnates like the Earls of Enniskillen and Roden, the leaders of the Irish Tory party in the House of Lords; and the more moderate, unofficial leaders of the Irish Conservatives in the Commons, Sir Frederick Shaw and J. D. Jackson, were scarcely representative of rank and file opinion. 'Conservative' and 'Conservatism', terms first widely used in Ireland during the 1832 Election, had connotations in Irish conditions and for Irish Conservatives rather different from the interpretation put on the words by Peel. For men seemingly surrounded by Catholic rebels and their Liberal 'fellow-travellers', an uncompromising

[1] John O'Connell, *Recollections*, II, 24, 26–40.
[2] In Dublin, the Irish Protestant Conservative Society (1831–3) was followed by the Conservative Registration Committee (1835) and the Metropolitan Conservative Society. For the aims and attitudes of Irish Conservatism, see McDowell, *Public Opinion*, 109–17, 204–28.

defence of the threatened established institutions of Church and State was the beginning and end of politics.[1]

In practice, the Irish Conservatives were left largely to their own electoral resources. Although London Tories raised £2,400 for the Dublin election of 1837 and probably helped to defray the immense costs of the petition against O'Connell's election in 1835, financial support from English sympathizers was limited and only obtainable for particularly important purposes.[2] A central Conservative fund in Ireland, part of which went to assist candidates outside Dublin, seems to have been raised only in 1832, but since it was the party's boast that it represented the bulk of the wealth and property of the country, the extent of this assistance was never emphasized.[3] In general Tories relied on their own efforts and influence or on local organizations. A committee of the party's leaders set up in London in 1832 to watch the Irish elections gave way in 1835 to a more general committee on which Shaw was the Irish representative; but the efforts in Ireland of Shaw, and in 1841 of Jackson, were jejune and almost unimportant in comparison with O'Connell's electoral activity and influence.[4]

In comparison with the other parties, the Irish Whigs and Liberals were a heterogeneous body ranging from 'right-wing' Whigs like Sir Charles Coote, the Hon. John Bruce O'Neill and the Hill brothers (all of whom were Conservatives by 1835) through Whig ministerialists like Lord Acheson, Lord Brabazon and the Hon. Cornelius O'Callaghan to radical Reformers like Richard More O'Ferrall, George Hampden Evans, James Grattan and T. B. Martin, even to conditional Repealers in 1832 like Henry Lambert and Sir Richard Keane. Although some distinction may be made between

[1] See, as a specimen of Tory views, 'An Appeal by the Protestants of Ireland to their Brethren, the Protestants of England and Wales', presented in the Lords by Lord Roden, in *Times*, 14 February 1832; 2 January 1833.

[2] See Hardinge to Peel, 20 January [1837], Peel Papers, Add. MSS 40314, 177.

[3] This fund raised £1,926 in one week, which compares favourably with the sum of £1,000 collected in one day for O'Connell; *Times*, 15, 29 October; 10 March 1832. The Tory candidate successful in Waterford City in 1832 was apparently supported by £1,300 sent down from Dublin; *D.E.P.*, 18 December; *Times*, 29 December 1832.

[4] Ellenborough, *Diary*, 20 May 1832, Aspinall, op. cit., 266; Sir John Beckett to Lord Lowther, 11 December 1834, Lonsdale MSS., quoted by Aspinall, *Three Diaries*, lvii–iii; Fitzgerald to Peel, 2 January 1835; Hardinge to Peel, 20 January [1837]; Jackson to Peel, 15 June 1841, Peel Papers, Add. MSS. 40323, 201–2; 40314, 177; 40429, 337–40.

Whigs and Liberals (in that the latter generally stood on far more advanced and explicit programmes),[1] there are good precedents for referring to this whole body of Members as the Irish 'Liberal party', whose common bond was support of the Union as well as of the current Whig Government.[2]

This party never developed an independent organization of its own, even of the limited kind possessed by Irish Conservatives. Isolated in 1832 by the rise of the nationalist movement and excluded throughout the period from Dublin (a Liberal seat in 1831), the Irish Liberals were forced back on their reserves of local and landed influence and were ready in 1832 to enter into electoral coalitions with nationalists in Carlow, Tipperary and Roscommon or, as in Armagh, Antrim and Down, with Conservatives.[3] In later years, O'Connell's party organization tended to attract the body of un-committed Liberal opinion in Ireland, and the only serious attempt to create a body which would have included O'Connell and his sup-porters but which would have been permeated with safe, minis-terialist Liberalism was completely unsuccessful in 1839, wrecked by O'Connell's refusal to fall into an obvious trap and by the Whig Government's open disapproval of all party organizations in Ireland.[4]

The English Whigs took very little interest in Irish electoral politics and had little need to do so while the alliance with O'Connell

[1] Cf. the laconic, ministerialist addresses of Acheson and Brabazon (*D.E.P.*, 11 December; *Times*, 5 December 1832) with those of James Grattan, who stood for a series of reforms in Church and State and of Martin, a son of 'Humanity Dick', the celebrated duellist and protector of animals, who called for church reform, the abolition of tithes, church and vestry cess, a radical change in the grand jury system, additional facilities for commerce, agriculture and fisheries, suitable provision for the unemployed poor and a real identification in laws, liberty and interest between England and Ireland; *F.J.*, 3 October; *D.E.P.*, 27 December 1832.

[2] This phrase, describing the Whigs' supporting coalition of English Whigs, Liberals and Radicals and the Irish, occurs in the letters of the Radical Joseph Parkes, the Liberal Speaker Abercromby and the Whig Spring Rice; Parkes to Ellice, 16 September 1841, Ellice MSS, N.L.S., pkt. 2; Abercromby to Mel-bourne [n.d. early 1835], Melbourne Papers, Windsor Castle; Spring Rice to Sir R. Price, 30 September 1837, Monteagle Papers, N.L.I.

[3] See for example *F.J.*, 4 December 1832, on the situation in Roscommon; *D.E.M.*, 10 December; *F.J.*, 11 December 1832; 11 January 1833, for Armagh.

[4] McDowell, *Public Opinion*, 173–4. O'Connell had no objection to the Whigs forming a separate body; to Barrett, 8 May 1839, O'Connell Papers, N.L.I., 423.

brought them such handsome dividends. But another important reason lay behind the Liberals' organizational failure. It was widely held that the backing of an organization implied some renunciation of an M.P.'s much valued 'independence', reducing him to the status of the delegate of an extra-parliamentary body and placing him at the orders of O'Connell. Most Irish Whigs and Liberals would have repudiated O'Connell's statement: 'I am a public servant rendering an account of my Stewardship . . . if my constituents are dissatisfied with my conduct, I am quite ready to resign.'[1] They would instead have agreed with the Whig who brusquely refused an invitation from the National Political Union to attend a pre-session meeting of Irish M.P.s: 'Whenever the constituency of the county which I have the honour to represent shall instruct me to act in subserviency to a self-constituted association, I shall take the earliest opportunity of returning to them the trust which they have confided to me and which I should no longer feel I could hold with honour to myself or with credit to them.'[2] Smith O'Brien at Limerick was equally at pains in 1837 to deny any connection with O'Connell which would '. . . compromise the independence which as a Member of Parliament I never will cease to claim for myself'; despite 'a general coincidence of views upon questions of public policy', O'Brien strongly protested at 'placing Mr. O'Connell's name in such connection with mine as would make it appear that I am acceptable to the county only because it please him to tender his support.'[3]

Political interests and influences

Influence and interest arising from the ownership of land, an inevitable consequence of franchises which were tied to the ownership or tenancy of property, were fundamental features of the Irish electoral system. Indeed it might be said that electoral law merely sanctioned the exercise of an influence which many contemporaries,

[1] O'Connell to his Constituents, 11 September 1833, O'Connell Papers, N.L.I., 422.
[2] J. Hely Hutchinson to E. Dwyer, 7 January 1832, O'Connell Papers, N.L.I., 5242. See also Greville, *Journal*, 11 May 1834, III, 83: 'Independence now-a-days relates more to constituents than to the governing power.'
[3] W. S. O'Brien to Edward O'Connell, 21 July 1837, O'Brien Papers, N.L.I., 429.

English as well as Irish, regarded as the basis of the social and political order. A Tory landowner in Galway, Denis Daly of Dunsandle, reflected this attitude when he wrote to Peel about the county election of 1837, in which his son James was defeated partly 'by the extreme exertion of the priests but principally by a most extraordinary transaction. Lord Mulgrave sent down one of his aides-de-camp to canvass Lord Clanricarde's tenantry to vote against my son in opposition to the written wishes of their landlord. I think I never heard of anything so monstrously unconstitutional.'[1]

Many examples might be given of the workings of landed influence. For instance in 1840, concerning a by-election in Mayo, Bonham drew Peel's attention to 'a most delicious letter' quoted in *The Times*

> . . . from Lord Oranmore . . . to his Mayo tenantry, and remember that he is the uncle of Ben Stanley's wife, and one of Ld Melbourne's Peers, having neither birth, fortune, talent or weight of any kind except physical to recommend him to that honor—'Remain neutral if you can, but if *wanted*, vote for the *"pledged Repealer"* against the Conservative. The return of one more among the former can do no harm, but that of the latter may overturn the Government.' A happy commentary on Ld ·Ebrington's declaration and a finished specimen of Whig morality!!!![2]

In Wicklow, the powerful Fitzwilliam interest[3] was quite explicit in 1832. Lord Milton, the Earl's eldest son, announced publicly that

[1] Daly to Peel, 4 August 1837, Peel Papers, Add. MSS 40424, 5. He was perhaps as surprised by this rare instance of Government interference as scandalized by the canvassing of another man's tenantry. Cf. the wounded protest of one of the Grosvenors to Gladstone about the Flintshire election of 1841, '. . . that interference between a landlord with whose opinions you were acquainted and his tenants was not justifiable according to those laws of delicacy and propriety which I considered binding in such cases', quoted by John Morley, *The Life of W. E. Gladstone* (1908), 177–8.

[2] Bonham to Peel, 10 December 1840, Peel Papers, Add. MSS 40428, 451. Bonham was unfair to Oranmore, who as Dominick Browne sat for Mayo from 1813 to 1836 with a short break from 1826 to 1830, had been a useful and prominent Irish Member supporting Emancipation and Reform, and was related to the Tory Marquess of Sligo. Lord Ebrington's declaration was an announcement from the Irish Government in August 1839 that no Repealer would be considered in the distribution of official patronage.

[3] See F. M. L. Thompson, 'Whigs and Liberals in the West Riding, 1830–1860', *English Historical Review*, LXXIV, No. 291 (April 1959), 214–39, for this interest in its English base.

the family interest was behind the Whigs James Grattan and Colonel
Ralph Howard:

> Those who give plumpers either for Mr. Grattan or for Mr. Howard, I
> consider as friends, though I cannot rate their friendship so high as
> those who vote for Mr. Grattan and Mr. Howard . . . next I rate those
> who plump for Grattan, and then those who plump for Howard; those
> who split for Acton [the Tory candidate] or who plump for Acton I
> consider as opponents.[1]

In Ireland to a greater extent than in England the land agent was a
vital link in the chain of command from landlord to tenantry. In
December 1832 O'Connell produced in the National Political
Union, as an instance of a peer's interference in an election, a
circular letter signed by the agent of the Whig Lord Lansdowne and
addressed to the Lansdowne tenants, which announced that 'It is
the Marquess of Lansdowne's wish to give his interest at the ensuing
election for the county of Dublin, to Lord Brabazon and Mr. Evans.
As you have registered your lease, I hope that you have no objection
to vote for them.'[2]

Throughout the period, well over half of the total county electorate consisted of £10 freeholders and leaseholders, but while the £10
freeholders (over 34,000 in 1847)[3] were in theory independent of a
landlord's direct wishes or commands, in practice, in Ireland as well
as in England, these electors were subjected to as strong though
more subtle a pressure from above as the more obviously dependent
but far smaller class of leaseholders. In an almost wholly agricultural
community, the relationship between farmers with freeholds or
leases for a life or a term of lives and larger local landowners was a
crucial one, both in an economic and a social sense. For a small
farmer-peasant, dependent economically on his not very considerable holding and owing his possession of it in the first place to a
landlord, it often required considerable courage to vote for the
popular cause and frequently involved a man in a conflict of choice
between the clear sympathies or strong recommendations of his
priests and the equally plain wishes of landowners who as magistrates, grand jurors and Deputy Lieutenants were the official and
powerful rulers of the countryside.

An analysis of the voting support for Repeal candidates in 1832
shows, as might be expected, that the £10 electors voted in many

---

[1] *D.E.P.*, 22 January 1833; *Times*, 17 October 1832.
[2] *Times*, 8 December 1832.   [3] Dod, *Electoral Facts* (1853), 155.

constituencies against the wishes and certainly against the politics of their landlords. The great county of Cork, with a population (700,000) larger than that of any English county except Yorkshire or Lancashire and with the largest county electorate in Ireland (3,835 electors in 1832), had not been contested since 1812. In the fierce contest of 1832, Feargus O'Connor and Garret Standish Barry (a conditional Repealer) were triumphantly successful. O'Connor's effrontery deeply impressed his contemporaries. Without money or influence, an unknown backwoods, squireen with a remarkable talent for mob oratory defeated 'the most powerful and richest landed aristocracy in Ireland'[1] with the support of electors who were reliably reported to be subject to clerical influence and to be almost unanimous in support of Repeal and the abolition of tithes. O'Connor and Barry with 1,837 and 1,778 votes respectively, drew the bulk of their support from the 2,288 £10 voters. Indeed at one point in the election, the Tory candidates were urged by some of their supporters to give up an unequal contest and thus avoid further conflict between landlords and their tenants. It was surely not coincidental that the 994 votes for the leading Tory candidate tallied very nearly with the 926 £50 electors in the constituency, and this supposition is strongly supported by Madden's remark that in 1834 there were about 1,000 Conservatives in County Cork.[2]

The 1832 Election, the repetition on a grand scale of the Clare election of 1828, saw a great class revolt against the landlords and the landed interest which continued, less dramatically and on a smaller

[1] John O'Connell, *Recollections*, I, 24–7. For the election, see Madden, *Ireland and its Rulers* (1844), I, 171–84; W. J. O'Neill Daunt, *Eighty-Five Years of Irish History* (1886), I, 231–56; *F.J.*, 11, 27, 29 December; *Times*, 29, 31 December; *D.E.P.*, 29 December 1832. Daunt was O'Connor's collaborator in 1832.

[2] Madden, *Ireland and Its Rulers*, I, 213; Return of Electors, P.P. 1833, XXVII, under Co. Cork. Other clear examples of voting on class lines are to be found in the counties of Dublin, Carlow and Leitrim, and in Kildare where the £10 leaseholders either plumped for the nationalist or split their votes between him and the Liberal, *F.J.*, 24 December 1832. In Co. Wicklow, the Whig candidates owed their success to the Fitzwilliam tenantry and to Catholic £10 voters, but the fact that nearly 250 out of about 1,000 £10 electors supported the Tory candidate strongly suggests that it was only for Repealers that this class was prepared to vote *en bloc* against landlords or landlords' politics; *F.J.*, 19, 20 December; *D.E.P.*, 20 December; *Times*, 22 December 1832; Return of Electors, P.P., 1833, XXVII, under Co. Wicklow.

and decreasing scale, throughout the period. But its social effects, in terms of the reprisals taken by landlords, must not be exaggerated. In the counties only one person in every 115 was enfranchised, and even if landlords had resorted widely to eviction for political reasons, only a small proportion of the population would have been affected. In fact eviction for non-payment of tithe or rent and in the interests of consolidating estates was far more widely practised than eviction for political reasons. It is significant that while a fund for the compensation of those who suffered for their politics formed an important feature of O'Connell's organizations between 1826 and 1832, little is heard even of the existence of such a fund in later years.

County Longford, a convenient example, was the scene of a long struggle for political supremacy between the White family, the heirs of the Dublin bookseller who was reputed to have been the richest man in Ireland, and the Conservative family interests of Forbes (Earls of Granard) and Lefroy, the latter like the Whites a new county family rising on the profits of the legal profession. The county contained a large Protestant population of landlords and tenant farmers, an almost entirely Protestant magistracy and the seats or interests of several Conservative peers, including those of two die-hard Ultra Tories, the Earl of Longford and Lord Lorton. The political activity of the Catholic priesthood caused a great increase in the substitution of Protestant for Catholic tenants; even a Liberal landlord like Mr. Lovell Edgeworth said that he would never give land to Catholics if a foreign influence separated him from his tenantry, while Lord Lorton was accused of having practised eviction for political disobedience.[1]

Anthony Lefroy, one of the county Members, testified that his own ejectments were part of an agricultural experiment apparently popular with landlords towards the north of Ireland, by which Protestants were brought in to supplant Catholics, but the evidence of his own agent shows that Lefroy's motives were not entirely disinterested. Landlords, according to this man, had first claim on their tenant's votes; he admitted that there had been some 'political' ejectments on his employer's lands and that it was his own practice to reward disobedience with an early demand for rent: 'I have said to them [the tenants] myself, that if they did not vote as the landlord

[1] Third Report of Select Committee on Fictitious Votes, P.P. 1837–8, XIII, Qs. 12687, 7258–62, 12423–4. For evidence of evictions in Carlow, see Tocqueville, *Journeys*, 131.

chose, perhaps they would be sorry for it.'[1] On the other hand, Lord Forbes, the eldest son of the Earl of Granard and M.P. for Longford from 1820 until his death in 1836, was said never to have interfered with his tenantry because of their religion and voting habits. These tenants always voted for him, although after his death they fell away to some extent from their old allegiance.[2]

Longford was in some respects exceptional. But at least one important reason for the relatively small number of Irish leasehold electors was that landlords deliberately refused to grant the necessary leases. When in 1843 Peel and Graham were considering a reform of the Irish franchises, they received a protest from the Tory Lord Farnham on which Peel commented acidly:

> It amounts to this. We the Protestant landlords make a distinction between Protestants and Roman Catholics in respect to the grant of leases for the purpose of preventing the Roman Catholic from acquiring the right to vote at a County Election. We prohibit you the Govt. from qualifying the Roman Catholic in any other manner. What a persuasive to Repeal! Could a more cogent argument be used to a solvent, respectable Roman Catholic Tenant?[3]

In many Irish constituencies, a continuous revolt against landlords was made unnecessary, at least from 1835 to 1841, by the considerable strength of the Whig and Liberal landed interest. In Kerry the Kenmare and Lansdowne interests had no Tory equal; in Leitrim the interests of Samuel White and of the Earl of Leitrim were unassailable and in Monaghan the Liberal interest of Lord Rossmore divided the representation with that of the Conservative Lord Blayney. In Roscommon, a Whig and a Repealer, both representatives of entrenched local families, were returned in coalition throughout the period, facing weak opposition only once, in 1835. In King's County the Liberal landed interests of the Earls of Rosse and Rossmore shared the representation until 1840 with the Repealer Nicholas Fitzsimon, and in 1841 two Liberals were elected there without opposition.

A few Tory interests which had been powerful and active before the Reform Act, like that of the Beresfords in County Waterford,

---

[1] Ibid., Qs. 7263-5, 7184-234.

[2] Ibid., Qs. 12417-19, 12714-15.

[3] Peel to Graham, 22 December 1843, Peel Papers, Add. MSS 40449, 277. See also Third Report of Select Committee on Fictitious Votes, P.P. 1837-8, XIII, Part II, Qs. 15635-6.

seem virtually to have contracted out of politics.[1] Further, while the greater part of Irish land was owned by Protestants, in that they held the fee simple, they were rapidly losing their hegemony. It was calculated in 1834 that about one-fifth of Irish land was already owned outright by old Catholic families which had escaped forfeiture or by Roman Catholics who had bought land, and that nearly half of Irish land was held by Catholics on leases for lives renewable for ever, or for 99 years, or for 3 lives and 31 years, while many Catholics were investing their money in fee simple estates.[2] Land was in fact changing hands quite rapidly long before the operation of the Encumbered Estates Act of 1848, and while increased Catholic ownership of land went no way towards solving the land problem itself, it presumably made for some lessening of friction between landlords and tenants at election-time.

The finest examples of the great territorial interests were to be found in the north. In Ulster, where the religion and politics of landlords and their enfranchised tenantry generally coincided, a county election was usually a formality. From Cavan, Fermanagh, Londonderry and Tyrone, eight Conservatives were returned at every Election in the period. In the first three of these counties, there were no contests for the representation, while the contests in Tyrone in 1835 and at a by-election in 1839 were merely the results of some disagreement between the Tory interests of Earl Belmore, the Marquess of Abercorn and the Earl of Caledon. The counties of Antrim and Down, each returning a Whig and a Conservative in 1832, were solidly Conservative by 1835 and 1837 respectively. In County Armagh the strong Whig interest of the Earl of Gosford in the person of his eldest son, Lord Acheson, divided the representation with the diehard Tory Colonel William Verner in a firm coalition which was never opposed.

In these counties, party politics at election time was largely confined to boisterous manifestations of Tory Protestant feeling; tradition and class had given leading local families a prescriptive right to the representation, a right confirmed by the weight of landed influence. In Cavan, the Maxwells and the Youngs shared the representation. In Fermanagh, where the Coles, Archdales and

---

[1] *F.J.*, 21 December 1832, for the Marquess of Waterford's declaration that he would take no part in the county elections. Waterford, county and city, and Dungarvan borough remained Repeal-Liberal strongholds after 1832.

[2] Memo [n.d. October 1834], Wellesley Papers, Add. MSS 37307, 217-20.

Brookes provided the county Members, Viscount Cole, the eldest son of the Earl of Enniskillen, was M.P. from 1831 until 1840 when he succeeded his father in the peerage, and his seat was taken over by Sir Arthur Brooke. The other county seat was held first by General Mervyn Archdale, who had sat for the county almost uninterruptedly from the Union until 1834, and then by his nephew Captain Mervyn Archdale, whose grandfather had represented the county before the Union. The borough of Enniskillen was in the gift of the Earl, whose brother, the Hon. Arthur Henry Cole, represented it from 1828 to 1844 without the slightest sign of opposition. In Londonderry Sir Robert Bateson shared the representation with Captain Theobald Jones, who was probably the nominee of the Irish Society, an organization which managed much land in the county for twelve London companies. In Antrim, the Whig interest of the Marquess of Donegall lost ground after 1837 to the O'Neill, Hertford and Londonderry interests, while in Down the county representation was entirely possessed by the Marquesses of Londonderry and Downshire.

Most of the Ulster Members were highly placed in the organization of the Orange Order, but the dissolution of this body in April 1836 made no difference to the Conservative hold on the north, where the great majority of its lodges were situated and where its activities seem to have resembled the process of preaching to the converted. Its organization, whose ritual kept alive and symbolized the fiercest expression of the Protestant Ascendancy, was certainly too cumbrous to function as an electoral caucus.[1] In the north, the landed interests were virtually unchallenged and needed no electoral reinforcement. Some idea of their strength is shown by the position in Cavan. In the barony of Castleraghan, the Maxwells (Lord Farnham and his relations) were landlords of 150 out of 324 registered electors, and in a total county electorate of 1,996, their tenants numbered 402 potential voters. Similarly, Sir William Young of Bailieborough Castle, the father of the Peelite John Young who was M.P. for Cavan from 1831 until after 1847, was the landlord of 114 of the 304 electors in the barony of Clonkee.[2]

[1] McDowell, *Public Opinion*, 114–16, 227; Hansard, XXXI, 779–861, 23 February 1836, Debate. The Orangemen never forgave Peel for his failure to defend them in 1836 and re-constituted their Order in 1845 in dissatisfaction at his Irish policies.

[2] Returns ... Registered Electors, Co. Cavan, 1 January 1833–1 February 1841, State Paper Office, Dublin.

The Irish boroughs defy any of the relatively neat generalizations which can be made for the counties. The Reform Act, which was generally supposed to have opened up the majority of the Irish boroughs, did so only in a limited sense. Of the ten 'close' and eight 'nomination' boroughs existing before 1832, only three, Dungannon, Enniskillen and Lisburn, remained pure nomination seats after 1832 in the control respectively of the Earl of Ranfurly, the Earl of Enniskillen and the Marquis of Hertford. But the high £10 household franchise ensured that over half the Irish boroughs had registered electorates of under 300 in 1832, a proportion which was probably rather larger by 1847.[1] These small borough constituencies were in practice amenable both to the influence of local magnates and to every kind of illegal electoral activity, notably straightforward bribery. In Athlone for instance, although the interest of the Tory Lord Castlemaine received a distinct setback in 1832, when his nephew Richard Handcock, the Member since 1826, was defeated by a Liberal, it had recovered by 1835, and he was thought by 1841 to have the nomination of the borough completely at his disposal.[2] In Athlone between 1847 and 1856, bribes averaged £30 to £40. Recalling this, T. P. O'Connor wrote that with 'many of the people the periodic bribe entered into the whole economy of their squalid and weary lives . . . The very whisper of a dissolution sent a visible thrill through the town.'[3] There is no reason to suppose that things were any different during the earlier period.

Youghal, represented by John O'Connell from 1832 to 1837 and thereafter by nominees of the Whig Devonshire interest, wrung from Morgan O'Connell the heartfelt comment that 'Those boroughs are vile places, and I pity any man who has to do with them. That dirty little town of Youghal was more expensive to me than the County of

[1] The fairly high average for borough electorates (769 in 1832) was caused by the fact that over 16,000 electors out of a total borough electorate of about 31,000 came from Dublin, Cork, Limerick and Galway, all of them 'counties of cities and towns' (together with Carrickfergus, Drogheda, Kilkenny and Waterford). In the 26 plain boroughs, the average electorate was about 440 in 1835 and 600 in 1841. These figures also certainly conceal the truth since they include places like Belfast (1,659 electors in 1832, 4,234 in 1841) and the University (2,058 in 1832). See Appendix A, No. 6; Dod, *Electoral Facts*.

[2] Bonham to Peel, July 1841, Peel Papers, Add. MSS 40485, 357, cited by Gash, *Politics*, 401–2. In fact in 1841 Castlemaine's nominee lost his seat on petition, and a Liberal was subsequently elected.

[3] T. P. O'Connor, *Memoirs of an old Parliamentarian* (1929), I, 380.

Meath, where we had to bring voters from twenty-four miles and farther. As William Ford says, "In the towns, it's the ready money down".[1] This remark was literally true not only of places like Kinsale with its 206 electors in 1832, of which Dod in his handbook simply says that 'judicious pecuniary management' was important, or Portarlington with well under 200 electors throughout the period, where in 1832 Thomas Gladstone, W. E. Gladstone's brother, defeated the Whig Colonel George Dawson-Damer by one vote in an election in which 131 voters were polled out of a possible electorate of 137.[2] Money, local knowledge and no scruples were essential even in the larger boroughs. A by-election in 1834 at Dungarvan was the scene of one of Feargus O'Connor's most memorable early exploits. Acting as 'speechifyer, canvasser, lawyer, gutter agent and mobleader' for the nationalist candidate, Ebenezer Jacob, in a hard contest with a Whig who was supported by the interest of the absentee Duke of Devonshire, O'Connor concocted a letter purporting to come from the Duke's agent and at a critical point read it out on the hustings to the electors, informing them that 'his Grace's tenants have his entire assent to the fullest and freest exercise of their voting privilege . . . none of his tenants shall be punished . . . for supporting the repeal candidate at this election'. Only when the electors had responded by giving the nationalist an unassailable majority was it discovered that the letter was signed 'Ebenezer Humbug'.[3]

[1] Morgan O'Connell to Fitzpatrick, 15 April 1835, *O'Connell Corr.*, II, 14. Ford was a lawyer often retained by the O'Connells.

[2] Dawson-Damer, M.P. for Portarlington after 1835, was a Conservative by that year. A good example of an election in the smaller boroughs is provided by the bye-election in 1838 for the borough of Carlow. The only unusual feature was that the Liberal candidate was an Englishman. Thomas Gisborne, a sporting Staffordshire landowner, applied to Joseph Parkes for help in getting a seat, and in February 1839, Parkes arranged with O'Connell for Gisborne to stand for Carlow. In the election, Gisborne's Tory opponents went to remarkable lengths to defeat him. They bribed ten Liberal electors with £50 each, polled two stamp distributors and the county surveyor, all officials appointed by the Government and therefore ineligible to vote and sent ten more Liberal electors away to Liverpool and about the country at a cost of £30 each. 'We had cars out with their wives,' Gisborne wrote, 'following them in several directions often on the scent never overtook them.' Gisborne lost the election by three votes, but was eventually seated on petition; Gisborne to Parkes, 13, 19 February 1839, quoted by J. K. Buckley, *Joseph Parkes of Birmingham* (1926), 173–5.

[3] John O'Connell, *Recollections*, I, 98–102, who was present as the representative of his father.

At Carrickfergus, the Whig Lord Donegall and the Chichester family made a vigorous effort to realize the potentialities of the resident freemen as electoral pawns. By the Reform Act, freemen by right of birth, apprenticeship and marriage, if they were resident, remained in full and perpetual possession of their parliamentary franchise; honorary non-resident freemen, admitted by 'grace especial', retained the franchise only for their own lives and on condition that they had been admitted before 30 March 1831. This date-line effectively prevented most corporations from overwhelming the £10 householder constituency with non-resident freemen.[1] But in Carrickfergus no less than 919 persons in an electorate of 1,070 were resident freemen, and in 1832 half of the electors were bribed, generally at £5 a vote, though sums of £700 and £1,000 were supposed to have been offered for the votes of 40 fishermen. Claims to the freedom were allowed or refused by the mayor, in 1831 Lord Donegall, on political grounds or by acclamation. An alderman put the situation neatly: 'Now, when you see a beggar on crutches coming to vote for a Member of Parliament, some new qualification for freedom, in the nature of a property qualification, is requisite.'[2]

The 1832 election, after which the borough came close to disfranchisement, seems to have seen a last desperate fling by the Chichester interest. Carrickfergus remained a Conservative seat returning Peter Kirk, a local landowner who was significantly enough mayor for five successive years. But except in Carrickfergus, Dublin City with its 1,500 voting freemen, Cork City and perhaps Galway, the Irish municipal corporations had only marginal electoral importance, although in places like Bandon, Enniskillen and Armagh they served as useful props to Conservative interests.

Until 1833 the Tory Lord Bandon paid the salaries of the officials of the corporation of Bandon in return for complete political control. In that year, he found himself unable to fulfil an electoral agreement

[1] At Athlone, where the exclusively Protestant corporation was largely composed of Lord Castlemaine's relations, s. 9 of the Act made nearly 160 such freemen ineligible for the parliamentary franchise since they had been created on 24 June 1831, 'for the purpose of increasing the Constituency in the interest of his Lordship's family'; First Report, Corporations, P.P. 1835, XXVII, Part I [125–37]; and see above p. 106, and n. 2 for Castlemaine's difficulties in maintaining his interest.

[2] First Report, Corporations, P.P. 1835, XXVIII, App., 743–87, esp. 761–2; Hansard, XVIII, 96–9, 24 May 1833, O'Connell. By 1852, Carrickfergus was a pocket borough of Lord Downshire's. See Whyte, *Independent Irish Party*, 75.

made by his father with the Whig Duke of Devonshire, who owned most of the borough and all the property of the corporation. Despite this, the Devonshire interest was no match for that of Lord Bandon, whose local influence was buttressed by the 70 voting freemen in an electorate of 250.[1] Enniskillen corporation, entirely composed of Lord Enniskillen's close relations or friends, had apparently only two main functions: to provide a returning officer for parliamentary elections and to swell votes for its patron's nominee, though this support was never actually called upon. The corporation of Armagh, entirely controlled by the Protestant Archbishop who owned most of the borough, seems to have played an important part in the Archbishop's unsuccessful attempts to wrest control of the borough from the Liberals. The borough's M.P. from 1832 to 1837, Leonard Dobbin, said of his election in 1835: 'I had a hard battle to fight here, single handed, as to pecuniary matters, against the Church, down to the grave digger with all the appurtances thereunto belonging, which was a heavy business but I was nobly supported by my fellow citizens.'[2]

A few northern boroughs—Belfast, Coleraine, Newry, Londonderry, and Armagh—were the only exceptions to the Conservative hold on the north. But even Belfast, with its long liberal tradition, which before 1832 had been a close borough returning the nominees of Lord Donegall, was soon to become a Conservative stronghold in which Liberals could think themselves lucky if they returned one Member. In 1832 Lord Arthur Chichester, Lord Donegall's third son, was successful with James Emerson Tennent, even then a highly independent Liberal, against two Radical candidates, one of them William Sharman Crawford.[3] Tennent's heavy reliance in 1832 on Tory and Protestant support and his vigorous attacks on O'Connell no doubt hastened his conversion to Peelite Conservatism. In 1835 as a Conservative he was again successful in company

---

[1] First Report, Corporations, P.P. 1835, XXVII, Part I, 5–9. The M.P.s for Bandon were the patron's son, the Hon. William Bernard (1832–5), his nominee J. D. Jackson (1835–42) and his eldest son, Viscount Bernard (1842–52). See above pp. 92–3 for the position in Cork; and Sir Valentine Blake to Peel, 25 June 1838, Peel Papers, Add. MSS 40425, 178–80, for Blake's position as the Corporation's candidate in Galway.

[2] Dobbin to E. Dwyer, 2 February 1835, O'Connell Papers, N.L.I., 5242.

[3] *Northern Whig*, 25, 30 December; *D.E.P.*, 27 December 1832; *Pilot*, 4 January; *Times*, 8 January 1833; see also *The Belfast Election: Mr. Emerson Tennent's Claims and Conduct* (1832).

with a Liberal; in 1838 he and his fellow Conservative candidate
were seated on petition, and in 1842, he and David Ross, a prominent
Ulster Liberal of the Sharman Crawford school, were successful
in a second election after the first in 1841 had been declared void for
its 'gross and extensive' bribery and personation of voters. Despite
the size of Belfast, with 1,659 electors in 1832 and over 4,000 in 1841,
plentiful supplies of money and local influence were essential; and
the temporary success of Liberals in 1837 was partly attributed by
Tennent to 'the local influence of Lord Belfast [Lord Donegall's
eldest son] as lord of the soil (*personal* influence he has none) who
arrived here fraught with money, an extraordinary circumstance
considering his actual poverty; and this was lavishly expended in
buying out any necessitous voters'.[1] But northern Conservatives
could at least always take comfort from the almost complete failure
of O'Connell's movement to make any appeal in that part of Ireland.

With the exception of the larger southern provincial centres like
Cork, Limerick, Kilkenny and to some extent Waterford, the Irish
boroughs were generally much less nationalist and O'Connellite
than the counties. The explanation lay partly in the relatively high
£10 household franchise, producing a class of electors who often
supported Whigs and Liberals but only voted nationalist if great
pressure was brought to bear on them. Thus the steady decline in
Repeal borough Members was matched by a progressive increase in
Liberal borough representation throughout the period.[2] It may have
been that O'Connell's followers were less willing or able to bear the
inevitably high costs of a borough election, and also perhaps, that
the Irish towns, with a slightly higher level of prosperity than the
counties and with a far higher proportion of Protestants to Catholics
in their population, were less open to popular appeal and had less
incentive in the way of grievances to return extremist Members.[3]
This second explanation cannot be pressed too far. Protestants were
quite densely concentrated in Dublin, Cork, Limerick and Waterford, yet all these constituencies were places where Repeal was either

[1] Tennent to Peel, 9 August 1837, Peel Papers, Add. MSS 40424, 51–3; see
also Report of Select Committee, Belfast Election: 1841, P.P. 1842, V, 263 ff.

[2] See Appendix A, Nos. 1–4.

[3] T. W. Freeman, *Pre-Famine Ireland* (1957), 25–33, believes that Irish towns
suffered as much as the countryside from overcrowding and under-employment.
But the evidence he produces indicates that at least in the 18 cities and towns
with populations over 10,000 (most of them parliamentary boroughs), the
economic situation was somewhat healthier than elsewhere.

highly or at least intermittently successful; and again, Liberal successes in the Irish boroughs show that borough voters were prepared
at least to support Reformers and Whig Ministerialists, often on
quite radical programmes.

It was an axiom among O'Connell's opponents to attribute the
greater part of the electoral success of his party to the intimidation
practised in different forms by the Catholic clergy and by the unenfranchised peasantry. *The Times*, which throughout the period
constantly harped on this theme, fulminated in 1835 against 'the
indefatigable intrusion of spiritual power upon the rights and interests of civil life' and never tired of painting lurid pictures of
disciplined hordes of Catholic voters, completely submissive to the
commands of their spiritual and secular masters, the priests and the
agitators.[1] But it would be wrong to rely solely on the accusations of
their opponents in reaching an estimate of the political influence of
the Irish Catholic clergy. O'Connell's opponents had a case to make,
one which the great majority of Protestants were strongly disposed
to believe even if there had not been a considerable body of evidence
to support it; but while most Englishmen were probably hostile to
the Catholicism inherent in O'Connell's movement, it by no means
followed that their view of Irish politics as priest-ridden and priest-
controlled was completely accurate.

In a sense, as Mr. Strauss has pointed out, clericalism was 'the
inevitable form of a nationalist movement combining middle-class
purposes with lower-class support'.[2] In the struggle for Catholic
Emancipation and in the Repeal movement of the 1840's, the
Catholic priesthood played a vitally important part, and one which
has been fully investigated.[3] But the Church's part in O'Connell's
movement between 1830 and 1841 has received far less attention. In
part, this neglect is the consequence of a slight decline in priestly
participation in politics. By a Pastoral Letter of February 1830 and
the hierarchy's resolutions of January 1834 which were reinforced
by Papal discouragement, priests were strongly enjoined not to use
their chapels or altars for political purposes or for the expression of

---

[1] See, for examples, *Times*, 28 January 1835; 28 July; 3 August 1837; and
Annual Register (1835), 14–15; (1837) 93.

[2] E. Strauss, *Irish Nationalism and British Democracy* (1951), 93.

[3] See J. A. Reynolds, *The Catholic Emancipation Crisis in Ireland, 1823–29*
(1954); John F. Broderick, 'The Holy See and the Irish Movement for the Repeal
of the Union with England, 1829–47', *Analecta Gregoriana*, LV (1951).

political views and were urged not to join political organizations.[1]
These injunctions were certainly not uniformly obeyed. Indeed the
tacit co-operation at least of the parochial clergy was essential for
the collection of the O'Connell Tribute, which was largely taken at
the church doors. A police report of 1834 stated that it was gathered
in 'by Lay Collectors who stood on the Tribute Sunday at every
Chapel & collected as the congregation was assembling . . . ,' while
another report commented that 'the Recommendation of the Priests
is alone required to induce the great mass of the Population to
subscribe'. In Carlow, on the other hand, Bishop Doyle's opposition prevented collections being taken at the chapels and as a
result, according to one report, 'very little was collected in the
County'.[2]

The opposition of Dr. Doyle until his death in 1834, the cautious
neutralism of Archbishop Murray of Dublin, of the Primate, Archbishop Crolly of Armagh and of men like the Whig Dr. Abrahams of
Waterford was balanced by the radicalism of Bishops like Dr.
MacHale of Tuam, Keating of Ferns, Blake of Dromore, Nolan
(Doyle's successor in Kildare and Leighlin) and Browne of Galway.
The hierarchy was until after 1841 deeply divided on the question
of priestly activity in politics and officially favoured a policy of non-
interference at all levels. The parochial clergy, who had been the
staff officers of the Emancipation campaigns, to some extent reflected this division in the hierarchy and certainly risked censure if
they chose to ignore the Church's official policy. But it could never
be a question of total abstention from politics, for priests played a
considerable part in the agitation against tithes.[3] Nor was it simply
that the disfranchisement of 1829 so drastically reduced the number
of voters whom the clergy could influence that priests ceased to be
influential at election time. Ten-pound electors were numerous
enough after 1832 and were certainly in a position to be influenced.

[1] Broderick, op cit., 45–7, 59–65, 97–8, 99–108. But Cardinal Fransoni's
letters from Rome to Archbishops MacHale and Crolly in 1836 and 1839,
strongly deprecating priests' participation in politics, were apparently known
only to the hierarchy.

[2] Police Reports, Province of Leinster: C. H. Tuckey, 4 April 1834; H. W.
Thompson, 5 April 1834; James Battersby, 4 April 1834, H.O. Papers, 100/245,
137, 133, 125; but see Doyle to H. Lambert, 23 December 1833, Fitzpatrick,
Doyle, II. 480–1: 'We had no tribute collection or a word about it in any chapel
of this diocese, but the *employées* collected it *ostiatim*.'

[3] See below pp. 176–7.

Perhaps the most important single cause of the slight and temporary recession in clerical electioneering was that the functions performed in earlier elections by the parish clergy were taken over after 1832 by constituency organizations which were in many respects better adapted for the task. These bodies generally included priests, but it is perhaps significant that it was not until after 1850 that 'intimidation' by priests became the subject of election petitions, though this is certainly not strong proof that such forms of persuasion did not exist in the earlier period.[1]

In fact, in every Election between 1830 and 1847 numerous instances can be found of priests taking an active part in electoral politics, always on the Liberal side or, in 1832, in support of Repeal. In Kildare in 1832, a parish priest collected money with which voters had been bribed in the Conservative interest and handed it over to the National Rent Fund in Dublin. In 1837 a witness described to a Select Committee how country voters would come marching in to Cork City to vote, 'a fine, bold yeomanry; they are the finest fellows; you would be delighted to see them come in in their frieze coats' accompanied by their priests, in 'a kind of triumph'.[2] In Longford, the influence of the Catholic clergy was always exerted against the Conservatives and in favour of the Liberal-Repeal candidates. One priest considered it part of his duty as a priest to give general 'encouragement' to Catholic electors from the altar, to instruct the people in their moral duty and to notice publicly those who did not take his advice; and parish priests used to attend registry sessions and elections, riding to the polls at the head of their parishioners.[3]

Conservatives deeply resented what they regarded as the socially disruptive effects of clerical interference between a landlord and his tenants, but priests replied that in so doing they were simply safeguarding those tenants' consciences. In 1835 Hardinge as Chief Secretary received 'from various quarters reports of the intimidation exercised by the Priests on the Catholic voters, & many instances

[1] See J. H. Whyte, 'The Influence of the Catholic Clergy on Elections in Nineteenth-Century Ireland', *English Historical Review*, LXXV, No. 295 (April, 1960), 239–44, an informative article which perhaps underestimates the extent of clerical activity and influence between 1830 and 1841.

[2] *F.J.*, 22 December 1832; Whyte, art. loc. cit., 242–3, for other examples; First and Second Reports of Select Committee on Fictitious Votes, P.P. 1837–8, XIII, Part I, Qs. 3830–6; 5912–13.

[3] Third Report, Fictitious Votes, P.P. 1837–8, XIII, Part II, Qs. 11850–2; 12722–31; 12300–7.

have been communicated to the Government in which the desire on the part of the voters has been to support their Landlords, but [they] have been prevented by the denunciations of their Clergy'.[1] Of the same Election Lord Fitzgerald, who had been the victim in Clare seven years earlier, wrote that 'in the South & in Galway & Mayo, the conduct of the Priests is frightful, & as outrageous as it was in 1828'.[2] O'Connell was always ready to admit that priests took part in elections, though he was at pains to show that they would support a Protestant candidate, like Vigors at Carlow, as well as Catholics. Indeed at one point he found it necessary to congratulate the clergy, and particularly Dr. MacHale, 'for laying aside their pacific policy, which formerly dictated a course of non-interference in politics'. It is clear that O'Connell received as much support as he wanted or needed from the bulk of the parish clergy. As a body, they were, as he told the Commons, imbued with popular ideas and even had they wanted to, could not have gone against the people's wishes.[3]

Henry Goulburn, the Tory politician, was over-optimistic in thinking that the special power of the Irish Catholic priest, resting partly on the belief that he was 'vicarius Dei' and gifted with miraculous powers and partly on his being apparently unconcerned in the worldly interests of his own class, would be diminished by continued political activity. But Stanley's view on the other hand, one widely held by Englishmen, that 'the priests are connected with O'Connell for religious and political motives and with the people, whom they are obliged to lead from *pecuniary* considerations', was altogether too crude and simple.[4] The Catholic Church, then and later, was firmly opposed to any violent social or political revolution in Ireland. But in 1835 the observant Alexis de Tocqueville noticed the strongly democratic and liberal politics of most Irish priests, their deep distrust of any scheme, such as payment by the State, which would weaken their hold on the people and the fact that nearly all of them were recruited from the class of small tenant farmers, the same class which supported O'Connellite candidates at election time and which

[1] Hardinge to Major Miller, 31 January 1835, H.O. Papers, 100/246, 143-4.
[2] Fitzgerald to Peel, 2 January 1835, Peel Papers, Add. MSS 40323, 201-2.
[3] Hansard, XIII, 573; XXVIII, 896, 13 June 1832; 19 June 1835, O'Connell; *Times*, 29 December 1834.
[4] Goulburn to Peel, 14 November 1828, Peel Papers, Add. MSS. 40333, 55-9; Stanley to Melbourne, 26 March 1833, *Melbourne Papers*, 193-4.

had at least some stake in the existing land system.[1] After dinner with Dr. Nolan, Bishop of Kildare and Leighlin, in company with an Archbishop, three other Bishops and several priests, Tocqueville noted:

> The feelings expressed were extremely democratic. Distrust and hatred of the great landlords; love of the people, and confidence in them. Bitter memories of past oppression. An air of exaltation at present or approaching victory. A profound hatred of the Protestants and above all of their clergy. Little impartiality present. Clearly as much the leaders of a Party as the representatives of the Church.[2]

It would thus be wrong to underrate the electoral influence of the priesthood, even though, because £10 freeholders would support Repealers and Liberals without needing much encouragement, this influence was less sensational than in the struggle for Emancipation. At least three important cases can be quoted against the view that the clergy did not intervene directly in the selection and return of candidates. At Limerick, the Vicar-General of the diocese, Father Costelloe, was the great power in the Limerick Liberal Club; at O'Connell's suggestion, he tried without success in 1837 to oust Smith O'Brien from his seat, and as a staunch O'Connellite would gladly have defeated O'Brien in 1847 if the combination of his brother priests and the local landowners had not proved too strong for him.[3] In County Mayo and in Connaught generally, Archbishop MacHale possessed so considerable an influence throughout the period that in 1839 Graham and Bonham referred to Dillon Browne and Sir William Brabazon, the Members for Mayo, Patrick Somers, M.P. for Sligo and about four others as the 'MacHale faction'. In 1846 O'Connell thanked the Archbishop for his efforts in support of Joseph Miles MacDonnell in a Mayo by-election and repaid his expenses of £128.[4]

---

[1] Tocqueville, *Journeys*, 118–92, esp. pp. 132–6, 145–6, 150, 161–72. The College of St. Patrick at Maynooth, which replaced the continental colleges as the main seminary for Irish clergy, was widely regarded from the early years of the nineteenth century as being responsible for changes in the general character of the priesthood. Compared with many priests of the old school, Maynooth seminarists were generally more insular and more nationalist, certainly less well-educated and much less reactionary in politics.

[2] Tocqueville, op. cit., 20 July 1835, 130.

[3] Gwynn, *Young Ireland and 1848*, 126–7.

[4] Graham to Bonham, 23 December 1838; Bonham to Peel [August 1839], Peel Papers, Add. MSS 40616, 141; 40427, 381–2; O'Connell to MacHale, 15 April 1846, *O'Connell Corr.*, II, 371–2; MacHale to O'Connell, 30 April

The long correspondence of Father John Sheehan with O'Connell from 1826 to 1845 provides the best example of the activity of a priest in politics. Sheehan, parish priest of Waterford, was a staunch nationalist and remained always suspicious of independent Liberals like Wyse or of a Repealer like Henry Barron who was rightly suspected of being ready to deal in patronage. In 1834 he warned O'Connell that 'the honest repealers of this place feel quite disheartened that no proper candidate has yet been named for Dungarvan. I tell you that the Wyse party are here very busy about him—I understand that the Devonshire interest is likely to be arrayed in his support . . . If Wyse ever gets in, you will have another Luther to annoy you.'[1] In December 1834, Sheehan's position in Waterford City was typical of that of a conscientious nationalist in alliance with the Whigs:

> To secure unanimity here I have made up my mind to support Barron and Wyse at the election . . . I make a very great sacrifice of feeling. For Wyse's sense I have the poorest possible opinion. No man but a fool could in times like the present have a contempt for the people such as he has manifested. In Barron's honesty, I have very little confidence— He would forget the most solemn promises for one smile or courteous salute from *a great one* . . . However as the cause of reform requires that we should take them I am satisfied to do so . . .

Sheehan guaranteed 'to unite the democracy in his [Wyse's] favour provided he only address the constituency as an Anti-Tory' and he was prepared to support two such Liberals for the county;[2] but later he warned O'Connell 'not to recommend a coalition between Galwey and Power—[for the county]. If a Beresford started, Power would have immense difficulty in carrying Galwey thro' . . . It would be no harm whatever to get rid of your fat friend . . . [sc. J. M. Galwey]'.[3]

1846, O'Connell MSS, U.C.D. For MacHale's intervention in a bye-election in 1841 in Mayo, and in Mayo and Galway in the 1841 General Election, see *Pilot*, 18, 21 December 1841; Bernard O'Reilly, *John MacHale, Archbishop of Tuam* (1890), I, 510–19; O. J. Burke, *History of the Catholic Archbishops of Tuam* (1882), 316–18.

[1] Sheehan to O'Connell, 19 January 1834, O'Connell Papers, N.L.I., uncatalogued. O'Connell immediately sent money, a manifesto, a candidate and his son Maurice to Dungarvan; *O'Connell Corr.*, I, 403, 406–8, 411; O'Connell to Electors of Dungarvan, 29 February 1834, O'Connell Papers, N.L.I., 423.

[2] Sheehan to O'Connell, 8 December 1834, O'Connell Papers, N.L.I. uncatalogued.

[3] Sheehan to O'Connell, 7, 14 January 1835, O'Connell Papers, N.L.I. uncatalogued. Galwey was in fact dropped.

Sheehan continued to take a close and active interest in the electoral politics of the county and city of Waterford and of Dungarvan. By 1840, unable to break the hold on the city of the sitting Members and true to his original fears, he lamented to O'Connell that 'Barron's votes . . . have given great outrage to some of his constituents. I wish he was a little less selfish or that the representation of the city were out of his and Wyse's hands.' Seven years later, when cracks were beginning to appear in the nationalist movement, he is found writing full of admiration for O'Connell's 'saying that you would not bring about the greatest possible good at the expense of one drop of human blood. This is the principle of the true moral revolutionist . . . ,' assuring him that the Waterford Repeal Association was not disunited and that there was neither 'a Wyse party' nor, 'thank God', an 'Infidel Colleges Bill party' in the city.[1] It was to men like Father Sheehan, watchful, censorious and rather puritanical, devoted personally to O'Connell and intensely suspicious of his rivals, that O'Connell's movement owed much for services which were not the less valuable for being often private and unpublicized. The letters of this priest add weight and substance to Tocqueville's penetrating analysis of the political attitudes of the Catholic priesthood.

Irish elections were fought against a background of simmering agrarian discontent. Yet politics as understood inside the insulated electoral system (only one in every 70 or 80 of the population having the vote) played little part in the life of the great mass of the peasantry, who were preoccupied in a struggle for existence on the narrow margin between subsistence and starvation. Peasant secret societies and factions had no direct political aims, and the nearest the peasantry came to participation in politics, before their numbers were mobilized in the Repeal campaigns of the 1840's, was during the tithe agitation. Even then their general protest against agrarian conditions was governed by very different aims and motives from those of O'Connell and the middle-class politicians, who might profit electorally by the physical and financial support of voteless peasants but who, as men closely connected with the land system, could hardly afford to use too often or too carelessly a weapon which might perhaps be turned against themselves.[2]

The excitement of a contested election, when the passions and

---

[1] Sheehan to O'Connell, 3 March 1840; 30 October 1845, O'Connell Papers, N.L.I. uncatalogued.　　　　　　　　　　　　　　[2] See below, pp. 175 ff.

grievances of the countryside came suddenly to a head, undoubtedly provided opportunities for the peasantry to pay off old scores and frequently turned elections into bloody and riotous affairs. At Dungarvan in 1832, Lord Melbourne's brother George Lamb, the successful Whig candidate, was said to have had 'at least a hundred votes in reserve, but was unwilling to expose them to the danger they would have run in coming to the Hustings': a wise enough move when it was reported that

> The country people from distant parts of the county assembled in multitudes, and carried sticks and stones in their hands and pockets . . . stones were thrown in every direction . . . The Hotel where Mr. Lamb and his friends were, was assailed, and the windows broken by Mr. Galwey's party . . . All the tenantry on Lord Cremorne's property came in with sticks . . . threatening all with destruction who would vote for Mr. Lamb.

It is only fair to add that in an election in which three lives were lost, the nationalists claimed that their opponents had hired a band of fellows who were supplied with spirits, armed with bludgeons and set on to a quiet crowd which was listening to a speech from O'Connell.[1] Five men were killed in the 1832 election in Queen's County, two by dragoons escorting Sir Charles Coote to his home after his victory. At Newry a mob of 3,000 peasants from Louth encamped on a hill outside the town for two days and might well have carried out their threat to 'exterminate' every Tory voter if the local Catholic priest had not prevented them from entering the town.[2] In Mayo, after two men were shot dead by policemen, the peasants retaliated by breaking down the pontoon bridges leading to Sligo and Tyrawley, cutting off communication for wheeled carriages with Castlebar, and by cutting an immense trench across the road to Ballina. A party of freeholders, escorted by police, were rushed by a crowd of peasants swearing that they would 'have the freeholders alive or dead'. The police opened fire and wounded six persons.[3]

In 1835 nervous magistrates in Newry, Queen's County, Tralee, Kilkenny and Mayo requested military reinforcements. In 1841 the authorities in Belfast, Cork and County Carlow needed cavalry and infantry to prevent violence, and 'exclusive dealing', which *The Times* called 'the last invention of social enmity', was a feature of

---

[1] *D.E.P.*, 15, 18 December; *F.J.*, 15 December 1832; *D.E.P.*, 10 January 1833.
[2] *Times*, 2 January 1833; *D.E.P.*, 27 December 1832.
[3] *D.E.P.*, 27 December; *Times*, 29 December 1832.

elections in Dublin City and Mayo in 1832, in Kerry and Tralee in 1835 and in Longford in 1837.[1] Intimidation by the voteless no doubt contributed to the solidarity of 'left-wing' voters, but it could not by itself save the nationalist cause from the electoral disaster of 1841.

The electoral influence at the disposal of the Irish Government was extremely limited, and seems in practice to have been confined to Dublin. In 1831, a Select Committee reported that 'Certain persons holding high official stations, or considered to be connected with the Irish government, did use undue influence to promote the return of the two [Liberal] members'.[2] In 1832, Lord Anglesey issued a public statement that 'the Government takes no part whatever in the Dublin election', although the Under-Secretary, Sir William Gossett, seems to have made an unauthorized promise that the Government would support the Conservatives. This promise was not apparently kept and O'Connell himself was unable to produce any real evidence of the Government's partiality.[3] In 1842, Sir James Graham thought that for the Dublin by-election of that year,

... the Government must enter the lists forcibly and give to the Conservative Candidate the full measure of their support and influence. If the Antagonist be a Repealer, I think that every man receiving the Pay of the Crown should be required to vote in favour of the Government candidate: if Morpeth [the Whig ex-Chief Secretary] be brought forward, then I would use against him *exactly* the same degree of pressure and of influence, which he himself applied at the last Election in favour of O'Connell and against West & Grogan ...

But whatever truth there was in Graham's allegations about the 1841 election (and his letter sounds somewhat over-excited), Peel was most cautious and damping.[4]

[1] *Times*, 2 January 1833; Correspondence between Lieutenants of Counties and Magistrates, Ireland, relative to the late elections, P.P. 1835, XLV, 385 ff.; R. B. McDowell, 'Ireland on the Eve of the Famine', in *The Great Famine*, ed. R. D. Edwards and T. D. Williams (1956), 76.

[2] Report of Select Committee, Dublin City Election, P.P. 1831, IV, 447; Sheil, *Sketches*, II, 329–31, alleging Government interference in the Police Offices and Paving Board.

[3] Anglesey to Alderman Darley, *Pilot*, 15 December; *F.J.*, 22 December 1832; 3 January; *Pilot*, 4 January 1833.

[4] Graham to Peel, 1 January; Peel to Graham, 3 January 1842, Peel Papers, Add. MSS 40446, 270–2. Morpeth, who was actually seconded on the hustings by O'Connell himself as Lord Mayor, was defeated by William Gregory. See Sir William Gregory, *An Autobiography*, ed. Lady Gregory (1894), 58–67.

In fact allegations from any quarter about the use of official influence in Ireland were few and isolated, and there were no constituencies in any way comparable to the six English 'Government' boroughs investigated by Professor Gash.[1] On the other hand, there was no doubt that largely because of its command of patronage, the Government of the day possessed a slight general advantage over the Opposition in Irish Elections. In 1835 and in 1837, gains by Conservatives and by Liberals respectively were attributable in part to this advantageous position, and in 1840 Bonham advised Peel that 'in *Ireland*, *your* Election might make a difference of five or six seats in our favour' and that a Whig dissolution would adversely affect Conservative fortunes only in Ireland.[2]

The whole subject of electoral finance is beset with difficulties. Reliable evidence is rarely available even for the finances of O'Connell's movement, for although O'Connell was certainly not plagued by scruples about dependence on popular subscriptions, very few either of his personal or public accounts seem to have survived. In practice, the two main sources of his funds (the Tribute collected for his personal use and the National, Justice or Repeal Rents which theoretically went to finance his political organizations) seem to have overlapped and to have been confused with each other. Some hint of this state of affairs is given by his remark to Fitzpatrick in 1840 that 'a Repeal Association . . . will injure your operations for me, as the parishes in general will not make double contributions', and a year before, he had been attacked for refusing to allow the funds of the Precursor Society 'to rest in the hands of the treasurer and trustees ostensibly appointed to take charge of them, instead of being lodged in a country branch bank to his personal credit'.[3] In 1845 he calculated that the Repeal Association owed him, as its Treasurer, over £15,000, yet in his will two years later he left £1,000 to the Association 'as in full satisfaction of any demand that body may or could have upon me'.[4] In view of O'Connell's complete control of

---

[1] Gash, *Politics*, 444–59. Cf. Hansard, XVII, 195–7, 16 April 1833, William Roche, on alleged Government interference in Limerick in 1832, which was denied by Stanley and by the magistrates concerned.

[2] Bonham to Peel, 14 January 1840, Peel Papers, Add. MSS 40428, 13–16.

[3] O'Connell to Fitzpatrick, 9 April 1840, *O'Connell Corr.*, II, 238; Duffy, *Young Ireland*, I, 6–7.

[4] O'Connell's Will [n.d. 1847]; a later codicil changed the sum to £630, O'Connell MSS, U.C.D. John O'Connell, *Recollections*, II, 23–4, states that in election years more than half the O'Connell Tribute went for electoral purposes.

his organizations and of P. V. Fitzpatrick's relationship towards both them and O'Connell, it can be assumed that the O'Connell Tribute and the movement's finances were in practice fused together to serve as a central political fund as well as to maintain large and hospitable establishments at Darrynane, at 30 Merrion Square in Dublin and in London during parliamentary sessions.

For most of the years between 1830 and 1845, it is possible to establish the amount of funds at O'Connell's disposal.

Date	Sum	Sources
1831–2	£26,065	Fitzpatrick to O'Connell, 21 February 1831, O'Connell Papers, N.L.I. uncatalogued.
1832–3	£12,242	*Pilot*, 2 January 1833.
1833–4	£13,908	Report: Contributions to the O'Connell National Annuity 1833–1834, N.L.I.
1829–34	£91,800	*O'Connell Corr.*, I, 212, apparently the full total of receipts between these years.
1835	£13,454	*Pilot*, 7 September 1835.
1840	£2,688	
1841	£8,685	For 1840–5, Abstract of Repeal
1842	£5,705	Rent, December 1845, O'Connell
1843	£48,706	Papers. N.L.I. uncatalogued.
1844	£43,884	
1845	£17,824	

These figures provide a remarkable index to the electoral history of O'Connell's party. Between 1829 and 1834, the years of independence and increasing electoral success, O'Connell had at his disposal between £90,000 and £100,000, and in 1835, the annual fund showed no signs of decline following an Election which generated much popular enthusiasm. Yet no figures of any kind can be produced for 1836 to 1839, the years of the Whig alliance. Money was still being collected, but neither O'Connell's supporting newspapers nor his correspondence throw any light on the finances of those years. If funds had been at all impressive, details would certainly have been published in the O'Connellite press; but during the 1837 Election the *Pilot* and the *Freeman's Journal* gave no totals of contributions and concentrated much less attention on the progress of the Tribute than they had in 1832 and 1835. Shortage of funds between 1836 and 1840 was not disastrous, because at least for the Dublin election petition English sympathizers came to O'Connell's rescue. But early in 1841 O'Connell had every reason to be seriously worried by the financial situation,[1] and the disaster of that year must have been partly caused by an acute shortage of money for electoral expenses. The great funds of 1843 and 1844, swelled by American contributions, were never used in a General Election.

But while some candidates, nearly all of them members of his family or close followers, were undoubtedly helped from O'Connell's funds or by public subscription, the costs of an Irish election often fell largely on the candidates themselves. Local clubs might defray the expenses of registration, but at election time a candidate was expected to dip into his own pocket. There were the official election expenses—the payment of assessors, the provision of polling booths and poll books, the expenses of sheriffs or returning officers, which were shared between candidates who paid a lump sum down to the returning officer before the election, and little attention was paid to the statutory limitations on these expenses.[2]

An uncontested election (hence its great attraction) could mean no official expenses at all. In 1832, ten Conservatives in Down, Fermanagh, Sligo, Londonderry and Tyrone and ten Repealers in Kerry, Kilkenny County and City, Meath, Louth and Roscommon paid no deposits to the returning officers and incurred no official expenses. In Dublin, on the other hand, the official bill came to about £460 towards which the two Repealers paid £132 each, the two Conservatives £150. A contested county election, requiring a large number of polling booths, was nearly always more expensive officially than a contested borough. In the county and city of Limerick, the bills came to £441 and £391 respectively; Clare cost the candidates £500, for although the actual bill came only to £149 the sheriff kept the balance, by Irish custom, for his expenses. The average for official expenses in all Irish constituencies was £290 in 1832, a considerably higher figure than the average of £134 in England and Wales.[3]

[1] O'Connell to Fitzpatrick, 19 February 1841, *O'Connell Corr.*, II, 260–1.

[2] These were £40 and £25 respectively for each county and borough polling booth. After 1835, by the 5 & 6 Will. IV, c. 36, candidates were no longer put to the expense and trouble of paying for the administration to voters of the oaths of allegiance, supremacy and abjuration.

[3] Return of all Monies deposited with Sheriffs etc. . . . and of the Expenditure of the same, P.P. 1833, XXVII, 255–86; Gash, *Politics*, 116.

But these official expenses only represented a small part of a candidate's expenditure. Even with the support of a club, the cost of employing agents, of placing addresses in local and Dublin newspapers, of canvassing, of bringing electors to the polls and entertaining them, even of paying for their support, could be very large indeed.[1] Estimates of £20,000 and £11,000 for elections in Queen's County and County Limerick in 1832 may have been exaggerated, but when Pierce Mahony planned to stand for Limerick City in 1832 he gave £1,500 to the Catholic Bishop for 'charitable purposes' and was rumoured to have set aside £10,000 for the election.[2] The counties, where voters generally needed no great inducement to give their support, were on the whole less expensive for Repealers and Liberals than the boroughs. But even in County Kilkenny, where there was no vestige of Conservative opposition, the sitting Repeal Members were supposed in 1837 to put down £250 each, when 'arrangements would be made to return them free of further expence'.[3] For Carlow, where his son Maurice would enjoy a higher status than as M.P. for Tralee, O'Connell was ready to put up £500 or if necessary £1,000; and for the same county, in the bargain made between O'Connell and Alexander Raphael, O'Connell was to receive £1,000 before the election and £1,000 afterwards if Raphael was successful; in return O'Connell, who sent the £2,000 to Nicholas Vigors, Raphael's fellow-candidate and the election manager, guaranteed Raphael against any further expenses. This arrangement collapsed when Raphael, for whom O'Connell was unable to obtain the baronetcy which he had held out as possible solace, was also called upon to meet the further expenses of defending his election against a petition.[4]

Most election petitions (13 out of 17 between 1830 and 1847) were concerned with the boroughs, and it was in these places that the

---

[1] In Carlow in 1835 addresses in newspapers cost between £300 and £400, Fagan, *O'Connell*, II, 456.

[2] *D.E.P.*, *F.J.*, 27 December; *F.J.*, 5 December; *Times*, 8 December 1832. In 1830, for his election at Waterford City, Wyse was prepared to spend £5,000, Auchmuty, *Wyse*, 95.

[3] Richard Sullivan to O'Connell, 14 July 1837, O'Connell Papers, N.L.I. uncatalogued.

[4] O'Connell to Fitzpatrick, 4 January 1835, *O'Connell Corr.*, I, 511–12. For the whole Raphael episode, see Fagan, *O'Connell*, II, 429–73; Hansard, XXXIII, 22–114, 192–7, 21, 22 April 1836, Debate and Divisions; Report, Select Committee, Co. Carlow Election, P.P. 1836, XI, 1 ff.

really large sums were spent. The 1832 Dublin election cost the defeated Tories £8,000 in all, about £2,000 a day. In the 1842 Dublin by-election, William Gregory himself put up £4,000 and the rest of the Conservatives' expenses (about £5,000) were met by subscriptions in Dublin and London; £4,500 alone was spent in 'gratifications' of £3 for each of the 1,500 freemen, the Tory 'Macedonian phalanx'.[1] Examples have already been given of the importance of plentiful supplies of money in the Irish boroughs, but the situation in Tralee, where the O'Connells employed a permanent agent, provides a final comment. In 1841, his bill came to a moderate £58, including rent of rooms, refreshment (there were 82 teetotallers out of 258 electors), pollbooks and stationery. But it occurred to the agent that 'it would be desirable to lodge . . . £150 or £200 by way of a *loan* fund to be advanced from time to time on good security to such of the voters who may stand in need of assistance, and secure their votes in future. They have faithfully discharged their duty.'[2]

Finally, the cost of defending an election could be exorbitant. In 1835, when the Conservatives petitioned against the return of O'Connell and Ruthven for Dublin, O'Connell expected at first that his defence costs would be between £1,000 and £1,500, most of which would have to be found by himself as 'we shall get but little money from Dublin'. By September 1835, his estimate for the defence of his own and John O'Connell's election at Youghal was £7,000, though even this, he claimed, was only one-fifth of the cost to his opponents. By May 1836, with the Dublin result still uncertain, the total was £10,000 and seems finally to have been about £12,500.[3] O'Connell, who was seriously considering mortgaging his property, would have been ruined but for the timely help of a fund of between £8,000 and £9,000 raised in England and sponsored by the Radicals Joseph Hume and Henry Warburton.[4] Compared with

[1] *D.E.P.*, 5 December; *Times*, 21 December 1832; Gregory, *Autobiography*, 58–67.
[2] Daniel Supple to O'Connell, 9 August 1841; Bill of Expenses, July 1841, O'Connell MSS., U.C.D.
[3] O'Connell to Fitzpatrick, 27 February; 7, 13 March; 14 April; 29 June; 4 September 1835; 13 May 1836, *O'Connell Corr.*, I, 523, 525, 528; II, 13, 29–30, 35, 54.
[4] Fagan, *O'Connell*, II, 537–9, who gives a figure of £8,489 for the fund, to meet expenses of £12,500; Hume to Ellice, 17 January 1837, Ellice MSS., N.L.S., pkt. 34, for a figure of £9,300 for the fund. Only a few Whigs and no Ministers contributed. For the Duke of Bedford's explanation of his gift of 100

these expenses, £1,000 for an expected petition in 1837 was almost reasonable, but this time the publicity given by O'Connell and Smith O'Brien to a London Conservative fund, in which Sir Francis Burdett as well as the Conservative leaders were implicated, no doubt made use of the fund more difficult and helped O'Connell to retain his seat.[1] But his bitter experiences led him to attack the whole system of hearing and deciding election petitions. He believed that election committees were invariably partisan, their decisions reflecting the political composition of each committee and having no reference to the merits of each petition. For this aspersion on its dignity, O'Connell was censured by the Commons, but since even opponents substantially agreed with him, a victory was won in 1839 when on Peel's initiative the old Grenville committees were replaced by a single committee nominated by the Speaker.[2]

guineas, see Bedford to Lord John Russell, 12 June 1836, Russell Papers, P.R.O. 30/22/2B: 'Mr. O'Connell is a powerful man in that country and as long as he acts aright, and for the real interests of Ireland, he ought to be supported.' When he heard of this, the King ordered the Duke's bust to be removed from Windsor Castle.

[1] Hansard, XXXIX, 687-94, 695-6, 699-701, 6, 7 December 1837, O'Brien, O'Connell, Burdett; 747-844, debate and division on O'Brien's unsuccessful motion to declare the so-called 'Spottiswoode Conspiracy' a breach of privilege; Greville, *Journal*, 8 December 1837, IV, 31. For the Tory leaders' connection with election petition funds in 1836 and 1837, see Hardinge to Peel, 7 January 1836; Lord Francis Egerton to Peel, 29 September 1837; Graham to Bonham, 9 October 1837, Peel Papers, Add. MSS 40314, 118-19; 40424, 180-1; 40616, 9.

[2] Hansard, XLI, 105-17, 172-5, 263-70, 26, 28 February 1838, O'Connell, Division, 293 to 85 in support of the Tory censure motion, Censure by Speaker; Gash, *Politics*, 134-5.

CHAPTER IV

The Irish Party in British Politics

The Repeal question in Parliament

THE first session of the reformed Parliament in 1833 had disappointed O'Connell's hopes for the political effects of Parliamentary Reform and placed him in a most difficult position in relation to the Repeal question, to which he and his party were irrevocably pledged. Repeal of the Union would certainly be opposed by an overwhelming majority in the Commons; and faced with the choice either of advertising his movement's weakness in Parliament or of exposing himself and his followers to charges of insincerity, O'Connell first played for time. In June 1833, at a meeting of the party in London, a narrow majority (12 to 10, with 10 abstentions) supported his policy of postponing the question. O'Connell's view, that the debate would be badly reported in the English press, that any motion would be inevitably defeated and would serve only to strengthen the Whigs, was realistic enough; and at a second meeting later in June he had a large majority in favour of postponement. But the extremists, led by Feargus O'Connor, were supported by a section of the Irish nationalist press, including the *Freeman's Journal* in Dublin and newspapers in Cork, Waterford and Tipperary; and O'Connell, much against his will, was finally forced to maintain the unity of his party by promising a future discussion.[1]

On 22 April 1834 O'Connell finally introduced his motion for a

---

[1] Fagan, *O'Connell*, II, 243–52; McDowell, *Public Opinion*, 158. See also Donald Read and Eric Glasgow, *Feargus O'Connor* (1961), 34–5, who see O'Connor's manoeuvres at this time as a bid to oust O'Connell from the leadership.

Committee to inquire into the effects of the Union. His speech, over five hours long, was not one of his most impressive efforts. The case required analysis and exposition of a kind which scarcely suited his own brand of oratory and he was painfully conscious that he could expect no sympathy from his audience.[1] Ireland's claim to legislative independence within the Empire was advanced by him in largely economic terms. He argued that the country had steadily prospered between 1782 and 1800 under the protection of the Irish Parliament, that the Act of Union had been carried by force and corruption, despite the incompetency of the Irish Parliament to vote for its own extinction, and that the economic, social and political consequences of the Union had been disastrous. Ireland, forced by the fiscal terms of the Union to provide two-seventeenths of the imperial revenue, had been impoverished by a steady drain of capital in over-taxation and in the loss of absentees' rents. The gradual repeal after the Union of the protective duties on Irish manufactures and the opening of free trade between England and Ireland had stifled the rapidly developing industrial sector of the Irish economy; and the silk, woollen, linen and cotton industries outside Ulster (an area he was ready to admit as an exception) had been exposed to and killed by superior British competition. Finally, a predominantly English Parliament which had required coercive legislation to govern Ireland for twenty years in the thirty-four years of the Union's existence inevitably ignored Irish interests: 'How . . . can the men sitting in London know our wants and our wishes', he was reported to have said earlier in Ireland, 'Why, if the Parliament were sitting in Dublin, you could take your short sticks in your hands some fine morning, and go up and tell them to vote honestly and rightly'.[2]

O'Connell scarcely developed a coherent doctrine of Ireland's right to national self-determination. With an almost instinctive feeling for the country as an entity, a possessive pride in its people and in an historical past in which fact and myth were sometimes imperfectly distinguished, he had no time for a nationalism based on the old Gaelic traditions and culture. Although personally tolerant of religious differences and genuinely concerned for the rights of politico-religious minorities, the identification of the Irish nation with Irish Catholicism was so complete in his mind and so evident

[1] John O'Connell, *Recollections*, I, 82, 85; *O'Connell Corr.*, I, 423–30.
[2] Hansard, XXII, 1092–1158, 22 April 1834, O'Connell; *Pilot*, 2 December 1832.

in many of his speeches that his attempts to secure Protestant support
and co-operation were largely condemned to failure; and in calling
for the restoration of a Parliament inseparably connected with the
name of Henry Grattan, for whom he had a lasting admiration, he
demanded limited self-government on strictly utilitarian and economic grounds, always insisting that he was not a separatist.[1]

He made no impression in 1834 on a wholly Unionist Parliament.
Thomas Spring Rice, answering for the Government, argued from
official figures that Ireland had actually prospered under free trade
with 'the best and richest market for agricultural produce in the
world'; he pointed out the great weaknesses of the 1782 constitution,
notably as they affected the sovereignty of the Crown, dilated on the
corruption of the Irish Parliament and contended that Repeal,
ushering in 'democratic liberty' in Ireland, would mean separation
within a year.[2] For the opposition, Peel readily admitted the existence of widespread distress and increased absenteeism, but in his
view Repeal alone would not solve these problems and by threatening
the security of the United Kingdom it would be tantamount to the
dissolution of the Empire.[3] After five days of debate and speeches
from fourteen Repealers, O'Connell's motion was defeated by 523
votes to 38, only one English Member voting with the Irish party.[4]

The Government took the motion seriously enough to carry an
address pledging both Houses to the maintenance of the Union; but
in reality, O'Connell's cause in Parliament was powerless against an
entrenched Unionism deriving its strength from religious as well as
political sources and against an English nationalism reinforced by
laissez-faire economics, which saw O'Connell's somewhat inexplicit
demands for the protection of an Irish Parliament as poorly-dis-
guised separatism. The defeat in 1834 was decisive for the immediate
future not only of the Irish nationalist movement but also of the
Irish party. There was now no real alternative for O'Connell but
alliance with the Whigs in exchange for liberal policies towards

[1] W. J. O'Neill Daunt, *Personal Recollections of Daniel O'Connell* (1848), I,
14–15, for O'Connell's remark on the Gaelic language: 'I am sufficiently utilitarian not to regret its gradual abandonment.' See further R. Dudley Edwards,
'The contribution of Young Ireland to the development of the Irish national
idea', in *Féilscríbhinn Tórna* (1947).

[2] Hansard, XXII, 1164–1283, 23 April 1834, Spring Rice.

[3] Hansard, XXIII, 69–95, 25 April 1834, Peel.

[4] Hansard, XXIII, 286–7, 29 April 1834, Division. The extremist O'Connor
and the moderate Sheil were the only absentees on the Irish side.

Ireland; and on their side, the Whigs could never have considered alliance with a party committed to the cause of Irish self-government. The inevitable parliamentary defeat of Repeal, which Melbourne in January 1834 had hoped might lead to 'the bare possibility of the People of Ireland at last opening their eyes to their true interest',[1] marked the first step on the road to Lichfield House, to an alliance with the Whig Government.

The disruption of the Grey Government

The division within Lord Grey's Government on the subject of Appropriation epitomized a struggle for power which had been dividing the Government since the first discussions on Irish Church reform, perhaps even from its formation in 1830. By September 1833 the nine members of the Government inclined, in Graham's words, 'to court Radical and Irish aid' (including Althorp, Russell, Duncannon, Brougham, Ellice, Poulett Thomson and Holland) almost balanced the six former Canningite Tories and six more or less conservative Whigs, including Grey himself, Stanley and Graham. It was inevitable that if any issue should divide the two smaller sections, the balance of power within the Government would tip decidedly in favour of the larger and more liberal group.[2]

The policy of O'Connell and his party between June 1833 and May 1834 was clear and consistent. Formally independent of the Whigs though supporting them on most important issues, they attempted to exploit the well-known divisions inside the Cabinet by maintaining a constant pressure on Appropriation. Stanley's departure from Ireland in March 1833, followed in September by Anglesey's retirement, were encouraging signs.[3] O'Connell, mitigating his public attacks on the Whigs, set about establishing good relations with E. J. Littleton, the new Chief Secretary, a Staffordshire country gentleman of conciliatory manners and decidedly liberal opinions now placed in what he regarded, not unjustifiably,

[1] Melbourne to Wellesley, 7 January 1834, Wellesley Papers, Add. MSS 37306, 311–12.

[2] Parker, *Graham*, I, 169. The losses of Durham, Anglesey and Hobhouse in the liberal group were balanced by the accessions of Littleton and Wellesley.

[3] Sir John Hobhouse lasted little more than a month as Chief Secretary. His over-scrupulous resignation on the house and window taxes was regarded partly as an admission of failure in office, 'his temper . . . unequal to the demands made upon it by the constant attacks of the O'Connell tribe': Le Marchant, *Diary* [n.d. May 1833], Aspinall, op. cit., 326–8.

as 'incomparably the most arduous [office] under Government'. They were soon on good terms, O'Connell praising Littleton in public and thanking him privately 'for having muzzled in some degree the Irish newspapers, as far as personal abuse of him went', though Littleton feared that 'he will go over to Ireland and apologize for his silence and the unpopular part he has sometimes taken, by saying, "Oh, I have never done so much for you heretofore, I have the new Irish Secretary in my pocket".'[1]

To the Opposition, Littleton seemed 'little more than a tool in the hands of the Roman Catholic Party'. Hardinge wrote of a 'most disgraceful intrigue' and prophesied that there would soon be 'a collision which must afford him [O'Connell] great Parliamentary chances & that at any rate, his friends think he may be keeping terms with L[ittleton], [may] renew the negotiation & [seek] in the interval [to] exasperate the Protestant party with the Govt'.[2] But the Government was in fact deeply divided in its attitude to O'Connell. Against Brougham's and Littleton's view that 'a great effort should be made to propitiate him', Melbourne still believed that O'Connell's activities concealed, whatever their 'ulterior objects',

> those still more dangerous & desperate designs, which it must be clear to all he really entertains . . . But . . . we have to deal with a man of very extraordinary & unusual character, possessing throughout the greater part of a populous country that unquestioned power & un-bounded influence which has been enjoyed temporarily & in single cities by Tribunes of the People and Demagogues heretofore, & who . . . turns all the privileges of the Constitution agt. the Constitution, & makes the safeguards of the law his principal means of destroying the law itself.

For Grey also, there was 'really nothing for it, as far as he is con-cerned, but determined & uncompromising resistance'.[3]

---

[1] Littleton, *Diary*, 18 May; 24 July; 5 August 1833, Aspinall, op. cit., 331, 351, 355. See also *Lady Morgan's Memoirs*, ed. W. Hepworth Dixon (1862), II, 378, for Lady Morgan's prescient warning in December 1833 to Littleton of the dangers of becoming entangled with O'Connell.

[2] Goulburn to Peel, 27 November 1833; Hardinge to Peel, 16 November [1833], Peel Papers, Add. MSS 40333, 166–7; 40313, 172–3.

[3] Littleton to Graham, 30 September 1833, Parker, *Graham*, I, 183; Melbourne to Wellesley, 7 January; Grey to Wellesley, 9 January 1834, Wellesley Papers, Add. MSS 37306, 311–12, 314–17. For Brougham's views, see Brougham to Althorp [n.d. Spring 1834], Spencer MSS., cited in *Two Centuries of Irish History*, ed. R. B. O'Brien (1907), 349.

The Government crisis of May 1834 hinged on the determination of the liberal section of the Cabinet to press for a more radical policy towards the Irish Church, as an essential preliminary to an understanding if not to an alliance with O'Connell and his party. In January 1834 Althorp told Littleton confidentially that he had been convinced for a long time that 'this Church Question in Ireland must, either in this session or at no very distant period, dissolve the present Cabinet. It can be postponed but for a very short time, & whenever it is really forced on, we shall be obliged all of us to take our own line . . . We can now break up the Government, if we like, on this question . . .'[1] Althorp, whose solid liberalism, devotion to Grey and honest, somewhat pedestrian conscientiousness had made him a successful leader of a difficult House of Commons, was not the man to make the vital move. But Lord John Russell could no longer restrain himself. Highly temperamental, possibly jealous of Stanley and intensely disliking the illiberalism with which Stanley had tainted the Government and Whiggism in general, he suddenly declared on 6 May 1834 during a debate on Irish tithes, without consulting even his liberal colleagues, that Irish Church revenues were too large for the Church's purposes and that when Parliament had settled the tithe question, he would be prepared to assert his opinion on the appropriation of these surplus revenues.[2]

He had indeed 'upset the Coach'. Littleton 'saw from the moment Lord John had finished, that Stanley had decided on his Line—retirement—or the ejection of Lord John'.[3] Russell's resignation would have involved Althorp's and the collapse of the Government, and Brougham's proposal for a commission of inquiry into Church revenues, while it allowed the Whigs to block Radical and Irish attempts to force their hands, could not prevent the resignations of Stanley, Graham, the Duke of Richmond and Lord Ripon.[4] The whole episode was in one sense a triumph for the liberal section of the Government, now strengthened by the promotions of Edward

[1] Althorp to Littleton, 5 January 1834, Wellesley Papers, Add. MSS 37306, 308-9.

[2] Hansard, XXIII, 666, 6 May 1834, Russell.

[3] Stanley to Graham [n.d. 6 May 1834], Parker, *Graham*, I, 187; Littleton to Wellesley, 7 May 1834, Wellesley Papers, Add. MSS 37307, 26-9.

[4] For details of the three-week Cabinet crisis, see Le Marchant, *Diary* [n.d May 1834], Aspinall, op. cit., 378-81; Littleton to Wellesley, 8, 14, 17 May 1834, Wellesley Papers, Add. MSS 37307, 30-2, 43-8, 64-8; Parker, *Graham*, I, 187-92.

Ellice and James Abercromby to Cabinet rank,[1] as well as a personal victory for Russell, who had eliminated a powerful rival. But it was also a triumph for the Irish party, whose constant and irritating pressure had brought on the crisis. On 2 May, Althorp and Littleton were in 'some difficulty' about resisting an Irish motion calling for Appropriation, and Russell's outburst may well have been directly caused by an apparent improvement in the relations between Stanley and O'Connell, when O'Connell's proposal on 6 May to reduce tithes by two-thirds had been received with remarkable friendliness by Stanley.[2]

Stanley and his friends believed, in Graham's words, that true Whiggism was not incompatible with the firm maintenance of the Established Church, 'that religion of perfect freedom, which the Revolution of 1688 bore triumphant over Popery and regal tyranny'.[3] They were ready to carry out limited ecclesiastical reforms but they were also convinced that the Church's existence, the symbol of all property and institutions, was endangered by a sinister alliance of English and Irish Radicalism and by 'the growth and boldness of Dissent', and they believed that the Government was moving under these pressures towards the destruction of the Irish Church.[4] If their fears were somewhat exaggerated, they were undeniably right in thinking that the crisis of May 1834 had changed the whole orientation of the Government towards the Irish party.

Immediately after Russell's outburst, O'Connell informed the Government through Sir Francis Burdett that if his own tithe plan were adopted 'he would answer for quieting the whole country', and admitting that his position was a disagreeable one, virtually offered his services as Irish Attorney-General. Grey was at first surprisingly favourable, though he did not see how O'Connell and Stanley could be colleagues; but a week later, perhaps realizing that Stanley's resignation was now virtually certain, Grey definitely refused the

[1] For O'Connell's pleasure at Abercromby's promotion, see O'Connell to Fitzpatrick, 29 May 1834, *O'Connell Corr.*, I, 438–9.

[2] Littleton to Wellesley, 2, 7 May 1834, Wellesley Papers, Add. MSS 37307, 26–9, commenting on O'Connell's 'extraordinary Speech & proposal ... conveyed in language & a tone perfectly novel in him', and on Stanley's 'most complimentary' answer.

[3] Graham to Lord Stanley, 4 June 1834, Parker, *Graham*, I, 195–6.

[4] Graham to Francis Aglionby [n.d. May 1834], Parker, *Graham*, I, 198; Broughton, *Recollections*, 11, 30 May 1834, IV, 340, 345, for Graham's remark: 'My position is a difficult one; I am a believer! ! ! !'

offer. O'Connell's tithe plan, objectionable in itself, would only be a prelude to further demands, involving the Government in sacrifices 'ruinous to the party making them in public opinion'.[1]

Within little more than a month the Government faced a second internal crisis. In January 1834 Grey and Melbourne had decided to postpone any parliamentary discussion on the renewal in whole or in part of the Coercion Act of 1833, partly to wait for the Repeal motion and partly to avoid beginning another session with 'a six weeks discussion, to the obstruction of all other business'.[2] By June, Grey was reluctantly prepared to drop the courts-martial clauses on the recommendation of the Marquess Wellesley, Wellington's brother, the former Governor-General of India who had replaced Anglesey in September 1833. But the Prime Minister made it clear that he considered the ban on public meetings indispensable, since 'If this control were taken away . . . you would see Mr. O'Connell first taking credit with the People of Ireland for having compelled the Government to relinquish it', and then using the liberty to renew the Repeal agitation. It would not diminish his opposition on tithes and on the rest of the Coercion Bill, and 'it would give new grounds for the reproaches of the Tories.'[3]

But on this issue the section of the Cabinet anxious to conciliate O'Connell were prepared to go to any lengths. Wellesley, who from January to 11 June 1834 had advised renewal of the meetings clauses in a stream of dispatches, suddenly and in response to an appeal by Littleton recommended their abandonment on 21 June.[4] Littleton, who had written to Wellesley at Brougham's instigation and with Althorp's knowledge, next saw O'Connell, again with Althorp's approval, and left him with the strong and quite mistaken impression that the liberals in the Cabinet had carried the day.[5] As soon as it was

----

[1] Broughton, *Recollections*, 11 May 1834, IV, 339–40; Patterson, *Burdett*, II, 621–3; see also Note by Disraeli [n.d. 1836], W. F. Monypenny, *The Life of Benjamin Disraeli* (1910), I, 389.

[2] Melbourne to Wellesley, 7 January; Grey to Wellesley, 23 January 1834, Wellesley Papers, Add. MSS 37306, 311–12, 335–6.

[3] Grey to Wellesley, 23 June 1834, Wellesley Papers, Add. MSS 37307, 90–2.

[4] Grey to Wellesley, 30 June 1834, Wellesley Papers, Add. MSS 37307, 100–8, a general review of Wellesley's correspondence.

[5] For the whole affair, see *O'Connell Corr.*, I, 445–7; Halévy, *History*, III, 173; Parker, *Graham*, I, 207; *Creevey Papers*, II, 287. Brougham later tried, quite inaccurately, to brand Ellice as the instigator of Littleton. Wellesley's defence, that he was quite uninformed as to the opinions of Grey and the Cabinet, seems

clear that this was not so and that Grey had in fact overruled the
liberal minority, O'Connell promptly and justifiably brought his own
private transactions with Littleton before the Commons.[1] The
revelation that part of the Government had been in negotiation with
O'Connell behind the Prime Minister's back led to the resignations
of Grey and Althorp and to the reconstruction of the Government
under Melbourne, with the indispensable Althorp back in his original
post; and the Coercion Bill, much modified and shorn of the meetings clauses, was passed without difficulty.

Lord Grey, ageing, out of touch with his more liberal colleagues
and unable to stomach any alliance with O'Connell, who had
recently attacked him as 'a wretched old man with a childish hatred
and maniacal contempt for the people of Ireland', seized the chance
of longed-for retirement.[2] Althorp, Brougham and the liberals had
not plotted to drive Grey out, but they had certainly profited by the
loose ministerial discipline which was so marked a feature of Grey's
system, and they showed themselves ready to lose their old leader,
even as the result of a damaging ministerial indiscretion, in order to
gain O'Connell. 'We are on the way', O'Connell wrote, 'from a half
Whig, half Tory Government to one half Radical, half Whig'.[3]
There was no reason why he should not come to terms with such a
combination.

plausible, and is borne out by Melbourne's own apologies for 'indolence &
negligence'; see Draft Memo by Wellesley [n.d. July–August 1834]; Melbourne
to Wellesley, 30 June 1834, Wellesley Papers, Add. MSS 37307, 129–30, 98–9.
  [1] Ebrington to Newport, 9 July 1834, Newport Papers, N.L.I., 796, for the
minority in the Cabinet consisting of Althorp, Ellice, Abercromby, Spring Rice
and Grant. See *O'Connell Corr.*, I, 446–7, for O'Connell's cross-examination of
Littleton in the Commons.
  [2] *Address to the Reformers of England and Ireland* (Spring 1834), quoted by
Donald Southgate, *The Passing of the Whigs, 1832–1886* (1962), 42; Grey to
Wellesley, 8 July 1834, Wellesley Papers, Add. MSS 37307, 112–13.
  [3] O'Connell to Barrett [n.d. July 1834], *O'Connell Corr.*, I, 451. Brougham
may have been erratic and unbalanced, but Althorp was neither, and furthermore
he was devoted to Grey who was supposed to have acquired a complete ascendancy over him; yet it was Althorp's 'voluntary pledge' to Littleton (who passed
it on to O'Connell) that the meetings clauses would be abandoned, which effectively drove Grey out of the Government. See Littleton, *Diary*, 5 March 1835,
Hatherton MSS in A. Aspinall, *Lord Brougham and the Whig Party* (1927),
App. C, 292.

The Lichfield House Compact

The events of November 1834 to April 1835—the dismissal of Melbourne's Ministry, the short interlude of Peel's Conservative Government and the return of the Whigs to power—decisively affected not only English political alignments but also and even more dramatically the future of the Irish party. Melbourne's Government made no move towards an open alliance with O'Connell. They considered the possibility of making him Irish Attorney-General only to reject it, Melbourne remarking that even if they could bring themselves to give him a position 'adequate to his station and influence in Parliament and in the country', office would not shake O'Connell's hold on his countrymen since 'the people of Ireland are not such damned fools as the people of England'.[1] Ministers had come to no decision on the question of Appropriation when, on the death of the aged Earl Spencer and Althorp's removal from the Commons to the Lords, they were abruptly dismissed from office by the King.

William IV had not concealed his strong disapproval of the Whigs' increasingly liberal approach towards the Irish Church, and, though he did not say so publicly, of their equivocal relationship with O'Connell. Distrusting and disliking most of the ministers, particularly Brougham and Russell, he had convinced himself that the loss of Althorp's leadership in the Commons was fatal to the Government.[2] Melbourne helped to destroy his own Government. By emphasizing to the King 'that there was a serious division in the Cabinet' on the Irish Church question between reluctant reformers like Lansdowne, Spring Rice and by implication himself, and 'the Radical part' led by Russell and Duncannon who were prepared, if defeated in their attempt to bring forward 'very strong measures', to join Hume and O'Connell, Melbourne encouraged William to

---

[1] Melbourne to Russell, 23 August 1834, *Melbourne Papers*, 209–11.

[2] *Annual Register* (1834), 43 ff., for the King's speech to a delegation of Irish clergy on the day after the resignations of Stanley and Graham, expressing his attachment to the Church and his hostility to its enemies; William IV, Memo, 14 November; to Melbourne, 14 November 1834, Parker, *Peel*, II, 253–5. William had been disgusted by Brougham's undignified and megalomaniac speaking tour in Scotland, and according to Lord George Bentinck, 'had got to feel' about him 'as some people do when a cat is in the room.' Shocked by Russell's 'declared opinions on the Church', the King also thought him incapable of leading the Commons; Bentinck to ?, 18 December 1834, Welbeck MSS, quoted by Aspinall, *Three Diaries*, xxxii, n. 1; Lady Salisbury, 20 November 1834, Salisbury MSS.

believe that the Whig party was breaking up and that a Conservative Government would enjoy the support of many Whigs and Liberals who were not Radicals in disguise.[1] The rumour that the Queen had done it all was quite unnecessary, even given the Queen's opinions, as well as untrue.[2] William was perfectly willing, as Melbourne recognized, to act on his own. He had always been, despite the political moderation which he had shown during the Reform crisis, a bluff and unsophisticated Tory at heart. He was intelligent enough to recognize the Radical menace when Melbourne pointed it out, and, as Wellington told Lady Salisbury, the King 'had naturally looked forward to the event of Lord Spencer's death as likely to afford him a good opportunity of changing his ministers'.[3]

The Opposition had not been directly consulted. Peel, on holiday in Italy at the time, had disappointed many of his followers by the patience and moderation of his policy in opposition. Still to some extent nursing his past disagreements with Wellington, he was ready to wait for the Government to break up 'though its own differences and misunderstandings' and caustically condemned 'eternal fussy manoeuvring' and any suggestions of alliance with the Radicals.[4] He was now saddled with office and with uncomfortable and pressing legacies. 'The Duke or rather Peel', Spring Rice wrote, 'has to choose between two opposite resolutions—he must become a Liberal, a Church and Corporation Reformer—losing some character with his party and some Tory support—or he must make up his mind to a very short duration of his restored office or honour.'[5] The new Government was entirely Tory due to the refusal of Stanley and Graham to join it, but its programme, as laid down in the Tamworth Manifesto of December 1834, proclaimed a moderate reformism as

[1] Salisbury, 20 November 1834; 22 February 1835, Salisbury MSS; Melbourne to William IV, 12 November; to Grey, 14 November 1834, *Melbourne Papers*, 219-21, 224-6; to Wellesley, 15 November 1834, Wellesley Papers, Add. MSS 37307, 290-1. Over a year earlier, Macaulay thought it common knowledge that the Government would eventually break up; to Hannah Macaulay, 17 August 1833, in G. O. Trevelyan, *Life and Letters of Lord Macaulay* (1908), 235.

[2] For the leakage of the rumour, see *The History of the Times* (1935), I, 334-5. According to Creevey, the Queen thought of herself as another Marie Antoinette; *Creevey Papers*, II, 300.

[3] Salisbury, 26 November 1834, Salisbury MSS.

[4] For the difficulties with Wellington, see Parker, *Peel*, II, 227-42; Peel to Goulburn, 25 May; to Arbuthnot, 27 May 1834, Ibid., II, 243-4, 247.

[5] Spring Rice to Lord Suffield, 24 November 1834, Monteagle Papers, N.L.I.

the basis of the Conservative cause and thus marked an important stage in Peel's own political development.[1] For its immediate electoral purposes, as an appeal to the large body of non-Radical opinion which had hitherto supported Whig reforms, the Manifesto was undeniably effective; reinforced by Government and Crown influence, it caused a considerable swing in the Conservatives' favour in the General Election of December–January 1834–5.

Great gains in the English counties and boroughs together with an increase of nine seats in Ireland had cut the huge Whig majority of 1833 to one on paper of 80 or less. Ellenborough, for instance, calculated on between 280 and 290 firm Government supporters as against 150 Radicals and 218 Whigs and Stanleyites.[2] The Whigs might hopefully claim these results as promising 'much less for the government than for their opponents,'[3] but for orthodox ministerialist Whiggism the elections had been little short of disastrous. Three ex-ministers, including the unfortunate Littleton, were defeated, and moderate Whigs had lost seats principally to Tories but also to the English and Irish Radicals whose total representation in the House had perhaps even been doubled. One estimate, making Radical and Whig strengths almost equal at 170 and 180 Members respectively,[4] may have erred in favour of the Radicals; but it is at least certain that the results completely transformed the relationship of the Whig leadership to Radicals and Liberals whose previously doubtful support or even opposition, as in the case of the Irish party, had not decisively affected the stability of the Whig Government. If the Whigs ever returned to power, it would be on Radical votes and in particular with the support of O'Connell, who now virtually controlled over 60 Irish Members or somewhere between one-third and one-half of of the entire Radical contingent.

Between July and November 1834, O'Connell's guarded overtures

---

[1] Parker, *Peel*, II, 257–9; Ellenborough, *Diary*, 11, 12 December 1834, P.R.O. 30/12/28/5, 56, 59, on the attempt at 'a broad based Govt.' incorporating 'Leporello' [Graham] and 'Don Juan' [Stanley]; Peel to Graham, 9 December; Graham to Peel, 14 December 1834, Peel Papers, Add. MSS 40318, 7–9. For the composition, text and impact of the Manifesto, see. G Kitson Clark, *Peel and the Conservative Party, 1832–41* (1929), 209 ff.; Halévy, *History*, III, 178–9; Greville, *Journal*, 20 December 1834, III, 183–4.

[2] Ellenborough, *Diary*, 30 January 1835, P.R.O. 30/12/28/5, 155.

[3] Spring Rice to T. Drummond, 16 January 1835, Monteagle Papers, N.L.I.

[4] Sir John Walsh, *Chapters of Contemporary History* (1836), 184, quoted by Halévy, *History*, III, 180, n. 1.

of friendship, interlaced with threats, had met with little response from the Whig Government.[1] He failed to persuade Duncannon, Home Secretary from July 1834 and his one firm contact with the Whig leadership, to purge Irish central and local government in favour of Liberal Protestants and Catholics, and the appointment in October of Sergeant Michael O'Loghlen as Solicitor-General, the first Catholic to hold office in Ireland since the reign of James II, was made by the Whigs largely on their own initiative.[2] The dismissal of the Whigs completely altered the situation. Convinced that Tory government meant a return to the Protestant Ascendancy and the certain proscription of himself and his movement, O'Connell at once entered into an informal electoral alliance with Irish Whig-Liberalism. A shady journalist in the Tories' pay informed Wellington from Dublin that 'the most striking feature' of one of O'Connell's meetings 'was the presence of a good many of the Whig lawyerlings. Conway, the editor of the [Dublin Evening] Post, the government organ, appeared and made his peace with O'Connell—so that your Grace may be prepared for an *unprincipled* agitation—I repeat one of the most [sic] ever witnessed . . .'[3]

But an electoral alliance in Ireland contained no guarantee of future co-operation in Parliament and could not solve the urgent problem facing the Whig leaders, as summarized by Spring Rice:

> If questions are proposed which split the opposition into sections, Sir Robert's fortune is made, for he will have no opponents of sufficient strength to replace or carry on the Govt. if he is defeated; his would then become a government of *necessity*, as Ed. Ellice was accustomed to call

[1] O'Connell to Duncannon [n.d. August 1834]; to W. S. Crawford, 27 September 1834; to Duncannon, 11 October 1834; to Lord Durham, 21 October 1834, O'Connell Papers, N.L.I., 423; *O'Connell Corr.*, I, 489–92, 497–8; App. I, 536–8.

[2] O'Connell to Duncannon, 30 August; 2, 6, September; 2, 11 October 1834, *O'Connell Corr.*, I, 465–86, 489–92; Melbourne to Wellesley, 7 October 1834, Wellesley Papers, Add. MSS 37307, 198. O'Connell's attitude even to Duncannon was equivocal; while publicly welcoming his appointment, he wrote to the Radicals at Nottingham, where Duncannon was standing for re-election, a letter which might be interpreted as recommending opposition to Duncannon and certainly described the Whigs as 'cruel drags on the wheels of improvement'; O'Connell to B. Boothley, 17 July 1834, Rylands Library MSS quoted by Aspinall, *Brougham and the Whig Party*, App. C., 290–1.

[3] James Birch to Wellington, 22 [November 1834], Apsley House MSS, in Aspinall, *Politics and the Press*, 483. For the Election, see above pp. 58–62.

ours; and he would be justified in carrying on the public business even
after serious defeats.[1]

The first considered plan for uniting the Opposition came significantly from Radical circles, and envisaged not a monolithic union of
all the Opposition sections under Whig leadership but the formation
of three independent 'brigades' in a parliamentary coalition.
Towards the end of January 1835 Henry Warburton, a successful
Lambeth timber merchant and Radical M.P. for Bridport since
1826, wrote to O'Connell asking for his views on such a plan. He
explained that this 'brigading' was necessary to secure 'concert and
co-operation', which had been sadly lacking in the past two sessions
among the Opposition groups; it would be based on common interest
at least until the Tories had been defeated; and it was the only
alternative to serving under a Whig leadership in which the English
Radicals placed little confidence. Warburton, who was acting as
whip for the Radical brigade headed by George Grote, Joseph
Hume, Henry Ward and William Clay, asked O'Connell most tactfully for the names of any Irish Members likely to join 'our crew'
'rather than your party or that of the Whigs', and he at once secured
O'Connell's firm support for a united Opposition front.[2]

This Radical move, a distinct threat to the Whig leadership, forced
the Whigs seriously to consider their position and future tactics.
Melbourne, hoping for eventual reunion with Stanley and Graham
and worried by the possible consequences of leading a majority of
the Commons into 'a political warfare with the Crown, with the
decided majority of the House of Peers, with almost the whole of the
clergy and . . . with three parts at least of the gentlemen of the
country', strongly favoured, like the retired Grey, a moderate 'wait
and see' policy.[3] The liberal Whigs, essentially the same group which
had had its way in the crises of May and July 1834, were less
dominated by Melbourne's Radical bogy and much more realistic
about the effects of their dismissal and the Election results, which

[1] Spring Rice to Drummond, 16 January 1835, Monteagle Papers, N.L.I.

[2] Warburton to O'Connell, 20, 30 January 1835, O'Connell MSS, U.C.D.;
O'Connell Corr., I, 520; Graham Wallas, *The Life of Francis Place, 1771-1854*
(1951), 335-6. The plan seems to have originated with Warburton himself, who
was already corresponding with O'Connell on Irish election matters.

[3] Melbourne to Grey, 23 January 1835, *Melbourne Papers*, 239; Grey to
Melbourne, 1 February 1835, *Early Correspondence of Lord John Russell*, II, 84;
Halévy, *History*, III, 178, n. 3, for Melbourne's violent attack at this time on the
radicalism of the Dissenters.

had, as Duncannon bluntly remarked to Melbourne, 'imparted an almost sovereign sway to O'Connell'.[1] There was no chance of regaining office, and hence of initiating those liberal policies to which they were now committed, without a united Opposition which would begin offensive operations immediately.

The Speakership provided the first issue. Even Melbourne was ready to allow organized opposition to Charles Manners-Sutton, the present Speaker, who was generally suspected of having been concerned in the fall of the Whigs and the construction of Peel's Government;[2] but a strong candidate would certainly be needed against a man who had been for seventeen years a dignified and impartial Speaker. Thomas Spring Rice, an Irish landowner, an *Edinburgh Review* Whig and Colonial Secretary after Stanley, was most anxious for the position, but his universal affability and ingratiating manners had not increased his popularity.[3] The candidate of the Radicals and finally of the Whig Leaders was the experienced, respected and independent-minded Liberal M.P. for Edinburgh, James Abercromby. Writing to O'Connell to gain his support, Warburton emphasized that 'All on this side of the water agree in thinking Abercromby the fit man' and assured O'Connell that without Abercromby the Opposition would probably be defeated.[4] O'Connell certainly replied supporting Abercromby; he had no liking or respect for Spring Rice, who had been his official opponent on the Repeal motion, while Abercromby had supported O'Connell on the Coercion Bill and had recently been in touch with him over government policy. Abercromby's initial reluctance was overcome, a very disappointed Spring Rice was pacified, and the Opposition was now united behind a strong candidate.[5]

The liberal Whigs, having satisfactorily settled this preliminary issue, now set about organizing general opposition unity and sym-

[1] Duncannon to Melbourne, 18 December 1834, *Melbourne Papers*, 230.

[2] Melbourne to Grey, 6 February 1835, *Melbourne Papers*, 244–6; Spring Rice to C. Wood, 14 January 1835, Monteagle Papers, N.L.I., giving Russell's similar opinion.

[3] See the sharp comments of Le Marchant, *Diary* [n.d. May 1833], Aspinall op. cit., 326; and Lyndhurst's deadly witticism, reported by Creevey to Miss Ord, 7 January 1838, *Creevey*, ed. John Gore (1949), 383.

[4] Warburton to O'Connell, 20 January 1835, O'Connell MSS, U.C.D.

[5] O'Connell to Abercromby [n.d. September 1834], Walpole, *Russell*, I, 206–7; Spring Rice to Russell, 20 January 1835, Monteagle Papers, N.L.I.; Ellenborough, *Diary*, 2 February 1835, P.R.O. 30/12/28/5, 161.

bolizing it by a great party meeting. Much depended on Lord John Russell. The King was not alone in doubting his fitness for the post of leader of the Commons. Even in the inner circle of Whiggery, by no means prone to criticism of its members, old Lord Holland was worried by Lord John's inaction and incommunicativeness.[1] Russell may have been aloof and difficult, but he was also extremely ambitious. His pride must have been deeply wounded by the King's low opinion of his capacity and standing, and he made it clear, in a successful and widely reported speech at Totnes and in private letters, that he favoured an agressive opposition.[2]

The Irish party was the vital factor in the Opposition leaders' plans. Warburton, hearing with some impatience early in February that the Irish required individual invitations to the Opposition meeting planned for 18 February (the day before the beginning of the session) at Lord Lichfield's house in St. James's Square, sent off a bundle of circulars to O'Connell for distribution.[3] He did so not on his own authority but with the permission of Duncannon and Hobhouse. Russell himself must have known of Warburton's action and can scarcely have been surprised to receive an extremely friendly and co-operative letter from O'Connell, promising the support of some 60 or 62 Irish Members on the Speakership and wholeheartedly accepting Lord John's leadership in the name of his party. Russell characteristically drafted a cold and formal acknowledgment of this support, but he took the precaution of showing it first to Duncannon who knew O'Connell and the Irish well and bluntly pointed out that Russell would not last long as the Opposition leader if he began 'by trembling at shadows and quaking at the names of O'Connell and every other Radical who may tender you assistance'. Duncannon re-drafted the letter, slightly expanding it, emphasizing the common interests of the Whigs and the Irish party and virtually accepting O'Connell's co-operation.[4]

Russell's biographer attempts to absolve him from any direct share in the making of the Lichfield House Compact. But before

[1] Holland to Melbourne, 22 January 1835, *Melbourne Papers*, 232–3.

[2] Walpole, *Russell*, I, 212–13.

[3] Warburton to O'Connell, 3 February 1835, O'Connell MSS, U.C.D.

[4] O'Connell to Russell, 13 February 1835; Hobhouse to Russell, 3 February 1835; Russell, Draft, and as revised; Duncannon to Russell [n.d. February 1835], Walpole, *Russell*, I, 219–23. See also A. H. Graham, 'The Lichfield House Compact, 1835', *Irish Historical Studies*, XII, No. 47 (March 1961), 209–25, a valuable article.

Warburton sent out the circulars, Hobhouse, in the thick of the plot as the liaison between the Whigs and the English Radicals, told Ellenborough that the Opposition had formed two committees, 'one of Whigs [Russell, Spencer, Spring Rice, Duncannon and Hobhouse himself], the other of Radicals [O'Connell, Warburton, Hume and Gillon] which were to communicate upon every measure prepared by either Party'.[1] Russell was in fact implicated in the Opposition's plans. But he knew that the old Whigs, notably Grey and to a lesser extent Lord Lansdowne, disapproved particularly of an open alliance with the Irish party and he possibly feared that his own reputation might be damaged by any open communication with O'Connell. Most important, Melbourne, who naturally knew and did not approve of the liberal Whigs' activities, was less likely to make difficulties if Russell as well as himself could appear to be unconnected with them.[2] Thus on 11 February, some time after the circulars had gone out, Russell was able to pretend to Melbourne with some show of truth that he had only just heard of the plan for the great meeting on the 18th and that he had some doubts about it. Russell was covering the official Whig leadership from any possibly harmful effects of the plan; he could if necessary deny any part in negotiations which had been carried out by underlings; and he was allowing Melbourne to deny, as he did forcefully in April 1835, that he personally had come to any terms with O'Connell.[3]

The first short meeting at Lichfield House, involving only formal agreement on Abercromby's candidature, passed off successfully. But Russell's request that the Opposition, out of respect for Manners-Sutton, would not cheer a successful result went unheeded when Abercromby defeated his opponent by 316 votes to 306. Manners-Sutton had, on the combined English and Scottish vote, a clear majority of 10, and the Irish who had carried Abercromby to victory were 'particularly uproarious and disorderly'.[4] The Whig managers had known their numbers with astonishing accuracy,[5] on an issue which in view of the old Speaker's high reputation was

[1] Ellenborough, *Diary*, 2 February 1835, P.R.O. 30/12/28/5, 158.

[2] Grey to Russell, 23 February 1835, Walpole, *Russell*, I, 223–4, and n. 1, for Lansdowne's view; Melbourne to Grey, 6 February 1835, *Melbourne Papers*, 246.

[3] Russell to Melbourne, 11 February 1835, *Early Corr. of Lord John Russell*, II, 90; Hansard, XXVII, 997 ff., 18 April 1835, Melbourne.

[4] John O'Connell, *Recollections*, I, 129–30; Halévy, *History*, III, 181–2.

[5] Greville, *Journal*, 15, 20 February 1835, III, 211, 219. He won £55 by a judicious bet on Abercromby.

scarcely a true trial of strength; but they now knew that they were strong enough, provided that they could keep their Radical and Irish support, to overturn the Government.

If the first meeting was only the overture to alliance, the alliance itself was forged in the destruction of Peel's Government. Russell had made it clear that he would take no part in any future Whig Government in which Appropriation was left an open question.[1] The issue was bound to be raised in debate on the Tories' Irish Tithe Bill and apart from its intrinsic importance, Appropriation provided a plank on which the Whigs under Russell, the English and Scotch Radicals and the Irish under O'Connell could co-operate. An unexpectedly small majority of only seven against the Government on a moderate Whig amendment to the Address showed that without some drastic action on the Opposition's part, Peel might yet obtain the fair trial for which he had asked. Russell's hand was forced by the impatience of the Radicals.[2] Setting the seal on his growing reputation as a leader, he decided to take the vital Appropriation issue out of Radical hands and to lead the Opposition in a frontal attack on the Government.

On 27 March, he notified his intention to move for a Committee of the whole House to consider the application of the surplus revenues of the Irish Church 'to the religious and moral instruction of all classes of the community'. For Peel, increasingly unhappy with his position, this was equivalent to a motion of want of confidence. Most of his colleagues, including Wellington, wished to struggle on with the Government at all costs, and Ellenborough even suggested whipping up anti-Catholic feeling in England by meeting Russell's motion with one 'to the effect that the House would not adopt any measure which by weakening the Protestant Church would contribute to Roman Catholic Ascendancy in Ireland'.[3] But as Peel realistically explained to the King, there was no hope in an appeal on the Irish tithe question to the country or in reliance on the House of Lords. As he saw it, the only alternative to resignation was to abdicate responsibility for settling the tithe question to an Opposition bent on carrying on Appropriation; and, he asked

[1] Russell to Melbourne, 11 February 1835, *Melbourne Papers*, 254–5.

[2] Notably Henry Ward, with notice early in March of a motion on Appropriation and Hume, ready to limit supplies for three months as a motion of censure.

[3] Salisbury, 28 March 1835, Salisbury MSS; Ellenborough *Diary*, 25, 26 March 1835, P.R.O. 30/12/28/5, 230–5; Kitson Clark, *Peel*, 247.

cogently, 'shall we, beaten on [this] principle, still undertake the responsibility of government in Ireland'?[1]

After two defeats by majorities of 33 and 25, Peel finally resigned after Russell's motion on 7 April linking Appropriation with a final settlement of the tithe question had been carried by 27 votes.[2] Peel's short tenure of power, which saw a remarkable increase in Conservative strength and no doubt helped to efface bitter Tory memories of the 'betrayals' of 1829 and 1832, had been worth all its difficulties. 'Most Members', Littleton wrote at the end, 'felt the respect due to a fallen Enemy, who had combated throughout with honor.'[3] Throughout the struggle the Irish party voted solidly with the Opposition and had indeed, through the O'Connellite majority of 32 in the Irish representation, been the guarantee of final success. They had attended the great Opposition meetings in March and April at Lichfield House, in what John O'Connell called 'the dusty unfurnished drawing-rooms of that dingy-fronted mansion', and at a dinner given for Russell on 28 March, O'Connell had officially acknowledged the Whigs' leadership, declaring that 'it was the most delightful evening he ever passed in his life'.[4]

The making of the Lichfield House Compact was one of the most decisive events in British political history between 1832 and 1847. For its creators 'an alliance on honourable terms of mutual co-operation',[5] for its opponents an unprincipled league of office-hungry English Whigs with destructive Radicals and dangerous Irish separatists, the Compact was the subject of prolonged and vehement political controversy. There was no written agreement (though Tories did their best, by emphasizing an ambiguous phrase in one of Sheil's speeches,[6] to suggest that one existed) but an alliance based on an exchange of political advantages. The Whigs secured the defeat of Peel, their own return to office and the guarantee of a viable majority; they did so moreover without capitulating to the English Radicals or surrendering more, beyond lay Appropriation, than they were anyway prepared to yield; and on the basis of this alliance, they were to retain power for over six years.

[1] Peel to William IV; Memo, 29 March 1835, Parker, *Peel*, II, 298–302.

[2] Hansard, XXVII, 772, 861, 878 ff., 2, 6, 7 April 1835, Divisions.

[3] Littleton, *Diary*, 7 April 1835, Staffs. Record Office.

[4] John O'Connell, *Recollections*, I, 135; Greville, *Journal*, 31 March 1835, III, 244–5.

[5] Earl Russell, *Recollections and Suggestions* (1875), 135.

[6] Torrens, *Sheil*, II, 209.

O'Connell seemed to secure quite as real advantages. For five years he had occupied personally a remarkable and isolated position in the Commons, for three of those years as the leader of an independent party. The results of independence, at the cost of great efforts and much unpopularity in England, had probably disappointed him. He was now the leader of a less homogeneous, less united but larger Irish party allied to a Government dependent on his support, irrevocably pledged to carry through a sweeping Irish Church measure and tacitly accepting a generally reformist programme laid down by himself.[1] Like all political alliances, this one was temporary and terminable. O'Connell might take credit for its achievements; for its failures he would bear no immediate responsibility; and he had no difficulty in carrying the mass of Irish public opinion with him on this new departure of co-operation with a British Government. He could not have guessed, when on 18 April he and his sons took their seats on the rear minsterial benches, that the alliance would also involve submission, that it would deprive him of all freedom of manoeuvre and that it was to lead directly to the disruption of his independent party.

The Lichfield House Compact created a broad two-party system in British politics. Under the stress of this new system, the 'Derby Dilly', O'Connell's brilliantly derisive epithet for the attempt of Stanley and Graham to found a third party, rapidly disintegrated, its leaders gravitating steadily towards the Conservative party while many of their followers straggled back into Whiggism.[2] For the English Radicals, the Compact was in reality a decisive defeat. Their plan for an Opposition of independent 'brigades' was ruined largely by O'Connell's readiness to place himself and his party at the complete disposal of the Whig leadership, but also by the insistence of Hume, egged on by Brougham, that the Irish party should form an integral part of the general Liberal body.[3] Leaderless and with no national party organization to fall back on, the English Radicals had

[1] See Hansard, XXVI, 408, 26 February 1835, O'Connell. The programme covered, besides Appropriation, an unspecified extension of the Irish Reform Act together with Municipal Reform.

[2] Hansard, XXVI, 398, 26 February 1835, O'Connell. See D. W. J. Johnson, 'Sir James Graham and the "Derby Dilly"', *University of Birmingham Historical Journal*, IV (1953–)4, 66–80.

[3] Mrs. Grote, *The Personal Life of George Grote* (1873), 99. See John O'Connell, *Recollections*, I, 135, for Irish resentment at what they regarded as the Radicals' attempt to ostracize them.

been effectively nullified as a united and independent force in politics. They could make trouble, but they could not make or break Governments.

O'Connell's loyalty to the new alliance was immediately tested during the construction of Melbourne's second Government. He might reasonably have expected office and was ready to accept it, but Melbourne had long before decided to have nothing to do either with him, Brougham or Durham.[1] For a time O'Connell held the Government's future in his hands. Thomas Young, Melbourne's secretary and factotum, admitted to Littleton that O'Connell was 'the stumbling Block', and Russell was ready to break up the Government by renouncing office himself if O'Connell thought his exclusion an injustice. But O'Connell 'in the handsomest manner' made no difficulties, and the inevitable rumours that he had 'waived office on condition of nominating the Attorney and Solicitor-Generals for Ireland and of having a veto on the Lord Lieutenant' were largely unfounded.[2] The Liberal Protestant Louis Perrin had already been promised the Attorney-Generalship, and O'Loghlen, O'Connell's candidate for the post, had to be content with his old position as Solicitor-General.[3] But the Whigs were at least careful not to appoint anyone of whom O'Connell disapproved. Melbourne's ruthless exclusion of Lord Wellesley, which the furious victim himself attributed to O'Connell's influence, showed at least that the old Whig regime in Ireland was not to be resurrected.[4]

The Price of Alliance

To most English contemporaries, the Irish party seemed accurately to fulfil Henry Grattan's bitter prophecy that the Union would give Ireland 'revenge for all her wrongs; she will send into England, and into the bosom of her parliament, and the very heart of her con-

[1] O'Connell to Fitzpatrick, 10, 14 April 1835, *O'Connell Corr.*, II, 10–12; Melbourne to Grey, 23 January 1835, *Melbourne Papers*, 237. The King was quite as adamant on the subject of O'Connell.

[2] Littleton, *Diary*, 10 April 1835, Staffs. Record Office; Walpole, *Russell*, I, 234; Greville, *Journal*, 11 April 1835, III, 258; Ellenborough, *Diary*, 12 April 1835, P.R.O. 30/12/28/5, 260.

[3] Littleton, *Diary*, 11 April 1835, Staffs. Record Office; cf. O'Connell to Ellice, 14 April 1835, Ellice MSS, N.L.S., pkt. 48: 'You should promote O'Loughlin NOT Perrin.'

[4] *The Wellesley Papers*, ed. The Editor of 'The Windham Papers' (1914), II, 272–308.

stitution, a hundred of the greatest rascals that can be found anywhere'.[1] The hostility of English public opinion, embracing not only
the Repealers of 1832–5 but also the larger Irish Liberal party of
1835–41, forms a distinct theme throughout the party's history. The
traditional and deep-seated antipathy to Catholicism, transcending
class-barriers and forming an important element in the political
philosophy of most Englishmen, was confirmed by the general if
inaccurate view of the Irish party as wholly Catholic in composition
and also by direct acquaintance with the growing numbers of Irish
in England and Scotland. At least half a million by 1841, or about
one in 36 of the population in England and Scotland, concentrated
largely in the great cities of London, Liverpool, Manchester and
Glasgow and rapidly increasing both as permanent and seasonal
immigrants, the Irish remained unassimilated and highly unpopular,
the victims of economic fears and politico-religious prejudice. The
Irish party not only shared the unpopularity of their poverty-
stricken, immigrant countrymen, but also, as a party of landlords,
they incurred special odium with the steady hardening of English
opinion, from the late 1830's to the Famine, towards their class in
Ireland.[2]

In the narrower world of the politicians at Westminster, 'the
Irish Members', by tacit but widely accepted convention the
O'Connellite Members, were by almost universal consent the
pariahs of politics. The epithet of 'the Tail', in use as early as 1831
and throughout the period, exactly expressed the contemporary
view of the party's subservience to O'Connell and strongly implied
that its members, if not actually dishonest and disreputable, certainly
lacked any individual distinction. Set apart from the rest of the
House by undoubted differences of speech, manners and appearance,
O'Connell's followers were regarded as alien intruders and treated
as such, and John O'Connell's somewhat priggish complaints of the
rudeness of English Members were not unjustified.[3]

---

[1] Quoted by Lord Advocate Jeffrey, in *Memoirs, Journal and Correspondence
of Thomas Moore*, ed. Lord John Russell (1854), 25 April 1831, VI, 183–4.

[2] On the whole question of the numbers, unpopularity and economic status
of the Irish in England before 1847, see Freeman, *Pre-Famine Ireland*, 37–50,
who quotes from Engels' classic *The Condition of the Working Classes in England
in 1844*. For English opinion on Irish landlordism, see Black, *Economic Thought*,
32, 101–3, and below pp. 208, 292–3.

[3] *D.E.P.*, 5 April 1831, quoted by Whyte, 'O'Connell and the repeal party',
loc. cit., 297, n. 2; John O'Connell, *Recollections*, I, 47–57.

The 1830's undoubtedly witnessed a sharp decline in parliamentary manners and behaviour, yet because the Irish were frequently involved in disorderly scenes, some of which they undoubtedly instigated, it did not follow that they or the Radicals were always the chief culprits. John Arthur Roebuck wrote in 1833 of 'the *élite* of the great nation in the character of legislators', crowded into the 'small ill-conditioned room' of St. Stephen's Chapel, with Members 'lying at full length on the benches, talking, laughing, hooting, coughing, sleeping . . . '; noting with disgust the yells, groans and animal noises which frequently disfigured debates, Roebuck, who was no friend to O'Connell or to his party, still thought that the rudest and most boisterous elements were the young Tories. In 1840, O'Connell protested at the 'beastly bellowings' of Members; in his view at least the Irish were as much sinned against as sinning.[1]

The common accusation that the Irish Members lacked status and property might have constituted, if true, a valid criticism of their political value in the early nineteenth-century House of Commons. But it has already been shown that the Repeal party, like the Irish Whigs and Liberals, was strongly landed in composition and that most of its members came from Protestant and Catholic gentry families; in an age of unpaid M.P.s and expensive elections, the majority of Irish Members in this period seem to have been able to afford the very considerable expenses of political life. Only two, Feargus O'Connor and A. C. O'Dwyer, actually lost seats for lack of the necessary property qualifications.[2]

There seem to have been few parallels to the case of John O'Connell of Grenagh, (Daniel's brother, High Sheriff of Kerry in 1839 and the father of Morgan John O'Connell, M.P. for Kerry from 1835 to 1847), whose daughter-in-law, recording that he once spent £9,000 on one of his son's elections, wrote sadly that 'Hounds, open house,

[1] Halévy, *History*, III, 65, seems too hard both on the Irish and the Radicals; *Life and Letters of John Arthur Roebuck*, ed. R. E. Leader (1897), 52–3; John O'Connell. *Recollections*, I, 258–66. See also [James Grant], *Random Recollections of the House of Commons* (1836), 1–13, 61–2, 64, 75–9. Conditions and behaviour did not immediately improve in the new House after 1835.

[2] See above pp. 73–7; and Helen E. Wilmer, *The Property Qualifications of Members of Parliament* (1943), 130–5. Le Marchant, *Diary* [n.d. March 1833], Aspinall, op. cit., 314, in describing the Repealers as 'not [a] very creditable looking set', picked unerringly both on O'Connor and O'Dwyer and also on Patrick Lalor and W. J. O'Neill Daunt, who were both strongly suspected of lacking the qualifications and who both had short careers as Members.

my dear husband's London life and contested elections ruined him'.[1] The criterion of a gentleman was doubtless less strict in Ireland than in England; and Thackeray, whose first successful pieces in *Vanity Fair* concerned The O'Mulligan of Ballymulligan, a charming, feckless and amorous rogue closely modelled on The O'Gorman Mahon, found abundant material in Irish snobbery.[2] But the House of Commons was itself an intensely snobbish place, especially in its general reaction to Irish 'outsiders', and Irish obstreperousness was in part a reaction to English misunderstanding, ridicule and prejudice.

The general charge of the party's subservience to O'Connell was scarcely deserved. Revolts against his leadership occurred on Repeal in 1833, on the Tithe question and on the Poor Law. Indeed during the period of the Whig alliance O'Connell emerges as a leader remarkable more for tolerance than for ruthless punishment of independence, and this despite the fact that for members of his own family, personal followers and M.P.s with large and radical constituencies, discipline was to some extent built into the electoral origins of the party. Nonetheless, in an age when both Government and Opposition relied rather on a highly-skilled management of individuals than on any strict and over-riding party allegiance, even a general acceptance of O'Connell's leadership seemed both novel and deplorable. Together with the party's sensitivity to Irish opinion, it constituted a violation of the Burkeian doctrine of Members' independence as enunciated by the High Church Tory Sir Robert Inglis in 1831: 'This House is not a collection of deputies ... We are not sent here day by day to represent the opinions of our constituents. Their local rights, their municipal privileges we are bound to consult at all times; but not their will, unless it shall coincide with our own deliberate sense of right.'[3]

---

[1] Mrs. M. J. O'Connell, *The Last Colonel of the Irish Brigade, Count O'Connell*, II, 307–8.

[2] Gwynn, *The O'Gorman Mahon*, 159–67; see W. M. Thackeray, *The Book of Snobs* (1889), 98–101.

[3] Hansard, II, 1096, 1 March 1831, Inglis. Radicals no doubt regarded these views as archaic and inadmissible, but many Whigs would have sympathized strongly with Inglis, and most M.P.s, even some Radicals, cherished their personal independence and believed in the exercise of individual judgement while often submitting to the claims of party discipline. It was this independence in particular which his followers were accused of having lost to O'Connell and which a Liberal like Smith O'Brien was so anxious to preserve; see above p. 98.

Even regular attendance was held against the Irish. Greville contrasted the voting habits of Conservatives whose busy social life presented problems to their party's whips with a large section of their opponents, 'a dense body of fellows who have no vocation out of the walls of the House of Commons; who put up in the vicinity; either do not dine at all, or get their meals at some adjoining chophouse, . . . and never think of moving till everything is over . . . these blackguards, the chief of whom are O'Connell's Tail and the lower Radicals'.[1]

The party's reputation was undoubtedly damaged by its quota of rascals, men such as Patrick Somers and Robert Dillon Browne who according to Charles Gavan Duffy, 'would have professed themselves Mormons rather than be excluded from Bellamy's and the smoking room of the House of Commons';[2] or Sir Valentine Blake, a shifty and impecunious baronet who wrote to Peel in 1838 with 'a high respect for your extraordinary talent & vast experience', deploring as a Catholic the priesthood's interference in politics which had cost him two defeats in Galway and advising Peel to impose a high municipal franchise in order to neutralize it. In 1845 he went further, offering in exchange for office to test Irish feeling on Peel's policy by seeking the necessary re-election. In 1847 he obliged the Whigs by resigning his seat for the borough of Galway so that James Monahan, the newly-appointed Solicitor-General, could stand for Parliament.[3] Sheil, a speaker of great eloquence and one of the few Irish Members to take an active and informed interest in foreign affairs, was not in this low category, but in February 1834

[1] Greville, *Journal*, 26 March 1835, III, 241. See also Charles Dickens, *Sketches by Boz* (1890), 118, for the complaints of the butler that Bellamy's actually lost by the patronage of the Irish Members who each ate 'more dinner than three English Members put together . . . drank table-beer by the half-gallon; and went home to Manchester Buildings or Millbank Street for [their] whiskey-and-water'.

[2] Duffy, *Young Ireland*, I, 27. For Somers' later high reputation as a manipulator of patronage, which seems ironically to have brought about his downfall, see Whyte, *Independent Irish Party*, 46. Browne, drunken and recklessly extravagant, the traditional Western gentleman, was also a fine popular speaker; O'Neill Daunt, *Journal*, 7 July 1845, N.L.I., 2040.

[3] Blake to Peel, 25 June, 1838, [n.d. April 1845], Peel Papers, Add. MSS 40425, 178–80; 40564 (latter ref. from McDowell, *Public Opinion*, 138, n. 3); Gwynn, *Young Ireland and 1848*, 100–1. This Galway by-election saw the first and unsuccessful attempt by the Irish Confederates to unseat a Government placeman.

he was accused by Althorp of having used language in private on the Coercion policy very different from his public utterances. Although he was formally acquitted by a Select Committee, the accusation had been made by a man with an enviable reputation for sincerity and honesty, and the episode, besides causing yet another disorderly scene in the Commons, was a blot on Sheil's character and a further blow to his party's reputation.[1]

Yet the party as a whole scarcely deserved its violent treatment at the hands of Young Ireland, who had no time for a collection of 'scamps, drivellers, fribbles and placehunters' representing, in Madden's words, the 'Donnybrook Fair school of patriotism'.[2] The Repealers included serious, able and public-spirited men like the formidable Dr. Baldwin, whose knowledge of Irish conditions deeply impressed Littleton; Henry Grattan, described by one observer of politics as straightforward, bold and generous, 'the best type of wild Irishman'; the earnest and eccentric Edward Southwell Ruthven and Andrew Lynch, an able lawyer who took an active interest in public works in Ireland.[3] None of O'Connell's sons inherited their father's genius, although John later revealed considerable and unsuspected gifts as a political tactician; but The O'Conor Don, Richard Bellew, the Macnamaras, N. A. Vigors, J. H. Talbot, Charles Walker, William and David Roche constituted, with several others, a highly respectable rank and file in the party.

It is undeniable that with the exception of O'Connell himself and perhaps Sheil, the Repeal party produced no men of the calibre and distinction of William Sharman Crawford, Thomas Wyse and William Smith O'Brien and that the relations between O'Connell and these outstanding Liberals were by no means always good. By December 1836 Crawford, the father of tenant right and of federalism, had regained his political independence to become O'Connell's

---

[1] Torrens, *Sheil*, II, 152–73. It is unlikely that Sheil was entirely innocent, but his fears that O'Connell would use the incident in order to ruin him were unfounded. See O'Connell to Barrett, [n.d. February 1834], O'Connell Papers, N.L.I., 10523: 'Sheil *must* be triumphant—There is not the least danger of his reputation suffering permanently . . . the most brilliant and honest public man that ever represented their County [sc. Tipperary]'.

[2] *Nation*, 26 December 1846; Madden, *Ireland and Its Rulers*, I, 247–50.

[3] Littleton, *Diary*, 11 July 1833, Aspinall, op. cit., 346–7; Grant, *Random Recollections of the House of Commons*, 324–9; for Lynch, see below p. 205, n. 2. Grattan produced, between 1839 and 1846, a five-volume biography of his father, the Anglo-Irish leader.

fiercest Irish critic.[1] Wyse, a well-informed, cultured but entirely
humourless man whom his biographer describes as 'the most important figure in the whole history of Irish education', was scarcely fitted
for the rough world of Irish politics and though often personally on
good terms with O'Connell kept aloof from any close political association.[2] Smith O'Brien, who had a useful parliamentary career behind
him before he finally joined the nationalist movement in 1843, was
actively interested in emigration, education and the construction of
Irish railways. In 1837 he clashed with O'Connell on the issues of
ballot and state payment for the Catholic clergy, but reasonably good
relations were restored after 1839 when he received the usual request
from O'Connell for his attendance in Parliament. In April 1839
O'Connell persuaded him most tactfully to drop his Bills for reform
of voting regulations and an annual revision of the registries, because
'. . . . if they pass, they annihilate the liberal interest in Ireland. I
know that I have no influence nor have any right to have influence
over you but surely you cannot doubt that I am thoroughly
acquainted with the present system'.[3]

The return of the Whigs to power in 1835 was one of the few
occasions in modern British political history when a small party,
holding the political balance of power, virtually dictated which of the
two major parties should constitute the Government.[4]

How did this action affect the Government and the Irish party?
Melbourne's second Administration to some extent deserved the
harsh judgements of its opponents. With notable exceptions including Melbourne himself and Russell, few of its members increased
their reputations.[5] The Whigs' handling of finance was extremely

[1] See B. A. Kennedy, 'Sharman Crawford's Federal Scheme for Ireland', in
Essays in British and Irish History, 235–54; and the references to Crawford in
R. Barry O'Brien, *Parliamentary History of the Irish Land Question* (1880).

[2] Auchmuty, *Wyse*, 101, 135–9; Auchmuty, *Irish Education*, 68–123.

[3] O'Connell to O'Brien, 5, 13 April; 29 June 1839, O'Brien Papers, N.L.I.,
430. There is regrettably and surprisingly no life of Smith O'Brien; but see
Gwynn, *Young Ireland and 1846*, esp. 14–21 et seq., a book which makes valuable
use of the huge and largely unpublished collection of O'Brien's Papers in the
National Library.

[4] A similar position was enjoyed by the Peelites and the Irish party in 1852, by
the Irish again in 1885–6 and by the Liberals in 1929–31.

[5] This was admitted even by Whigs; see Normanby to Russell, 29 July 1838;
Duke of Bedford to Russell, 24 August 1838, Russell Papers, P.R.O. 30/22/2B,
632–7, 663–4. Both writers excepted Melbourne and Russell, Bedford added
Howick, Lord Grey's prickly eldest son who resigned in September 1839.

inept. While they were perhaps merely unlucky in their near-defeat and temporary resignation in May 1839 on the suspension of the Jamaican constitution, it was certainly not due to the Government's general policy that the Canadian revolt of 1837 produced in the Durham Report a document of great importance for the future of the Empire. Palmerston's hard-earned diplomatic victory over France in 1840–1 almost disrupted the Government. Yet even apart from the Whigs' general policy towards Ireland, a legislative record in England which included a complete reform of borough government, the administration of the new Poor Law of 1834, much needed reforms in the finances of the Church, the creation of a registry of births, deaths and marriages, the grant of a charter to London University, the reduction of newspaper taxation and the introduction of penny postage was by no means contemptible. It was achieved despite a political position of increasing difficulty and uncertainty.[1]

William IV's attitude was at best one of suspicious and grudging co-operation. After 1837, the Whigs relied heavily on the active goodwill and firm support of the young Queen Victoria, which while it could not solve their problems in the Commons could at least bring them back to office, with their reputations somewhat tarnished, after the Bedchamber crisis of May 1839. Their entire legislative programme was at the mercy of forces beyond their control. The overwhelming Tory majority in the Lords[2] could never be coerced by the threat of large ministerialist creations, and while Wellington was in general more moderate than most of his followers, on Irish questions in particular he was often under strong diehard pressure emanating largely though not exclusively from the Irish Tory 'interest' in the Lords.[3] The entrenched Toryism of the peers not only directly affected the Government's Irish measures but tended

See Howick to Ellice, 6 September 1839, Ellice MSS, N.L.S., pkt. 32, a formidable indictment of the leadership, personnel and policies of 'a government of departments'.

[1] For general histories and judgements of the Government, see Halévy, *History*, III, 185–351; E. L. Woodward, *The Age of Reform, 1815–1870* (2nd edn. 1962), esp. 94–103; and Southgate, *Passing of the Whigs*, 61–75.

[2] See Salisbury, 26 February 1835, Salisbury MSS, for Wellington's happy remark on the Lords to Count Esterhazy: 'Ah . . . c'est le bon vieux temps là—nous avons une majorité de trois à un—all gentlemen there.'

[3] David Large, 'The House of Lords and Ireland in the Age of Peel, 1832–50', *Irish Historical Studies*, IX, No. 36 (September 1955), 367–71, for figures on Irish landownership of peers generally and on the almost wholly Tory politics of the 27 Irish representative peers.

constantly to cause damaging splits in the Conservative leadership, as Peel followed a policy of cautious forbearance and moderate reform which he called 'making the Reform Bill work . . . , falsifying our own predictions . . . [and] protecting the authors of the evil from the work of their own hands'. One vital aspect of Peel's policy of waiting for the tide to turn finally in the Conservatives' favour was, as Greville noted, the settlement of outstanding Irish questions and the establishment of the Irish government 'on a footing from the practice of which he could not deviate, and that once effected up to a certain point (as far as the Whigs can go) he would be enabled to go a good deal farther . . .'[1]

The constant support of the Irish party, important enough from 1835 to 1837 when the Government enjoyed a majority only a little larger than the size of the whole Irish Liberal contingent, became a vital necessity after the 1837 Election, when this majority was cut to perhaps 40 on paper and to rather less, between 20 and 40, in practice.[2] Lady Holland summed up the position succinctly: ' "The fact is we have nothing to rely upon but the Queen and Paddy" ' ; and in May 1839 on the Government's temporary collapse, Russell told O'Connell that 'It is a pleasure which I cannot refuse myself to acknowledge the constant & disinterested support which you have given to the Ministry in which I held a Department closely connected with the Affairs of Ireland'.[3]

It was indeed a well deserved tribute. Until 1841 O'Connell acted as an additional but vital whip for the Government. His party's organization in London seems always to have been informal, but the Irish now attended the official Whig meetings and most of them belonged to Brooks's or after 1836 to the Reform Club, those vital adjuncts to party organization.[4] Indeed the Whigs' 'capture' of the

[1] Peel to Croker, 5 March 1833, Parker, *Peel*, II, 216; Greville, *Journal*, 18 February 1838, IV, 65.

[2] K. B. Smellie, *A Hundred Years of English Government* (1950), App. III, 327, gives figures for 1837–41 of 339 'Reformers' and 319 Conservatives; Betty Kemp, 'The General Election of 1841', *History*, XXXVII (June 1952), 150, estimates the pre-1841 Whig majority at 24; but see below p. 193, for the slightly larger majorities on the vital Appropriation question.

[3] Greville, *Journal*, 23 September 1839, IV, 250; Russell to O'Connell, 9 May 1839, Russell Papers, P.R.O. 30/22/3C, 1044, printed by Walpole, *Russell*, I, 321.

[4] The earlier separate meetings of the party had been usually held at O'Connell's different London houses in Langham Place, Albemarle Street and 9 Clarges Street, or at the British Hotel, Jermyn Street, 'the old quarters'; James Tighe to T. M. Ray, 31 January 1847, O'Connell Papers, N.L.I., 696.

latter Club, which was originally planned as a Radical centre, was symbolized by Ellice's insistence that O'Connell should be a member of the Club's founding committee.[1]

But retention of power on Irish support, involving the Whigs in long and uphill parliamentary struggles on Irish questions, also largely contributed to the gradual loss of prestige and popularity which had been inherited from the great days of the Reform Bill. The Opposition's campaign to persuade English public opinion that the Whigs, as Disraeli wrote later, were in 'dark but baffled confederation with an Irish section, not viewed without distrust by the great body of the liberal party', was remarkably successful.[2] *The Times*, finally throwing off its Whig proclivities during Peel's first Government and appealing to English consciences and Protestant prejudices against Irish landlordism and political Catholicism, regaled its upper and middle class readers with constant and violent attacks on the 'Crim-Connell Administration', the 'O'Connell Cabinet and Household', and on O'Connell himself, the 'scum condensed of Irish bog', a man 'whose principles we hold in abhorrence, as those of the worst being in human form that ever disgraced the floor of an English Senate'.[3]

O'Connell was at least partly to blame for this damaging feud with *The Times* and for the general lack of support from the English press. In July 1833 he had attacked the English newspapers, particularly *The Times* and the Liberal *Morning Chronicle*, for distorting or failing to report his speeches and had attempted, when *The Times* staff declared that they would not report any of his speeches until he apologized, to call the owners and printers of the paper to the bar of the House.[4] Although he failed and finally apologized, this attack, regarded as an abuse of his privileges as an M.P. and as a deliberate victimization of the newspapers in their exposed and uncertain

[1] Gash, *Politics*, 408.

[2] B. Disraeli, *Lord George Bentinck* (1852), 14.

[3] *Times*, 16 June 1836. See *History of The Times*, I, 333–89, for the whole feud between the paper and O'Connell and for the paper's opposition to the Whigs. The first phrase is a particularly unscrupulous allusion to the unsuccessful action brought against Melbourne for criminal conversation in June 1836. See *Campbell*, II, 82–5, 89, who was convinced that Tories were behind the action.

[4] Hansard, XIX, 1242–52; XX, 6–7, 67–95, 25, 26, 29 July 1833, Debates on O'Connell's motion, which was lost by 48 votes to 153. O'Connell exploited the fact that newspapers only reported speeches in Parliament on sufferance and were technically committing a breach of privilege in doing so.

position, was not forgotten; and in 1836 he proceeded to make an enemy of John Walter II, the owner of *The Times* who took an active interest in the paper's policy after 1841 and loathed O'Connell, his programme and his religion.[1] The paper hounded O'Connell until his death, and there is little doubt that while its opposition helped to sap the Whigs' position in the country, it also robbed O'Connell's party and movement of the sympathy of informed English opinion.

Personal attacks on O'Connell, as the most convenient method of discrediting the Whigs, became an accepted convention of political life. From his quarrel with O'Connell in May 1835 the unknown young Disraeli at least secured valuable publicity. Earlier, in April, Lord Alvanley, a Whig wit apparently disappointed of place, attempted to disrupt the new Whig-Irish alliance by inconvenient questions in the Lords; foiled by Melbourne and insulted by O'Connell, who called him 'a bloated buffoon' but would not give him satisfaction, Alvanley tried to organize O'Connell's expulsion from Brooks's.[2] In November Sir Francis Burdett, never an admirer of the Whigs, now moving rapidly towards Toryism and disgusted by what he regarded as the vulgarity of O'Connell's Lords Reform speeches in Scotland and the north of England in September, made a similar appeal. On both occasions, the club's managers, who included Duncannon and Ellice, refused to adopt the doctrine that a club was responsible for the private and political behaviour of its members; but their second refusal cost them the resignations of 100 members including Stanley, Graham and Burdett himself.[3]

Personal hostility to O'Connell, based on disgust at the coarseness of his attacks on opponents, on intense disapproval of his political methods and on a general fear of his real as opposed to his apparent intentions, became almost an obsession with many

[1] *History of The Times*, II, 8.

[2] For Disraeli's breach with O'Connell, his connections with Lyndhurst and with *The Times*, and his political activities against the Government, including his authorship of the *Runnymede Letters*, see *History of The Times*, I, 368–9, 438–441. For the Alvanley episode, see Fagan, *O'Connell*, II, 373–88; Hansard, XXVII, 997 ff., 1009, 18, 20 April 1835, Alvanley, Melbourne, O'Connell; Creevey to Miss Ord, 5 May 1835, *Creevey Papers*, II, 304–5. Morgan O'Connell, representing his father and the Irish party, fought an inconclusive duel with Alvanley in Regent's Park.

[3] Patterson, *Burdett*, II, 636–44; Greville, *Journal*, 22 November 1835, III, 327. In April 1837, Burdett made O'Connell and the Irish-Whig alliance the theme of his successful re-election as a Conservative for Westminster, the traditional Radical stronghold.

politicians. The correspondence of Lord Ripon, at any moment expecting the Whigs 'to advance under the impulse of O'Connell at a rail-road Pace to a Republick', and of Sir James Graham contains many variations on this theme, while old Lord Wellesley wrote to Peel in 1837 describing the Irish Government as 'Folly & Vanity mutually offering incense to each other, & then kneeling together in joint adoration at the bloody shrine of O'Connell.'[1] From his some-what costive retirement at Howick, Lord Grey protested constantly and bitterly at an alliance which seemed to disgrace the fair name of Whiggism. Unable in 1835 to 'understand the security which the Ministry derives from the majority of 35 depending upon such an unprincipled villain as O'Connell', Grey was much amused in 1839 by the difference in Whig attitudes towards Louis Papineau and the Canadian rebels on one hand and 'O'Connell & his fellow scoundrels in Ireland and Scotland' on the other. In his view, Papineau was undoubtedly 'the lesser villain of the two'.[2] The young Tory Glad-stone, though later a warm admirer of O'Connell, admitted to being hotly prejudiced at this time against him, while Wellington's circle was shocked by O'Connell's unusual presence at Lansdowne House in May 1835, 'the first time', Lady Salisbury wrote, 'I have heard of him in a gentleman's house'. Later she reported Melbourne's remark, 'Why, you know, after one has had O'Connell, one may have anybody!'[3]

In reality the Whig leadership kept its social contacts with O'Con-nell to a minimum, leaving any necessary entertainment of him to Duncannon or to Mulgrave and his successor in Dublin, Lord Ebrington. It was not until three years after the making of the alliance that Lady Holland met O'Connell at Duncannon's, 'liked him much' and hoped (but apparently did not succeed) to have him at Holland House. During his embassy in 1840 Guizot was surprised at not meeting O'Connell in Whig circles, and a special dinner had to be arranged by the wife of E. J. Stanley, one of the Secretaries of

[1] Ripon to Graham, 20 October 1835, 26 December 1836; Graham to Stanley, 25 April 1835, 21 January 1838, Graham MSS; Wellesley to Peel, 20 February 1837, Peel Papers, Add. MSS 40423, 46–8.

[2] Grey to Ellice, 26 November 1835, September 1837, 2 January 1839, Ellice MSS, N.L.S., pkt. 11. In 1837, he wrote of his own Reform Bill as having raised 'a new Rienzi, . . . his dictatorship & the democracy of the Towns para-mount to all the other interests of the State'.

[3] O'Rourke, *Life of O'Connell*, 283–6; Salisbury, 28 May; 1 November 1835, Salisbury MSS.

the Treasury, to bring Guizot, O'Connell, Russell and Duncannon together. Guizot, who was much impressed by O'Connell, left an interesting and perceptive description of him, 'tall, bulky, robust, animated, his head a little sunk between the shoulders, with an air of strength and shrewdness, . . . [he] was neither elegant nor vulgar, his manner a little embarrassed yet firm, with even a tincture of suppressed arrogance', his politeness to Englishmen tinged with a mixture of humility and pride.[1]

Whatever the effects in England of the alliance with O'Connell, in Ireland it allowed the Whigs to attempt to prove that the Union could provide a government sympathetic to the outlook of the majority, and one, moreover, which for six years accomplished the rare and difficult feat of remaining both efficient and internally united.[2] The combination of Mulgrave as Lord Lieutenant until 1839, when he was succeeded by the equally liberal Ebrington, Lord Morpeth as Chief Secretary, Thomas Drummond as Under-Secretary and Russell at the Home Office was a remarkably happy one. In Drummond, the ex-officer of Engineers and protégé of Althorp, the Whigs produced the most outstanding civil servant, with the possible exception of Sir Anthony MacDonnell, ever to grapple with Irish problems. He reformed the entire police system, freely recruiting the new Royal Irish Constabulary from the Catholic population, infused a new spirit of impartiality into the administration of justice and was largely responsible for the important Report of the Commission on Irish Railways, whose plan for state aid in the construction of trunk lines, though incorporated in Morpeth's Bill of 1839, unfortunately foundered on parliamentary indifference and en-

[1] Earl of Ilchester, *Chronicles of Holland House, 1820–1900* (1937), 236; F. Guizot, *An Embassy to the Court of St. James's in 1840* (1862), 135–8. For evidence that O'Connell was not at his best in polite society, see *Lady Morgan's Memoirs*, II, 291; cf. Disraeli's description of O'Connell at Queen Victoria's coronation. He 'looked very well, and was deeply interested in everything, but was hooted greatly, *on dit*, by the mob': to Sarah Disraeli [2 July 1837], Monypenny, *Disraeli*, II, 32.

[2] See R. B. McDowell, 'The Irish Executive in the nineteenth century', *Irish Historical Studies*, IX, No. 35 (March 1955), 264–80. The record of disagreements and disharmony between Viceroys and Chief Secretaries, stemming from a governmental structure which was fatally unclear as to individual and final responsibility, lasted as long as the Union; attempts to reform the system were never successful and, at ministerial level, never very whole-hearted; and O'Connell himself always opposed, on logical nationalist grounds, the abolition of a separate executive which was the last vestige of legislative independence.

trenched *laissez-faire* dogmatism.[1] His refusal to tolerate magistrates who flaunted their Orangeism or to co-operate with importunate tithe-owners and, even more notably, his courageous reminder to Irish landlords that they had duties as well as rights delighted liberals as much as they infuriated Tories; and the Government successfully weathered the inevitable counter-attack from the House of Lords, where the Irish Tories under Roden broke free from Wellington's control in March 1839 and appointed an investigatory committee of inquiry into the state of Ireland.[2]

The least original aspect of Whig administration, a patronage policy designed to conciliate all shades of liberal and nationalist opinion as well as to maintain vital Irish parliamentary support, profoundly affected the Irish party. This deliberate policy was greatly facilitated by the centralization of patronage at the Castle, itself a growing bureaucratic machine which controlled the appointment to all judgeships, paid and unpaid magistracies, legal posts in Dublin and assistant-barristerships (for legal and specifically electoral work) in the provinces, posts under the Irish Poor Law Commission after 1838 and to all ranks in the army and in the rapidly growing police force. In January 1836 Russell reported that he had had 'a good deal of correspondence' with the King 'respecting the employment of Roman Catholics—& even of the more violent Party in Ireland, which I contended was right & necessary with caution & selection.

'It ended by an admission of what I said but with the more homely than royal jest that if only the sound parts were to be cut off, the Tail would be but little diminished!'[3]

The correspondence of Russell and Mulgrave between 1835 and 1839 abounds with the minutiae of patronage. In January 1836, to still the fears of Lansdowne and Spring Rice, Mulgrave strongly contradicted reports that '"the last four Assistant Barristers have been *all* named from the Repeal Party"', though he admitted that

[1] See J. F. McLennan, *Memoir of Thomas Drummond* (1867); R. Barry O'Brien, *Life and Letters of Thomas Drummond* (1889); Woodward, *Age of Reform*, 347–8; McDowell, *Public Opinion*, 177–203; and Black, *Economic Thought*, 191–4.

[2] Large, 'House of Lords and Ireland', loc. cit., 379–80. Mulgrave left Ireland for the Colonial Office soon after the episode of the Roden Committee, but Drummond, who emerged triumphant from an unpleasant cross-examination, remained until his death in May 1840.

[3] Russell to Mulgrave, 15 January 1836, H.O. Papers, 100/251, 145.

these appointments had O'Connell's approval; in October, he was anxious to gratify Christopher Fitzimon, M.P. for County Dublin, since 'this would be one of the very few unobjectionable ways of pleasing O'Connell. Fitzsimon is a man of excellent character and good family and is married to Dan's favourite daughter. I am told that upon vacating the Co. Dublin [the Whig Lord] Brabazon would come in without a contest. This in itself would be a triumph.'[1] Fitzsimon was duly provided for as Clerk of the Hanaper in Ireland. Sheil, whose attack on the dying Duke of York in 1826 had never been forgiven, could not be helped during William IV's lifetime. Mulgrave found him 'very reasonable' about his exclusion in 1836 during a general reshuffle of the legal appointments, but by September 1837 thought he had become 'a little fidgetty'. Besides, with an English office (and a rich wife), 'he would keep exactly the sort of open house which is so wanted for Irish Members on our side particularly at the dead time of year'.[2] In February 1838 Sheil was appointed Commissioner of Greenwich Hospital, a sinecure worth, according to a delighted O'Connell, at least £1,200 a year in '"money and marbles"', and in August 1839 he was promoted to the Vice-Presidency of the Board of Trade.[3]

O'Connell himself became deeply implicated in the Government's patronage policy, sending his recommendations directly to Drummond and pressing the claims of his own family as well as of friends and supporters.[4] His son Morgan became in 1840 Assistant Registrar of Deeds in Dublin; Nicholas Fitzsimon, Christopher's brother, was settled with a knighthood and a police magistracy; another son-in-law, not an M.P., was helped in hard times by appointment to a

[1] Mulgrave to Russell, 9 January; 27 October 1836, Russell Papers, P.R.O., 30/22/2A, 2C.

[2] Mulgrave to Russell, 27 October 1836; 2, 16 September 1837, Russell Papers, P.R.O., 30/22/2C, 2F; Torrens, Sheil, II, 251–7.

[3] O'Connell to Fitzpatrick, 15 February 1838, O'Connell Corr., II, 128. Sheil was later Judge-Advocate (1841), Master of the Mint in Russell's first Government (1847–50) and British Minister at Florence (1850–1), where he died.

[4] O'Connell to Drummond, 24 March; 20 June; 9 July; 13 October 1836; 17 August; 25 September; 1 November 1837; 2 February; 16 July 1838; 8 April; 30 July 1839, O'Connell-Drummond Papers, N.L.I., 2152, a correspondence covering proposals for reforms on Trinity College lands, criticisms of various law appointments and of the distribution of honours to Catholics, suggestions for purging Commissions of the Peace and including recommendations for the posts of Teller in the Stamp Office, Auditor for Dublin under the Poor Law and Paymaster.

magistracy, and Richard Barrett, the editor of *The Pilot*, was recommended to Drummond's notice as 'a man of the purest integrity and of the best principles'.[1] The extent of O'Connell's influence was perhaps exaggerated by contemporaries, but despite occasional difficulties the Government did its best to gratify or at least to consult him. In 1837, writing to inform O'Connell that the Repealer Andrew Carew O'Dwyer was to be made Filacer of the Exchequer, Drummond assured him that 'If there are persons who have represented to you, that your recommendations do not receive that fair consideration to which they are justly entitled, I shall only say that I hope they have done so in ignorance of the facts, and not from a desire to promote their own selfish ends, at the risk of more important ends.'[2] When the Whigs contemplated making Sir John Campbell Lord Chancellor in Ireland in place of Lord Plunket they first obtained O'Connell's approval.[3]

The original Repeal party, rigidly excluded from the spoils system in the early years of its existence and unprotected by any specific pledges against office or patronage, was disrupted by its place-hunger and by the Government's willingness to gratify it. Ten of its thirty-nine members received offices, places or titles. In addition to the places found for Morgan O'Connell, the Fitzsimons and O'Dwyer, Henry Barron and David Roche acquired baronetcies and Andrew Lynch an English Mastership of Chancery, while Sheil, The O'Conor Don and Richard Bellew later became junior ministers as naturally as orthodox Catholic Liberals such as Wyse and Richard More O'Ferrall.[4] A firm offer of high judicial office, the Mastership

[1] O'Connell to Drummond, 16 March; 4 September 1836, O'Connell-Drummond Papers; *O'Connell Corr.*, II, 381. Morgan O'Connell got his place from D. R. Pigot, the Attorney-General, who had been an O'Connellite Liberal.

[2] Drummond to O'Connell, 23 September 1837, Drummond Papers, N.L.I., 2149, 431–5. The Raphael case (see above p. 123) nicely illustrates the limitations of O'Connell's influence. He applied to Melbourne through Mulgrave for a baronetcy for Raphael; Melbourne's answer was 'anything but favourable', and Mulgrave wisely did not communicate again with O'Connell on the subject; Mulgrave to Russell, 12 February 1836, Russell Papers, P.R.O. 30/22/2A.

[3] *Campbell*, II, 200–1, n. 1; see also Duncannon to O'Connell, 19 October 1836, O'Connell MSS, U.C.D., on filling a vacant judgeship.

[4] Madden, *Ireland and Its Rulers*, II, 290–1. O'Conor Don and Bellew were Lords of The Treasury in Russell's first Government, as Wyse and O'Ferrall had been under Melbourne. Office-holders and placemen in a sense represent only part of the full picture. Less conspicuous but almost as good evidence of the

of the Rolls in Ireland, was made to O'Connell himself in June 1838. His reluctant refusal, based largely on an accurate estimate of the effects of acceptance on Irish public opinion, undoubtedly saved his political career.[1]

Like O'Connell, several of his followers took the opportunity to provide or to attempt to provide for their families. Pierce Butler was accused of attempting to blackmail the Government into satisfying his demands for patronage in the Navy and the Church by abstaining from critical divisions, while Barron succeeded in obtaining a baronetcy for himself and places in government service for a son, a brother and three cousins.[2] No doubt there were others as successful though less conspicuous. But it was a recognized convention of early nineteenth-century politics that one of an M.P.'s duties was to submit his constituents' claims for patronage to the Government. Smith O'Brien, whose rectitude was unimpeachable, insisted that the mere performance of this duty did not guarantee his future support. The consequence of past support had been, he wrote, 'to create a belief among my constituents that I have it in my power to be useful to individuals seeking situations under Government'. Certain recommendations of his had not been successful, and he added: 'I do not urge any request of this kind as a means of conciliating my support [which] . . . will be given to the measures of Government, as long as I approve of them, without reference to patronage.'[3]

Failure to gratify constituents could seriously affect an M.P.'s

party's readiness at least to accept favours was the stream of local offices and magistracies which descended on its members after 1835 (see below Appendix B; O'Connell himself was not a J.P. until 1835). It is of course true that the mere possession of a magistracy, unlike the holding of office or place, did not prevent men, as O'Connell and others showed after 1841, from holding and expressing extreme nationalist opinions; but the Tory Government which deprived Repealers of their Commissions in 1843 was merely following a strict and conventional logic.

[1] Morpeth to Russell, 7 June; Ebrington to Russell, 11 June; Russell to Melbourne, 14 June 1838, Russell Papers, P.R.O. 30/22/3B. Only Ebrington seems to have been concerned about the possible effects of the appointment, especially on Grey and the old Whigs. For O'Connell's refusal, see Greville, *Journal*, 21 June 1838, IV, 106; and the vivid account in O'Neill Daunt, *Personal Recollections of O'Connell*, I, 36–7.

[2] McDowell, *Public Opinion*, 137; C. Gavan Duffy, *Four Years of Irish History, 1845–1849* (1883), 320.

[3] O'Brien to E. J. Stanley, 4 September 1835; to Melbourne, 20 October 1836, O'Brien Papers, N.L.I., 428.

position. Sheil made enemies by his blunt replies to suitors, and one of the reasons for his transferring to Dungarvan in 1841 was to escape the clamour against him in Tipperary 'for not having gorged my friends with patronage'.[1] In view of this pressure, stronger perhaps in Ireland than elsewhere, it was scarcely surprising that Repealers succumbed. Their failings in this respect were not so much personal as those of a class and a generation, of a nationalist movement at a certain stage of its development, and at least it may be said that Irish jobbery, common to the two Liberal Members who besieged Littleton in 1833 and to the Tories who plagued Peel after 1841, knew no strict party barriers.[2]

O'Connell's alliance with the Whigs, while it hardly gave him a commanding influence on policy and certainly forced him to accept moderate, even conservative solutions to Irish problems, also severely restricted his freedom of manoeuvre and prevented any successful attempt at political re-insurance. The Precursor Society of August 1838, which was to be if necessary the fore-runner of a new nationalist campaign, was initially far less successful than earlier organizations had been, and in an attempt to attract Liberal support all mention of Repeal was dropped from its programme by December 1838. The Government first brought much private pressure to bear on him to drop the whole plan and then in August 1839 announced that no Repealer would be considered for official appointments.[3] The Precursor organization was dissolved and O'Connell, in a long interview with the Lord-Lieutenant,

> expressed the best disposition both towards the Govt. & me & though he said he could not dissolve the Precursor [Society] without holding out Repeal in the distance as his remedy for the political grievances of his countrymen, he assured me that he would agitate as little as he could, & would not be a party in forming any Society except that which he had announced for revising the Registration . . .[4]

The Whigs could not so easily kill the revived Repeal Association of

---

[1] Torrens, *Sheil*, II, 300–1.

[2] Littleton, *Diary*, 27 [July] 1833, Aspinall, op. cit., 354–5; McDowell, *Public Opinion*, 208–9; and Peel to De Grey, 23 November 1841, Peel Papers, Add. MSS 40477, 17, a warning that De Grey would become very familiar in Ireland with the expression: 'My father over and over again refused a peerage.'

[3] Normanby to Russell, 6 September 1838; Russell to Melbourne, 2 December 1838; Ebrington to Russell, 20 May 1839, Russell Papers, P.R.O., 30/22/3B, 3C.

[4] Ebrington to Russell, 8 September 1839, Russell Papers, P.R.O., 30/22/3D.

April 1840 by a crude use of the weapon of patronage, but the Association's existence, extremely weak at first, made no difference to O'Connell's continued support of the Government.

He seems indeed never to have considered at any time the possibility of withdrawing his vital support from the Government (no doubt the alternative seemed to him infinitely less preferable); and although he occupied the classic position which Parnell and the Home Rule party later exploited with such efficiency, it was he and not the Whigs who made sacrifices and concessions.[1] Thus, while his support of the ballot (by 1839 an open question with the Whigs themselves) and his active part in the growing movement against the Corn Laws did not endanger the Government's existence, an independent line on the Canadian question, with its close political and religious analogies to Ireland, would have been extremely serious. But in January 1838 Mulgrave was able to report that O'Connell, while disliking the Government's suspension of the Candian constitution, also disapproved strongly of the Canadians' attempts at rebellion and that he 'will be alright (or at least will do no mischief) on the Canadian Question. The line he proposes to take is not to discuss the Question at all in public before the meeting of Parliament, [and] to abstain from attending the House during the first few days of its sittings . . .'.[2] He kept his word, but thick-and-thin support of the Government on all vital questions further estranged him from the English Radicals in Parliament, professionally and fanatically anti-Whig but leaderless and divided on tactics, who came to dislike him almost as much as they did the Whigs, ostracized him socially and not infrequently attacked him for betraying the Radical cause.[3]

[1] Parnell was of course much more determined and uncompromising than O'Connell, with none of O'Connell's respect for the nature and processes of parliamentary government and none of his strong preconceptions about the relative merits of English political parties. In addition, it must be said that in Parnell's time, it was at least conceivable that one of the major English parties might be converted to Home Rule. In O'Connell's time (and with O'Connell's methods), no such conversion to Repeal was even remotely possible.

[2] Mulgrave to Russell, 6 January 1838, P.R.O., 30/22/3A.

[3] *Life of Roebuck*, ed. Leader, 74–108; Mrs. Grote, *Personal Life of George Grote*, 99, 105–6, 120. See Michael St. J. Packe, *Life of John Stuart Mill* (1954), 195, for the Radical Sir William Molesworth's description of the Whig Government: 'the miserablest brutes that God Almighty ever put guts into.' Even Joseph Hume, who favoured a general policy of co-operation with the Whigs and was the only Radical helped by O'Connell after the Radicals' electoral disasters of

Alliance with the Whigs was at least partly responsible for his failure to give promised parliamentary support in 1836 to the Ten Hours movement, for which he was bitterly attacked by Richard Oastler as no friend to the working classes but 'a political-economist Malthusian Whig' in the pay of the mill-owners,[1] and it may well have affected his whole attitude towards Chartism. His initial friendly patronage soon changed to disapproval and hostility as the movement became increasingly dominated by the character and policies of his former follower, Feargus O'Connor. O'Connell's opposition to Chartism, together with his active support of the Anti-Corn Law League, split the political sympathies of the Irish in England and certainly ensured that there would be no great alliance between Irish nationalism and English discontent.[2]

It was appropriate that the Whigs ended, as they had begun, on an Irish issue. In February 1840 the Opposition leaders, cheated of office in May 1839 and conscious that their party required action, took up the question of Irish registration in a frontal attack on the Government.[3] Stanley's Bill, which provided for the annual registration of voters, the abolition of certificates of registration (a fertile source of corruption and impersonation) and the imposition of fines for frivolous or unreasonable claims and objections was at once

1837, rebelled on the Canadian question, causing the Government, to O'Connell's anger, to lose six vital Irish votes; O'Connell to Fitzpatrick, 7 May 1839, *O'Connell Corr.*, II, 177.

[1] Fagan, *O'Connell*, II, 561–76, quoting *Blackwood's Magazine* and *London Mercury*. These accusations of bribery arose from the election fund raised for O'Connell in 1837 (above p. 124). O'Connell's strictly orthodox economic views, which led him to regard trade unions as disrupting the economic process and infringing the freedom of contract of worker as well as capitalist, certainly would not have inclined him to enthusiastic support of the statutory limitation of working hours. For his onslaught in 1838 on trade unions, which exposed him to a bitter counter-attack from George Julian Harney, see A. R. Schoyen, *The Chartist Challenge* (1958), 23–6.

[2] See Read and Glasgow, *Feargus O'Connor*, 48 ff.; S. Maccoby, *English Radicalism, 1832–1852* (1935), 163, 200, 204–5; Edouard Dolléans, *Le Chartisme* (1949), 95, for O'Connell's changing attitude to O'Connor, the Chartists and the Charter. His relations with William Lovett and the London Working Men's Association were good in 1837. For his support of the League, and for the important consequences in Manchester itself of the alliance of the League and O'Connellite Irish against the Chartists, see Norman McCord, *The Anti-Corn Law League, 1838–1846* (1958), 99–103.

[3] Thomas Fremantle to Peel, 18, 30 December; Stanley to Peel, 18 December 1839, Peel Papers, Add. MSS 40427, 333, 366–8.

denounced by O'Connell and the Irish as a deliberate attempt to restrict the franchise and to increase landlord influence. The Government, forced by the claims of its alliance to defend a system full of acknowledged abuses, was repeatedly defeated before Stanley withdrew his Bill at the end of the session.[1]

The session of 1841 repeated the Whigs' humiliation. Their own measure in February, though similar in most respects to Stanley's, proposed also to reduce the county franchise from £10 to a £5 rating to the Poor Law and thus clearly violated Russell's famous declaration in 1837 on the 'finality' of the Reform Bill. After a full-dress debate they carried its Second Reading by only five votes in a division for which both sides brought down 'the sick and the dying without remorse';[2] and in April, failing even to carry an £8 franchise, they had no choice but to withdraw their Bill. On this issue, the Government could not resign and appeal to the country; skilful Opposition tactics had caused the Whigs a series of humiliating defeats; and the struggle provided an indispensable prelude to the final *coup de grâce* a little over a month later, when Peel carried by one vote in a very full House his motion of no confidence in the Government.

[1] See W. B. Jones, *Lord Derby and Victorian Conservatism* (1956), 74–6, and references; Greville, *Journal*, 26 March 1840, IV, 228–9.
[2] Greville, *Journal*, 27 February 1841, IV, 388.

CHAPTER V

The Question of Irish Tithes

The problem

THE years between 1830 and 1838 saw in Ireland a long campaign of resistance to the payment of tithes to the clergy of the Established Church. Most Englishmen saw this movement as an insidious politico–religious conspiracy on the part of the Catholic population, organized by O'Connell and his henchmen, against the revenues and hence against the existence of the Church. This view, at best half true, could only have been the product of a deeply-ingrained suspicion of Catholicism combined with great ignorance or at least misunderstanding of Irish social and economic conditions. Official concern was clearly reflected in the 114 Commissions and 60 Select Committees which investigated Irish problems between 1810 and 1833;[1] but these detailed inquiries into particular problems, issuing forth in unwieldy and indigestible Reports of strictly limited circulation, did little to increase general knowledge of or interest in Ireland. If these official documents had stood alone, they would have constituted some excuse for English ignorance.

But long before the first complete, official description of the Irish predicament in the Reports of the Devon Commission of 1843–5, there existed a mass of easily accessible literature on Ireland, much of it of an exceptional order of literary merit and technical excellence, including Arthur Young's magnificent pioneering work, *A Tour in Ireland* (1780), Edward Wakefield's *An Account of Ireland, Statistical and Political* (1812), quite as observant, as frank and as full of

---

[1] Woodward, *Age of Reform*, 335.

information as Young though less fertile in suggestions and rather less well-written; Henry Inglis' *Journey Throughout Ireland* (1835), in some sense Wakefield improved and modernized; Gustave de Beaumont's *L'Irlande sociale, politique et religieuse*, translated in the year (1839) in which it was published and an attempt, rather less successful though with many interesting and perceptive passages, to do for Ireland what Beaumont's friend Alexis de Tocqueville had done for America; and Mr. and Mrs. S. C. Hall's *Ireland, its Scenery and Character* (1841–3), an attractive and thorough book written with much sympathetic insight.

If we add to this list of descriptive and analytical books, none of which could be described as ephemeral in size or nature, the popular novels of Maria Edgeworth, Lady Morgan and Charles Lever, the lyrics and prose-works of Thomas Moore, particularly his *Memoirs of Captain Rock* (1824) and *Travels of an Irish Gentleman in search of a Religion* (1833), and William Makepeace Thackeray's *An Irish Sketch-book*, first published in 1842, then it is clear that Ireland in all its aspects formed an important literary subject of its own.[1] The facts were obtainable and indisputable. Yet English public opinion steadily refused to absorb the uncomfortable lessons of these facts, to put them into practice or to allow the Irish to do so in their own way. In 1843 Nassau Senior said of Ireland that 'the great majority of the Members of each House . . . know less of that country than they know of Belgium or Switzerland'.[2] It required the catastrophe of the Famine to jolt English consciences and to arouse wide public interest for the first time in the social and economic as opposed to the political wrongs of Ireland.

The question of tithes provides a perfect epitome of the history of Anglo-Irish relations. Resistance to the tax was fundamentally agrarian in origin, a spontaneous and prolonged revolt by the Irish rural population against its conditions of life, and every legislative and administrative expedient which did not take account of this vital fact was doomed to failure. Religious or political motives may have been uppermost in the minds of O'Connell and his middle-class

---

[1] This list is by no means exhaustive. It might be lengthened by solid works like S. Lewis, *A Topographical Dictionary of Ireland* (1837) and Sir Robert Kane, *Industrial Resources of Ireland* (1844–5), and almost indefinitely extended by pamphlets, articles in the great *Reviews*, etc.

[2] N. W. Senior, *Journals, Essays and Conversations relating to Ireland* (1868), I, 130; cf. Peel's remark, quoted by Gash, *Peel*, 197, that M.P.s knew as much about Ireland as they did of Kamchatka.

associates. But both they and the reforming Whigs would have preferred to settle the question of the Established Church in Ireland (and to remedy the gross injustice by which the great majority was forced to contribute towards the upkeep of a minority and to Catholics, an heretical religion) without the disturbing and anarchic accompaniment of peasant agitation, when landlords' rents were fully as much endangered as parsons' tithes. If the Irish middle class participated actively in the resistance, it was partly in an attempt to control it and partly because tithe was an economic grievance for landowners and tenant farmers as well as for the peasantry; and it is significant that by 1838, O'Connell and the bulk of his party were prepared to accept a limited, conservative and somewhat unsatisfactory solution of the problem.

Tithes, 'the tenth part of the increase, yearly arising and renewing from the profits of lands, the stock upon lands, and the personal industry of the inhabitants',[1] were formally introduced into Ireland in the reign of Henry II but were not paid outside the Pale until the reign of Elizabeth. As early as 1612, it was noted that 'the poorer sort of papists groan under the many priests, in respect of the double tithes and offerings, the one paid by them unto us, and the other unto their own clergy', while a century later, Dean Swift declared that 'The payment of tithes in this kingdom is subject to so many frauds, wrangles and difficulties, not only from papists and dissenters, but even from those who profess themselves protestants, that by the expence, trouble and vexation of collection or bargaining for them, they are of all other rents, the most precarious, uncertain and ill-paid.'[2]

The most effective protest against the payment of a particular kind of tithe came from the Protestant House of Commons in

[1] Sir William Blackstone, *Commentaries on the Laws of England* (1811), II, 24. Tithes were divided into praedial (such as corn), mixed (such as lambs) and personal (money, etc.); they were further customarily divided into the 'great' or rectorial tithe (on corn, hay and wood) and the 'small' or vicarial tithe (on other praedial crops, such as flax, garden produce and potatoes). In Ireland, two-thirds of the tithes of corn, hay and wood frequently constituted the 'great' tithe, the rest the 'small'. See Richard Burn, *The Ecclesiastical Law*, ed. R. Phillimore (9th edn., 1842), III, 680; Sir Robert Phillimore, *The Ecclesiastical Law*, ed. Sir W. Phillimore (2nd edn., 1895), II, 1752.

[2] John D'Alton, *The History of Tithes* (1832), 28, quoting a Bishop of 1612; Anon., *State of Ireland Considered, with an Enquiry into the History and Operation of Tithes* (1810), 52, n. 1, with no source in Swift's works given.

Ireland, which in 1735 passed resolutions forbidding the payment of the tithe of 'agistment', or the tithes on pasture and its produce.[1] This event, described in 1828 as 'that enormous and unparalleled act of injustice committed by the gentry of Ireland, . . . which gave the great landholder an exemption from tithe, on the mere condition of depopulating his estate, and substituting cattle in the place of human creatures',[2] was a concession to the increasingly powerful grazier interest, represented by landowners who for much of the eighteenth century were substituting pasture for tillage in Ireland until the French wars produced an increased demand for cereals. This exemption of pasture meant that the liability for tithe devolved exclusively on tillage lands, occupied for the most part by a Catholic peasantry which was of all the classes in Ireland the least able, even if it had been willing, to pay the tax.

Before 1823 there were three ways of paying tithes in Ireland: in kind, or by a fixed annual payment based on acreage, or by 'view' of the growing crops, in which case the demand for tithe rose or fell in proportion to the output. A fairly general arrangement was the payment of 10/- an Irish acre for wheat and potatoes and 7/- to 8/- for oats,[3] but the payment of tithe in kind or by view was still quite common even after 1823. In that year, an attempt was made to establish the incomes of tithe-owners on fixed principles. By a Composition Act, known after its parliamentary sponsor as Goulburn's Act, composition for tithes was to be agreed upon by special parish vestries held by order of the Lord Lieutenant on the application of the tithe-owner or of five landholders occupying land of £20 value. The vestry, consisting of persons paying county rates of £1 or over, elected a commissioner to treat with the tithe-owner's commissioner; together these men agreed on sums to be paid by the whole parish and by each of its inhabitants according to the extent and quality of his land. They were to reach this sum by simple agreement, or by taking the average annual amount paid for tithes during the seven years from November 1814 to November 1821, or by calculating a rate based on the corn prices within the same period.

[1] These resolutions, immediately acted upon, were confirmed by the 40 Geo. III c. 23 at the time of the Union.

[2] John Finlay, *A Treatise on the Law of Tithes in Ireland* (1828), 477.

[3] Select Committee on Irish Tithes (Commons), P.P. 1831-2, XXI, App. I, 623-4. Higher figures (12/-, 8/- to 9/- respectively) are given by Robert C. Simington, 'The Tithe Applotment Books of 1834,' in *Journal of the Eire Department of Agriculture*, XXXVIII, No. 2 (1941), 243.

An amending Act of 1824 laid down that compositions reached by mutual agreement were to last twenty-one years while those based on prices and averages could be changed every seven years. Composition, payable in two instalments a year, was a first charge on land, taking precedence over rents, parliamentary and local taxes; it was to be paid by the same class of occupiers or owner-occupiers which had paid tithe in the past; and finally, it was to be paid on pasture as well as on arable lands.[1]

In these Composition Acts, the Government adopted Paley's recommendation that tithes, 'a tax not only upon industry, but upon that industry which feeds mankind', should be converted into corn-rents.[2] But in rationalizing the system of payment without distinguishing between tithe and rent, indeed by fusing the two, the Acts ensured that opposition to tithes and to rents would be concurrent and simultaneous. The voting regulations in the vestries weighted the balance in favour of the larger landowners, many of them graziers whose interest lay in defeating a scheme by which pasture became liable for tithe; and there is ample evidence that these powerful interests were not slow to take advantage of their voting rights and of the fact that composition was voluntary.[3] Compositions were still paid by the occupying tenantry; the so-called 'tithe-free' leases[4] simply meant that rents were increased by the amount of the composition and that the clergyman was implicated still further in the landlord-tenant relationship. Moreover, corn prices between 1814 and 1821 were comparatively high, since they included the phenomenal figure of 49/– in 1818 and covered several years of scarce harvests. Compositions made on this high average on terms favourable to tithe-owners and variable only after seven years were naturally unpopular when corn prices were markedly

---

[1] 4 Geo. IV, c. 99, amended later by the 5 Geo. IV, c. 63 and also by the 7 & 8 Geo. IV, c. 60. See Finlay, *Treatise*, 476–579; Joseph O'Leary, *The Law of Statutable Composition for Tithes in Ireland* (1834), 16–19.

[2] William Paley, *The Principles of Moral and Political Philosophy* (1811), II, 407–9.

[3] In vestries, payment of £10 county cess carried 1 vote, £10–20 2 votes, and above £20, 1 vote for each £10 up to a maximum of 6. For examples of successful grazier opposition to composition, see Select Committee, Tithes, P.P. 1831–2, XXI, 19, 26, 50, 70, 98, 167–8; Second Report, P.P. 1831–2, XXI, 245–v.

[4] In all future leases in compounded parishes, tenants were allowed to deduct from rents what they previously paid for tithes; the landlord then added the new composition to the rent.

lower after 1824.[1] In practice, many compounding parishes preferred to reach private agreements with tithe-owners. Unfortunate bargains, from the tithe-payers' viewpoint, were easily made
if small tillage farmers managed to outvote large graziers in the
vestries and agreed to compound for sums which, although they
equalized the burden between tillage and pasture, yet gave tithe-
owners increased incomes.

By 1830 over half of the 2,450 Irish parishes had entered into
compositions which, if they did nothing to change a system by which
an immense number of small sums were demanded from the peasantry, had at least done away with one of the most flagrant features of
the old system by which tithe proctors, paid by percentage and often
open to bribery, would value crops in good years by quantity and
in scarce years by price. As a tax, composition was considerably less
heavy than the old tithe, a fact which was much resented by the
clergy, the Primate Beresford denouncing Goulburn's Bill as 'in
principle sinful and unconstitutional, and in operation . . . irritating,
vexatious and impracticable'.[2]

But Irish tithe law, in all its rigour, remained otherwise unchanged. In England tithe could only be recovered in the Courts of
King's Bench, Common Pleas and Exchequer or before magistrates
for sums under 40/-. In Ireland tithe was recoverable by a cumbrous
process in ecclesiastical courts, in the Exchequer by a bill of equity,
when a number of defendants could be proceeded against at a time,
by summary proceedings before two magistrates for sums up to £10
or by distress, when an individual's goods could be seized and sold.[3]

[1] For evidence on this point, Select Committee, Tithes, P.P. 1831–2, XXI,
10, 87, 110, 177.

[2] Beresford to Lord Wellesley, 13, 15 February 1823; and to Lord Liverpool
[n.d. February 1823], complaining that he had not been consulted, Beresford–
Leslie MSS, N.L.I., 4838, letters 38, 39, 41. See also 'Mediensis', *Tithes No Tax*
(1823), and 'S.N.' [Thomas Elrington, Bishop of Ferns], *An Inquiry whether the
Disturbances in Ireland have originated in Tithes* (1823), two clerical broadsides
reaching conclusions implied in their titles.

[3] For the history of tithes in England, see J. A. Venn, *Foundations of Agricultural Economics* (1923), 96–123; V. A. Lavrosky, 'Tithe Commutation as a
Factor in the Gradual Decrease of Landownership by the English Peasantry',
Economic History Review, IV, No. 3 (October 1933), 273–89. The comparison
with Ireland is most illuminating. Even allowing for the greater degree of
religious unity, tithes in England seem to have pressed much less heavily on
agriculture and the land system. Much land was statutorily exempt, there was
no inequality between tillage and pasture, and commutation of land for tithes

This latter method was in fact the stock remedy in Ireland for arrears of tithe and tithe composition and for rent. Tithe was thus an integral part of the land system, closely identified with all the hateful features of rents without any of their benefits; and since the tithe-owner was a first claimant whose charge up to a year's amount must be paid before the landlord's rent, the tax was obnoxious to a Catholic tenant not merely because it was paid to a Protestant heretic (who might be an amiable and charitable man) but, far more important, because it could drastically reduce a tenant's vital rent-money, plunging him into arrears with his landlord and exposing him to all the horrors of eviction. There was indeed no escaping a tax from which very little Irish land was statutorily exempt after 1823 and which might well have pressed hard on food supplies. In all uncompounded parishes it could be levied on wheat, oats and barley, on potatoes in Munster, Connaught and in four counties of Leinster, on hay everywhere except Galway and on sheep and lambs in Leinster.[1]

Apologists for the Church's tithe revenue relied heavily on the theory advanced by Adam Smith that 'taxes upon the produce of land are in reality taxes upon the rent; and, though they may be originally advanced by the farmer, are finally paid by the landlord. When a certain portion of the produce is to be paid away for a tax, the farmer computes . . . what the value of this portion is likely to amount to, and he makes a proportional abatement in the rent which he agrees to pay to the landlord.'[2] In England a tenant would deduct tithes and other charges when coming to terms with a landlord, but in Ireland a tenant from year to year or 'at will' was not in this position, and rents were fixed by the intensity of competition. An Irish witness, asked in 1832 whether the Irish tenant 'would not

took place simultaneously with the many enclosures by Act of Parliament between 1793 and 1815, before all tithes were converted by Acts of 1836-9 into rent-charges subject to gradual redemption.

[1] For tithing areas and rates, see George Dwyer, *A View of Evidence on the subject of Tithes in Ireland* (1833); Select Committee, Tithes, P.P. 1831-2, XXI, 177, 445, 623-4; XXII, in Index [458-9] (a map showing areas where potatoes were titheable which wrongly exempts Connaught). Ulster was remarkably well-treated in the matter of tithes. Potatoes were subject only in Londonderry, sheep and lambs nowhere, while tithes on flax, hemp and wool, raw materials for a growing industry, were small and in some areas non-existent.

[2] Adam Smith, *An Inquiry into the Nature and Causes of the Wealth of Nations* (1828), III, 386-7.

calculate that a tenth would be liable to tithe', replied, 'Yes, he would; but he takes the chance of paying for that as he can: the proctor tries to jockey him, and he tries to jockey the proctor . . .'[1] Thus the argument of Archbishop Whateley, the Whig ecclesiastic and economist, that tithe operated as a reduction of rent was quite inapplicable to Irish conditions. Tithe was an additional rent, and as William Smith O'Brien pointed out, it would be impossible to convince the Irish Catholic peasant that it was the Protestant landlord alone who paid the tithe with the argument that the latter's rent receipts would be higher if tithes did not exist. It was of course possible that rents would rise still higher if tithes were abolished, and this argument was also used by Whateley and others as a strong reason for retaining them.[2]

Tithes were thus indissolubly bound up with the inter-connected problems of the land system and of a population which had more than doubled in the space of sixty years, amounting by 1841 to over eight millions.[3] The willingness of landlords to condone the fragmentation of even the smallest holdings, largely in the interests of their rent-rolls but also for political and even often for mildly humanitarian reasons, must have provided an important incentive for early peasant marriages; and the potato, easily raised on the smallest area and generally in abundant supply, provided a nutritionally adequate basis for the people's diet. In a stark and comfortless world, marriage might well be seen as offering a vital companion-relationship, a priority above all considerations of prudence, and children might well constitute a form of insurance against old age in a country without any kind of a poor law until 1838. Those without land or for whom no parental plot could be spared could settle on

[1] Select Committee, Tithes, P.P. 1831–2, XXI, 287.

[2] Richard Whateley, *Introductory Lectures on Political Economy* (4th ed., 1855), 186; W. Smith O'Brien, *Thoughts upon Ecclesiastical Reform* (1833), 7–11. See also Henry Cotton, *Cui Bono?: A Letter to the Right Hon. E. G. Stanley* (1836), 42–6; Sir Robert Wilmot Horton, *The Object and Effect of the Oath in the Roman Catholic Relief Rill* (1838), 52.

[3] See K. H. Connell, *The Population of Ireland, 1750–1845* (1950), 1–3, 24–5, and *passim*, a seminal work which together with his other contributions has revolutionized the whole question of Irish population growth, its history, causes and connection with the land system. See also K. H. Connell, 'Some Unsettled Problems in English and Irish Population History, 1750–1841', *Irish Historical Studies*, VII, No. 28 (September 1951), 225–34; 'Peasant Marriage in Ireland after the Great Famine'; and 'The Potato in Ireland', *Past and Present*, Nos. 12 and 23 (November 1957, November 1962), 76–91, 57–71.

the reserves of mountain and bog land; or tenants, without reference to a landlord, might take for their own support land which had formerly grown a cash-crop to provide rents. Whatever the full explanation, it is undeniable that from the last quarter of the eighteenth century a proverbially wretched peasantry subsisted and multiplied on a more or less reliable potato crop, and that despite some severe regional potato famines in later years, notably in 1817, 1822 and 1826, the birth-rate was apparently still well in excess of the rate of mortality until the onset of the Famine.

With the end of the Napoleonic wars, steadily falling corn prices after 1818 inclined landowners once again to see the attractions of a pastoral economy.[1] Clearance and consolidation of estates involved the eviction of squatting cottier tenants, but landowners were encouraged in this general policy not only by the almost unanimous recommendations of the economists and experts on Ireland, who hoped to see there an agricultural economy of medium to large farms held by capitalist and preferably grazier tenants and who looked to this policy as the basis of a solution to the population problem;[2] but also by the Government in the Sub-letting Act of 1826, which prohibited sub-letting without a head landlord's express consent, and less directly, by the disfranchisement in 1829 of the forty-shilling freeholders. Consolidation was not by any means a general practice before the Famine, but the process helped to create a situation in the countryside where the slightest spark might set off a general explosion.[3]

Resistance to tithes, a prominent feature of the long series of agrarian risings which made violent outrages against persons and property an endemic phenomenon of Irish rural life, had a long history before 1830.[4] In the law of public opinion dispensed by the

[1] It must be emphasized that this process was a gradual one and that Ireland still continued after 1815 to export large and increasing quantities of cereals. See Connell, *Population of Ireland*, 268, App. III, Table D, from which it appears that the export of oats alone rose from an annual average of 388,546 barrels in 1800–9 to over 1,000,000 in 1810–19, to nearly 2,000,000 in 1820–9 and to 2,373,235 in 1830–9.

[2] See esp. Black, *Economic Thought*, 1–24; and below pp. 202–3.

[3] For evidence on the probable extent of consolidation, see Connell, *Population of Ireland*, 175–81.

[4] See George Cornewall Lewis, *On Local Disturbances in Ireland and on the Irish Church Question* (1836), 3–44, and *passim*, the best single source, which shows clearly that many of the outbreaks between 1761 and 1832 were concerned

peasantry through secret societies of Whiteboys, Whitefeet and Blackfeet, Rockites, Molly Maguires and Lady Clares, Terry Alts, Shanavests, Carders, Threshers and (in Ulster) Ribbonmen, the abolition of tithes and of rents were fundamental issues in a great general protest against intolerable conditions. But while the war against landlords, agents, middlemen and new tenants was liable to break out at any time and in every part of Ireland, the great anti-tithe campaign which began in 1830 and which was to dwarf all previous attempts at resistance can be traced to its origins in a particular area.

This was a section of south-east Ireland, comprising Kilkenny, Carlow and Queen's County, and in particular the parish of Graiguenemanagh on the borders of Kilkenny and Carlow. This parish of 500 Catholics and 63 Protestants had compounded for tithe at what was agreed to be a high rate, but the immediate cause of the trouble was the unusual and tactless action of the curate, who was acting as tithe-proctor for his rector and who was extremely unpopular for his proselytizing activity, in distraining the cattle of the local Catholic priest, Father Martin Doyle.[1] Encouraged and advised by his diocesan Bishop Doyle, this priest, who was described by a government spy as 'clever, ingenuous and intriguing, and who has proved himself to be capable of doing some good, or a great deal of mischief', had personally organized by November 1830 an almost completely successful resistance.[2] In two months Sir John Harvey, Inspector-General of Police in Leinster, with 350 policemen and two military detachments had collected only one-third of the tithe arrears, by which time a further half-year's tithe was due. Cattle could only be seized for distress between sunrise and sunset; the peasantry and farmers, by a system of signals, drove their beasts

with tithes. See also Sydney Smith's remarkable and sympathetic article in the *Edinburgh Review* (1820), in his *Works* (1850), 296–307, where tithes are placed firmly in the general agrarian context.

[1] The curate was a member of Lord Farnham's Association for Promoting the Second Reformation, one of a number of proselytizing bodies. Bishop Doyle almost certainly exaggerated their importance as a cause of resistance to tithe; Select Committee, Tithes, P.P. 1831–2, XXI, 294, 327, 381, as also did R. B. O'Brien, *Fifty Years of Concessions to Ireland*, I, 376–7.

[2] Bishop Doyle to Fr. Doyle, 28 October; 10 December 1830, Fitzpatrick, *Doyle*, II, 222, 231–2, emphasizing the importance of getting the confidence and support of the magistracy. For the report on Father Doyle, see Memo, 16 October 1833, H.O. Papers 100/244, 557. He replaced in Graigue 'a quiet, easy Priest of the old School', a nice comment on the new generation of priests trained at Maynooth.

home at the approach of the military, and once under lock and key, no doors could legally be broken down. In March 1831 Father Doyle told the under-sheriff of Kilkenny that 'it would be a tenacious thing to now advise them to pay tithe, as the system had become general throughout . . . Kilkenny, Carlow and Wexford not to do so, and that all Ireland was awaiting the result of Graigue'.[1]

In Graigue the resistance was organized by the local priest with the support of his bishop, and at least as far as the parochial clergy were concerned, this became a familiar pattern all over Ireland. But the area which led the resistance was not one of acute sub-division or of excessively concentrated population. Farms were certainly very small; in North Kilkenny and Carlow, two-thirds of the holdings were less than 15 acres and in Queen's County three-quarters were in this category. But south-east Ireland in general has been described as being 'in many ways . . . economically stronger than most of the remainder before the Famine'.[2] In Kilkenny the leaders of resistance were the more substantial farmers who objected primarily, in the compounded parishes, to the high rate of composition.[3] For this class, Protestant and Catholic, whose economic problems were not those of peasants in need of land for subsistence, it was not principally a question of maintaining their hold on the land by direct action. For tenant-farmers, the lower the current price of corn (and prices were steadily falling between 1829 and 1835), the higher the proportion which a composition calculated on the higher prices of 1814–21 bore to rents and produce, and the more its payment, eating into profits and rent-money, was regarded as an inequitable burden. It was surely not coincidental that resistance to tithes began to

---

[1] For resistance in Graigue, see Select Committee, Tithes, P.P. 1831–2, XXI, 7–16, evidence of Sir John Harvey; Report of Henry Devereux, 7 March 1831, ibid., App. I, 185.

[2] Freeman, *Pre-Famine Ireland*, 183; and ibid., 193, 196 and Fig. 29, 184, for Graigue's population of between 101 and 200 persons to the square mile. For Queen's County, see Select Committee, Tithes, P.P. 1831–2, XXI, 376–90, evidence of Patrick Lalor, Catholic farmer and later Repeal M.P., one of the organizers of opposition in the county.

[3] Joseph Greene to Sir W. Gossett, 31 March 1831, Select Committee, Tithes, P.P. 1831–2, XXI, App. I, 191; 40, Greene's evidence; ibid., 12–17, 52–7, 110 for the situation in Knocktopher, Co. Kilkenny, where the composition of £1,700 p.a. was thought even by a Protestant clergyman to be very high. See also Bishop Doyle to Lord Darnley, 30 December 1830, Fitzpatrick, *Doyle*, II, 236–8, who says that in Kilkenny, Wexford and Tipperary farmers were joining the peasantry 'either avowedly or covertly'.

subside during a period when wheat prices were again steadily rising and when compulsory compositions were calculated on a lower scale. This is not the only explanation for the rise and fall of agitation, since it could apply only to men with some profits to lose; but it certainly helps to account for the participation of Protestants who had no strong religious reasons, as all Catholics had, for refusing to pay the Protestant clergymen.

This phenomenon, that resistance to tithes produced a temporary alliance between a large section of the agricultural middle class and the mass of the peasantry ought not to obscure the fact that the parties in the alliance were pursuing different objectives, for different economic reasons and by different methods. As the resistance spread through Ireland, it became more obviously a spontaneous protest against agrarian conditions. In Donegal, 'the peasants . . . went . . . to all the respectable landowners resident here, *threatening* and *demanding* that the rents should be lowered . . . [and] entered into resolutions to "pay neither *rent, tithes, nor taxes*, until O'Connell got new laws for them . . .".'[1] In Armagh, the attempts of the Rev. James Blacker to collect his arrears of tithes in 1834 in the parish of Keady brought out 'upwards of 1,000 men . . . in the townland of Carrickaduff, on two different hills, numbers of them armed with guns and pistols, others with pikes and different weapons, who shouted "No rents, no tithes"; and continued blowing horns and firing shots . . .'[2] No distinction was made by the peasantry between tithes and rents. Both were regarded as oppressions, both were proceeded for in the same way and often collected by the same person. An agent writes to a lay tithe-owner in November 1837, to explain that 'the harvest has been so late that I have not been able yet to collect either Rent or Tythes unless in part, and those who paid I was obliged to take notes from for the tythe payable 1st January'.[3] Non-payment of tithes could easily lead to eviction if a man was also in arrears with his rent. The same tithe-proctor writes again to his employer, to inform him that

[1] Lieut. Conyngham Ogilvie to Gossett, 24 January 1832, Select Committee, Tithes, P.P. 1831–2, XXI, App. I, 225, quoted by the Irish Attorney-General in the Commons, Hansard, XI, 176–7, 13 March 1832, Crampton.

[2] Chief Constable Hill to Sir F. Stoven, 12 December 1834, Tithes, Keady, P.P. 1835, XLVII, 99 ff.

[3] F. Malcolmson to Colonel Anthony Weldon, 3 November 1837, Weldon Papers, N.L.I., 486, relating to two parishes in Co. Carlow of which Weldon owned the tithes.

. . . the tenants are poor and their holdings small, with the exception of Hennessy who you have in prison [for tithe arrears], and whose wife has requested me to write to you to know if you wd compromise the debt and receive it by instalments as he is unable to pay the full amt . . . he now owes me a year's rent £116/10 and unless he be discharged soon he will loose [sic] the Interest (if any) on his farm as I will serve an Ejectment on the premises.[1]

It was widely believed by the peasantry that the abolition of tithes would lead to a reduction in the exorbitant rents which many witnesses saw as the immediate cause of the resistance to tithes. For example, the tenant of a Crown estate in Galway had sub-let 50 acres of arable land of inferior quality valued at 15/- per acre to 222 under-tenants at a rent of 45/6 an acre. Any further demand before and on top of this inflated rent, the payment of which might prevent a man's retaining the land on which his life depended, was naturally fiercely resisted. Bishop Doyle's remark that 'it is universally admitted that the first object of the Whiteboys was to dissolve the tithe system' was not simply a piece of good propaganda against the Protestant Church.[2] Catholic peasants could be called on twice a year each for tithe composition, landlords' rent, dues for their own clergy, grand jury cess and, until their abolition in 1833, for church rates. At their economic level, distress for tithes was indistinguishable from and could be as disastrous as distress for rent.[3]

The methods of resistance varied from place to place and with the different classes of tithe-payers. With the peasantry, particularly in the densely populated areas of the south and west, opposition took the form of a wholesale war against property. Threatening notices would appear:

1. Remarke the Concequence Thomas Wardren dant pay the tithe for if you do you may prepare your coffin you may be assured that you will loose your life either at home or abraad.

    No Tithes
    No Tithes   COFFIN
    No Tithes   Captain Rock

[1] Malcolmson to Weldon, 15 December 1837, Weldon Papers, N.L.I., 486. This case nicely illustrates the primacy of a tithe-owner's claim before a landlord's rent.   [2] Lewis, *Disturbances*, 25, note.
[3] Catholic dues were extremely moderate, from 5/- to 1/- a year. See Select Committee, Tithes, P.P. 1831–2, XXI, 167; and The Rev. David Croly, *An Essay . . . on Ecclesiastical Finance as regards the Roman Catholic Church in Ireland* (1834), 26–45, a highly coloured account of their collection.

2. There are spies through the parish looking on to see who dare pay
   1s. tithe to any man whatsoever; any person violating my rules and
   regulations will receive the most rigid punishment . . . If Mr.
   Kennedy insists on driving or distraining the parish, I will come at
   him very easy; all the military in Templemore will not save his life.
   Given under my hand,
   Captain Kill Proctor.[1]

Outrages, committed frequently by strangers, varied from murder
and assaults to the houghing of cattle, burning houses or, as in
Limerick with the Terry Alts, the turning up of grasslands for sow-
ing potatoes. Middlemen or new tenants, nearly always Catholics,
were the chief victims, while those most active in disturbances were
the poorest farmers or labourers, cottiers or tenants at will, though
small farmers in better circumstances who believed that without
outrages their lands would be taken away either joined or were
passive and friendly if not frightened spectators. Bound together by
secret oaths and with a remarkable communications system, the
peasantry were both ready and able to wage an agrarian war in which
they made little distinction between the different grievances to which
they were subject.

   Middle-class resistance to tithes was a very different affair. The
small and substantial farmers and landlords who attended the local
meetings against tithes and often led the opposition in their own
areas certainly had strong economic reasons for their actions. As the
Protestant landholders of the parish of Dronard in County Down
put it, they were willing to pay a reasonable tax but 'the tithe composition . . . comes upon the landholder after his means are already
exhausted by the payment of an oppressive rent'.[2] Yet while the
abstract rights and wrongs of a Church Establishment were the last
things which the peasantry cared about, the most prominent
national opponents of tithes—O'Connell and Bishop Doyle, Protes-

---

[1] Select Committee, Tithes, P.P. 1831–2, XXI, App. I, 201, 227; see also ibid.,
206, 214–15; *Annual Register* (1832), 281–2. Some notices mingled threats and
hard economic facts with an abstract religious argument. For a most interesting
example, which cites Paley on Church Establishments and refutes Adam
Smith's argument (above p. 173) by saying that landlords add tithes to the
rent, see Select Committee, Tithes, P.P. 1831–2, XXI, App. I, 224.

[2] Select Committee, Tithes, P.P. 1831–2, XXI, App. I, 220–1. See *D.E.P.*,
29 June; *Times*, 2 February 1832, for typical anti-tithe meetings in Kilkenny
and Carlow, large and orderly affairs attended by peasantry and farmers and
presided over by local landowners.

tant and Catholic nationalist politicians like Feargus O'Connor, Henry Grattan, the Ruthvens, Pierce Butler, Sir Richard Nagle, Sheil and Ronayne, Whigs and Liberals like Wyse, More O'Ferrall and James Grattan—were campaigning against the Church and its income on grounds of right and public policy. Feargus O'Connor saw 'the assumption of Tithes by the Protestant Clergy as their own exclusive property . . . [as] a gross violation of their self-assumed trust, . . . a complete subversion of the law of GOD which invests the people with a right to support from the land'.[1] From journalists in Dublin and in the provinces a stream of damaging propaganda and satire poured out against the Church, epitomized by the parson's song to the police before 'The Battle of Skibbereen' in July 1831:

> Brave Peelers, march on with the musket and sword
> And fight for my *tithes*, in the name of the *Lord*!
> Away with whoever appears in your path—
> And seize all each peasant in Skibbereen hath![2]

Bishop Doyle was certainly aware of the intolerable position of the mass of tenant-cottiers and had done his best to draw the attention of the authorities and of public opinion to it. More than any other man he was responsible for swinging the priesthood into a campaign which he hoped would lead to the destruction of the 'Juggernaut Establishment' and to the creation of a Poor Law from its revenues. But he wanted a movement of passive, legal resistance, and before his death in 1834 he had become horrified and bitterly disillusioned by the violence and lawlessness which were the inevitable outcome of peasant agitation.[3] Neither he nor O'Connell, who

---

[1] Feargus O'Connor, *Letter to the Marquis of Anglesey* (1832), 5; see also Pierce Butler, *Letter to the Landlords of Kilkenny*, in *Kilkenny Moderator*, 29 April 1837.

[2] John Cornelius O'Callaghan, *The Green Book* (1845), 285–6; and ibid., 20–8, for the founding and success of the *Comet* newspaper in 1831 and of various anti-tithe publications like *The Parson's Horn Book*, whose author was imprisoned in 1832.

[3] J.K.L. [John Kildare and Leighlin], *Letters on the State of Ireland* (1825); *Letter to Thomas Spring Rice* [March 1831], in Fitzpatrick, *Doyle*, II, 278–85; *Letter to Lord Anglesey on Tithes, Times*, 1 September 1832. See also his evidence before the Select Committee, Tithes, P.P. 1831–2, XXI, 290–337; his pastoral of 1831, sympathetic to tenant grievances but condemning agrarian combinations, in ibid., P.P. 1831–2, XXII, 235–9; and Fitzpatrick, *Doyle*, II, 403, 413–14, 458–9, 480–1; Cloncurry, *Personal Recollections*, 459–60, for the change in his attitude.

was ready by 1837 to accept a compromise solution to the tithe question, wanted a revolution in the Irish countryside. A complete abolition of tithes as the result of an uncontrollable peasant movement rather than by Act of Parliament would have seriously endangered the position of every landlord, Catholic and Protestant, in Ireland.

But if by 1833 O'Connell was uncertain of controlling a movement for which he and Bishop Doyle had originally accepted full responsibility, it was not for want of middle-class participation, no doubt strengthened by the Government's savage offensive against anti-tithe newspapers.[1] In 1833 Stanley told Wellesley that

. . . The great difficulty which I have always found in my way, was how to overcome the combination between Landlord and Tenant to rob the Church, the third party, for the purpose of dividing the plunder between them; and the absence of that mutual understanding between them (where the former motive did not exist) which would enable us, by mutual consent, to deal with existing interests. If you have found the means of securing the cooperation of the Landlords, the work is done.[2]

The Government later set itself deliberately to obtain this cooperation. But in the meantime landlords as well as tenants were defaulting on their payments. The revenues of the Established Church were officially reckoned at £815,331 a year in 1835, of which £531,782 was due from tithe composition, only about one-fifth (£113,550) payable to lay tithe-owners.[3] Well over half the Church's revenue, representing practically the whole of the income of the parish clergy, was thus obtained from tithes. By 1833 a total of £818,518, or more than half the full amount, was owing in tithe arrears since 1831; in 1834 only one-third of the tithe composition was paid; in 1835 only 12 per cent, with landlords still defaulting though to a lesser extent than tenants; and by 1844 the gross arrears still amounted to £866,011, of which £114,192 was due from land-

[1] O'Connell to Duncannon, 14 January 1833, O'Connell Corr., I, 317-18. See Inglis, Freedom of the Press, 195-204, for prosecutions against the Freeman's Journal, Pilot, Comet, Waterford Chronicle, Tipperary Free Press, Carlow Morning Post and Castlebar Telegraph.

[2] Stanley to Wellesley, 20 November 1833, Wellesley Papers, Add. MSS 37306, 188-9.

[3] P.P. 1835, XLVII (461), 2-5; P.P. 1831-2, XXII, App. K., 365; P.P. 1831-2, XXX (326), 3-23.

lords and £751,818 from occupying tenants.[1] It is clear that land-lords, whose rents had always been to some extent endangered by the existence of tithes, frequently joined with tenants in refusing to meet their obligations, though their methods were invariably less dramatic, more peaceful and even legalistic.[2]

In Ulster, much less heavily taxed and with a higher proportion of Protestants of the Established Church, Presbyterians objected as strongly as all Catholics and many Anglicans to paying tithe.[3] The whole western sea-board—Kerry, Clare, Galway, Mayo and Donegal—was deeply affected, while the south-eastern counties of Kilkenny, Carlow, Tipperary, Wexford, Waterford and Queen's County remained the centre as they had been the source of resistance. In Queen's County, over 11,000 decrees were obtained against defaulters; there were more imprisonments for tithe offences in Kilkenny than anywhere else in Ireland, though Kerry and Kildare were not far behind; and between 1829 and 1832, the worst areas of non-payment were the dioceses of Ossory, Leighlin, Cork and Ross, Ferns and Cashel, the region from Cork to the south-east coast, including Tipperary and Queen's County.[4] If the southern half of the country was most deeply affected, there was virtually no region where between 1831 and 1837 tithes were paid either willingly or in full.

---

[1] Return of Claims for Relief, 1831–3, P.P. 1833, XXVIII, 319; P.P. 1836, XL, 135; P.P. 1844, XLIII, 555. In 1835, only £29,056 was forthcoming out of a total of £103,880 owing by landlords, £8,776 of the £148,873 due from tenants.

[2] In Colpe, Co. Meath, the resistance was organized by local landowners led by Thomas Brodigan of Pilltown, a Catholic; the parish refused to pay composition in 1830, got up a subscription to defend their case and to pay for legal opinions, and finally won. But it is clear that while resistance here was covered over with legal opinions, definitions and parish history, the spirit was the same as in those parishes which could put up no legal claim to exemption; a correspondent to Thomas Brodigan, 10 March 1832; F. Brodigan to Thomas Coleman, 28 November 1835; Petition to Lord Anglesey; Legal Opinion of the Whig-Solicitor-General, Crampton, 15 June 1831, advising against opposition, Pilltown Papers, N.L.I. 635.

[3] Select Committee, Tithes, P.P. 1831–2, XXI, 433, evidence of Rev. Henry Montgomery, the Presbyterian leader.

[4] A Return of the total number of persons imprisoned for Tithe offences etc., since 1 January 1831 [to 1837]: P.P. 1837–8, XXXVIII, 319; Return of Arrears of Tithe due since 1 May 1829; P.P. 1833, XXVII, 499–517.

Towards a solution

The Whig Government, apparently convinced that disturbances and resistance to tithes were political in origin, resorted first to the use of force, but the policy of protecting process-servers and of assisting in distraining for tithes soon led to a series of disastrous clashes between the peasantry and government forces. In June 1831 cattle seized for tithe by the rector of Newtownbarry in County Wexford were put up for sale under police escort; but the local magistrate, alarmed at the threatening crowds of peasantry, ordered out a force of yeomanry which fired on the crowd and killed twelve people. This massacre caused an immense public outcry. The yeomanry were generally and rightly believed to be Ascendancy, while the local grand jury of landowners refused to convict the captain and sergeant of murder. But although the police had not fired on this occasion, Bishop Doyle was right in thinking that 'the Newtownbarry affair was a certain if not necessary effect of the proceedings of Government with respect to the magistracy, the constabulary and yeomen'.[1]

This massacre, followed in September and December 1831 by collisions between police and peasantry at Castlepollard in West-meath, and at Knocktopher in Kilkenny, provided Irish politicians and newspapers with abundant material for constant attacks on the Government, which was unable even to carry through a successful prosecution of the peasants led by a hedge schoolmaster, an old United Irishman, who caught a party of police and soldiers in a 'bohreen' called Carrickshock in Kilkenny and killed eleven of them. In September 1832, after four peasants had been killed as the result of attempts by the vicar of Wallstown in Cork to carry out a tithe valuation, O'Connell virtually charged the Government with murder. His letter, originally published in the Radical *True Sun* in England, was reprinted, despite his strong warnings to these newspapers, in the *Pilot* and the *Freeman's Journal*. Blackburne, the Attorney-General ,would gladly have proceeded against both papers and was only deterred by the refusal of the English law officers to prosecute the *True Sun*, since they feared that O'Connell stood a very fair chance of proving his contention at common law.[2]

[1] Doyle to Sir Henry Parnell, 8 July 1831, Fitzpatrick, *Doyle*, II, 300–1; O'Brien, *Fifty Years of Concessions to Ireland*, I, 383–5, et seq., for subsequent clashes between government forces and peasantry.

[2] Inglis, *Freedom of the Press*, 199–200; O'Connell to the Reformers of Great Britain [September 1832], *Annual Register* (1832), 296–7.

Earlier, in June 1832, an Act had been passed which placed £60,000 at the Lord Lieutenant's disposal to be paid to tithe-owners in difficulties and empowered the Government, through the Irish Attorney-General, to collect the arrears due for 1831,[1] a scheme which was strongly opposed by Irish Liberals and Repealers who thought it unjust to pay the clergy's arrears and then to obtain repayment of these advances by harsh measures against defaulters. Several denied that the clergy were distressed or suggested that they should be relieved out of church property, and Sheil, in a speech in which he attacked the exclusion of Catholics from the Select Committee on Irish Tithes which had so far examined only one Catholic witness, summed up the Irish opposition to a policy of 'Coercion to the people and largesses to the clergy . . . and Ireland exasperated for the sake of certain persons of the establishment!'[2]

In reply, Stanley said that the Government was merely taking the place of the tithe-owner in enforcing payment and in vindicating the law. He was strongly supported by Peel, who emphasized that while disturbances had not arisen exclusively from tithes (and here he voiced the fears of those few English politicians with any knowledge of the country), particular disputes soon became general in Ireland, and if the Government did not act at once, the resistance would spread to landlords' rent and grand jury cess.[3] The attempts of Irish Members to delay the bill, though they drew from Stanley the angry remark that public business was being brought to a standstill, were unsuccessful, and in O'Connell's absence Sheil wound up the hopeless opposition of Irish and English Radicals by trusting that the Church 'consisted in something better than vast episcopal territories, numerous sinecurism, bloated pluralities, offensive rates, insulting cesses, pulpits occupied with cobwebs, altars encompassed with loneliness, and churches with clerks for a congregation'.[4] Under the Act, a vigorous campaign was launched from June 1832 to June 1833, which was from every point of view a total and expensive failure. Over 43,000 decrees were issued and only £12,316 were collected, at a rough cost of £26,000.[5]

[1] 2 Will. IV, c. 41 (1 June 1832), generally known as the Attorney-General's Act; see Thomas Daly, *An Outline of a Plan for the abolition of Tithes* (1834), 3–5.
[2] Hansard, X, 1344–9, 8 March 1832, Sheil.
[3] Hansard, XI, 135–55, 181–98, 13 March 1832, Stanley, Peel; see also Melbourne to Wellesley, 8 September 1833, Wellesley Papers, Add. MSS 37306, 72.
[4] Hansard, XII, 577, 16 April 1832, Sheil.
[5] Return of all sums recovered . . . to 1 May 1833, P.P. 1833, XXVII, 491–7.

Grey, Stanley and Melbourne were determined to uphold the law before legislating for grievances. Anglesey in Dublin, infuriated by importunate tithe-owners, had worked out a radical scheme for the abolition of tithes, the resumption by the state of church lands and their letting or sale to provide church income, any surplus to go towards education and the establishment of the Catholic Church. But Stanley, clear as early as January 1832 that he would resign rather than allow any confiscation or diversion of Church property, not only won his point about an early coercive measure but also imposed his own solution for Irish tithes.[1] This was announced in June 1832 in the Second Report of the Select Committee on Tithes, which had already established 'the existence of an organized and systematic opposition to the Payment of tithe' in Ireland and had recommended, in an unfortunate phrase, 'a complete extinction of tithes' by 'commuting them for a charge upon Land . . . or an investment in Land'.[2] Stanley's distinction that it was the old system and not the charge itself which was to be abolished was generally disregarded in Ireland, and from the standpoint of authority, Peel was no doubt right to object to the expression.[3]

Stanley's Tithe Composition Act of 1832 swept away the privilege of compounding by private agreement; a single official commissioner was to fix the total amount payable by the parish and to applot each individual's share; these compositions, compulsory and permanent for at least twenty-one years, were to be reached by discovering the value of each man's land and by fixing a set proportion for tithe composition with reference to the lower corn prices of the years 1823 to 1830. In view of the immense number of small payments and the difficulties of collection, tithe composition was in future to be paid by the landholder immediately above the class of tenants holding land at will or from year to year. At the expiry of each lease in the often long chain between a head landlord, middleman and sub-tenants, the tenant next above was to become responsible for payment, which he could add to the rent of his sub-tenant; any person in this chain could 'undertake' the liability, from the

---

[1] Cloncurry, *Personal Recollections*, 437–8, 440, 442, 445, 450–2; Le Marchant, *Diary*, 26 January 1832, Aspinall, op. cit., 186, for Stanley's explicit declaration in Cabinet against Appropriation.

[2] Select Committee, Tithes, P.P. 1831–2, XXI, 3–5.

[3] Hansard, XI, 184, 13 March 1832, Peel. See also Ellenborough, *Diary*, 15 February 1832, Aspinall, op. cit., 196: 'Peel's opinion was that tithes were gone —at least in Ireland.'

head landlord downwards, for which the 'undertaker' was to be granted a rebate of 15 per cent.[1]

Under this Act and despite the general opposition to tithes, applotments for tithe composition were completed throughout the country and produced, quite by accident, 'a great national survey, . . . the first complete register of the people in relation to the working and tenancy of the land'.[2] But in its real aim the Act was not by any means successful. Landlords were not immediately attracted by a bonus when they might easily not be able to recover any tithe composition in rents. In the northern diocese of Derry nearly all tithe composition was being paid by landlords in 1835, but in the dioceses of Cork and Ross, Cloyne, Waterford and Lismore, and in the south generally as has already been shown, landlords showed a marked unwillingness to co-operate.[3] Middlemen and tenants with leases short enough but longer than from year to year were often almost as economically insecure as their cottier sub-tenants and were not necessarily to be induced to pay a more moderate and fixed composition. To expect them to do so showed Stanley's optimism or, as Sir Henry Parnell thought, his lack of understanding of 'the true circumstances of the case'.[4] Again, and perhaps most important, a tithe composition payment of between one-thirtieth and one-fiftieth of the productive capacity of a piece of land was too heavy for small farmers with extremely low profits, if any, and with relatively high rent obligations.

Stanley's full tithe plan included a measure by which tithes would be redeemed for land. Tithe-payers would redeem all their obligations by a single money payment. If carried out by all tithe-payers at sixteen years purchase, this would produce a capital sum of £9,600,000, assuming a gross annual tithe income of £600,000; and this capital, invested in land by diocesan corporations, would bring in 'a safe and complete rental' of £510,000, a reduction of 15 per cent in tithe-owners' incomes. If landlords would not redeem, the State

[1] 2 & 3 Will. IV, c. 119, esp. sections 12, 13, 17, 20.

[2] Note by R. C. Simington, *Analecta Hibernica*, No. X (July 1941), 296–7. See also his 'The Tithe Applotment Books of 1834', *Journal of Department of Agriculture*, XXXVIII, 289–343, for further comments on the agricultural, topographical and genealogical importance of these 2,500 MS volumes of 1823 to 1837.

[3] Three Returns of Tithe Composition, P.P. 1835, XLVII (405), 2–7; Return, P.P. 1834, XLIII, 263–319, shows that nearly all parishes had compounded by 1834.

[4] Parnell to Bishop Doyle, 20 September 1832, Fitzpatrick, *Doyle*, II, 419.

might purchase the claims of the clergy for tithes and leave the corporations to distribute the sums invested. This was as far as Stanley would go in settling the tithe question, and he made it clear that far from proposing to abolish tithes, he was only seeking by this commutation to substitute one kind of property for another.[1]

The whole of Stanley's plan met with opposition from O'Connell and Irish Members. James Grattan, as a landlord, would not 'undertake' the tithe composition, and he was supported by the Whig Robert Carew, himself a tithe-owner, on an amendment to abolish tithes in substance and name, with compensation, and to make property contribute to a fund for the provision of the clergy and for charitable purposes. Sheil called Stanley's scheme 'this petrified piece of legislation' which 'would but East Retfordize the Church', and O'Connell bitterly attacked the Bill, asking whether 'a whole nation can be guilty of a combination' and declaring with some justice that 'to give them [the clergy] more law is to give them nothing but a mouthful of moonshine'. He called for a tax on all property to be used for the maintenance of all religions and for the relief of the sick.[2] The strategy of O'Connell and his followers, to keep up pressure on the question of Appropriation in the hope of bringing to light the divisions in the Cabinet on the subject, was, for the present, unsuccessful; and although Stanley dropped his bills for commutation of tithes and ecclesiastical corporations in deference to Irish opposition, he actually made it a merit of the Composition Bill that 'it left the whole question of the appropriation of the revenues of the Church just precisely where it found them'.[3]

In June 1833, Government policy on the actual collection of tithes took a new turn. By the Church Million Act, tithe-owners were to be advanced sums up to a total of £1,000,000 subject to reductions of 25 per cent for arrears of 1831 and 1832 and of 15 per cent on arrears for 1833, which together with the suspension of government aid in enforcing payment meant that for all practical purposes the arrears of 1831, 1832 and 1833 were given up.[4] A new policy of preserving a cautious neutrality between the importunities

[1] Hansard, XIV, 95–112, 5 July 1832, Stanley.

[2] Hansard, XIV, 112–28, 360–74, 5, 13 July 1832, Grattan, Carew, Sheil, O'Connell.

[3] Hansard, XIV, 227–9, 10 July 1832, Stanley; see above pp. 39–41, for the Appropriation issue in the Irish Church Temporalities Bill.

[4] 3 & 4 Will. IV, c. 100; see P.P. 1836 (420), XL, 7, for Sir William Gossett's circular, 17 June 1833, ordering the suspension of government aid.

of tithe-owners and the resistance of tithe-payers was laid down by Melbourne for Littleton, the new Chief Secretary, in August 1833. By 1835, magistrates could not order police attendance in distress cases on the unsworn, verbal statements of tithe-owners. Such protection could be given only on the Lord Lieutenant's instructions, and Hardinge, as Chief Secretary in Peel's short Government, maintained exact continuity with this policy.[1]

In January 1835 a group of lay tithe-owners headed by the Tory Lords Roden, Enniskillen, Farnham, Bandon and Lorton hit on a new legal expedient of applying to the Court of Exchequer for power to recover tithes. Sheil, who with O'Connell was proceeded against in this way, managed to throw considerable doubt on the legality of this procedure and on the Court's decision to hold the police liable for not carrying out the orders of commissioners of rebellion.[2] But the most effective answer to this new and brutally direct remedy was provided from the Castle by Thomas Drummond, who purposely refrained from giving the necessary instructions to police authorities and was quite ready to refuse assistance to tithe-owners.[3]

Most politicians, with the exception of the Irish and the Radicals, favoured some kind of commutation scheme.[4] The Tithe Bill

[1] See Melbourne to Littleton, 29 August 1833, Wellesley Papers, Add. MSS 37306, 61–4; Morpeth to Inspectors of Police, 17 October; 24 December 1835; Memo. by Drummond, 26 October 1835, directives laying down the policy; Copies of orders made by H.M.'s Government 1833–5, etc., P.P. 1836 (420), XL, 7–8; and Hardinge to Goulburn, 21 January 1835, P.P. 1835, XLVII, 128–9.

[2] By a simple process, Exchequer bills were filed and served; if these were ignored, writs of rebellion were issued and commissioners empowered to call on local authorities to arrest defaulters until they had paid; see Hansard, XXXIII, 1403–12; XXXIV, 8–12, 2, 3 June 1836, Sheil, Jackson, who defended the Exchequer and tithe-owners. Sheil paid up, but not O'Connell: O'Brien, *Fifty Years of Concessions to Ireland*, I, 565. For Colonel Weldon's use of the remedy in Carlow, see Thomas Butler to Weldon, 27 October; 29 November 1837, Weldon Papers, N.L.I., 486.

[3] *Two Centuries of Irish History*, ed. O. Brien, 358–9; O'Brien, *Drummond*, 202–3, 224–7, 228. See also Littleton to Rev. James Blacker, 14 November 1834, H.O. Papers, 100/245, 203; and Mulgrave to Russell, 2 February 1836, Russell Papers, P.R.O., 30/22/2A, fulminating against the Exchequer's decision and worried about its possible effects on the police.

[4] Peel to Goulburn, 26 April 1833, Parker, *Peel*, II, 218–20. Whig Ministers from Stanley to the left approved the principle, but Archbishop Whateley of Dublin was probably in advance of Irish clerical opinion: A. R. Blake to Bishop Doyle [n.d. 1831], Fitzpatrick, *Doyle*, II, 324–5; Whateley to Wellesley, 30 January 1835, Wellesley Papers, Add. MSS 37307, 349–56.

proposed by Littleton in February 1834 aimed at converting tithe composition into a crown rent or land tax payable for five years up to November 1839 at the full rate of compositions already established and redeemable during this period by a money payment or land; any crown rent unredeemed by 1839 was to become a rent-charge, also redeemable, paid by the head landlord at 80 per cent of the composition. Landlords could recover this charge by adding it to rent, and tithe-owners were to be paid by the Ecclesiastical Commissioners who were to invest the produce of crown rents, rent-charges and redemptions in land.[1] Littleton was enthusiastic about his scheme by which 'the clergy and peasantry will be relieved from pecuniary collision at once, and at the end of 5 years the Government would only have to deal with such owners in Fee or Perpetuity as had not redeemed'.[2]

Even before it entered committee, the Bill offered substantial inducements to Irish landlords to co-operate, and Littleton had managed to 'come to terms with the Primate, the Archbishop of Cashel, Shaw and Lefroy, about the principal details of the Bill. I have agreed to take an uniform rate of Deduction of 15 per cent [on tithe incomes].'[3] But the scheme was strongly attacked by O'Connell and the Irish party as transferring the odium of tithes from the clergy to the landlords. O'Connell warned the Commons that 'Government was about to turn the landowners of Ireland into tithe-proctors ... They should recollect that tithe agitation already threatened to extend to rent. They were to a certain degree necessarily mixed ... [but] Let them [landlords] be turned into tithe-proctors, and the spirit which had continued the present agitation for seventy years, would be applied to rent as well as tithes.'[4] Grey might comfort himself that 'The violent censure, at once

[1] Hansard, XXI, 572–91, 20 February 1834, Littleton. The Irish administration (Wellesley and Littleton, supported by Duncannon) originally wanted a single land tax to supplant tithes, county rates and all other taxes; but their plan was defeated in Cabinet by the opposition of Lord Lansdowne, the personification of the Irish landed interest. See Duncannon to Littleton 17 October 1833, Wellesley Papers Add. MSS 37306, 130–3; Littleton, Diary, 7 July; 11 August 1833, Aspinall, op. cit., 344, 356.

[2] Littleton to Sir John Newport, 31 December 1833, Newport Papers, N.L.I., 796, an interesting letter showing that Littleton, an advanced Whig, was anxious to satisfy both landlords and clergy.

[3] Littleton to Wellesley, 2 May 1834, Wellesley Papers, Add. MSS 37307, 1–7.

[4] Hansard, XXI, 596, 20 February 1834, O'Connell.

pronounced upon it [the Bill] by O'Connell & his Tail was, I think advantageous', but it was a good deal less convenient when the Irish were continually pressing the Government on Appropriation or when, during the Bill's Second Reading,

> Every Irishman in the House returned by a R. Catholic Constituency, with the exception of Ld. Oxmantown and some one other, voted . . . for postponing the 2nd Reading . . . Each member was afraid of having it said that 'he voted against even a week's delay'—so they mustered a good Division. The Irishmen will agree to no measure in the H. of Commons which they cannot defeat in Ireland—unless it be one that shall at once surrender to them or their Tenants the Property of the Church—[1]

At the committee stage the new relationship between O'Connell and the Whigs, following the resignations of Stanley and his friends and of Lord Grey, was immediately apparent. In February, Russell had called O'Connell's plan to reduce tithes by two-thirds 'a direct act of robbery', but in July the Government accepted an amendment of O'Connell's to make the rent-charge 60 per cent instead of 80 per cent of the existing tithe composition, guaranteeing an income of £77/10 per cent to tithe-owners by offering to pay the difference of £17/10 per cent out of the Consolidated Fund.[2] O'Connell's' amendment had in fact sealed the fate of the Bill in the Lords, where it was rejected by 189 votes to 122. Peel was strongly in favour of its being read and if necessary amended, but as Wellington explained to Aberdeen, 'the bill itself was abominable and I could not have commanded a majority in the Lords if I had allowed the second reading unopposed'.[3] The reactionary and obscurantist Tory peers fully deserved Greville's bitter strictures. They had not only caused a rift in their own party's leadership but by rejecting instead of amending this Bill, they had also killed what was to be the last chance of a relatively early solution to the tithe problem. Indeed, in one

---

[1] Grey to Wellesley, 1 March 1834, Wellesley Papers, Add. MSS 37306, 377–8; Littleton to Wellesley, 3 May 1834, Wellesley Papers, Add. MSS 37307, 8–12.

[2] Hansard, XXI, 606, 621, 20 February 1834, O'Connell, Russell; XXV, 771, 30 July 1834, Division. For Duncannon's connivance at this change, see Greville, *Journal*, 7 August 1834, III, 120; Hansard, XXV, 1200–1, 11 August 1834, Duncannon.

[3] Wellington to Aberdeen, 4 September 1834, Add. MSS 43060, cited by Large, 'House of Lords and Ireland', loc. cit., 375.

historian's opinion, they had made the disendowment of the Irish Church 'a mere question of time'.[1]

All new Whig schemes for dealing with the Irish Church and tithes were rendered academic by the dismissal of the Ministry in November 1834. But as the Whigs had gone in some sense because of their Irish Church policy, so they returned triumphantly in April 1835 on Russell's resolution 'that no measure upon the subject of tithes in Ireland can lead to a satisfactory and final adjustment, which does not embody the principle [of Appropriation] . . .'[2] This resolution was Russell's answer to the Conservatives' own Tithe Bill, which was closely modelled on Littleton's original Bill of February 1834 except that rent-charges, redeemable after three years, were to be 75 per cent instead of 80 per cent of the composition, a scheme which had the support not only of Irish Tory M.P.s but also of the Archbishop of Armagh, and this despite the fact that it involved a larger reduction in clerical incomes.[3] But while Appropriation served to force Peel out of power, it completely destroyed any chance of an early settlement of the tithe question. Included in any Tithe Bill, it was certain to be opposed by a growing Conservative Opposition in the Commons and by the solid Conservative majority in the Lords. Yet the Whigs could not quietly drop the principle on which they had returned to power. Graham was angry but right in saying that 'A Tithe Bill, without the Appropriation Clause, introduced *by the present Government* would be a Monster of Political Deformity revolting even to the lax Morals of the days of political Expediency, in which we live'.[4] The Whigs had tied Appropriation and the Irish tithe question firmly together. They had made the settlement of one urgent and serious problem dependent on the assertion of a principle which while it was strictly irrelevant to that problem, yet had provided the Whigs with the parliamentary strength to defeat their opponents and to maintain themselves in office.

[1] Greville, *Journal*, 8, 24 December 1834, III, 177, 187; S. Walpole, *History of England from the Conclusion of the Great War*, III, 266, n. 1, quoted by A. S. Turberville, *The House of Lords in The Age of Reform*, 346.

[2] Hansard, XXVII, 880, 7 April 1835, Russell.

[3] Hansard, XXVII, 13–22, 24–8, 20 March 1835, Hardinge, Shaw. Peel was largely responsible for the plan, an answer to what he called 'the tremendous difficulties of Irish Tithe', to Haddington, 13 February 1835, Peel Papers, Add. MSS 40314, 53. For Church support, see Hardinge to Peel, 6, 7 February 1835, ibid., 40314, 41–4, 47–8.

[4] Graham to Hardinge, 24 January 1836, Peel Papers, Add. MSS 40314, 139–40.

Appropriation was a feature of every Tithe Bill between 1835 and 1837. In the Bill of June 1835 fixing rent-charges at £68/5 per cent of the tithe composition, a surplus of £58,000 'for religious and moral instruction' was to be raised by suspending presentation to benefices with less than 50 Episcopalian parishioners and by deducting income over £300 a year in these parishes. The Bill of April 1836 was practically identical except that it produced a theoretical surplus of £92,612, and in May 1837 in his third Tithe Bill, Morpeth proposed to institute a tax of 10 per cent on the clergy for educational purposes.[1] In 1835, after Peel had failed to divide the Bill in two and the Government's Bill had only been saved by the Irish ministerialist majority of 29, the House of Lords passed the Bill in so far as it regulated tithes and rejected the appropriation scheme by 138 votes to 41. The Government immediately dropped the Bill.[2] In 1836, the Second Reading in the Commons was carried by 39 votes against an amendment by Stanley, whose scheme differed from Morpeth's only in excluding Appropriation and in including redemption, but a majority of only 26 on the Third Reading was 'a grievous disappointment' to the Government.[3] The Lords inevitably rejected the appropriation clauses by much the same majority as in 1835; and Russell, advised by Speaker Abercromby that the Lords' amendments infringed the Commons' privileges on money bills, persuaded the Commons to reject the Bill.[4] A well-established process might have been repeated in 1837 if the death of William IV had not interrupted it.

Throughout these vicissitudes O'Connell and his party solidly supported the Government, and it was scarcely O'Connell's fault if by 1837 any solution of the tithe problem seemed as far away as ever. Indeed his support of schemes which aimed only at replacing tithes by more moderate rent-charges finally provoked a rebellion within his own party when in July 1836 Sharman Crawford moved to abolish tithes altogether. In a speech in which he criticized the Composition Acts, pointed out that while tithe was combined with

[1] Hansard, XXVIII, 1319–44; XXXIII, 204–21; XXXVIII, 408–21, 26 June 1835; 25 April 1836; 1 May 1837, Morpeth.

[2] Hansard, XXIX, 790–822, 1067–72; XXX, 934–6, 21, 23 July; 24 August 1835, Peel, Divisions.

[3] Hansard, XXXIV, 117–122, 1259–64, 3 June; 4 July 1836, Divisions; Greville, *Journal*, 9 July 1836, III, 361.

[4] Hansard, XXXV, 516, 760–92, 25 July; 2 August 1836; Abercromby to Russell, 25 July 1836, Russell Papers, P.R.O. 30/22/2B.

rent it would continue to be paid by the people and asserted 'the right of conscience against the tyranny of establishments', he appealed for support to Irish Members, who though publicly pledged to the complete abolition of tithes, were now voting for Morpeth's Bill. O'Connell opposed Crawford's motion, implying that unlike Crawford with his concern for 'eternal justice', he (O'Connell) was prepared to accept a compromise, and using the curious argument that if tithes were abolished there would be no surplus revenues available for educational or charitable purposes. Only 18 Members, including Repealers like Henry Grattan, Butler, Finn, Callaghan, Sir William Brabazon and Dillon Browne with a few Liberals like Sir Richard Musgrave and Westenra and some English Radicals, supported Crawford, and O'Connell with the rest of his own party found himself voting with Irish Tories and Whigs.[1]

Crawford carried his opposition to O'Connell from Westminster to Dublin. In the General Association he attempted in October and December 1836 to carry resolutions in favour of the complete abolition of tithes, and accused O'Connell of sacrificing the interests of Ireland to the convenience of the Whig Government.[2] He found little support either then or in 1837 and 1838, when he kept up a series of attacks on O'Connell and his 'Castle-hacks' and on the details of the final Tithe Bill of 1838. Ulster Liberals and a few Catholic priests like Father Davern of Tipperary and Archbishop MacHale might agree with him, but they were quite unable to shake O'Connell's firm hold on his party or to force him to change his policy.[3] In July 1836 it was the English Radicals and not O'Connell who would have made trouble if Appropriation had been dropped. In June 1837 only seven Irish Members joined Crawford in opposing the current Tithe Bill, and O'Connell replied to Archbishop Mac-Hale's protest against the measure by saying that he thought the

---

[1] Hansard, XXXIV, 1135-44, 1147-8, 1149-50, 1 July 1836, Crawford, O'Connell, Division.

[2] O'Brien, *Fifty Years of Concessions to Ireland*, I, 514. For Lord Cloncurry's unsuccessful attempts to patch up the quarrel, see W. J. Fitzpatrick, *Life and Times of Cloncurry* (1855), 440-3.

[3] *Northern Whig*, 2, 10 June 1837; 4, 16 August 1838; *Kilkenny Moderator*, 2, 6, 13, 23, 27 September 1837. O'Connell handled the stern and uncompromising Crawford badly, alienating him finally by his rough banter at a meeting of the Precursor Society in August 1838. See Duffy, *Young Ireland*, I, 8, 17-18, who probably exaggerates the extent of clerical suspicion of O'Connell but quotes a vitriolic letter to him from Fr. Davern.

Bill 'a valuable instalment'. As a politician he knew how it would aid his next move.[1] By this evasive remark, he meant that he had decided to accept a Tithe Bill without Appropriation.

Six months ealier Henry Warburton had passed on to Russell a letter from O'Connell from which it was clear that the Whigs could depend on his support if they dropped Appropriation and in which he had written that 'If there were a proper deduction from the burthen of the tythes, there would for the present be no surplus; and it is really too bad to risk *on such* a point, a Ministry who are for the first time in History conquering the 'Anti-Saxon' spirit of Ireland and adding Eight Millions to the King's subjects'.[2] Greville and others had noticed distinct signs that O'Connell's attitude was not an exceptional one among ministerialists, even Duncannon, a strong appropriator and in Stanley's words 'the âme damnée' of O'Connell, confessing in November 1836 that the policy 'would not pacify'. 'Pretty well', Stanley thought, 'for a Cabinet Minister on the healing Measure.'[3] Russell was under strong pressure from his elder brother Lord Tavistock, who thought that the whole question could now only be settled by a compromise with Peel and cogently asked whether the Government could re-introduce in Parliament 'a measure which you *know positively* that one branch of it will reject, and to connect it with another measure which you are in duty bound to settle if you can? Is it not almost criminal to persist in such a course—if not criminal, is it statesmanlike?'[4]

On this issue at least, Peel, Wellington and the Conservative majority in the Lords were in complete agreement after 1835; no Tithe Bill would be passed which contained Appropriation in any form. Even when Peel did not oppose the Bill of May 1837, he was

---

[1] Greville, *Journal*, 24 July 1836, III, 364; O'Connell to MacHale, 31 May 1837, *O'Connell Corr.*, II, 93; MacHale to O'Connell, 20 May 1837, O'Connell Papers, N.L.I., uncatalogued, enclosing a petition against the Bill from the clergy of Tuam diocese and stressing 'how great is the dissatisfaction of the people at the prospect of being obliged to pay the full amount of the Tithes after the hopes so often held out to them of being released from the odious impost'.

[2] O'Connell to Warburton, 29 December 1836, Russell Papers, P.R.O. 30/22/2D.

[3] Stanley to Graham, 10 November 1836, Graham MSS; Greville, *Journal*, 18 July 1836, III, 362; A. Bannerman, M.P. to Russell, 8 July 1836, Russell Papers, P.R.O. 30/22/2B, astonished at 'the talk' of some English and Irish Members on the Irish Church question.

[4] Tavistock to Russell, 12 December 1836, Russell Papers, P.R.O. 30/22/2D.

quite clear that its tax of 10 per cent on clerical incomes, 'a principle of vital interest to the Establishment', was unacceptable; on the other hand if the Whigs dropped Appropriation, he and Wellington were prepared to make a settlement of the tithe, municipal reform and poor law questions.[1] With the fate of these three measures resting in the hands of the House of Lords, the Tory leaders were in an excellent position to drive their bargain and the Whigs had the strongest of incentives to come to terms.

The first sign of a possible arrangement on these lines came in February 1837, when Peel and Wellington agreed not to take any initiative on 'the Irish Church Question' both on general and on party grounds,[2] and when Russell's postponement of the Tithe Bill was seen by the King and Melbourne and by Greville as a preliminary move to drop Appropriation.[3] From Mulgrave in Ireland came the encouraging view that 'If the Government thought it desirable with reference to their own stability to postpone the Question altogether and that such a course was on the other side of the water prudential, I am sure for such an object the popular party here would cheerfully acquiesce'. Even Crawford had apparently told Mulgrave that 'if it would maintain the Government in power', he would actually be prepared to recommend payment of tithes; as for O'Connell, wrote the Lord Lieutenant, 'the more I think on *this* subject you will have in *fact* the vote of O'Connell'.[4] Mulgrave thought that Appropriation was only 'a badge of attachment to the Party at present in power', that no one in Ireland saw it as '*a triumph*' or anticipated 'any solid advantage from it' and that it was essentially a matter for the consciences of those Irish M.P.s heavily committed to it.[5]

By May 1837, Melbourne's opinion, expressed to Wharncliffe and passed on to Peel, was that '"I can't help thinking that things are *soothing* down . . . and as to the appropriation Clause I can't [say] so publicly yet, but we should give that up without much

[1] Peel to Wellington, 9 April 1837, Parker, *Peel*, II, 344–6; see further below pp. 250 ff.

[2] Wellington to Peel, 29 (sic) February 1837, Peel Papers, Add. MSS 40310, 164–6, wrongly dated by Parker, *Peel*, II, 339–40.

[3] Sir H. Taylor to Russell, 2 January 1837; Melbourne to Russell [February 1837], Walpole, *Russell*, I, 274–6; Greville, *Journal*, 22 February 1837, III, 396.

[4] Mulgrave to Russell, 8 April 1837, Russell Papers, P.R.O. 30/22/2E.

[5] Mulgrave to Russell, 16 December 1836, Russell Papers, P.R.O. 30/22/2D.

difficulty".'¹ In September, after the elections showed clearly the decline in the Whigs' support in England, Russell finally capitulated. Wellington's compromise was, he thought, 'in principle a fair one, & . . . we should not be justified in keeping unsettled the three Irish questions, unless the details were very unfair, & unequal'.² The final plan for Irish tithes, outlined by Russell in March 1838, was to convert tithe composition into a rent-charge at 70 per cent of the composition; the proceeds of this tax were to go to the payment of the Irish constabulary and other secular purposes, while the Consolidated Fund was to bear an equal sum for the payment of clergy and tithe-owners.³

With this last ingenious attempt to maintain the appearance of Appropriation without meeting the old difficulty that Church funds were to be used entirely for the education of Catholic children, the Government immediately came under attack from Conservatives and Radicals. The Tory Sir Thomas Acland's motion formally to expunge the famous resolution of 1835 failed by only 19 votes,⁴ but a Radical move to re-insert Appropriation in the Bill was heavily defeated by 270 votes to 46, with 14 Irish Members, most of them supporters of Crawford's attempt to abolish tithes, voting in the minority. Most of the Irish party under O'Connell voted against the motion, their leader declaring that the Irish people now did not want appropriation and that, if they did, a reduction of 25 per cent to 30 per cent in tithes would effectively provide it.⁵

The Government accepted some drastic amendments in committee. The quasi-appropriation clauses were given up and plans for redemption by the State and by tithe-payers were dropped. Shaw, the Irish Conservative, proposed to increase the rent-charge to 75 per cent of the composition, and his suggestion was finally incorporated in the Bill. O'Connell's proposal to remit all arrears of tithe was

¹ Wharncliffe to Peel, 13 May 1837, Peel Papers, Add. MSS 40423, 227–9, reporting Melbourne's conversation.

² Russell to Melbourne, 13 September 1837, Russell Papers, P.R.O. 30/22/2F; Melbourne to Russell, 15 September 1837, Walpole, *Russell*, I, 292.

³ Hansard, XLI, 1315–18, 27 March 1838, Russell. The scheme failed to meet the approval of the Archbishop of Armagh: Walpole, *Russell*, I, 298–9.

⁴ Hansard, XLII, 1203–13, 1353–8, 14, 15 May 1838, Acland, Division. Greville thought that Acland's was a pre-concerted move, despite the Opposition's offer of a compromise, but added: 'I cannot help thinking Peel likes to see his party defeated in this way': *Journal*, 13, 18 May 1838, IV, 96–8.

⁵ Hansard, XLIII, 1202–5; 1188–94; 2 July 1838, Division, O'Connell.

virtually conceded when Russell agreed to use £260,000 (the residue of the Million Act) to indemnify tithe-owners.[1] The Bill passed the Commons by 148 votes to 30 against a last wrecking amendment by Dillon Browne, one of Archbishop MacHale's Members, supported by English Radicals like Hume, Ward, Grote and Daniel Whittle Harvey, 'an opposition', according to Russell, 'small in numbers but bitter in spirit'.[2] Peel, Stanley and O'Connell all supported the Bill, with nearly the whole of the Irish party and including many former followers of Crawford, whose absence from Parliament perhaps allowed them to come more easily to terms with their consciences and with a measure which passed the House of Lords almost as a formality.

As a legislative climax to eight years of resistance to tithes, the Act of 1838 was disappointing. A rent-charge, three-quarters of the old composition and payable twice yearly by head landlords, took the place of tithe composition; but the landlords, who received a bonus of up to 25 per cent for their trouble, were entitled to add the charge to the rent of their immediate sub-tenants and the liability travelled downwards, stopping only at tenants at will or from year to year, the largest single class of the Irish peasantry, whose exemption by Stanley's Act was confirmed in 1838. Further, the Act provided that rack-rents (full rents, without fines or deductions of any kind) should be reduced by a quarter of the tithe composition, the difference between the old composition and the new rent-charge. These rent-charges were liable to variation with reference to the average price of corn in the seven previous years. Finally all arrears for 1834 to 1837 were written off, and provision was made for the collection of future arrears by the Government, although this was never carried out with any vigour.[3]

---

[1] Hansard, XLIV, 84–90, 368–72, 10, 19 July 1838, O'Connell. Stanley and Peel, to their surprise, found themselves in agreement with him, Stanley remarking that the whole benefit of the Bill depended on the clergy's not demanding payment directly from the people. In fact, the arrears had been given up in every Tithe Bill since Hardinge's in 1835.

[2] Russell to Normanby, 27 July 1838, Russell Papers, P.R.O. 30/22/3B; Hansard, XLIV, 693–5, 26 July 1838, Division.

[3] 1 & 2 Victoria, c. 109. See Daniel Kinahan, *A Digest of the Act for the Abolition of Tithes* (1838), v–xxxiii. Between 1839 and 1844, £42,000 in arrears, only a fraction of those outstanding, were paid to the Government, over £28,000 through legal proceedings; Return of . . . Tithe Arrears, P.P. 1844 (305), XLIII, 2.

For eight years, the greater part of the income of the Established Church in Ireland had been withheld at the considerable cost of over £1,000,000 to the State. Archbishop Whately's balanced description in 1835 of the clergy's position was probably accurate enough, that 'in some instances they are left quite destitute, and are relieved by a pittance out of the liberal subscription raised for them in England. In some instances again, they are pretty well paid; but the greater part of them are, I believe, in an intermediate state—i.e. a few of the landlords pay the composition, and the rest not.'[1] Yet the Act of 1838 seems to have met with little resistance. The poorest peasants were exempted from actual payment, and more moderate charges in a period of rising corn prices inclined more prosperous tenants and middlemen to pay the additions to their rents with less hostility than they had shown to the payment of tithe composition.[2] Above all, a scheme by which, with a considerable bonus for their trouble, landlords collected the tithe in rents was certainly more convenient than a system which placed the clergy in direct conflict with their unwilling Catholic and Protestant debtors. The landlord possessed stronger sanctions than even the most determined parson had enjoyed. He could evict or at least refuse to renew a lease and the mere threat to withhold land was in itself a powerful weapon. But while the Act of 1838 saved the Church from extreme popular hostility and postponed its downfall for thirty years, it did so at the expense of Irish landlordism. When the campaign against tithes ceased, it was followed by the war of tenants against landlords, when rent (increased by the hidden payments to the clergy) became the sole focus of agrarian discontent and opposition.

Thus the Act had consequences very far from the intentions either of the Whig Government or of their Irish supporters. The Whigs had set out to solve the question principally by breaking the direct and disastrous relationship between the clergy and the rural population while still maintaining the axiom that tithes, a species of landed property, must be paid by all persons with anything resembling a

[1] Whately to Melbourne, 16 October 1835, *Melbourne Papers*, 298. By 1838 only £3,238 out of £635,712 advanced to tithe-owners under the Million Act had been repaid, about two-thirds of it by the Duke of Devonshire. By 1844, nearly £1,000,000 had been advanced; Returns, P.P. 1836 (355), XL, 2–19; 1837-8 (266), XXXVIII, 1–2; 1844 (305), XLIII, 2.

[2] Mulgrave to Russell, 11 May 1838, Russell Papers, P.R.O. 30/22/2B, thought that 'all sides . . . so long accustomed to *lie* that I don't believe they could speak truth if they would', were now 'heartily tired of the Question'.

permanent interest in the land. By confusing what was at bottom an economic problem with the whole question of the existence of the Established Church in Ireland, they delivered themselves into the hands of the Conservative Opposition, who saw in Appropriation a threat to disestablish the Church and who could rely on overwhelming support in England for their successful rearguard action. As Russell explained, the Government had finally given up Appropriation partly because of its weak majority in the Commons, partly because of the English public's hostility to the principle and partly because of the indifference of the Irish people.[1]

He was undeniably right in this last point. Appropriation as such received little support in Ireland, and as leading ultimately to a Catholic Church endowed by the State, it would have certainly been as strongly opposed in Ireland as by public opinion in England.[2] The Irish people, for religious and for even more pressing economic reasons, wanted a complete abolition of the tithe system. Why then did O'Connell and most of his party, who had supported and encouraged this demand, agree to a compromise solution in 1838? It would no doubt be an over-simplification to say that as landlords they too participated in the bribe of one quarter of the tithes and thus helped indirectly to shore up the Established Church; but at least from any landlord's point of view, moderate tithe payments collected in rent were greatly preferable to no tithes at all and perhaps no rents. There had always been a wide cleavage between the aims of middle-class politicians who wanted to pull down a Church Establishment and of a peasantry in revolt against a whole social and economic system. But the history of the tithe question also shows clearly that for O'Connell and his party, alliance with the Whigs required great sacrifices of opinion and consistency in the interests of discipline and support. Political compromise was the inevitable consequence of alliance with an English Government.

[1] Lord John Russell, *Letter to the Electors of Stroud on the Principles of the Reform Act* (2nd edn. 1839), 20–1, 42.

[2] Macaulay was right on the opposition to Catholic Establishment: 'no combination of statesmen', Whig and Tory, 'is a match for a combination of fools', 'High Church and Low Church, . . . Oxford and Exeter Hall; all the champions of the voluntary system; all the English Dissenters; all Scotland; all Ireland, both Orangemen and Papists'; to Macvey Napier, 25 November 1843, Trevelyan, *Macaulay*, 444–5.

CHAPTER VI

The Irish Poor Law

The controversy : participants and alignments

IN 1844, in a short analysis of the Irish agrarian problem, Engels insisted that Irish poverty and distress were not principally due to English exploitation of the country or to the financial exactions of the Established Church or to the 'hundreds of other reasons' which had been suggested, but were 'the inevitable consequences of the existing state of society'.[1] Nothing illustrates so well the truth of this remark (which Engels himself scarcely substantiated) as the terms of the vigorous public controversy, conducted through pamphlets, journals, newspapers and in evidence before Select Committees of Parliament, which preceded and accompanied the final introduction of a Poor Law into Ireland in 1838.

In contrast to the problem of tithes, whose social and economic origins were often obscured by factors of religion and politics, the Poor Law question was ideally suited for such a discussion. It was concerned with the great certainty of Irish poverty. There was no question, as in England, of working out schemes to reform an existing system, for the Irish poor were largely dependent on private charity. There was no compulsory or uniform assessment for poor rates and although the sick poor were reasonably well provided for in county infirmaries, fever hospitals and dispensaries, there were only twelve houses of industry for the homeless and unemployed in the whole of Ireland. All parties could safely assume that existing

[1] F. Engels, *The Condition of the Working Class in England*, eds. W. O. Henderson and W. H. Chaloner (1958), 308.

arrangements for poor relief were ineffective and haphazard, dependent largely on private contributions or on government grants to
supplement grand jury presentments, and very unequally distributed
in favour of the more prosperous Dublin area as against the
heavily-populated, occasionally famine-stricken parts of the west.
These arrangements did not deserve the name or dignity of a
system.[1]

Beginning in the 1820's, serious discussion of the problem of Irish
destitution came to involve men as different as economists and
theorists of politics such as Thomas Malthus, David Ricardo,
James McCulloch, James and John Stuart Mill, Nassau Senior and
Isaac Butt, Members of Parliament like the Evangelical Tory
Michael Thomas Sadler, the Whig George Poulett Scrope and the
Radical Colonel Torrens, ecclesiastics like Bishop Doyle, Archbishop
Whately and the Presbyterian Dr. Thomas Chalmers, and Irish
agricultural experts and reformers like the Irish Whig M.P.,
Viscount Clements, William Sharman Crawford, William Conner
and William Blacker. But an interest in the basic poverty problem
led inevitably to a discussion of the whole economic and social
position of Ireland—the causes and consequences of the growth of
population, possible changes and reforms in the land system, the
questions of emigration and public works—to a debate about the
role of the State in economic life, an issue more familiar to the
laissez-faire nineteenth century than is often supposed.[2] Those who
opposed an Irish Poor Law were forced to suggest other remedies
for the problem of poverty while those who favoured a Poor Law
went on to suggest other ways in which the state might usefully
intervene in the Irish economy. Both sides were compelled to set out
their theoretical positions in order to justify their conclusions.

The opponents of an Irish Poor Law made two basic assumptions.
They believed that Irish poverty was the inevitable result of an
excess of population over the demand for labour and that it could
only be remedied by ensuring that capital, whose agency would
satisfy the demand for labour, increased faster than population.
They believed with some justice that sub-division of land and a

---

[1] See George O'Brien, *Economic History of Ireland from the Union to the
Famine* (1921), 162–9.

[2] An important recent treatment of the whole question of the inter-action of
theory and policy on Ireland is R. D. Collison Black's *Economic Thought and The
Irish Question, 1817–70* (1960). See esp. pp. 86–133 on the Poor Law.

potato diet had enabled the Irish to increase rapidly while still just supporting themselves and therefore that the cottier system must be abolished and replaced by a capitalist agriculture on the English model. This would entail the consolidation of estates and the eviction of cottier tenants, who would become wage-labourers dependent on employers instead of on themselves; in this state of dependence the Irish would cease to make 'imprudent' marriages and the growth of population would be checked. Increased capital invested in a profitable system of agriculture would swell the wages-fund and hence multiply opportunities of employment; and those ex-cottiers not absorbed into agriculture would find alternative employment in industry or in public works, or would be encouraged to emigrate.[1]

This prescription did not take any account of the peculiar temperament or wishes of the Irish peasantry. It assumed that Irish landlords would, given only the capital, become 'English' landlords overnight; it took little account of the huge numbers of Irish who would necessarily be involved or of the difficulties certain to arise in exchanging one system of agriculture, one type of society for another. An increase in capital investment might actually lessen opportunities for employment, since grazing, creating much less employment than tillage, was always the better investment in Ireland in the early nineteenth century, even before the Repeal of the Corn Laws. But this scheme had the merit (given its premises) of being coherent and plausible. Any legislation which might increase population without increasing capital investment was therefore to be condemned, especially if, as its opponents alleged, a Poor Law actually swallowed up funds which might be used to employ productive labour.

This general attitude towards the Irish economy stemmed from a synthesis of Malthus' population-thesis, Ricardo's capitalist theories and Bentham's view of a spontaneous economic system in which interests must be allowed to find their own natural harmony with the minimum of outside or governmental interference. When the question of Irish poverty first came up seriously with the fall in agricultural prices after 1815 and the partial famines of 1817 and 1822, Malthus and Ricardo both declared against any plan of giving

[1] The Malthusian recommendation of 'moral restraint' was thus to be supplemented, if not entirely replaced, by severely practical checks on population growth, such as eviction, consolidation, wage-labour and emigration. See Black, *Economic Thought*, 18–20, 239–42.

relief to the able-bodied poor.[1] The Benthamites, without a direct lead from the master, were divided. Nassau William Senior, a close associate of Bentham and, with Edwin Chadwick one of the leading members of the English Poor Law Commission, consistently opposed a general Poor Law in Ireland. He conceded that medical treatment with provision for the blind, the chronically infirm and the mad should be available, but he believed that provision for the relief of the aged and able-bodied poor would destroy industry, providence and mutual benevolence, an argument frequently used by all opponents of the measure.[2]

Senior also held (and here he was strongly supported by a rigid Malthusian like Colonel Torrens) that a Poor Law would lead to an increase in population without increasing the country's resources. As Torrens put it, 'the whole rental of the country would be inadequate to the maintenance of those for whose labour there would be no demand', and Irish poverty would become England's responsibility.[3] Opponents of an Irish Poor Law were always inclined to argue from English analogies and experiences. For those, like Senior himself, who had carried through in 1834 the reform of the English Poor Law it seemed madness to inflict anything like the old unreformed English system on Ireland, where the problem of poverty was comparatively so much worse. Senior always assumed that when his opponents talked of a Poor Law they meant outdoor relief given out of workhouses to the able-bodied in the shape of allowances to supplement wages. Some of them did mean this, but in 1837 Senior was not even prepared to accept the workhouse system for Ireland.

Arguing against what he called Bishop Doyle's 'clap-traps on the rights of the poor, and the duties of the state, the law of nature and the law of the gospel', Senior accused Doyle of being almost a Saint-Simonist and of wishing to turn Ireland into Paraguay under the Jesuits 'where the law punished idleness and sinfulness, and the priest divided among the people the whole produce of the soil'. To

---

[1] For Malthus' explicit opposition, which had not changed by 1833, see Select Committee, Emigration, P.P. 1827, V, Q. 3228, quoted by Black, *Economic Thought*, 92. Ricardo subscribed to the Report of a Select Committee in 1823 which came down against such a plan.

[2] Nassau William Senior, *A Letter to Lord Howick on a Legal Provision for the Irish Poor . . .* (1831), 14–16, 24–5. See also Second Report, Select Committee, Irish Poor, P.P. 1830, VII, Qs. 3394, 3569–79, evidence of Dr. Thomas Chalmers.

[3] Hansard, VI, 821–2, 29 August 1831, Torrens.

Senior's *laissez-faire* philosophy, state intervention in the shape of a Poor Law was equated with commercial protection, censorship and the attempt to control men's minds as well as their bodies.[1] His own recommendations—large-scale, state-aided emigration and an ambitious programme of public works—could be defended on strictly orthodox grounds by arguing that the state might provide those essential facilities (roads, harbours, for instance) which private enterprise would not or could not profitably undertake.[2] But a Poor Law would halt the essential and healthy trend towards the consolidation of estates; without such a Law, the process would gather speed and momentum.

The supporters of a Poor Law for Ireland are not so easily categorized as its opponents, partly because they did not all make the same general assumptions, partly because they were divided on the nature and scope of the measure. Bishop Doyle, the weightiest member of this school, argued that since the social state is natural to man, a community is obliged to provide for those of its members who cannot provide for themselves.[3] But this strict right of the poor to support was, he emphasized, 'a right to get but not to take'.[4] Eloquently and from first-hand knowledge, Doyle described the desperate condition of the Irish poor, which even his opponents did not underestimate; a Poor Law which also provided employment would give the poor that 'bare sufficiency of necessaries' without which they would have no incentive to improve their condition.[5] He was necessarily and violently anti-Malthusian. Even admitting the present superabundance of the Irish people, which he was most reluctant to do, he argued that the country would certainly not be

[1] Senior, *Letter to Lord Howick*, 25–7, 38, note; see also his *Journals*, I, 147–9.

[2] Black, *Economic Thought*, 159–62. It might be noted here that the Irish party's contribution to parliamentary discussion of the questions of emigration and public works was small. Exceptions were Andrew Lynch, a strong advocate of a public works policy and Chairman of a Select Committee on the subject in 1835, and Smith O'Brien, personally as well as publicly interested in emigration and railway construction. See Black, op. cit., 196, 224.

[3] J.K.L. [John Kildare and Leighlin], *Letters on the State of Ireland* (1825), Letters XI, XII.

[4] Letter XI, 318–20, 327–33. Doyle argued that the Protestant Establishment, having taken over Catholic Church property, had never fulfilled its obligation to support the poor and should now be made to do so.

[5] Letter XII, 355, 356–9. Doyle saw this provision of employment as leading to an increase in capital investment (i.e. in land improvement, growth of new industries and stimulus to internal trade).

over-populated if its resources were fully exploited, and that a Poor Law, by raising the people's condition, would automatically check improvident early marriages.[1]

Sadler and Poulett Scrope, the most prominent spokesmen of this school in Parliament, owed much to Doyle not only in their insistence on the right of the poor to subsistence but also in their anti-Malthusian attitudes and in their demand for a Poor Law giving relief in return for labour.[2] Scrope, like Doyle, saw poor relief essentially as a programme of public works which would increase the country's prosperity, lessen insecurity and stimulate investment.[3] Another supporter of a Poor Law was Lord Clements, the Whig M.P. for Leitrim, a dim figure in politics but the author of an able and well-informed pamphlet in which he argued for small tillage farms worked by improved methods, as against consolidation, the latter being a process which did not necessarily entail more capital investment but simply the extension of grazing. A Poor Law was not a panacea, but 'it will give us', he wrote, 'a new social element, by which it will become the direct interest of the landlord, to foster the growth of capital vested in labour, instead of capital vested in cattle'.[4] Fear of being financially swamped by poor rates would drive landlords and farmers to find employment for the able-bodied poor.

The real interest of Clements' pamphlet lies in his advocacy of small farms as the proper basis of the Irish rural economy. Those like Scrope, Clements and William Sharman Crawford who rejected the possibility of transplanting the English agricultural system to

[1] Letter XII, 363-4; and Letter V, 112: 'Poverty and population act reciprocally upon each other like cause and effect; remove the one, or lessen it, and you will thereby check the other.'

[2] Hansard, VI, 783-816, 29 August 1831, Sadler. Both Scrope and Sadler agreed with Cobbett in admiring the Elizabethan Poor Law, which enshrined the right to relief; see *Cobbett's Manchester Lectures* . . . [and] *A Letter to Mr. O'Connell* (1832), 154-79.

[3] Scrope's pamphlet output was remarkable: G. Poulett Scrope, *Plan of a Poor-Law for Ireland* . . . (1833); 'Foreign Poor Laws—Irish Poverty', in *Quarterly Review*, LV (December 1835); *How is Ireland to be Governed* (1846); *Letters to Lord John Russell on the expediency of enlarging the Irish Poor-Law* (1846); *Remarks on the Irish Poor Relief Bill* (1847). Orthodox opposition to any plan of State intervention to cure under-employment is well shown by Spring Rice's remark to Bishop Doyle, 26 April 1829, Monteagle Papers: '. . . I cannot see that Poor Laws tend to augment the demand for labour in any respect.'

[4] Lord Clements, *The Present Poverty of Ireland* (1838), 119.

Ireland were forced to suggest an alternative solution.[1] They found it, as later did John Stuart Mill and Isaac Butt,[2] in the creation of a peasant proprietary owning small farms or holding them on secure copyhold tenancies—a line of thought less revolutionary in economic and social terms than the orthodox prescription of consolidation, far better adapted to existing Irish conditions and to the peculiar psychology of the Irish peasantry and destined to lead to the Tenant League agitation of the 1850's, to a partial victory in Gladstone's Land Acts of 1870 and 1881 and to final success, after Ashbourne's and Balfour's Acts of 1885 and 1891, in the land legislation of 1903. Most of this school of thought were also supporters of an Irish Poor Law, and indeed their agrarian theories were a direct result of their participation in the debate on the Poor Law question.[3]

The protagonists of an Irish Poor Law were supported, to the immense advantage of their cause, by public opinion in England. Archbishop Whately thought that 'The feeling of the English was a mixture of revenge, compassion and self-love. They pitied the suffering poor of Ireland; they had a fierce resentment against Irish landlords, whom they hastily judged to be the sole authors of those sufferings; and they dreaded calls on their own purse'.[4] A huge fund of information was available through the Reports of four Select Committees in 1819, 1823, 1827 and 1830. The academic controversy found its way into the English newspapers, with the *Morning Chronicle* supporting Bishop Doyle against Dr. Chalmers, and *The Times*, consistent with its opposition to the English Poor

---

[1] Scrope saw Ireland's future as 'a Belgium on a large scale, with its Catholic population, its five to ten acre farms, cultivated . . . by a prudent, thrifty, contented and comfortable peasantry': *How is Ireland to be Governed*, 65. See also W. S. Crawford, *A Defence of the Small Farmers of Ireland* (1839).

[2] For earlier writers like William Conner and William Blacker, working on the same lines in the 1830's, see Black, *Economic Thought*, 24, 29. Engels, in opposing the idea of a smallholder economy in Ireland on the grounds that it would scarcely provide a livelihood for most peasants and that any improvement would be lost by a consequent and rapid population-increase was merely repeating the arguments of the Malthusians and orthodox economists. See his *Condition of the Working Class*, 307–8.

[3] Isaac Butt, then a Tory barrister, Professor of Political Economy at Trinity College, Dublin and later the first leader of the Home Rule party, in fact opposed the Poor Law proposals as wholly inadequate. See his *The Poor-Law Bill for Ireland Examined . . . in a Letter to Lord Viscount Morpeth* (1837), and below p. 220, n. 4.

[4] E. J. Whateley, *Life and Correspondence of Richard Whateley* (1866), I, 401–2.

Law, carrying Senior's pamphlet.[1] More important than the terms of Bishop Doyle's disagreement with Senior, (whose claims to pontificate on Irish issues Doyle dismissed with the remark that Senior was 'buried in the dens of the Inns of Court or vending political economy to beardless youths at a *coterie* in the "west end"'), the leading articles of John Black in the *Morning Chronicle* converted James Mill and most of the Political Economy Club to support of an Irish Poor Law. Economists were the more encouraged to change their views because they thought they saw in the English Poor Law Act of 1834 a system which if applied to Ireland, might check the growth of population, or at least do nothing to increase it.[2]

Popular resentment in England against Irish landlords stemmed partly from the belief that measures like consolidation inevitably worsened the condition of the poor but also in part from the conviction that cheap Irish labour, now easily transported by steamships, provided unfair competition to English labour in agriculture and in industry. If Irish landlords did their duty, so it was argued, this flood of immigration would stop. 'Irish landlords should be *compelled* to do their duty', Lord Shrewsbury told Bishop Doyle, 'if they will not do it otherwise.'[3] Herded together in large and growing slum-communities in the industrial cities, living and working in conditions of dense overcrowding and almost unrelieved squalor which yet provided more in wages and food than were obtainable at home, the Irish seemed to threaten the standard of living of a large section of the English working class. Carlyle's violent prejudices were not always unrepresentative. To him in 1839 the Irishman, continually forcing down wages in occupations where he competed with native labour, was 'the sorest evil this country has to strive with . . . There abides he, in his squalor and unreason, in his falsity and drunken violence, as the ready-made nucleus of degradation and disorder. Whosoever struggles, swimming with difficulty, may now find an example how the human being can exist not swimming but sunk.'[4]

In reality, English working class fears of Irish competition

---

[1] *Morning Chronicle*, 18 January; *Times*, 3 September 1831, cited in Fitzpatrick, *Doyle*, II, 318.

[2] For Black's achievement, see *Letters of John Stuart Mill*, ed. H. Elliott (1910), II, 14; for Doyle's remark, see Fitzpatrick, *Doyle*, II, 319.

[3] Shrewsbury to Doyle, 5 April 1831, Fitzpatrick, *Doyle*, II, 287.

[4] Thomas Carlyle, *Chartism* (1839), 28–9, quoted by Engels, *Condition of the Working Class*, 104–5.

were largely unjustified. The Irish were almost entirely employed in the roughest, most unskilled industrial activities, as 'navvies' in railway and bridge construction, builders, labourers, porters, odd-jobs men and handloom weavers; and George Cornewall Lewis, who made an official inquiry into the subject, concluded that far from depressing the rate of wages the Irish actually raised it by providing a constant supply of strong mobile labour, without which industrial expansion could not have taken place. Both he and Senior were agreed that without Irish seasonal migration, English and Scottish harvests would have been much reduced.[1] There was perhaps more justification for middle-class fears that unemployed or sick Irish might be a burden on English poor rates. But however irrational popular opinion may have been on this subject, there can be no doubt of its strength nor that, economic reasons apart, religious and political prejudice contributed powerfully to the demand that Ireland, and in particular Irish property, must support her own poor. Professor O'Brien's view, that the Government proposed the Irish Poor Law largely with the object of facilitating the expulsion of Irish immigrants from England is perhaps exaggerated; but certainly English public opinion was almost unanimous in hoping that a Poor Law would in future keep the Irish in Ireland, or at any rate out of England, and this view found considerable support in Parliament.[2]

Many Irish landowners, particularly those in the House of Lords, opposed any measure of relief for the able-bodied poor on the grounds that its cost would swallow up the rental of the country. But in reality the landed interest, at least as represented by the great majority of Irish M.P.s of all parties, was not by any means united on this issue, and debates on the final measure in the Commons produced some interesting and unexpected alliances. O'Connell was always fundamentally opposed to a Poor Law, and if he was incon-sistent on this issue it was because the Catholic clergy, so crucial an element in his political support, generally favoured some measure of poor relief.[3] Professor O'Brien's view that Irish opinion was

[1] G. C. Lewis, Report on the State of the Irish Poor in Great Britain, P.P. 1836, XXXIV, App. G., esp. xxxiii–viii, xliii–viii; Senior, *Letter to Lord Howick*, 47.

[2] O'Brien, *Economic History*, 173.

[3] Hansard, V, 1105–7, 10 August 1831, C. Brownlow, presenting a petition of 24 Catholic Bishops for provision for the destitute and labouring population.

unanimous against a Poor Law is plainly untenable.[1] It might indeed be said that practically all classes in Ireland were in favour of relief to the helpless poor, that the Catholic clergy together with a substantial section of the landed interest (represented in the Commons by Whigs and Liberals like Clements, Sir Richard Musgrave and Wyse, Tories like Jackson, Shaw and Perceval, and a large proportion of O'Connell's own party) favoured a more sweeping measure which would provide some form of relief to the able-bodied but unemployed poor; and that popular opinion in the countryside was either apathetic or as George Nicholls thought, generally in favour of property being assessed for poor relief. Only when the workhouse system was established and in full operation did popular opinion in Ireland express itself in sporadic and disorganized opposition.

Before 1833 the opponents of an Irish Poor Law held their own in the face of growing demands for the measure. In 1830, a Select Committee presided over by Thomas Spring Rice reported against any system of compulsory relief.[2] In 1831, Smith O'Brien introduced a Bill to relieve the aged, helpless and infirm poor, Sadler a resolution in favour of a general legal provision; both failed to make any progress.[3] But on three separate occasions in August 1831 O'Connell wavered from his earlier position of hostility, and in asking Sadler to

[1] O'Brien, *Economic History*, 173–4. See, for instance, Drummond to Morpeth, 6 January 1838, Russell Papers, P.R.O. 30/22/3A: 'With regard to the whole plan I do not think it has excited much interest here. The people . . . know nothing of it; the farmers and cottiers who are *to pay* know as little—and at *present care* little; by & bye they will care a great deal.' There is no evidence either that they did care passionately later or that, as some Liberals feared, the Poor Law Bill would prove electorally disastrous to Liberals who supported it.

[2] The Committee's recommendations (19 Bills covering public works, emigration, local county government, parochial education and the reform of existing institutions for poor relief) were not proceeded with. See Fourth Report, Select Committee, Irish Poor, P.P. 1830, VII, 55–7, which also contains Bishop Doyle's plan for a Poor Law based on the 43rd Elizabeth (Q. 4449–71) and his explicit rejection of a workhouse system (Q. 4472). Peel himself at this time doubted the expediency of introducing any Poor Law into Ireland, while the Whig Government remained quite unmoved by Anglesey's suggestions of a Poor Law and a compulsory Labour Rate. See Gash, *Peel*, 626, and Black, *Economic Thought*, 100–1.

[3] Hansard, II, 246; VI, 783–816, 8 February; 29 August 1831, O'Brien, Sadler. In a small House, Sadler was only defeated by 64 votes to 52, with Sheil, More O'Ferrall and James Grattan supporting him against the Whig Spring Rice and the Tory Lefroy.

withdraw his motion until the Reform Bill had passed, he actually promised him the assistance of the Irish party.[1]

At last in 1833, in debate on a resolution moved by Richards, the Member for Knaresborough, Althorp proposed to set up a commission of inquiry. He was seconded surprisingly by O'Connell, who admitted that his interest lay in supporting a Poor Law since the Catholic clergy favoured it but went on to attack it in principle as certain to dry up private charity and to destroy 'the sense of personal independence which still remained in the country'. When Henry Grattan spoke in favour of a Poor Law, it was clear that the Repeal party itself would be divided on the issue.[2] Some M.P.s believed that a Commission was the Government's device to shelve the subject and certainly while the Commission went slowly about its work, the Government was easily able to resist attempts by Smith O'Brien, Musgrave and Scrope to bring in their own Bills. In 1832 and again in 1835 and 1836, O'Connell returned to his old position of hostility to the 'perfectly visionary' idea of providing relief for the able-bodied poor. His rigidly orthodox economics would not tolerate the provision at public expense of employment which could not be provided by private capital, while in social terms and with more justification, he feared that a Poor Law would deepen the divisions already existing between landlord and tenant.[3]

The making of the Poor Law

For chairman of the Commission of inquiry the Government chose Richard Whately, Archbishop of Dublin, who had been Nassau Senior's tutor at Oxford and somewhat surprisingly succeeded him as Professor of Political Economy before coming to Dublin in 1831.[4] The immense thoroughness with which the

---

[1] Hansard, V, 1109–10; VI, 157–8, 224–5, 10, 17, 18 August 1831, O'Connell. He had been temporarily 'converted' by Doyle's advocacy and wrote to him 'as an unwilling, but not the less sincere convert to your opinions'; 29 March 1831, Fitzpatrick, *Doyle*, II, 283–5.

[2] Hansard, XVII, 846–64, 867–71, 871–9, 882–6, 2 May 1833, Richards, Althorp, O'Connell, Grattan.

[3] See Fitzpatrick, *Doyle*, II, 362–70, for the public controversy with Bishop Doyle in January 1832 after O'Connell had strongly denounced any plan for a legal provision. Fagan, *O'Connell*, II, 124–5, calls this 'the most painful affair in O'Connell's political life'.

[4] Senior actually recommended Whately for the post; Senior to Spring Rice,

Commission went about its work resulted in what one authority has called 'the most important document in existence for the student of Irish economic history'.[1] Its three Reports contained information on existing relief facilities, including the estimate that no less than 2,385,000 persons were out of work or distressed for thirty weeks of the year, much statistical data on institutions and finally, in 1836, its recommendations. After two years, only the First Report had been published, and the Government's growing impatience was reflected in Spring Rice's remarks to Drummond that it would be 'disgraceful if we have not an actual report before the next Session upon which some definite opinion may be pronounced . . . The Commissioners should be compelled to say Aye or No, and to inform *when if ever* their Report is to be made.'[2] Whately was indeed under very strong pressure, and later remembered 'receiving a pretty broad hint, once or twice while the inquiry was going on, what Government expected us to report; and I replied at once . . . that I, for one at least, should make no report but just what seemed to myself the best, for which of course none of those in power liked me all the better'.[3] The Government wanted a simple recommendation to introduce the reformed English Poor Law into Ireland and received instead a scheme of 'enactments calculated to promote the improvement of the country, and to extend the demand for free and profitable labour'.[4]

The Commission concluded that the workhouse test, the basis of the English system, would not suit a country where there was no alternative employment to agriculture, that its cost would be enormous, about £5,000,000 a year, and that the workhouse would be regarded by the Irish poor 'as a stratagem for debarring them of [the] right to employment and support'. Outdoor relief or money allowances in lieu of wages would require nearly £7,000,000 a year (about 7/10 of the estimated gross rental of the country) to raise the average weekly wage from its present 2/- or 2/6 to 4/6, and the

5 May 1833, Monteagle Papers. Whately was a Church and education reformer of orthodox economic views. The most prominent of the other Commissioners were the Catholic Archbishop of Dublin, Dr. Daniel Murray, Richard More O'Ferrall, Catholic Liberal M.P. for Kildare, A. R. Blake, a Catholic government official, and J. E. Bicheno, F.R.S., a political economist.

[1] O'Brien, *Economic History*, 181.
[2] Spring Rice to Drummond, 13 September 1835, Monteagle Papers.
[3] Whateley, *Life of Richard Whately*, I, 199.
[4] Third Report, Poor Commissioners, P.P. 1836, XXX, 8.

Commission believed that this charge, falling on the landlords, would ruin both them and the country.[1]

Rejecting any kind of Poor Law except that providing relief in institutions to the helpless poor, the Commission recommended a system of subsidized and organized emigration, the establishment of a Board of Improvement to supervise the reclamation, drainage and fencing of waste lands and to set up agricultural model schools and an unspecified programme of public works with capital provided partly by the State through the Board of Works and partly by county boards.[2] Even before the Third Report was published Mulgrave told Russell that he was 'very much afraid . . . that the Archbishop has done incalculable mischief in that Board and that the Report will disappoint everyone'. Its recommendations, according to the Lord Lieutenant, would have no attraction 'for the English landowner who objects to the unchecked inroads of Irish labourers—The provision to satisfy them or indeed to mean anything . . . must be compulsory in its nature . . .'[3] Spring Rice, an orthodox amateur economist as well as a landowner in Limerick, deeply disapproved of the Report, describing it as 'the most sotto sopra affair I ever read in my life . . . Bds. of Improvement exercising unrestrained dominion over all property and a system of letting down and building up cottages, fencing—everything except new theories— and draining everything including patience. These strange propositions have actually taken away my breath & I Cry Hélas & Hélas!'[4]

In the Government's eyes, Whately had committed two grave offences. He had proposed a complex series of measures valuable in themselves but going beyond the immediate condition of the poor and he had rejected the workhouse system which, following English precedents, could be simply and quickly drafted for legislation. This was the Government's case and they quickly set out to make it. Senior, whose general thesis had been upheld by the Commission,

[1] Third Report, 4–7.
[2] Third Report, 17–33.
[3] Mulgrave to Russell, 1 February 1836, Russell Papers, P.R.O. 30/22/2A. The emphasis on English landowning opinion is interesting.
[4] Spring Rice to Morpeth, 4 April 1836, Monteagle Papers. Cf. Melbourne to Spring Rice [n.d. November 1837], Monteagle Papers: 'This comes of appointing university professors to great offices', written after reading Whately's protest at the Government's action in passing over the Commission's recommendations.

could hardly criticize its Report in fundamentals.[1] But George Cornewall Lewis, the eldest son of the chairman of the English Poor Law Commission and George Nicholls, an English Commissioner, both submitted official memoranda in favour of the workhouse system. Lewis argued against the Commission's view that the duty of the State was to find employment for the people by declaring that 'A Government can only . . . attempt to accelerate the improvement of the soil by *indirect* means.' In his view, the main purpose of a Poor Law in Ireland would be '. . . by offering the poor man a sure prospect of maintenance in case of absolute need, to loosen his hold upon the land, and thus to relieve the landlord from the incubus which now presses upon him'.[2] Absolute need would be determined, as in England, by the test of the workhouse.

Nicholls was promptly sent to Ireland (a country he did not know) with instructions from Russell to compare the practicability of the Commission's proposals with his own suggestions. He was indeed virtually told by Russell to ignore the Commission's recommendations.[3] Whately's reaction was reported by Mulgrave: 'I hear that the Archbishop of Dublin *poo-pooed* him [Nicholls] unmercifully and now speaks of him with sovereign contempt as indeed he does of everyone who crosses his path and refuses to mount behind on the cruppers of the hobby he happens to be then riding.'[4] Morpeth, the Chief Secretary, found Nicholls' views 'very satisfactory, very much because they coincide with those which I have ventured to form', though how far Nicholls and Spring Rice 'may coalesce is not I think so sure'. He believed that 'The Archbishop & Mr. Blake would be found rather sore & intractable upon any question of reconsidering or superseding their recommendations', and quoted a bitter letter from Whately to Blake, his fellow Commissioner: ' "So Mr.

[1] Letter from N. W. Senior to [Russell] on the Third Report . . . , 14 April 1836, P.P. 1837, LI, 244–52. He did not approve of the proposed emigration depots, though approving generally of emigration.

[2] Remarks of G. C. Lewis on Poor Laws, Ireland, P.P. 1837, LI, 266, 282. See also G. Nicholls, *A History of the Irish Poor Law* (1856), 129–30, for his Suggestions to Lord John Russell, 21 January 1836, before the Third Report emerged.

[3] Russell to Nicholls, 22 August 1836, H.O. Papers, 122/17, 31–6; Nicholls to Russell, 3 September 1836, Russell Papers, P.R.O. 30/22/2C, finding his instructions 'full & complete'.

[4] Mulgrave to Russell, 22 September 1836, Russell Papers, P.R.O. 30/22/2C, also approving of Nicholls' approach to the problem.

Nicholls is sent here to get one bottle of water out of the Liffey, & one out of the Shannon, & then persuade the English people that he can give them a better Poor-Law than we who have been 3 years considering it".[1]

Nicholls, after two weeks of his tour, told Morpeth that he had 'not met with anything to cause a well-grounded doubt as to the sufficiency of the Workhouse Test' and he confidently informed Russell three weeks later that 'Ireland stands in need of a system of Poor Laws based upon that principle fully as much as England itself . . . in every instance but one, I have found the Catholic Hierarchy disposed heartily to concur in all that I propose'. Doctors, Protestant and Catholic clergymen he thought generally favourable and he claimed to 'have also gone amongst the People, into their Cabins—in the Markets, into the Fields . . . & I found a similar feeling to prevail with them'.[2] The English Poor Law as applied to Ireland 'would not give employment or capital, but it would, I think, help the country through what may be called its transition period . . . from the system of small holdings, conacre, and the sub-divisions of land . . . to the better practice of day-labour for wages'.[3]

Nicholls thus assumed the orthodox economists' prescription for Irish agriculture not only as a correct but also as an inevitable process, although unlike Senior, he believed that it would have to be accompanied by some immediate provision for the victims of this policy. He argued that while it would be impossible to make life in workhouses of a lower standard than the normal life of the Irish peasantry, the workhouse would still provide an efficient test of destitution because the Irish, as a migratory people, would do all they could to avoid confinement. In his first Report in November 1836 dealing with the proposed workhouse system, its cost and administration, he emphasized the need for a powerful central authority to establish the Unions and to control the Boards of Guardians, and recommended that the English Poor Law Commission should administer the Irish system through a joint Commission.[4]

The Irish administration—Mulgrave, Morpeth and Drummond—

[1] Morpeth to Russell, 27 September; 5 October 1836, Russell Papers, P.R.O. 30/22/2C.

[2] Nicholls to Morpeth, 23 September; to Russell, 17 October 1836, Russell Papers, P.R.O. 30/22/2C.

[3] Nicholls, *History of Irish Poor Law*, 166.

[4] Nicholls, First Report, 15 November 1836, in condensed form in *History of Irish Poor Law*, 160–88.

were whole-heartedly in favour of Nicholls' scheme, as also were
Howick and Duncannon.[1] Spring Rice and Lansdowne, the representatives in the Cabinet of the Irish landed interest, opposed it, but
were no match for their colleagues on the principle of the measure.
Spring Rice was convinced that 'to adopt any plan undertaking the
relief of the *able-bodied* poor of Ireland will . . . strike a blow at the
whole social system of the country—check industry, retard civiliza-
tion & introduce an uncertainty with respect to all property. It
supplies the only element of mischief from which we have hitherto
been protected.'[2] Both agreed to it, as Spring Rice wrote philosophi-
cally, 'on the principle of treating it *as an experiment*—one necessary
to be tried no doubt, but where I do not anticipate success . . . I
think those who differ with me will be convicted by their own
experiment, & for that demonstration I am willing to wait'.[3] On the
important detail of the composition of the Central Board, the Cabinet
agreed that it should be predominantly English though based of
course on Dublin. Mulgrave argued convincingly that

> . . . we shall have to encounter, if not the continued opposition, the
> very unwilling consent of some of the most popular Personages in
> Ireland and I really believe that the active support of others who can
> neutralize any obstacles from these Quarters depends very much upon
> this point of its being under the management of a perfectly independent
> Board in Ireland. There is a great deal of sensitiveness on this subject
> in the whole of the Liberal party . . . the persons comprizing it being
> English would not I believe at all excite that morbid national feeling
> which would be roused by the name of subjection to the English Board.[4]

[1] Morpeth to Russell, 19 November 1836, but conveying More O'Ferrall's
prophecy that confining relief to workhouses 'would produce a rebellion in Ireland'; Russell, Memo, 16 November; Howick to Russell, 18 October; Duncannon to Russell, 19 October 1836, Russell Papers, P.R.O. 30/22/2C, 2D.

[2] Spring Rice, Memo, 20 November 1836, Russell Papers, P.R.O. 30/22/2D;
Lansdowne to Spring Rice, 15 December 1835, Monteagle Papers, wanting the
Whately Commission's scheme for emigration 'to work ahead of the workhouse
system, and it should if possible be made sweet in proportion as the other must
be bitter to the national taste'. But Russell was firmly opposed to all schemes of
emigration; see his Memo, 21 November 1837, Monteagle Papers.

[3] Spring Rice, Memo, 16 March 1837, Russell Papers, P.R.O. 30/22/2E. Cf.
Althorp's remark to Hobhouse on Lansdowne, 'an Irish landlord . . . [and]
whenever his pecuniary interests interfere, his opinion is sure to be swayed by
them', in Broughton, *Recollections*, 31 July 1834, IV, 360.

[4] Mulgrave to Russell, 4 December 1836; and Opinions of Howick, Duncannon and Spring Rice in favour of an 'English' Board, Russell Papers, P.R.O.
30/22/2D.

In Ireland, the whole issue attracted much less popular attention than either tithes or municipal reform. O'Connell did not organize any opposition because such a campaign would certainly have been unsuccessful and would only have divided his own supporters. His whole attitude was uncharacteristically defensive; he spoke on the subject rarely and only in Dublin where the Trades' Union, representing a class least likely to benefit from a Poor Law, supported his views. His slogan, 'Repeal of The Union or a Poor Law', was based on the belief that an Irish Parliament dominated by the landed gentry would know its own interest well enough to avoid crippling itself with poor rates, or with 'that most destructive of all experiments, employment for the able-bodied out of the poor-rates! ! !'[1] He had quarrelled in the past with Cobbett as well as with Bishop Doyle on the merits of the Elizabethan Poor Law and as a landowner in a poor and thickly populated part of Ireland, this remained with him a constant nightmare.[2] Even though he thought the English Act of 1834 'a great improvement; of course not perfect, but giving *us* a model wide indeed of the 43d Eliz.', he was very unwillingly resigned to seeing it transferred to Ireland: 'We *must*, however, have a Poor Law, and *poorhouses*, and much of moral degradation and of change in *the mode* of suffering', and this because of the pressure of English public opinion and of those in Ireland who were, in his view, 'benevolent and humane at the expense of others'.[3]

O'Connell's real position, when he was not being forced by political considerations to moderate his public statements, was one of extreme hostility to a substantive Poor Law for the able-bodied of any kind, whether dispensing outdoor relief or confining it to workhouses; nor does there seem to be any evidence for the view, put forward by Sir Llewelyn Woodward, that he regarded the recommendations of the Whately Commission favourably.[4] If he

[1] O'Connell to Fitzpatrick, 1 April 1836, *O'Connell Corr.*, II, 52. See also O'Connell to Barrett, 11 July 1831; to T. M. Ray, 13 February 1847, ibid., I, 268-9, II, 405-6.

[2] O'Connell to Barrett, 2 October 1834, *O'Connell Corr.*, I, 487.

[3] O'Connell to Fitzpatrick, 1 April 1836, *O'Connell Corr.*, II, 52, on a meeting in Dublin in favour of a Poor Law.

[4] Woodward, *Age of Reform*, 347. A. R. Schoyen, *The Chartist Challenge*, 23-4, n. 1, seems also to misunderstand O'Connell's position. Chartists and Tory Radicals regarded him as a heartless 'Malthusian Whig' not because he publicly defended the New Poor Law (given his views this would have been unlikely), but because he attacked the old system of outdoor relief.

approved of the Commission's rejection of the workhouse system as well as of outdoor relief, he was certainly never a supporter of subsidized emigration, while the proposed Board of Improvement might well have offended his *laissez-faire* principles; and it was not until the crisis of the Famine that he appealed with any urgency for a programme of public works.

Morpeth gave Russell a vivid picture of an interview with O'Connell and 'a tail of 20 of the Trades Union' who came 'to ask what sort of a Poor Law it was intended to bring in'. Morpeth would only say that it would be 'a substantive measure . . . "Quite enough", says Dan, jumps up, & whisks them at once away; except [that] one man fired a shot in retreating which rather surprized me, "that the great majority of us agree with Mr. O'Connell, that the measure ought to be confined to the sick, aged & infirm". All present seemed to assent, but I suppose he has packed his Tail.' In fact the Whigs could feel confident that O'Connell, with his party divided on the issue and unable to appeal to the country, would give no trouble; without a united party he could never seriously embarrass the Government, which showed its confidence by not troubling to consult him on the principle, or even on the details of the measure.[1]

The Whigs had in the attitude of the Conservative leaders a further reason for confidence. Early in 1836 Viscount Sandon, one of the Members for Liverpool (after London the city with the biggest Irish population in England) wrote to Peel hoping that

> . . . some step will be taken for the purpose of laying an early claim to the question of a Poor Law in Ireland . . . It is called for by the interest & public feeling of certainly two out of the three kingdoms—it is looked to as a source of relief by the agriculturists; & it is surely unwise to leave it to be appropriated by the readily-converted Government, or still worse to O'Connell. The Conservatives have not too many popular questions, questions which excite the interest & sympathies of all Classes, to be able to spare one useful and desirable in itself as well as popular.[2]

[1] Morpeth to Russell, 12 December 1836. Mulgrave to Russell, 14 November 1836, Russell Papers, P.R.O. 30/22/2D, reporting that O'Connell would not be supported by 'some of the most influential of his usual adherents or by the middling classes generally'. Drummond to Morpeth, 6 January 1838, ibid., 30/22/3A: 'O'Connell is hurt at not being consulted on the Poor-Law.' Drummond thought his co-operation could be obtained by 'yielding some immaterial points of detail', but the Government felt strong enough not even to do this.

[2] Sandon to Peel, 12 January 1836, Peel Papers, Add. MSS 40422, 22-3.

Peel, true to his belief that an Opposition ought not to initiate legislation, made no move, but both he and Wellington agreed with the Government in finding the Commission's recommendations 'absurd',[1] while Stanley, not yet fully ensconced in the Conservative party and himself a landowner in Ireland, obligingly wrote to Russell: 'I believe you are on the right tack if you adopt Mr. Nicholls' plan in the main . . . but you must be prepared, I think, to find much of the measure unpopular and the unpopular parts of it the most essential.'[2]

Like the Conservative leaders, Stanley was primarily interested in the question of the Poor Law rating. Duncannon told Russell early in 1837 that he had had 'a good deal of correspondence with Stanley on the subject of rating. He seems very anxious about the measure.'[3] But this was a special kind of anxiety, having little to do with the main principles of an Irish Poor Law on which there was no great difference between Government and Opposition. The latter were always eager, in contrast to their attitude on tithes and municipal reform, to settle the Poor Law question without a prolonged struggle, and as Graham put it, 'an efficient Poor Rate with a sure test of Value and a stringent check on the Franchise itself' would actually allow them to concede municipal corporations to Ireland.[4]

When in February 1837 Russell introduced a Bill framed largely by Nicholls, Peel supported its principle, as did the Irish Tory Shaw, the Liberal James Grattan and The O'Conor Don in a debate remarkable for its unanimity and absence of party feeling. Even O'Connell was ready to say that he 'cheerfully acceded to the proposed plan'; though he made it clear that he would propose alterations in committee, he was aware that 'efficient or not, a Poor-Law

---

[1] Peel to Goulburn, 12 September 1836, Parker, *Peel*, II, 326. See Wellington to Peel, 8 September 1836, Peel Papers, Add. MSS 40310, 155–8, for Wellington's opposition to any scheme of employment for the able-bodied, his fear of priestly control, and his extreme tenderness for the interests of Irish landowners.

[2] Stanley to Russell, 18 December 1836, Russell Papers, P.R.O. 30/22/2D. He even suggested making 'the occupation of land of more than a very small extent a bar to parochial relief', an idea translated into legislation in 1847 as the notorious 'quarter-acre' or Gregory clause.

[3] Duncannon to Russell [n.d. ? January] 1837, Russell Papers, P.R.O. 30/22/2E.

[4] Graham to Peel, 27 March 1837, Peel Papers Add. MSS 40318, 64–9. For the relevance of the Poor Law rating to the municipal franchise, and its part in Opposition tactics, see below pp. 250–1.

they must have'.[1] The prorogation of Parliament on the King's
death enabled Nicholls to make a second journey to Ireland in order
to confirm his earlier views and to report against both outdoor
relief, for which Smith O'Brien had asked, and a law of settlement,
which in Nicholls' view would impede the free distribution of
labour.[2]

On the Second Reading in February 1838 of the slightly modified
Bill, O'Connell changed his tactics. He could not now agree to any
proposal beyond that of relief to the helpless poor, since 'Ireland
was too poor for a Poor-law'.[3] It was ludicrous, he felt, to try to
distinguish as Nicholls did between poverty and destitution, and
made much of this point in his speech moving the postponement of
the Bill for six months.[4] He was supported by only 25 members, a
strange combination of English Radicals like Thomas Attwood and
Thomas Duncombe, his own followers like Brabazon, Bodkin, Fitzsimon, Macnamara, and John and Maurice O'Connell, a few Irish
Conservatives and independent Irish Liberals against a majority of
277 which numbered many of his usual followers, including Henry
Grattan, Butler, Bellew, Callaghan, Hutton, Morgan John O'Connell, the Roches, Talbot, Vigors and Maher, most of the Irish
Conservatives and Liberals and a solid host of English Members of
all political views.[5]

O'Connell was quite justified in fearing that he would be unable to
carry any changes in the Bill.[6] A long series of amendments—to

[1] Hansard, XXXVI, 479–82, 482–5, 504–5, 497–504, 485–92, 13 February
1837, Shaw, O'Conor Don, Grattan, Peel, O'Connell.
[2] Nicholls, *History of Irish Poor Law*, 196–209.
[3] Hansard, XL, 779–80, 5 February 1838, O'Connell.
[4] The wide discrepancy between Nicholls' estimate of 80,000 destitute persons
who would qualify for his workhouses and the Commission's figure of over
2,000,000 unemployed or in distress for most of the year was noticed also by
Fitzstephen French, the Whig M.P. for Roscommon, and by Isaac Butt, who
called the Bill 'a piece of forced legislation' dealing with destitution 'as if it were
the accident of individuals, instead of considering it as the essential and general
condition of a class': *The Poor Law Bill for Ireland Examined*, 5, 8; Hansard,
XXXIX, 496–9, 1 December 1837, French.
[5] Hansard, XL, 947–65, 9 February 1838, O'Connell, whose speech was
praised by the usually unfriendly *Annual Register* as 'of much force and
ability'.
[6] O'Connell to Fitzpatrick, 10, 15 February 1838; to Barrett, 15 February
1838, *O'Connell Corr.*, II, 127–9. Through Warburton, O'Connell protested at
the plan of charging occupiers with the poor-rate but the Cabinet decided not

substitute an Irish for a predominantly English central Board, to include Protestant and Catholic clergymen in the proposed Boards of Guardians from which they had been specifically excluded, to transfer liability for poor rates entirely from occupiers to landlords or at least to make the latter pay two-thirds instead of half the rates, to abolish the system of plural voting for Boards of Guardians and to substitute ballot—were all lost decisively.[1] Small minorities of O'Connellites and Irish Tories could make no impression on the overwhelming English support for a measure which passed the Commons by 234 votes to 59. But the minority's claim that the Bill had been forced forward by the English parties against the weight of Irish opinion was answered by Morpeth, who remarked that 56 Irish M.P.s had voted for the principle of the Bill while only 16 had opposed it, and that only in 8 out of 25 divisions in committee were there majorities of Irish Members against particular details of the measure.[2] The opposition to the Bill could now only look for salvation to the House of Lords.

For O'Connell, who had failed so completely in the Commons, it can scarcely have been much consolation that the Bill 'elicited the only serious demonstration made by the "Irish interest" as a whole in the Lords in the thirties'.[3] This rebellion of Whig and Tory peers against both their parties' leadership and in defence of their threatened Irish rentals must be distinguished from the much more frequent rebellions and private crusades on other issues of Irish Tory peers. The compromise by which the Government dropped Appropriation in return for the Lords' passing the Irish Municipal and Poor Law Bills was bitter enough for most of the Tory rank and file. One of them, Maurice Fitzgerald, the Knight of Kerry, believed that Wellington 'had involved himself under the false impression of men who know nothing of Ireland—the whole policy is one of compromise on all points at issue. They attach too much importance to the appropriation clause and will in return sacrifice us in the poor law and municipal bill. The scheme at bottom is to clear away those

to change the Bill; Warburton to Russell, 16 November 1837; Memos of Spring Rice, Duncannon, Howick and Lansdowne, Russell Papers, P.R.O. 30/22/2F.

[1] Hansard, XL, 1023–5, 1240–1, 1245–6; XLI, 979 ff., 12, 16 February; 16, 19 March 1838. Inconsistently, on the grounds that it would mitigate the harshness of the Bill, O'Connell also supported Smith O'Brien's unsuccessful motion for outdoor relief.

[2] Hansard, XLIII, 684–6, 30 April 1838, Morpeth.

[3] Large, 'The House of Lords and Ireland', *Irish Historical Studies*, IX, 390–1.

troublesome measures which might upset a new ministry.'[1] But on the Poor Law even a staunch Peelite and Irish landlord like Lord Fitzgerald and Vesci was at loggerheads with his party's leadership.

The Second Reading of the Bill was carried easily enough, but Tories like Fitzgerald, Londonderry and Westmeath and Whigs like Earl Fitzwilliam and Clanricarde all spoke out strongly against a measure which Fitzwilliam called 'the production of "the humanity-mongers" . . . an English Bill, . . . a great and hazardous experiment'.[2] The real conflict came in committee, when on the 41st clause Fitzwilliam moved to omit the able-bodied poor from relief in work-houses and thus attacked the basic principle of the Bill. He was supported by Fitzgerald and Haddington, both regretting their difference of opinion with Wellington, and by Whigs like Clanricarde and Fingall, most of them naturally emphasizing the cost and un-popularity of a measure which, Lord Roden declared, 'must be destructive to the property of half the gentry of Ireland'.[3] But the 'Irish interest' could in the end only muster 41 votes against 107 on Fitzwilliam's amendment and the Bill passed in July by 93 votes to 31.[4] Amendments to it were few and unimportant, agreed upon beforehand by Wellington and by Nicholls himself acting with the Government's approval, and were finally settled by conferences between the two Houses. Without Wellington's co-operation the Bill might not have passed at all, as Nicholls later acknowledged; and it was due to Wellington and to the compromise between Government and Opposition that it passed into law so quickly and so smoothly.[5]

If the opponents of a Poor Law had failed in their main object, they had at least managed to impress the subject on Irish opinion. But Drummond's warning that 'Nicholls will be anything but popular here, and *pray be cautious* as to sending *him over* to carry it into effect', was disregarded by Russell, who sent Nicholls over to

[1] Knight of Kerry's Diary, 23 May 1838, N.L.I., MS. 2077, quoted by Large, op. cit., 391. Cf. Melbourne's own attitude: 'I rather accede to Poor Laws in Ireland than approve of them', to Russell, 4 September 1837, Russell Papers, P.R.O. 30/22/2F.

[2] Hansard, XLIII, 15-19, 21 May 1838, Fitzwilliam.

[3] Hansard, XLIII, 352-3, 366-9, 475-7, 28, 31 May 1838, Roden, Fitzgerald, Clanricarde.

[4] Hansard, XLIII, 501; XLIV, 28-9, 31 May; 9 July 1838, Divisions.

[5] Nicholls, *History of the Irish Poor Law*, 220-1. The main issue was that of the rating. No details of the conferences are given in Hansard.

put the Act into operation.[1] Nicholls may have lacked tact, but he was an administrator of formidable drive and efficiency. In less than two years nearly all the Unions had been formed and half the workhouses were being built; by 1842, over 15,000 people were being relieved, a number which had increased by January 1845 to over 40,000.[2] Spring Rice, critical of the methods of Nicholls and his assistants, told Wellington that 'I do not anticipate that they will have much support and countenance from my brother Squires, who of all parties & creeds are alarmed at the measure'. But by 1839 the Lord Lieutenant could assure Russell that 'our excellent Nicholls ... will have told you ... how entirely the opposition which was made to the Measure in Parliament has disappeared after it once became Law, & how Ld Londonderry was among the first to complain of delay in the formation of a Union on his property'.[3] If the Irish landed interest now looked with more favour on the system, it may have been because the building of workhouses provided some local though temporary employment. Later, particularly in 1843 at the time of the Repeal campaign, there was some resistance notably in the west and in Waterford and Tipperary to the payment of poor rates, and in some places opposition on the part of the poor themselves to confinement in the workhouses, though there was nothing in Ireland to match the great anti-Poor Law campaigns in the north of England.[4] By and large the Irish poor, or that small proportion of them who came into contact with the system, seem to

[1] Drummond to Morpeth, 6 January 1838, Russell Papers, P.R.O. 30/22/3A, calling Nicholls 'a *conceited* man' and lamenting his 'ponderous, leaden articles' on the Poor Law in the *Morning Chronicle*, which had made O'Connell 'indignant'.

[2] See Nicholls, *History of Irish Poor Law*, 234–303, 323 for the administration of the Poor Law from 1838 to 1846; Freeman, *Pre-Famine Ireland*, 130–2, for details of workhouses, Unions, and poor-rates, for which more than 1,000,000 persons were liable, over half from property with an annual valuation of less than £5.

[3] Spring Rice to Wellington, 29 September 1838, Monteagle Papers; Ebrington to Russell, 26 June 1839, Russell Papers, P.R.O. 30/22/3C.

[4] According to Freeman, *Pre-Famine Ireland*, 149, nearly 11,000 men were directly employed by the Commissioners. See Nicholls, *History of the Irish Poor Law*, 294–6, for opposition. Graham, himself more than doubtful about the Poor Law, was worried late in 1842 about O'Connell's renewed opposition to it, which might receive landlord support; Graham to Peel, 28 December 1842, Peel Papers, Add. MSS 40448, 152–4. But this particular grievance was soon swallowed up in the wider Repeal agitation.

have accepted the workhouses, those solid buildings in the Gothic style which can still be seen in many parts of the country.

But the creators of the system believed that partial or widespread famine was 'a contingency altogether above the powers of a Poor Law to provide for'.[1] To meet earlier local or partial famines, the authorities had evolved a special pattern of emergency relief measures. Employment on public works, paid for by special parliamentary votes, was always preferred to relief in food or money, but in 1822 and 1831 potatoes were imported from Scotland, Liverpool and the Channel Islands and distributed by government officials; at the same periods, the Irish Relief Committee, a private organization whose funds were supplemented by government grants, spent over £300,000.[2] In 1839 severe distress in the west was met by sending a government official who secretly spent over £2,000 in providing various kinds of help, but on this occasion the Central Board of the Poor Law specifically declared that its own system could not cover any extraordinary or even temporary measures of relief.[3]

Thus when in the late autumn of 1845 the country faced an impending general famine, the authorities could not look to the Poor Law system either to provide the necessary relief or even to act as a framework inside which emergency measures might be administered.[4] As conceived and carried through in 1838, the workhouse system, providing accommodation in theory only for a maximum of 80,000 persons, was scarcely an answer to a situation in which about a quarter of the entire population of the country was unemployed or in distress for well over half the year.[5] But the framers of the Poor Law had deliberately not designed it to meet this 'normal' situation. Under strong pressure from English public opinion and influenced by the orthodox economists' prescription for Irish agriculture, they had pushed through a piece of doctrinaire legislation by which a special system practicable in English conditions was applied to a country with a well-established pattern of

[1] Nicholls, Report, Poor Laws, P.P. 1837, LI, 223.

[2] Memo by T.A., 5 November 1845, on relief of distress in Ireland, P.P. 1846, XXXVII, 3–4.

[3] Minute of Board, 5 December 1839, in Nicholls, *History of Irish Poor Law*, 257–9.

[4] See also below pp. 284 ff.

[5] For figures of running costs, rising steadily from £110,000 in 1841 to £435,000 in 1846 and of persons relieved (an actual maximum of just over 100,000 in 1846), see Nicholls, *History of Irish Poor Law*, 263 ff.

chronic under-employment and periodic mass destitution, and where the insecure possession of minute plots of poor land provided the only guarantee of subsistence for most of the population. The workhouse system was applicable only to an economy offering a wide range of alternative employment outside agriculture. Yet 'doctrinaires' like Nicholls and Lewis and Whig Ministers like Russell and most of his colleagues cannot be excused on the plea of ignorance of Irish conditions. In isolation, uncombined with large programmes of productive public works (notably the reclamation of waste lands) and a state scheme of emigration, the whole tendency of the Poor Law was towards breaking up the fabric of rural society—a result which Nicholls, its principal architect, had expressly intended and which later allowed the economic historian of this period to treat the Act of 1838 as yet another of the systematic 'aids to depopulation'.[1]

The opposition to the measure, with the exception of those who attacked it as being too narrow and restricted, was largely grounded on economic interest. O'Connell no doubt feared that it would exacerbate the already difficult landlord-tenant relationship and perhaps, that it might provoke violent peasant opposition similar to that which the English working class had offered to the New Poor Law between 1835 and 1839. But there is also no doubt that he was obsessed by a fear that the Irish agricultural interest, tenant-farmers as well as landlords, could not afford the further burden of taxation entailed by a Poor Law, and by a conviction that a workhouse system would soon be found inadequate to cope with the extent of Irish poverty. 'So long ago as 1830', he told Ray in 1847, 'I warned the Irish landlords that they had nothing before them but the Repeal of the Union or Poor Laws; they laughed me to scorn, and the Poor Law was introduced, and the natural progress of that measure is going on. It must necessarily arrive at the out-door relief for able-bodied persons.'[2]

These fears, proved quite correct by the Poor Law Extension Act of 1847, were connected with his position as a head landlord and substantial leaseholder in Kerry. In addition to the freehold property which he inherited from his uncle, part of the Darrynane estate was rented for £292 a year from Lord Cork while other lands were held from Trinity College, Dublin. Even as a leaseholder he was liable for poor rates on an estate which was in anything but a flourishing

---

[1] See above pp. 214–15; O'Brien, *Economic History*, 189.
[2] O'Connell to T. M. Ray, 13 February 1847, *O'Connell Corr.*, II, 406.

condition and situated in an area with a dense population and extremely poor agricultural land.[1] Private preoccupations must certainly have served to strengthen an opposition which was also based on grounds of public policy and economic theory; and it is significant that most of those in his own party who followed him on this issue came, like O'Connell himself, from the west of Ireland.[2]

The Poor Law Question split the Irish party, cutting O'Connell off from those of his followers who perhaps without much enthusiasm were prepared to see the establishment of a workhouse system, and also indeed from those like Smith O'Brien who had consistently advocated a measure of outdoor relief. O'Connell's opposition was in no respect different from that of many Irish Conservative landowners. But while the issue touched the Irish party most closely in its economic interests, it never involved the existence of the Whig Government, and there was thus no overwhelming motive for party unity. Ireland, as O'Connell claimed, may have been 'too poor for a Poor Law' and certainly could not afford the impracticable and even harmful luxury of the 1838 Act. But apart from the general panacea of Repeal, O'Connell had very little to suggest as a substitute, and it was left to dissident Liberals like Sharman Crawford with his demands for tenant-right, and Smith O'Brien with his suggestions for peasant ownership of reclaimed land, to call for more realistic answers to the urgent problems of the Irish economy, of which widespread poverty was both a symptom and a result.

[1] Documents in O'Connell MSS, U.C.D., referring to O'Connell's leases of property and showing that his outgoings on the house at Darrynane, lands, policies and pensions amounted in 1846 to £2,428. His income from land, after meeting expenses and taxes, was in the region of £3,000. See John H. Horgan, 'O'Connell the Man', in *Daniel O'Connell, Nine Centenary Essays*, ed. Michael Tierney (1947), 272.

[2] Sir William Brabazon (Mayo), Bodkin (Galway), Macnamara (Clare), John and Maurice O'Connell (Kerry).

CHAPTER VII

Irish Municipal Reform

The case for reform

Reform of town government and administration in Ireland took no less than five years to achieve, and the Irish Municipal Corporations Act of 1840, as compared with its Scottish and English counterparts of 1833 and 1835, was a most limited and conservative measure. At an early stage the question ceased to be treated on its merits or demerits and became a pawn in the overall strategies of Government and Opposition, with the latter too deeply divided on the issue for a quick and convenient compromise to be possible. The Radicals who promoted English municipal reform saw no immediate political advantage in pushing forward a similar Irish measure. Many Whigs and moderate Liberals, increasingly compromised by alliance with the Irish party, were hesitant about openly supporting a measure by which O'Connell and his party would be the chief beneficiaries, while O'Connell's somewhat tactless declarations as to the probable results of reform were eagerly seized upon by Conservative publicists and helped to harden English public opinion against further dangerous concessions to O'Connell and the Irish. For these reasons, the Whig Government could not appeal to the country on this issue. In an Election fought on the rights of the House of Lords over legislation, even when the Ministry's case was prima facie a good one, it was anything but certain, at least after 1837, that the country would support the Whigs.

Soon after they had come to power, the Whigs intended to deal with 'the abuses of Corporations' in Ireland,[1] but the long struggle

[1] Melbourne to Stanley, 2 January 1831, H.O. Papers, 122/15, 59.

over the Reform Bills delayed any consideration of the problem until early in 1833, when a Select Committee was appointed to inquire into the state of municipal corporations in the whole Kingdom. For Ireland, the Committee concentrated its attentions on the corporations of Dublin and Belfast, hearing evidence from corporation officials and from a number of hostile witnesses specially brought over to London by O'Connell.[1] As a member of the Committee, O'Connell was delighted by the damaging admissions made by these officials and by the Committee's Report which drew attention to various abuses in the two corporations, remarked justly that they were not adapted to the present state of society and recommended a full commission of inquiry into the whole system of municipal government in Ireland.[2]

O'Connell believed that there was no need to wait for this Commission's Report before proceeding to legislate. In April 1833 he was pressing Hobhouse as Chief Secretary 'to immortalize himself by a Reform of the Corporation of Dublin' and in June he was confident that he would meet 'no opposition from Government against bringing in my bill to regulate the Corporations'.[3] He thought that in this way reform, 'if the leading Corporators would join me, we could have at once and amicably; but if it be postponed until next session, it will come under the English precedents and be *sweeping*, as the English corporation reform certainly will be'. His own demands in 1833 were limited to Dublin and involved the division of the city into wards, in each of which four aldermen and eight common councillors would be elected by £10 householders, and a thorough reform of the exclusively Protestant trade guilds, a scheme which would, he believed, destroy the Protestant monopoly of corporate

[1] See O'Connell to Fitzpatrick, 17 February; 6 March 1833, *O'Connell Corr.*, I, 321, 332–3, for his explicit instructions on the kind of witness needed. For his interest in the Committee, see letters of 11, 13 March 1833, ibid., I, 330–1, 339.

[2] Report of Select Committee appointed to inquire into the State of Municipal Corporations in England and Wales and Ireland, P.P. 1833, XIII, iii–vii; O'Connell to Fitzpatrick, 3 April 1833, *O'Connell Corr.*, I, 344–5. For Tory suspicions of the Government's motives, see *Morning Post*, 21 February 1833, which alleged that the Committee contained six Conservatives to five times that number of Whigs and Radicals, as cited by G. B. A. M. Finlayson, *The Municipal Corporations Act, 1835*, B.Litt. Thesis (Oxford, 1959), 37–9.

[3] O'Connell to Fitzpatrick, 18 April; 21, 26 June 1833, *O'Connell Corr.*, I, 346, 368, 370.

rights and of the administration of justice, 'the hinge on which the reformation of Corporations turns'.[1]

O'Connell saw the Irish corporations as symbols of the Protestant Ascendancy which had fought so hard against Emancipation and as political strongholds of the Toryism which constituted his main opposition in Ireland. But his public and private letters, although they contain many attacks on the Orange corporations, show no desire for an organic or radical reform of these institutions, at least until 1835. It is mainly a question of patronage, of infiltration, or of encouraging the Whig Government to make a few examples of troublesome Tory aldermen and corporators.[2] This somewhat surprising attitude, since the ten 'close' corporation boroughs constituted a major electoral obstacle before 1832 to the formation of a sizeable Irish party under his leadership, partly stemmed from his belief that the Irish Tories might join him in campaigning for Repeal.[3] In 1833, giving instructions to Fitzpatrick to negotiate with the Rev. Charles Boyton, a Fellow of Trinity College and the most important of the Dublin Conservatives, O'Connell wrote: 'Urge upon him the obvious tendency of the Government management. One day they strike down Protestant monopoly; next day, they trample on Catholic freedom. Let him see how, in the Corporation reform, they strike down the last but powerful remnant of Protestant ascendancy.'[4] A campaign to reform all the corporations would only alienate the Tories controlling them but a reform confined to Dublin, by depriving Tories in the city of their exclusive privileges, might convert them from diehard Unionists into Reformers and even Repealers.[5]

[1] O'Connell to Fitzpatrick, 21 June; 3 April 1833, *O'Connell Corr.*, I, 368, 344–5.

[2] See, for instance, O'Connell to James Sugrue, 14 April 1829; to Fitzpatrick, 17 February 1833, *O'Connell Corr.*, I, 180–1, 387–9; to James Dwyer, 27 September 1830, Peel Papers, Add. MSS 40313, 61, a public letter describing the corporations' abuses as 'an abominable and almost insufferable nuisance' and Cork Corporation in particular as 'a sink of corruption . . . a vile receptacle of bigotry'. But for O'Connell's actual policy towards them, see O'Connell to Knight of Kerry, 24 June 1827; to John O'Brien, 30 September 1830, mentioning two cases instituted by the Catholic Association 'to enforce the right of Catholics and Liberal Protestants to their freedom of the City of Dublin'; to Duncannon, 27 April; to Barrett, 8 October 1831, *O'Connell Corr.*, I, 148, 215, 255–6, 275–6.

[3] For his hopes before the 1832 Election, see above p. 57, n. 2; and O'Connell to William Scott, 25 October 1832, *O'Connell Corr.*, I, 309–12.

[4] O'Connell to Fitzpatrick, 21 February 1833, *O'Connell Corr.*, I, 325–6.

[5] O'Connell to Fitzpatrick, 13, 17 September 1833, *O'Connell Corr.*, I, 385, 387–9.

It was an ingenious and even a somewhat devious plan, and as late as February 1834, when he made a token attempt to present his private Bill dealing with Dublin, O'Connell was still hoping for a Conservative move. He was quite prepared to be conciliatory on this issue. Indeed to judge from his correspondence, he had little real interest in a reform of town government for its own sake and had given no thought to its social and political implications in Ireland, where it might have directly affected between one-fifth and one-sixth of the population.[1] Political considerations or the necessity of providing supporters with some immediate and tangible proofs of the benefits of Emancipation were in this case more than a match for his reforming enthusiasm; and it was not a coincidence that his attitude of extreme hostility to the corporations followed the bitter experiences of his own election at Dublin in 1835.

But in sharp contrast to the re-distribution of official patronage in favour of Catholics and liberal Protestants, municipal reform could never have been achieved, given the unco-operative attitude of the corporations themselves, without officially-sponsored legislation, and O'Connell's private schemes were useless once the Commission had been set up in July 1833. If the English Commission and the subsequent Act were primarily aimed at boosting Whig and Radical party fortunes at the Conservatives' expense,[2] the same motives did did not influence the Government when it set up the Irish Commission. To damage the Tory political interest in Ireland could only benefit O'Connell, and it certainly could not be said either of Grey or of his successor Melbourne that by 1833 or 1834 they were moving towards an understanding with O'Connell. The Whigs were principally interested in remedying obvious abuses and in increasing the efficiency of Irish town government without much regretting if this reform should happen to damage Conservative interests, and they were also no doubt aware that to deny Ireland a reform which was considered right and necessary for England would simply provide Irish nationalists with stronger arguments for their cause.

O'Connell, with a direct political interest in the results of the Commission, was delighted with its composition under Louis Perrin,

[1] See Freeman, *Pre-Famine Ireland*, 25–7, for a chart which shows that over 1,500,000 persons lived in towns with populations over 500–1,500 (places properly called 'towns' in Ireland); or, if this category is too low, that over 1,200,000 lived in places with over 1,500–5,000 inhabitants.

[2] A view convincingly argued by Finlayson, *The Municipal Corporations Act, 1835*.

a Liberal Protestant lawyer, of six Catholics and six Protestants, most of whom were what Sydney Smith once called 'the Whigs' favourite human animal, the barrister of six years' standing'. Although their selection was apparently the responsibility of Perrin and the Government, at least five of them appeared for O'Connell in his defence of the Dublin election of 1835, and Liberal M.P.s certainly pressed the Chief Secretary to select only reformers for the Commission.[1] Dividing the country into circuits, the Commission went about its work in 1833-4 with great thoroughness, collecting information from every corporation including those which had only a nominal existence. In an interim report Perrin complained strongly of some delay and obstruction, particularly as regards 'the appropriation and management of corporation property' when 'our inability to enforce the attendance of witnesses and disclosure of evidence has sometimes permitted those so inclined to baffle Inquiry'. His uninhibited criticisms, which shocked at least one Whig Minister, showed clearly that the corporations could expect little mercy at his hands.[2]

The Irish municipalities had from earliest times served as instruments of royal power, and, since the seventeenth century, of the Crown's Protestant policy. Sixty-two of the 111 municipalities existing between 1660 and 1800 had been created by the Stuarts to increase the Crown's parliamentary influence, and in James I's

[1] O'Connell to Fitzpatrick, 5 July; 5 August 1833; to J. J. Murphy, 8 May 1835, *O'Connell Corr.*, I, 372, 379; II, 24; Littleton to Anglesey, 9 July 1833, Plas Newydd MSS, cited by McDowell, *Public Opinion*, 181. The five concerned both in the election petition and in the Commission were Stephen Woulfe, M.P. for Cashel (1835-8), Irish Attorney-General and later Chief Baron of the Exchequer; D. R. Pigot, M.P. for Clonmel (1839-46), Irish Attorney-General (1839-41) and also Chief Baron (1846-73); W. E. Hudson, Philip Fogarty and Matthew Sausse, all three of whom went on to prosper in their profession as Taxing Master, County Court Judge for Antrim and a Knight and Colonial Judge respectively. Fitzpatrick, *O'Connell Corr.*, II, 24, n. 1, says that the promotions of all these men (except Woulfe) and of two others who were also counsel for O'Connell in 1835 were due to O'Connell's influence. This remarkable list is therefore further evidence of the extent of his implication in the Whigs' patronage policy. See above pp. 160-2.

[2] Perrin to William IV [n.d. February 1834], H.O. Papers 100/245, 188-90. Melbourne, always tender for loyal Protestant interests, wondered whether it was advisable 'to bring forward such very strong and sweeping charges against the corporations of Ireland before the inquiry into them is completed', and objected to Perrin's admitting 'the inability of a Royal Commission to enforce the attendance of witnesses': Melbourne, Memo, ibid., 100/245, 192-3.

reign, to further his plantation schemes;[1] and early in the eighteenth century all Catholics were officially excluded from membership of corporations as they already were in practice.[2] The model Stuart corporation was a closed, self-elective body, thirteen or less in number, with the exclusive right of voting for their town's burgesses in Parliament. But when in 1800 at the time of the Union many boroughs lost their rights of parliamentary representation, their patrons, handsomely compensated at a flat rate of £15,000 per borough, had no further incentive to keep corporations in existence except where they owned property, and by 1835, only 60 corporations were reckoned to be actually in existence.

The corporations, faithful to their original conception, were generally small (over half had less than twenty members, including both governing body and freemen), self-elective (in forty boroughs, the corporations were entirely self-elected) and exclusively Protestant in that only four contained Catholics in 1835. They were nearly all poor or in debt. Thirty had no annual income at all while only seven disposed of incomes of over £1,000 per annum and, twenty-one of the forty-one corporations with property were in debt, so that it was not surprising that in many boroughs few if any municipal services were provided. There was 'no general, uniform and absolute right to admission' into any of the corporations.[3] Inhabitancy was nowhere recognized as a title. Some corporations recognized rights of birth, marriage and apprenticeship but most used their powers of admitting freemen by 'grace especial' to maintain their exclusiveness for private or for political reasons.

The Commission's Report was a unanimous and scathing condemnation of the whole system, and although its authors can hardly be said to have been impartial, their conclusions were never challenged in essentials. The corporations had 'long become unpopular, and objects of suspicion. [They were] . . . in many instances, of no service to the community; in others injurious; in all, insufficient and

---

[1] John J. Webb, *Municipal Government in Ireland* (1918), esp. Ch. I, 85–182; O'Brien, *Fifty Years of Concessions to Ireland*, I, 577–84; First Report of the Commissioners appointed to enquire into the Municipal Corporations in Ireland, P.P. 1835, XXVII, passim, which provides short histories of each municipality and a valuable general survey.

[2] The Relief Act of 1793 proved a dead letter where admission of Catholics to the municipal franchise was concerned, since they were unable as a result of their long exclusion to prove any titles or rights to freedom.

[3] First Report, Corporations, P.P. 1835, XXVII, 13.

inadequate . . .' Their members 'frequently consist entirely of the
relatives and adherents of particular individuals or families . . . In
far the greater number of close corporations, the persons compos-
sing them are the mere nominees of the "Patron", . . . while in those
apparently more enlarged they are admitted . . . in support of some
particular political interest, most frequently at variance with the
majority of the resident inhabitancy'.[1] The Report laid considerable
stress on the corporations' judicial responsibilities. Corporate
magistrates appointed for life were neither under the direct control
of the Crown nor chosen by the inhabitants, the selection of juries
by sheriffs was frequently partisan and unsatisfactory, and the slow
and expensive borough courts whose civil jurisdiction was generally
limited to small debts were only thought to be worth retaining if
their proceedings were improved and their jurisdictional boundaries
re-defined to fit the actual limits of boroughs.[2]

The Commission thought that it would be useless simply to
reform the present system of admission to corporations, for while
freedom was a matter of right, inheritance and favour it would continue to serve sectional interests and to prevent the formation of a
'constituency' 'by which the property, the interests or the wishes of
the whole local community may be secured a fair representation'.[3]
With its eye on the Reform Act, the Commission was opposed to
perpetuating the existence of an exclusively privileged class, whether
these privileges included the freemen's parliamentary franchise or
a share in municipal property and patronage. The corporations' mis-
management of their property had been quite flagrant. Much alienation of property had taken place, though the insistence of most
corporations that they were entitled to their property in 'absolute
dominion' and did not hold it on trust obviously made the task of
tracing such alienation extremely difficult.[4] Accounts were generally

---

[1] First Report, Corporations, 39–40, 16.

[2] Detailed recommendations included simpler forms of procedure and plead-
ing, professional judges, regular sittings, reduction of costs and a proper appeal
system. Confusion over boundaries was increased by the fact that only in six
boroughs was the authority of the corporate courts independent of the county
in which they were situated. In some places, like Athlone and Portarlington,
borough jurisdictions extended into two counties.

[3] First Report, Corporations, 21.

[4] The best example was the Corporation of Cashel, its property entirely controlled by the Pennefather family, which put forward exactly this claim: Hansard,
XXIX, 1296, 31 July 1835, Perrin.

non-existent or else badly kept and unaudited; numerous instances were found of favouritism in the disposal of property and in most places the chief items of expenditure were the salaries of corporate officials. But in sharp contrast to contemporary English practices, there was no widespread use of corporate funds and charities for political or specifically electoral purposes in Ireland, partly because of the relative poverty of Irish corporations and partly because charities held in trust and administered by municipalities were indeed few and far between in Ireland.[1] In fact, the electoral importance of the corporations, considerable before 1832, declined sharply after the Reform Act. In a few boroughs like Carrickfergus, Galway, Cork City and also the vitally important Dublin City seat, the corporations and their freemen were of real electoral importance, but in many places, as indeed in Cork and also in Limerick, the freemen by themselves were no match for the £10 householders.[2]

Enniskillen under the complete control of its Earl was typical of many Stuart corporations whether in the north, like Lisburn under the Marquess of Hertford, Sligo under the Wynne family or Armagh under its Archbishop, or in the south, like Bandon under Lord Bandon or Athlone under Lord Castlemaine. Larger corporations like Dundalk under the Earl of Roden and Limerick under Lord Gort also had controlling patrons, and the best examples of corporations which were managed (and exploited) by exclusively Protestant caucuses were Drogheda, where they openly professed the principle of 'promoting Protestantism and encouraging Protestant settlers', and Cork under its 'Friendly Club' of some 500 Conservative freemen, where the corporation enjoyed a monopoly of municipal patronage and property in a city with important Catholic mercantile interests and a large Catholic majority.

Dublin's municipal government was in a class of its own.[3] The Corporation was entirely Protestant, the upper house of the Common Council strictly controlling admission to the freedom of the Corporation which conferred the parliamentary franchise. But Dublin was unique in possessing an elective lower house of Common Council

[1] Wherever such charities did exist, as in Belfast and Dublin, the Commission pointed out that 'great neglect and abuse' inevitably occurred, either for private interests or simply through inefficiency; First Report, Corporations, P.P. 1835, XXVIII, 701; XXVII, 36.

[2] See above pp. 92–3, 108–9, 124.

[3] See Report, Select Committee, Corporations, P.P. 1833, XIII, Qs. 4767–6255; First Report, Corporations, XXVII, App. 1–113.

and corporate officers some of whom were also elected, even though
in practice the system always worked to the complete exclusion of
Roman Catholics and Liberal Protestants from both the freemen's
franchise and the patronage of the Corporation.[1] O'Connell's severe
attacks on the Corporation's exclusive character and on its administration of justice and municipal services were never effectively
answered by Irish Tories. The grand juries, voting municipal taxes
of about £30,000 a year, were shown to be picked by the sheriffs on
politico-religious lines, while assize and quarter session juries,
picked in the same way, were notorious for their biassed verdicts in
political cases.[2] The Corporation possessed considerable judicial
responsibilities, yet in the Court of Record the office of judge was
often farmed out by the Lord Mayor, while the Recorder, at this
time Sir Frederick Shaw, the Tory leader, was used only in an
advisory capacity. As in many boroughs, an increase in population
meant that a large portion of the city was actually outside the jurisdiction of the Corporation's courts. The Corporation provided only
an inadequate police force, leaving the watching, lighting and repair
of streets to be superintended, as they were in many other places,
by commissioners under an Act of 1828. Finally, despite a debt
alleged to be £30,000, annual salaries of £4,000 and £2,000 were
being paid to the Lord Mayor and aldermen respectively.[3]

Confronted with a system so full of indefensible abuses, anomalies
and inequalities, the Commission called for 'a general and complete
Reform' and suggested that the Act of 1828 would be a possible basis
for the reconstitution of existing corporations. By this statute, 'An
Act to make provision for the lighting, cleansing and watching of
Cities, Towns Corporate and Market Towns in Ireland', the
inhabitants of any town living in houses of a value of £5 or over
elected a board of commissioners who levied rates for municipal
services. The Act had already come into operation in many places
and was both popular and useful.

[1] These elections were hardly popular, since the lower House of Common
Council was largely elected by members of the trade guilds, and the election of
mayor, sheriffs and aldermen went by a system of elective co-optation.

[2] See Report, Corporations, 1833, XIII, Qs. 5125, 5169, 5220–1, 5636, 5815,
for jury packing by sheriffs who often farmed out their duties to deputies; see
also First Report, Corporations, P.P. 1835, XXVII, 30–1.

[3] Report, Corporations, 1833, XIII, Qs. 5088, 5349, 5393, 5410, 5456–60.

The struggle for reform

'A thorough Reform of the Corporations of the Country, so as to place them under popular control' was one of O'Connell's terms of support in February 1835 to his future Whig allies, and in June 1835 during a debate on the English Bill, he said that since 'Ireland required Corporation Reform more than England' she must at least have similar treatment.[1] His pressure on the Government was effective, for Spring Rice told Sir John Newport that 'had it [the Irish Bill] stood alone, . . . it might have been otherwise framed in many most important particulars, and been much improved. But we were bound by English Bill analogies . . . If we depopularized the Irish Bill . . . we gave an immediate countenance to the cry of Repeal'.[2] The Ministry, disregarding a strong protest from the King, pressed on with the Irish Bill and on 31 July, Perrin now Irish Attorney-General, introduced it in a speech based directly on his own Report.[3]

He proposed to institute town councils elected by £10 householders in the larger cities and towns (those with populations of over 20,000) and by £5 householders in towns under this size. One-third of the councillors would go out of office annually, unless re-elected, while the mayor was to be elected at a different time of year to the rest of the council; and a property qualification of £1,000 in the seven larger cities and £500 in the smaller was to be required for council membership.[4] An important feature of Perrin's Bill of which much was to be heard later was the election by the councils of sheriffs in the eight cities and towns forming legal counties in themselves. The new councils were to take over the duties of lighting and watching boards or, where this was not convenient, the councils were to have the power to examine the accounts of every board levying or administering taxes within the boroughs. The cognizance of local courts was strictly defined and their proceedings regulated. Borough magistrates were to be chosen by the Lord Lieutenant out

[1] Hansard, XXVI, 408; XXVIII, 573–4, 26 February; 5 June 1835, O'Connell. For Parkes' relief that 'the mighty Dan' did not intend to 'endanger' the English Bill, see J. K. Buckley, *Joseph Parkes of Birmingham* (1929), 126–7.
[2] Spring Rice to Sir John Newport [n.d. post July 1835], Monteagle Papers.
[3] William IV to Russell, 14 August 1835, Walpole, *Russell*, I, 246–7; Hansard, XXIX, 1289–310, 31 July 1835, Perrin.
[4] The Bill also contained provisions for dividing towns into wards and for compiling voting lists.

of a list sent to him by each council, although since party feeling might still prevail under this arrangement he was also to have the power to appoint magistrates on his own responsibility. Finally, as a gesture to Conservative feeling, the Bill's provisions were not to affect the rights of existing freemen.

Perrin hoped that his Bill would lead to 'a fair and adequate municipal government', but although he claimed that the measure involved only 'a renovation and a restoration' of the original charters, it was clear from its exultant reception by O'Connell and from the shocked comments of Irish Conservatives that the Bill was, in its own context, a more drastic and radical measure than even the English reform had been.[1] The Irish Tory Shaw, pointing to deserted benches, protested at the Government's bringing in such an important Bill so late in the session. He admitted the existence of abuses in the corporate system but thought that 'every care should be taken not to increase the power of agitation'. The corporations had served in the past to secure the British connection and to encourage Protestantism, and he would strongly oppose placing them in the hands of Repealers and subverters of the Establishment. O'Connell, praising Perrin's speech, said that 'for the first time it is proposed to identify the people of Ireland with the British Constitution, and expressed his 'infinite pleasure and delight' at the Bill. The Government had given 'an earnest of better days for Ireland, . . . the days of the corrupt corporations are over'. He ended with an appeal that since this was not 'a question of Church or Religion', it should not become entangled with these topics. Colonel Sibthorp, the extremely eccentric English Tory, wound up the debate in an almost deserted House by prophesying, accurately enough, that the House of Lords would save the corporations.[2]

The Bill, which passed the Commons without a division, was then dropped owing to the lateness of the session and to the preoccupation of the House of Lords with the English Municipal Reform Bill. Peel had conspicuously taken no part in these debates and his

[1] The electoral arrangements, the necessity for property qualifications and the councils' power to supersede existing boards were directly modelled on the English Bill's provisions. The main points of difference were the £5 franchise and the provisions concerning local courts. The £5 standard in the Irish Bill of 1835 was considerably more liberal than the £10 franchise of the Scottish Act of 1833.

[2] Hansard, XXIX, 1311-13, 1314-19, 1325-6, 31 July 1835, Shaw, O'Connell, Sibthorp.

absence, together with the fact that his attitude to the Irish Bill was unknown, undoubtedly weakened the Opposition in the Commons.[1] During the recess, efforts were made by Sir Henry Hardinge and Charles Arbuthnot to heal the damaging split in the party leadership which had resulted from the treatment by Wellington and Lord Lyndhurst of the English Municipal Reform Bill. Hardinge told Peel that 'Lord M[elbourne] talked of his position as worse than precarious—that you could turn him out—but that he calculated upon a bad Tory attendance—upon your dislike of office—and your coldness towards the D. of W.', while Arbuthnot emphasized that 'the time has come when consultation is most desirable, if not indeed quite necessary'. An amicable meeting between Peel and Wellington took place at Drayton, Wellington subsequently writing to Peel that 'we are of the same opinion as to the course to be pursued in Parliament'.[2]

But if Disraeli's account is reliable, a reconciliation between Peel and Lyndhurst so soon after Lyndhurst's activities in 1835 was impossible. These activities had been directed as much against Peel's own moderate leadership as against 'the [Radical] Movement' which had been their original justification, and early in 1836 Lyndhurst and his friends were preparing, according to Disraeli, 'another and still more comprehensive plan for arresting the movement' which was to be based on the Irish Municipal Reform Bill.[3] *The Times*, with which Lyndhurst was closely connected, launched at the end of 1835 a long and intensive campaign against O'Connell and his party, who were held up as a threat not only to the good government of Ireland but also to the established institutions of England, a more immediate peril in the editor's view than the English Radicals, since Repeal of the Union involved the disruption of the Empire. The Whigs, by

[1] Greville, *Journal*, 27 August 1835, III, 304–5, who noted Peel's deliberate absence.

[2] Hardinge to Peel, 7 January 1836; Arbuthnot to Hardinge, 11 January 1836; Wellington to Peel, 18 January 1836, Peel Papers, Add. MSS 40314, 118–19, 127–30; 40310, 122.

[3] For Disraeli's account of Lyndhurst's plans in 1835, see Monypenny, *Disraeli*, I, 301–2. An ultra Tory Ministry, including Wellington but not Peel, was to be formed on the rejection of the English Municipal Bill in the Lords. This wild scheme was ruined when a group of peers led by Wharncliffe refused to go against Peel and his followers in the Commons. This in turn frightened Wellington off. For the 1836 plan, see Disraeli, Memo, 17 September 1836, op. cit., I, 327–9.

weakly forming a parliamentary alliance with O'Connell, were thus deeply implicated in a dangerous and subversive conspiracy. O'Connell's own replies to *The Times*' unmeasured attacks gave valuable publicity to the paper's campaign, which continued throughout the debates on Irish municipal reform and which helped to turn an alliance with considerable parliamentary advantages into a grave liability for the Ministry.[1]

The Times' campaign against O'Connell, together with Disraeli's ferocious invectives against the 'anti-national', oligarchical Whigs and their Radical and Irish allies and his eloquent defence of the House of Lords and the Tory party as the real repositories of representative democracy, provided most valuable reinforcements for the Tory peers.[2] But they were also very necessary replies to O'Connell's own pre-session campaign in 1836 in England. He had been advised by Henry Warburton 'to explain fully to Englishmen what all the evils of an Irish Corporation are: and inform your audience, that bad as Liverpool or Leicester of old may have been, they are angelic creatures as compared to the abominations of your Municipalities in Ireland'.[3] The reaction of many Whigs to O'Connell's campaign was no doubt similar to Lord Lyttelton's, who wrote to Russell about a speech of O'Connell's at Birmingham that 'some of his speeches have been *more violent* and *more offensive*, I daresay; but there was some very pretty Treason & plenty of deep mischief'. Lyttelton hoped that O'Connell's 'reception at Birmingham . . . would seem

---

[1] For examples of these violent attacks, see *Times*, 12 December 1835; 26 February; 16 June 1836; 9, 10 May 1839; 3 January 1840; and for O'Connell's replies, including attacks on Lyndhurst and John Walter, see *History of The Times*, I, 366–7, 368. For Lynhurst's connection with the paper, see Lyndhurst to Peel, 26 February 1835; Barnes to G. Winslow [n.d. 1835], Peel Papers, Add. MSS 40316, 164–5, 195.

[2] For Disraeli's Runnymede Letters, a series of nineteen published anonymously in *The Times* from 19 January 1836, and his *Vindication of The English Constitution in a Letter to a Noble and Learned Lord* [sc. Lyndhurst] (1836), see Monypenny, *Disraeli*, I, 306–26. O'Connell was described in Letter VIII, 'To the People', in the course of an attack which Monypenny thought exceeded 'all bounds in its savagery', as 'a systematic liar and a beggarly cheat, a swindler and a poltroon . . . His public and his private life are equally profligate; he has committed every crime that does not require courage.' The *Vindication* is on an altogether higher plane, an attack in the spirit of Burke and Bolingbroke on Utilitarianism and Whiggism and an eulogy of the Tory party as combining 'democratic liberty, aristocratic security and monarchical convenience'.

[3] Warburton to O'Connell, 22 January 1836, O'Connell MSS, U.C.D.

to be rather an indication of the prevailing feeling about Ireland, & in support of the measures of the present Ministry in regard to Ireland, than of any personal goodwill towards the fellow himself'.[1] But while in November 1835 Hardinge could tell Peel that some Ministers 'talk indignantly of the mischief which O'Connell has done the Govt.',[2] the results of the English municipal elections in January 1836 were thought to have restored the Ministry's position. 'I think', Holland told Ellice, 'they have even abated the O'Connell fever', and Ebrington went further in thinking that the results

> must have convinced the Tories that we have all the most intelligent of the middle class on our side, & though the House of Lords with the Hierarchy and Squirearchy on theirs will make it difficult enough for our Friends to govern the country, the opposition of the towns would I believe make it impossible for theirs, especially as the O'Connello-phobia will I trust in great measure abate after the meeting of the House of Commons, when Dan always appears to more advantage than in any other theatre, & where in the last session he did us far more good than any other five men not in the Government.[3]

The session of 1836 opened with a strong objection by Wellington to a passage in the King's Speech which, he argued, pledged the Lords to reform the Irish corporations on the same lines as had been adopted in England and Scotland. He carried instead an amendment that the House would merely consider any defects or evils in the Irish system and Peel, reluctantly following suit in the Commons, lost his motion by a majority of 41.[4] He was tactically justified in not

[1] Lyttelton to Russell, 2 February 1836, Russell Papers, P.R.O. 30/22/2A, adding that he thought Parkes' presence at the meeting was unfortunate 'because inferences respecting the Government in relation to O'Connell may be drawn from it'.

[2] Hardinge to Peel, 18 November [1835], Peel Papers, Add. MSS 40314, 108–9. See also Greville, *Journal*, 27 September 1835, III, 323, on the press war surrounding O'Connell's campaign in Scotland.

[3] Holland to Ellice, 5 January 1836, Ellice MSS, N.L.S.; Ebrington to Tavistock, 10 January 1836, Russell Papers, P.R.O. 30/22/2A.

[4] Hansard, XXXI, 4, 12–14, 4 February 1836, King's Speech, Wellington. Greville thought that Wellington, in theory right, should not have pressed an amendment 'on such a trifle'. In terms of Tory strategy, it was hardly a trifle. The Whig leaders accepted it even though a division might have been very close—an apt comment on Melbourne's diffident leadership in the Lords. Peel apparently had no intention beforehand of moving any amendment: Greville, *Journal*, 5 February 1836, III, 341.

wanting a division by the delight which the Government and its supporters took in the size of the majority. The debate had been remarkable not only for Stanley's support of Peel but also for O'Connell's remark, which was to be endlessly quoted by his opponents, that he saw in each corporate town 'a Normal school for teaching the science of peaceful political agitation'.[1] But Stanley had also said that he was inclined to adopt 'the radical remedy of total extinction' for some corporations, and Mulgrave, in congratulating Russell on the division, told him that 'if you had yielded to Peel's amendment particularly after the ground it was put upon by Stanley, *five* minutes would have destroyed all the popularity we had been thru as many months building up in Ireland'.[2]

Stanley's move had an immediate effect on Peel, who indicated to his followers that 'it was of great consequence to shape their proceedings so as to get the support of Stanley', and by 10 February Peel himself was converted in theory to 'the abolition of all corporations without exception'.[3] Wellington readily agreed, while Graham, acting as intermediary between Peel and Stanley, obtained the latter's complete approval.[4] This policy, originating in a chance remark by Stanley and adopted by Peel at least partly to cement his alliance with Stanley and Graham, had important consequences. It meant that the Tory peers had some justification for their high-handed treatment of later Irish Municipal Corporation Bills and further, that a compromise on this issue, which would have been relatively easy to arrange in 1836 with Peel's co-operation, would cause great difficulty and acute differences of opinion between 1837 and 1840.

The Bill of 1836, introduced by Michael O'Loghlen, the Irish Solicitor-General, was practically identical with that of 1835. Peel's speech, his first contribution on this issue, contained the scheme

[1] Hansard, XXXI, 63–8, 98, 4 February 1836, Stanley, O'Connell. This was the first occasion on which Stanley sat on the Opposition bench: Greville, *Journal*, 5, 6, 7 February 1836, III, 342–3.

[2] Mulgrave to Russell, 11 February 1836, Russell Papers, P.R.O. 30/22/2A.

[3] Greville, *Journal*, 6 February 1836, III, 342; Peel to Wellington, 10 February 1836, Parker, *Peel*, II, 322–3.

[4] Wellington to Peel, 11, 13 February 1836, Peel Papers, Add. MSS 40310, 125–8, 129–30, suggesting that the corporations might resign their charters while their property would be vested in trustees. This was originally Shaw's idea. Peel to Wellington, 10 February 1836, Parker, *Peel*, II, 322–3; Graham to Peel, 12 February 1836, Peel Papers, Add. MSS 40318, 54–5, giving Stanley's approval.

which the Opposition leaders had just decided upon. He was concerned not merely with the local effects of a reform but with its possible contribution to the administration of justice and to the efficiency of the civil power. The old system with its exclusiveness and partiality could not be maintained, but he denied that principles of parliamentary reform had any relevance to this question or that popular municipal elections would necessarily ensure the satisfactory administration of justice, and he therefore proposed the appointment of all borough magistrates by the Lord Lieutenant, the vesting of the corporations' property in a commission and the general application of the Act of 1828 to provide elected local authorities in place of the old corporations.[1] For the Irish party, Sheil accused Peel and the Conservatives of abandoning the Irish corporations 'because they could no longer serve their turn . . . This in England they did not dare to propose; this in Ireland, please God and the people, they shall never carry.' Russell, for the Government, accused Peel of an invasion of rights and property.[2]

At the committee stage, when Irish Tories continued to invoke the spectre of an Ireland dominated by O'Connell and the priests, and Graham, pointing to the danger of extending democratic liberties in a divided and diseased society, quoted Tocqueville to the effect that once this process had begun there would be no stopping it until universal suffrage had been achieved,[3] Lord Francis Egerton's motion to abolish the corporations and to implement Peel's scheme was defeated by 64 votes, an even larger majority than that on Peel's amendment to the Address. 'We were woefully beat', wrote the Tory Knatchbull, 'and the Government is consequently stronger than ever—it gains strength every day. O'Connell is a great Radical, but more powerful than ever. He will do much more mischief before his race is run.'[4] The strong Government majority was in part due to 'the Whig managers, who make their people attend', and in part, as

[1] Hansard, XXXI, 1050–76, 29 February 1836, Peel.

[2] Hansard, XXXI, 1097–1100, 1103, 29 February 1836, Sheil, Russell, who had earlier acutely observed that Peel 'was, in fact, a great lover of changes and innovations', Greville, *Journal*, 27 August 1835, III, 305.

[3] Hansard, XXXII, 43–65, 8 March 1836, Graham. Tocqueville provided texts for both sides. O'Connell's celebrated phrase was an echo of one of Tocqueville's. See also the quotation used by the Radical Ward, that municipalities 'are to liberty what primary schools are to science', Hansard, XXXII, 670, 28 March 1836, Ward.

[4] Knatchbull to Lady Knatchbull, 8 March 1836, *Kentish Family*, 227.

Hobhouse told Greville, to poor Tory attendance—a factor which was to trouble Peel later. This division and the majority of 61 by which the Bill passed in the Commons showed that however success-ful the O'Connell cry might be in the country, it had very little effect in the House of Commons. Indeed Greville thought that this slogan 'was now worn threadbare; it had been argued and ranted upon *usque ad nauseam*' and he doubted if O'Connell 'is as much hated in England as the Tories would have him. They have overdone their attacks on him, and as it has unluckily been their sole *cheval de bataille*, they have ridden it till it has not a leg to stand upon.'[1]

The Bill passed the Commons with only one important change, when O'Loghlen, despite O'Connell's protests and as a concession to the Opposition, agreed to put the appointment of sheriffs in the Lord Lieutenant's hands; but ministers refused to accept Peel's suggestion that elected mayors should not also be magistrates or to compromise on the franchises, which were the most important features of the Bill as far as O'Connell and his party were concerned. As soon as Russell knew that the Tory peers would move to abolish the corporations, he wrote to Mulgrave for his views on the attitude of Irish public opinion towards the Bill and received an encouraging reply. 'I believe', wrote Mulgrave,

> that there is no other question on which there is more general anxiety, not perhaps that they anticipate any very great actual advantages from it except in the large towns but because they consider it as embodying the principle of *equal justice to Ireland* . . . every division (?) of the Liberal Party will unite in counting the Municipal Bill as the last of equal Rights on points not connected with the Church, and it would be very difficult to ensure continued confidence in the Government with our submitting to be beat upon such a point without an appeal to the people. I'm thoroughly aware of the counterbalancing disadvantages of a Dissolution but I am sure in Ireland it will be expected if the Lords relying on the limited nature of our Majority in the Parliament throw out the Bill.[2]

There is no reason to doubt the correctness of Mulgrave's analysis of Irish opinion on this issue, and it is also clear that the slogan of equality of rights and legislation, on which O'Connell had based his alliance with the Whigs, was a popular one at this time in Ireland.

---

[1] Greville, *Journal*, 10 March 1836, III, 354.
[2] Russell to Mulgrave, 12 April 1836, H.O. Papers, 100/251, 140–1; Mulgrave to Russell, 15 April 1836, Russell Papers, P.R.O. 30/22/2B.

O'Connell's own belief that the Lords would pass the Bill was soon proved wrong.[1] The peers gave the Bill a Second Reading after listening to Melbourne's defence of the Commission's Report, which unlike its English counterpart had scarcely been challenged, and of a measure which had been supported by a considerable majority of the Commons and was with one or two exceptions identical with the English Bill. But at the committee stage Lord Fitzgerald and Vesci carried an instruction to abolish the corporations by 203 votes to 119. Other clauses of the Bill were lost by smaller but decisive majorities, and Lyndhurst later left no doubt of the grounds on which he and his friends were acting when he told the Lords that

> The application of the same principle . . . to different places must pro-
> duce dissimilar results, and could not lead to equal justice . . . One
> fourth of her [Ireland's] inhabitants were English by descent, English
> in their habits, English in their usages, Protestant in their religion, and
> unalterably attached to the English connexion . . . They had to contend
> with a population alien to Englishmen, speaking, many of them, a
> different language, professing a different religion, regarding the English
> as invaders, and ready to expel them at the first opportunity.[2]

This outburst, which was heard by O'Connell in person, was deci-
sive in hardening Irish opposition, for even after Fitzgerald's instruction had been carried the Irish party might still have accepted the amended Bill. Mulgrave in Ireland had seen W. F. Finn, the Member for County Kilkenny, who 'surprised me by volunteering to say that he hoped the Govt. would at any rate in the first instance accept the Municipal Bill as altered by the Lords . . . , that the great object was to destroy the existing corporations, that as to anything further the whole liberal interest would be quite satisfied to leave its management in my hands . . . This is confidence with a vengeance!'[3]

The Bill, now altered out of all recognition, was duly passed in the Lords after a final debate remarkable for the intervention of the neutral Duke of Richmond, whose motion to give corporations to the seven largest cities and towns, though accepted by Lansdowne for the Government, was rejected by 141 votes to 82.[4] Faced with a

[1] O'Connell to Fitzpatrick, 22 March 1836, *O'Connell Corr.*, II, 50.

[2] Hansard, XXXIII, 734-5, 9 May 1836, Lyndhurst.

[3] Mulgrave to Russell, 3 May 1836, Russell Papers, P.R.O. 30/22/2B; see also O'Connell to Barrett, 16 May 1836, *O'Connell Corr.*, II, 57-9.

[4] Hansard, XXXIII, 1055-7, 1059-61, 18 May 1836, Richmond, Lansdowne.

constitutional crisis which had in a sense been hanging over politics
since June 1835 and which, in the Whig view, was caused by the
determination of a majority in the Lords 'not to stop or alter a
particular measure, but to stop or alter all measures, which may not
be agreeable to the most powerful, or in other words the most
violent, among their own body', Russell now urged 'a steady and
gradual creation of Peers', the threat of which had coerced the
House of Lords in 1832. The ministry, 'in the position of confessing
the evil, and not consenting to the remedy', was at a disadvantage as
compared both to the Tories with their support of the Lords, and
the Radicals with their demand for an elective Upper House; and
public opinion was, on Irish questions, a very imperfect check on
the Lords.[1] But the large Commons majority of 1831-2, backed by
the forces of organized public opinion, represented a very different
state of affairs to that of 1836, when the Government's majority
depended to a considerable extent on an over-publicized Irish
alliance and when the Opposition had skilfully contrived the crisis to
revolve round a series of Irish measures which were very far from
being popular issues in England. Political realism (as well as his own
prejudices) was on Melbourne's side when he refused to create
the '8, 10 or twelve peers' suggested by Russell.[2]

Russell had no alternative but to offer a compromise. Although he
carried in the Commons a motion that 'The House do disagree with
the Lords' Amendments', he announced in his speech that the
Government now proposed to provide only the eleven largest cities
and towns in Schedules A and B with corporations. In all other
towns the Act of 1828 would be applied immediately, and boards
elected by £5 householders would replace the existing corporations.[3]
Mulgrave, consulted on Irish opinion, again replied encouragingly
that such a scheme would 'quite content the great majority of our
friends' in Ireland despite their 'deep and undeniable feeling on the
subject', while O'Connell told Pigot that the Bill 'was *amended* by

---

[1] Russell, Memo, 5 June 1836, Russell Papers, P.R.O. 30/22/2B.

[2] Melbourne to Russell, 5 June 1836, Russell Papers, P.R.O. 30/22/2B.

[3] Hansard, XXXIV, 218-31, 405-10, 9, 10 June 1836, Russell, Division. The
Government was clearly aiming at the neat solution of 1661 cited by Speaker
Abercromby, when the Commons disagreed with the Lords' amendments on a
Corporations Bill, a conference between the Houses postponed the question and
after a recess the Lords accepted the Commons' Bill: Abercromby to Russell,
5 June 1836, Russell Papers, P.R.O. 30/22/2B.

Lord John against my consent. I protested in private against any compromise but was driven in public to support the party.'[1]

The new Bill met with no effective opposition in the Commons, nearly the whole of the Irish party following O'Connell's lead when he emphasized that the main issue was the power of the Tory House of Lords and that it was 'a mere question of detail' whether 32 or 15 towns required corporations.[2] As over tithes, it was left to Sharman Crawford to protest against the acceptance by the Irish party of an insult and to attempt to restore the towns of Schedule C to the Bill on the grounds that no less than eight places with populations of over 9,000 would be excluded by Russell's proposal. As a gesture on behalf of Bandonbridge which he represented, the Tory Jackson seconded the motion which was lost by 148 votes to 8.[3] This was the first of two revolts against O'Connell's leadership on this question; they were much weaker than those over tithes and reflected the fact that Irish Members were not in this case under the same strong pressure of Irish opinion as they had been on the tithe question. The Lords duly rejected the Commons' amendments and Russell's offer of a compromise. But as Melbourne explained to Hobhouse in arguing that resignation would not be justified, 'we knew nothing now that we did not know before'; and Russell carried a motion on 30 June to take the Lords' amendments into consideration in three months' time, acting in the spirit of his brother's advice to 'prorogue Parlt. as soon as you can, to give the Lords an opportunity of reconsidering their votes'.[4]

O'Connell's support in the Commons was staunch and unquestioning, but his powerful demands outside the House for an elective House of Lords or its abolition had been dangerous enough in 1835 to draw from Russell two explicit and public declarations against any organic, constitutional reform.[5] Brougham stressed the embarrassment which O'Connell's campaign might cause, particularly for Ministers reputed to be in close touch with O'Connell: 'I see Lord Morpeth is resolved to keep in Dan's good graces . . . He is the only one at the Leeds meeting from whom not a word can be extracted

[1] Mulgrave to Russell, 7 June 1836, Russell Papers, P.R.O. 30/22/2B; O'Connell to D. R. Pigot, 2 July 1836, O'Connell Papers, N.L.I., uncatalogued.

[2] Hansard, XXXIV, 387-99, 10 June 1836, O'Connell.

[3] Hansard, XXXIV, 308-11, 520-2, 538, 10, 14 June 1836, Crawford, Jackson, Division.

[4] Broughton, *Recollections*, 26 June 1836, V, 57-8; Tavistock to Russell, 12, 15 June 1836, Russell Papers, P.R.O. 30/22/2B.   [5] Walpole, *Russell*, I, 250-1.

against pulling down the House of Lords. For why—if he had said any such word there's no man can answer for what Dan would have said the week after!' But the Government's semi-neutrality on this issue was not, as Brougham thought, tactically unwise.[1] Some Whigs like Morpeth and probably Russell, although opposed in theory to O'Connell's radical proposals, were prepared to tolerate his campaign as a possibly useful weapon in any future struggle with the Lords. They could not afford to alienate the Irish party or the English Radicals whose support was essential to the Government, particularly when politicians like Charles Buller were pressing the Whigs to concede the Ballot as an open question, which would 'excite every elector in England in favour of the Government [and] . . . rescue us for ever after from the Tories'. According to Buller, 'the apathy of the people towards the present ministry [was] . . . the necessary consequence of its taking its stand on its two weak points—its Irish Bills'.[2]

The Opposition had its own problems. A constitutional deadlock between the two Houses was bound to strain the loyalty of Conservative M.P.s to their leader in the Commons, particularly since Peel's cautious and reserved attitude towards 'the high-flying Tories' of the House of Lords was well known.[3] It was not surprising that the first suggestion of compromise on the part of the Opposition came from a member of the Commons and only strange that it should have come from Joseph Jackson, the staunch defender of the corporations. In August 1836 he informed Peel that there was 'a very strong feeling,

[1] Brougham to Russell, 3, 11, September 1836, Russell Papers, P.R.O. 30/22/2C, criticizing Holland's policy of 'wait-and-see' on the Lords reform question and saying also that 'a thorough reform of the Lords house' was 'the line the friends of Government take'. Tavistock may have rather exaggerated the strength of this movement: 'It is now becoming the topic of public meetings and speeches as much as Parlty. Reform was before 1830,' to Russell, 15 September 1836, Russell Papers, P.R.O. 30/22/2C. But Harriet Martineau, *History of England during the Thirty Years Peace* (1849), II, 258-60, who believed that O'Connell's campaign only helped the Tory peers, shows how seriously the topic was discussed and taken up by English Radicals like Roebuck, Hume and Buller.

[2] Charles Buller to Ellice, 12 January 1837, Ellice MSS, N.L.S., pkt. 43; cf. Lord G. Somerset to Graham, 7 December 1836, Graham MSS, expecting that Radical support would be conditional on 'Radical *English* measures as well as Radical Irish measures'.

[3] Ripon to Stanley, 26 December 1836, Graham MSS, who on a visit to Drayton found Peel 'a most cautious man', who would not agree to any plan of action unless the Government conceded open questions.

even amongst our Conservative friends, against the total annihilation
of Corporations' and suggested that corporations might be conceded
on certain conditions, including a high municipal franchise to give
Catholics a share but not a monopoly of municipal power and
clauses forbidding corporations to transact non-municipal business.
Wellington, when consulted by Peel, understood 'the feeling which
Sergeant Jackson mentions. It prevails to a certain degree in the
House of Lords.' But he refused to adopt the scheme and was
'astonished that Sergeant Jackson should think that supposing it
should be possible to carry an enactment to prevent discussions in
Corporations, such a Regulation could be carried into execution', nor
did he see how a franchise could be fixed which would not be
immediately evaded.[1]

The Whigs decided to make 'the Corporations . . . our Cheval de
Bataille next session', against the King's advice that the Bill should
be postponed until the Irish Poor Law Bill was passed.[2] Warburton,
the contact between the Radicals, O'Connell and the Government,
who himself took a realistic view of the weaknesses of the Radicals'
position and believed that their business was to keep up a 'steam-
pressure' on the Whigs without actually proposing conditions of
support, won over O'Connell, whose main interest was in tangible
legislative reforms. O'Connell wrote to him to say that 'you wrong
me in thinking that I would assist in throwing out *any* Corporate
Bill . . . At all events I will not do that', and he guaranteed that '. . .
the entire "Irish Legion" invalids excepted will be in the front of
the battle'.[3] This decision to give the Ministry thick-and-thin support on its Irish policies, rather than to use the Irish party's position
as the guarantee of the Government's majority to force the Government to concede to Radical demands, had important consequences.
The session of 1837 was to be the last great opportunity before the

[1] Jackson to Peel, 31 August; Wellington to Peel, 8 September 1836, Peel
Papers, Add. MSS 40424, 113–16; 40310, 155–8.

[2] Mulgrave to Russell, 13 September 1836; 3 January 1837, Russell Papers,
P.R.O. 30/22/2C, 2E; Sir H. Taylor to Russell, 2 January 1837, Walpole,
Russell, I, 274. Only Holland seems to have been ready to compromise on
Richmond's plan of May 1836; Holland to Russell [n.d. December 1836],
Russell Papers, P.R.O. 30/22/2D.

[3] Warburton to O'Connell, 17 December 1836, O'Connell MSS, U.C.D.; and
O'Connell to Warburton, 29 December 1836, Russell Papers, P.R.O. 30/22/2D,
in which he also abandoned Peerage Reform entirely, although still thinking
Ballot 'a suitable concession to the Whig Radicals'.

English Radicals, as a semi-independent parliamentary force, were decimated in the General Election of 1837.

O'Connell's co-operative attitude allowed him to obtain one important concession which constituted the only main difference between the original Municipal Bill of 1836 and that of 1837. In the 1836 Bill the sheriffs in counties of towns and cities were to be chosen by the Lord Lieutenant out of a list of three names put forward by the town councils. This method, of which O'Connell approved, was, he claimed, finally

> . . . abandoned as a concession to the Tories—who made use of it as an argument against any new Corporations in Ireland. They said 'you', the Government, 'concede that your Councils in the new Corporations would be unfit to be trusted with so trivial a function . . . when you admit that, is it not a proof that they ought not be trusted with higher functions'. Thus the Ministry tarnished their own plan and gave their and our Enemies a triumph in Argument . . . It really is too bad to give the Tories their only argument, and in doing so to offer an Insult to the Men who will compose the new Councils.[1]

The Government conceded his point in 1837, scarcely a trivial one in view of the sheriffs' responsibilities in selecting juries and superintending parliamentary elections, and a good illustration of the closeness of the relationship between O'Connell and the Whigs at this time.

Russell, in his speech introducing the Bill, called it 'a vital question to the present administration' and a test of English policy towards Ireland. With its details already well known, the debates centred on the more general aspects of Whig policy towards Ireland.[2] O'Connell had picked up a rumour that Peel would allow the Municipal Bill to pass both Houses if Appropriation was dropped, but Egerton's motion to abolish the corporations was again proposed and defeated by an unexpectedly large majority of 80.[3] Peel had

[1] O'Connell to Warburton, 29 December 1836, Russell Papers, P.R.O. 30/22/2D. See also Mulgrave to Russell, 17, 22 December 1836, Russell Papers, P.R.O. 30/22/2D, stressing the anxiety of Irish Liberal Members, especially Sheil, on this point, and asking Russell to meet their views if possible.

[2] Hansard, XXXVI, 206–69, 380, 7, 8 February 1837, Russell, Jackson, O'Connell, Graham.

[3] O'Connell to Fitzpatrick, 18 February 1837, O'Connell Corr., II, 78–9, agreeing that such a bargain might have advantages, but 'none of the Irish popular members could commit themselves' to it; Hansard, XXXVI, 958–62, 22 February 1837, Division.

already received a warning from Hardinge that 'the sluggish folly of many of our supporters' might produce a poor attendance, and on a certainly not very promising' division Wellington pointed out to him that 'the Absence of the Irish [Tory] Members particularly is to be attributed to their fears of offending certain of their constituents. They knew that the vote would be against the Amendment, and they did not care, or thought that it did not signify whether the Minority was stronger or weaker.'[1] For Peel and Wellington, both of whom took it for granted that the Whigs would resign and appeal to the country on the loss or postponement of the Bill in the Lords, this kind of behaviour was extremely annoying.[2] Wellington, needing support from the Conservatives in the Commons to strengthen his hand in dealing with certain 'waverers . . . even among the leaders' in the Lords, thought 'the probable Resignation of the Government the great Question of the Day . . . They will seize the first opportunity of running away; and found their Resignation upon the Question upon which popular opinion may be unfavourable to their Successors; and on which there may be a difference of opinion among the Conservative Party'. The whole question certainly went 'further than the mere Question of the Municipal Administration of Towns which are bankrupt in Property'.[3]

At this stage Sir James Graham and Lord Stanley, those recent and important recruits to the Conservative party, decisively intervened. They too thought that the Government might resign, that as Graham said, 'this Irish Municipal Question constitutes after all the principal difficulty which a Conservative Government, once formed, must overcome', and that therefore the Opposition had every interest in an acceptable compromise solution. They suggested that a moderate attitude on the part of the Opposition would make the Whigs'

[1] Hardinge to Peel, 17 January 1837; Wellington to Peel, 29 (sic) February 1837 (wrongly dated in Parker, *Peel*, II, 339–40), Peel Papers, Add. MSS 40314, 174; 40310, 164–6.

[2] Wellington to Peel, 22 February 1837, Peel Papers, Add MSS 40310, 162–3. For Peel's disgust at his followers and for the divided condition of the party caused by dissatisfaction with Peel's cautious and prudent attitude, see Greville, *Journal*, 25 February 1837, III, 396–8; and Malmesbury, *Memoirs of an Ex-Minister* (1884), I, 74, both of whom thought in fact that the Government majority put an end to any question of dissolution.

[3] Wellington to Peel, 23 March 1837, Peel Papers, Add. MSS 40310, 168–70. Wellington believed that the Whigs had forced themselves on the King in 1835 and had conspired to throw politics into confusion—conduct which he contrasted unfavourably with Grey's in 1831–2: to Peel, 24 March 1837, ibid., 172–3.

resignation indefensible, and most important, that the Lords should not reject but merely postpone the Municipal Bill for two months until a Tithe Bill without Appropriation and a Poor Law with 'a real test of value founded on rating and bearing immediately both on the elective and municipal Franchise' had been passed. The Lords could then concede corporations to Ireland.[1]

Peel was convinced by these arguments but he had now to win over Wellington, who was ready to consider any course 'which would save Ireland from evils and the two Houses from constitutional conflicts' but who saw no need whatever for Irish corporations where 'the lowest Rabble of the Town will be the burgesses, and will elect the Town Council. The Police of the Corporation must be in the hands of Priests and demagogues; . . . I confess that I could not bear to be instrumental in imposing upon Gentlemen of Property, particularly upon Irish Protestants, living in and in the neighbourhood of these Towns such a system of vexatious tyranny as will be imposed upon them by this Bill.' Postponement, which would be considered by friends as well as opponents as 'an abandonment of the Principle of our opposition', might well not avert the Government's resignation, and the Duke could not believe that the Conservatives would obtain 'a reasonable Poor Law; a reasonable Tithe Composition Act; and through them a reasonable Municipal Corporation Act. Read O'Connell's speeches and Letters; and you will see that we shall fail in attaining all these objects'.[2] Peel in one of his most masterly memoranda finally dissuaded Wellington from his obvious leaning towards Lyndhurst's policy of outright rejection, by arguing that postponement would free the Lords of the dilemma which the Government was trying to impose on them, 'by which the Lords would be invited either to reject the Bill absolutely and thus commit themselves to a permanent conflict with the House of Commons on a question of civil privilege for Ireland which exists in England and Scotland, or to make a settlement of the Municipal Bill separately from the Tithe Bill, and to part with a main instrument in their possession for ensuring a satisfactory settlement of the Tithe Bill'.[3]

The whole compromise policy was at last settled on, with at least

[1] Graham to Peel, 27 March 1837, Peel Papers, Add. MSS 40318, 64-9.

[2] Wellington to Peel, 31 March 1837, Peel Papers, Add. MSS 40310, 174-6. His point about police applied also to local taxation.

[3] Peel to Wellington, 9 April 1837, Peel Papers, Add. MSS 40310, 181-2; cf. Lyndhurst to Wellington, 6 April 1837, ibid., 183-4.

an appearance of unanimity, by the Conservative party leaders on
24 April.[1] It was as Graham said, a policy of '*limited* conditional
concession', a recognition that in Peel's words, 'less from the love of
Corporations in the abstract, than from the feeling, that the denial
of them to Ireland implied inferiority, and the intention to insult—it
was unwise to persist in opposition to the Reconstitution of them'.[2]
But the really decisive factor for Peel had been the need for party
unity in the likelihood of the Government's resignation. He and
Wellington perhaps exaggerated this possibility, but Russell at least
was ready to resign if the Lords rejected the Bill and Mulgrave was
clear that the Government ought also in this case to appeal to the
country, since 'your not doing so would be construed by Peel with
great plausibility into a candid acquiescence in the assertion that the
feeling of the country had come round to him whilst, depend upon
it, the popular party would consider it an unaccountable desertion'.[3]
In fact, the action of the House of Lords in twice postponing the
Bill in order to legislate on tithes and the Poor Law was far from
being outright rejection, and Russell withdrew his threat to resign
while the Government 'retained the confidence of the House of
Commons'.[4] The Bill had passed through committee in the Commons almost unchanged; the only attempt at amendment came again
from Crawford, who lost his motion to deprive the Lord Lieutenant
of his veto on the choice of sheriffs by 65 votes to 5.[5]

Despite his doubts and hesitation about this particular policy,
Wellington had managed to persuade the Tory peers to postpone the
Bill, but he could not prevent another outburst by Lyndhurst on the
second postponement in which he attacked the Whigs for their forbearance of O'Connell's General Association, called the £5 franchise
in the Bill 'no qualification at all' and said the Bill would 'hand over

[1] Peel, Memo, 23 April 1837, read at Lyndhurst's house, Peel Papers, Add.
MSS 40423, 176–9.

[2] Graham to Peel, 2 April; Peel, Memo, 4 July 1837, Peel Papers, Add. MSS
40318, 75–6; 40423, 301–4.

[3] Mulgrave to Russell, 12 April 1837, Russell Papers, P.R.O. 30/22/2E.
Russell was supported by Duncannon. The rest of the Cabinet seems to have
been against resignation, and Greville thought that Russell was unlikely to be
widely supported by the party. See Spencer to Russell, 12 April 1837, Russell
Papers, P.R.O. 30/22/2E; Greville, *Journal*, 31 March 1837, III, 401; and
O'Connell to F. W. B. Mullins, M.P., 22 April 1837, *O'Connell Corr.*, II, 89,
mentioning the 'split in the cabinet'.

[4] Greville, *Journal*, 13 May 1837, III, 405.

[5] Hansard, XXXVII, 672–5, 20 March 1837. Crawford, Division.

the Corporations of Ireland to the Roman Catholic agitators'. It had
been arranged to postpone the Bill 'in the most conciliatory way', and
the official leaders of the party were 'astonished as well as annoyed'
by this speech.[1] But Lyndhurst was representative of many Tory
peers who disliked both Peel's 'opposition on Conservative principles' and Wellington's declared wish to reach 'a final and satisfactory settlement' of the three Irish questions.[2] One of these peers told
Disraeli in February 1838 that Lyndhurst's 'party cannot allow his
bride to monopolize him, the Duke of Wellington appears to have
been buttered & palavered into literally giving in his adhesion to
these shabby Ministers, & I don't see who there is in the House of
Lords to look to but Lord Lyndhurst'.[3] In 1838 and 1839 these angry
and discontented men, anxious to assert the legislative independence
of their House and to cause the Government as much trouble as
possible launched a general attack on the Whigs' Irish policies; and
while they could not prevent tithe and Poor Law legislation going
through as the first instalment of the compromise, they were
entirely successful in blocking any legislation for Irish municipal
government.

Peel and his closest associates certainly wanted to reach a settlement, but they refused to enter into any secret negotiations with the
Government or to disclose their terms because, as Graham rather
sententiously put it, 'Unreserved confidence in political associates
and uncompromising war with political opponents is the course,
which the British Public approves; and they are right, since it is the
broad high-way of strict integrity'.[4] He might have added that with
the Tory peers on the edge of rebellion, any secret understanding
with the Whigs (which might not have long remained secret) would
have been fraught with danger. Indeed when Peel finally produced

[1] Hansard, XXXVIII, 1308–21, 9 June 1837, Lyndhurst; Greville, *Journal*,
11 June 1837, III, 409.
[2] Hansard, XXXVIII, 1682–3, 29 June 1837, Wellington; Peel, Memo, 4 July
1837, Peel Papers, Add. MSS 40423, 301–4.
[3] Londonderry to Disraeli, 1 February 1838, Hughenden MSS. In August
1837 Lyndhurst had married as his second wife, Georgiana, daughter of Lewis
Goldsmith.
[4] Graham to Peel, 17 May 1837, Peel Papers, Add. MSS 40318, 89–92. See
also Peel to Stanley, 19 May; Wellington to Peel, 17 May 1837, protesting
against 'any Private Communication'; and Graham to Peel [n.d. July 1837],
reporting that attempts to induce Stanley to negotiate separately on the Bill had
failed, ibid., 40423, 232–4; 40310, 204–5; 40318, 95–8.

his concrete reform proposals in May 1838, they were undoubtedly unpopular with Conservative back-benchers. In eleven of the largest towns, Peel proposed to create corporations elected on a franchise of £10 rateable value under the Poor Law, and in smaller towns a majority of such electors could apply to the Lord Lieutenant for a charter of incorporation.[1] Russell was prepared to accept all these proposals, except that under strong pressure from Sheil and O'Connell, he stood out for a £5 franchise in the second class of towns and carried the issue with Irish support by only 20 votes.[2] For the Conservative leaders, the franchise, both parliamentary and municipal, was all-important. Graham, the proponent of compromise, told Peel that 'if Ireland is to be governed by constitutional means, the battle for the restriction of the Qualification within sure and rational limits must be fought; and we shall fight it to some advantage, while we keep in hand this great concession of enlarged Municipal Privileges'.[3]

The parliamentary struggles in 1838 and 1839 over the Bill, after it had passed the Commons in June 1838, now assumed a wearisomely formal pattern, with the Government carrying a measure incorporating an £8 municipal franchise through the Commons only to see it mangled by the Lords. By August 1839 the peers' sweeping amendments, including the substitution of a £10 franchise and the rejection of clauses giving town councils the powers of grand juries in matters of taxation, had resulted in complete deadlock, the Commons refusing to accept the Lords' Bill and supporting Speaker Lefevre in his ruling that, by their rejection of the councils' taxation powers, the House of Lords had infringed the Commons' privileges over Money Bills.

For the Irish party as for the Opposition, the municipal franchise was the vital question, although O'Connell's attempts to lower it were always subordinated to his consistent support of the Government in its difficult and humiliating position. In 1838 he objected particularly to clauses introduced by the Lords ensuring the Dublin freemen their parliamentary franchise in perpetuity and continuing the administration by the present corporation of all charities in

---

[1] Hansard, XLIII, 439–60, 29 May 1838, Peel.

[2] Hansard, XLIII, 460–6, 515–20, 523–5, 534, 787–8, 29 May, 1, 18 June 1838, Russell, O'Connell, Sheil; 540–2, 651–6, 1, 11 June 1838, Divisions.

[3] Graham to Peel, 25 March 1838, Peel Papers, Add. MSS 40318, 123–6, referring specifically to the Government's Irish Registration Bill.

Dublin. On both these points the Government conceded his demands.[1] In August 1839 O'Connell used strong language in urging the rejection of the Lords' Bill:

> I don't mean to terrify nor even to threaten, but the stoutest heart might well be alarmed if the Chartist violence gained that firmness and courage which a reinforcement from Ireland would naturally impart. I rose to protest against the manner in which this country treats Ireland. I rose to declare that we demanded not what this aristocrat or that may be pleased to assign to us, but the common privileges of Englishmen, . . . the English franchise.[2]

But Russell decided instead simply to postpone the Bill once again, as Graham reported to Peel with his own opinion that if the Irish party 'could obtain this extensive taxing Power for the Corporations, and the Dublin Freemen's Clause, I really believe they would take the Bill'.[3] Graham was right. By acquiescing in Russell's acceptance of most of Peel's proposals in 1838, O'Connell was unable later to return to the more sweeping schemes of the earlier Bills even had he wanted to do so.[4]

The importance of the Irish party's steady support of the Government is clearly shown by an analysis of division lists on the Municipal Bills of 1838 and 1839. In 1838, divisions seldom gave the Whigs a majority of more than 35 and on one occasion the vital £8 franchise clause was only carried by 15 votes and a clause on boundaries by 8 votes.[5] On all those occasions when full lists are given, the Irish party was solidly behind the Government, but if O'Connell had withdrawn the support of the 60 to 70 Members who were either his immediate followers or liberals under his influence, the Government would have fallen immediately. It was no wonder that Russell

---

[1] See O'Connell to Barrett, 28 July 1838, *O'Connell Corr.*, II, 144–6, inveighing against the Bill; to his Constituents, 29 September 1838, O'Connell Papers, N.L.I., 423, on the Dublin Corporation's use of freemen for electoral purposes; Hansard, XLIV, 903, 986, 2, 3 August 1838, Ball, Irish Attorney-General.

[2] Hansard, L, 206, 12 August 1839, O'Connell.

[3] Graham to Peel, 7 August 1839, Peel Papers, Add. MSS 40318, 152–4.

[4] See O'Connell to Fitzpatrick, 5, 7, 8 August 1839, *O'Connell Corr.*, II, 191–6, for his reaction of impotent disappointment to the Bill of that year.

[5] Hansard, XLIII, 537–42, 651–6, 1070–5; XLIV, 907–9, 922–4, 1, 11, 25 June; 2 August 1838; XLV, 1141–3; XLVIII, 1226–7, 1227–31, 1 March; 4 July 1839, Divisions. Those in 1839, 86, 50, 46 and 45 respectively, were noticeably less close.

warmly thanked him in May 1839 for his 'constant and disinterested support'.[1]

With Crawford temporarily out of Parliament, O'Connell was able to maintain discipline within his party, but it was just as well that there was no strong feeling in Ireland on the specific issue of town government. The Government, harassed in 1838 by the rebellion in Canada and in 1839 by the Jamaican crisis and by the attack on its whole Irish policy in the Lords, was in no position to adopt an uncompromising attitude towards the Lords' treatment of its Irish Municipal Bills. The negative or unconcerned attitude of English public opinion towards these disputes between the two Houses prevented the Whigs and their supporters from making political capital out of the peers' campaign, and with a steadily increasing loss of credit and popularity, surrender seemed to some Ministers the only policy left to them. In August 1839, on the Speaker's quite proper ruling regarding the Commons' privileges, the Cabinet finally decided to support him, but it did so only by nine votes to four.[2]

The Opposition, for all the boasts of *The Times* that the party's power lay not in mere numbers but in 'the consistency and harmony of its parts',[3] had its own difficulties. Lyndhurst's sweeping amendments to the Municipal Bill in 1838 were not popular with moderates like Fitzgerald and Wharncliffe, and in March 1839 a group of 65 Conservative M.P.s, English and Irish backbenchers, staged a protest against the Bill of that year which was also a rebellion against Peel's leadership and a counterpart to the Lords' Committee of inquiry into the state of Ireland.[4] Graham became so worried that he tried to persuade Peel to start the session of 1840 with a vote of no confidence, on the grounds that the party could not be held together much longer 'without a direct and vigorous attack on the Government', adding that 'the scheme of governing in opposition cannot

---

[1] Russell to O'Connell, 9 May 1839, Russell Papers, P.R.O. 30/22/3C. See *Times*, 9 May 1839; Greville, *Journal*, 10 February 1839, IV, 168, for analyses of party strength: *Times*: 317 Conservatives to 280 Whigs and Radicals, 60 to 70 'O'Connell's Tail'.

[2] Walpole, *Russell*, I, 327, n. 1. See also Greville, *Journal*, 23 August 1838; 15 August 1839, IV, 131, 240, for the passivity of public opinion and for increasingly critical judgements of the Government.

[3] *Times*, 9 May 1839.

[4] Greville, *Journal*, 20 August 1839, IV, 130; Hansard, XLV, 1141–3, 1 March 1839, Division.

be durable: the power lasts as long as the hope of succeeding to office endures; but extinguish this hope, and the power vanishes: the leaders do not fly; but the Troops are disbanded, the camp is broken up, and the Nation is disheartened'.[1]

Graham's fears for party unity did not influence Peel to change his policy over the Municipal Bill, but that these fears were not groundless was shown when the Bill passed through the Commons between January and March 1840. Together with a £10 municipal franchise in the eleven largest cities and towns, the Bill allowed a majority of £8 householders in other places to apply to the Lord Lieutenant for a charter; pending this, their affairs were to be managed by Lighting and Watching Commissioners. In towns with corporate property under £100 a year, municipal government was to be entrusted to the Poor Law Guardians. Shaw's attempts with the support of the Conservative leadership to introduce a £10 franchise in all future corporations and to amend the clauses on freemen (which restricted voting rights to those admitted before April 1831) were unsuccessful; but there was also a last move to wreck the Bill entirely and to repeat the rebellion of March 1839, sponsored this time by Sir George Sinclair and Emerson Tennent of Belfast. For Sinclair, this was a measure increasing Papal influence, investing O'Connell with the Lord Mayorship of Dublin and undermining British supremacy, proving that the Whigs' attitude to the Irish party was one of conceding 'nothing that you will allow us to withhold, but . . . [withholding] nothing that you insist upon our conceding'. But his motion to postpone the Bill found only 34 supporters as against 65 in 1839, and Peel and Goulburn voted with the Whigs and the Irish party to give the Bill a majority of 148.[2]

Soon after the House of Lords had given the Bill a Second Reading and had heard an eloquent speech from Isaac Butt as counsel for the corporations, Wellington suddenly developed scruples. Graham wrote in alarm to Charles Arbuthnot asking him to use all his influence with the Duke. The party which had only reluctantly agreed 'to the grant of Municipal Institutions on certain terms'

---

[1] Graham to Peel, 16, 28 December 1839, Peel Papers, Add. MSS 40318, 163–6, 169–72. Stanley's Irish Registration Bill (see above pp. 165–6) thus provided in 1840–1 an essential focus of unity for a party in real danger of splitting apart.

[2] Hansard, LII, 1051–60, 1060–6; 1068–70, 9 March 1840, Sinclair, Tennent, Division.

would not stand for another change of policy. Peel had taken up the policy on condition 'that the line then taken was once for all', either in opposition or in office, and 'on the eve of success, with power almost within our grasp, such differences, once disclosed, would destroy the Conservative Party, and restore life and vigor to a Government which is now tottering to its fall'. Graham made 'great allowance for the age and infirmities of the Duke', his fears for his reputation and his unwillingness to run risks,[1] but it was also clear that Wellington had been powerfully impressed by Butt's defence of the corporations. He was now convinced, as he had always been, that 'the greatest danger to the Protestant interest in Ireland would arise from throwing the Power into the hands of the Catholics' and told Arbuthnot that he had never agreed to pass a Bill which might destroy the Union and break up the Empire.[2] But four days later all was well again. Arbuthnot, wrote Graham, 'appears to think that the Duke will pass the Irish Corporation Bill; and he is reported to have said . . . that "everyone knew it must pass into a Law".' Wellington had never seen eye to eye with Peel on this question; he finally agreed simply in the interests of party unity, and because, as Graham said, 'the suspension of this confidential intercourse is most injurious, if not fatal, to our future prospects'.[3]

The Duke took no part in proposing amendments to the Bill, which was done by Lyndhurst on a grand scale. The separate Bill giving town councils the power of grand juries to levy taxes within boroughs was again rejected; the voting rights in municipal elections of *all* freemen were preserved; the £8 franchise in future corporations was raised to £10 and the appointment of sheriffs was given outright to the Lord Lieutenant.[4] It was small comfort to the Government that a motion by Lord Wynford to omit Dublin from the provisions of the Bill was defeated by a coalition of Conservative and Whig peers and not surprising that the Whigs now had to consider whether they could accept these sweeping amendments, which

[1] Graham to Peel, 9 June 1840, Peel Papers, Add. MSS 40318, 196–9.

[2] Arbuthnot to Graham, 10 June 1840, Peel Papers, Add. MSS 40318, 202–5. See Isaac Butt, *A Speech in Defence of the City of Dublin* (1840), esp. 83–6, 90.

[3] Graham to Peel, 14 June 1840, Peel Papers, Add. MSS 40318, 200–1. Wellington had actually wavered in August 1839 and thought of throwing out the Bill, but by December he was back in line again; see Shaw to Peel, 8 August; Wellington to Peel, 18 December 1839, ibid., 40427, 93–4; 40310, 308–13.

[4] Hansard, LIV, 1101–5; LV, 163–92, 12, 29 June 1840, Divisions.

Peel certainly disliked.[1] But Lyndhurst, in two conferences, refused to make any major concessions and on 7 August, the Commons accepted the amended Bill without a division after only token protests by members of the Irish party.[2]

Greville, in a celebrated passage, concluded that the legislative history of the Irish Municipal Bill had shown that 'if there are evils and disadvantages incident to a weak government, these are also not without some counterbalancing good' in inducing both parties to deal with important questions in a spirit of compromise and concession.[3] But the real test of Greville's principle that 'Good Government may happen to be the result of a weak Ministry and a strong Opposition' must lie in the quality of legislation produced. The Act of 1840 was in reality a scheme of municipal disfranchisement by which 58 corporations were abolished, their property and duties in the sphere of local government taken over, where such boards existed, by commissioners under the Act of 1828. In towns with over £100 of property annually, municipal commissioners were appointed pending applications for full charters of incorporation or the election of lighting and watching boards, and in towns with less property, local government was handed over to Poor Law guardians.[4] In Dublin, Belfast and eight other places given elective town councils,[5] the £10 municipal franchise and high property qualifications for councillors ensured middle-class electorates and 'respectable' councils. With their powers strictly defined and limited, these councils had to contend not only with the powerful grand juries in the counties but also with the boards of guardians of the Poor Law, which were unlike the grand juries in being permanent bodies, meeting weekly and to some extent representative.[6]

Halévy's judgement that 'even in Ireland' the Act created 'what

[1] Hansard, LV, 438–40, 450–1, 6 July 1840, Wynford, Division. Peel's position is clear from Lyndhurst's defence of his conduct to Peel [n.d. ? August], 1840, Peel Papers, Add. MSS 40316, 220–2.

[2] Hansard, LV, 1216–18, 1389, 3 August 1840, Morpeth, J. Grattan, W. Roche; Melbourne to Russell, 6 August 1840, *Melbourne Papers*, 415, correctly supposing that Russell would not insist on amending the Lords Bill.

[3] Greville, *Journal*, 19 August 1840, IV, 306–7.

[4] Only two applications were received before 1842 for incorporation, good evidence of the attitude of Irish public opinion to the Act, while by 1854 65 towns had Boards of Commissioners under the 1828 Act, P.P. 1842, XXXVIII, 5.

[5] These were Limerick, Kilkenny, Waterford, Cork, Clonmel, Drogheda, Londonderry and Sligo, Galway being excluded by the Lords.

[6] The appointment of magistrates and sheriffs and control of police became

were nothing less than islands of representative democracy' cannot be sustained.[1] In reality it was as conservative and as limited as it was possible to make it, and the £10 franchise, dependent on the payment of all local taxes, contrasted most unfavourably with that created in England. The terms represented a victory for the right wing of the Conservative party, based primarily on the House of Lords, who wanted to assert the 'independence' of their House and picked on this issue as one important and controversial enough but not too dangerously popular. If they had gained a complete victory over the Whig Government and its Irish allies, whose original aim had been to give Ireland a system of municipal government on the reformed English model, they had also thwarted Peel, the official Conservative leader, whose policy of reaching a limited but reasonable settlement of the question would have meant, as one authority has said, 'a denial of the Independence of the House of Lords'.[2] Peel's attitude and aims were fundamentally opposed to those of the Tory majority in the Lords, whom Wellington was unable and at times even unwilling to control; and reflecting after 1847 on the difficulties of the Irish corporations question, Peel was 'much more surprised that the Union [of the Conservative party] was so long maintained than that it was ultimately severed'.[3] The issue had indeed provided a dress-rehearsal for the great crisis over the Corn Laws.

O'Connell might protest formally at the failure to give Ireland a full measure of municipal reform, but he had in fact connived at what was done.[4] The Whigs, nearly always ready to concede his demands on this question, could not and would not fight in the end for their original conception of reform, and the Irish party, almost unhampered by the pressure of Irish public opinion, certainly never contemplated breaking its alliance with the Government. O'Connell was able to use the new councils to some immediate political advantage, becoming himself Lord Mayor of Dublin in

Crown responsibilities, so that in many boroughs four or even five and in some three independent authorities overlapped each other, in a system of local government by confusion.

[1] Halévy, *History*, III, 295.

[2] Kitson Clark, *Peel and the Conservative Party*, 350.

[3] Notes by Peel [n.d. post 1847], on Papers relating to discussions over Irish Municipal Bill, Peel Papers, Add. MSS 40423, 301-4.

[4] O'Connell to MacHale, 8 April 1840, *O'Connell Corr.*, II, 235-7; O'Connell, Notes on Policy, 10 August 1846, O'Connell Papers, N.L.I., uncatalogued.

1841 and later incorporating nationalist councils in his Repeal campaigns. But in the long run the failure to provide Ireland with a coherent or adequately representative system of municipal government meant that it was not until 1898 that a comprehensive reform of all local government was achieved. The whole issue provided Young Ireland and the opposition to O'Connell with another powerful instance of his apparent readiness to sacrifice Irish demands to the interests of a parliamentary alliance.

CHAPTER VIII

In Opposition and in Decline

O'Connell and Peel

THE General Election of 1841 brought the end of over ten years of almost continuous Whig rule and the accession to power of a Conservative Government under Sir Robert Peel. With an overall majority in the Commons of 80 or 90, Peel was in an incomparably stronger position than his opponents had been between 1835 and 1841. Indeed from 1841 until the great crisis inside the Conservative party on the Corn Laws in 1845–6, he was perhaps more favourably placed than the Whigs had been even from 1832 to 1835, since he was not confronted by the special problems of a huge and unwieldy majority in the Commons or by a crippling lack of strength in the Lords. Quite as important, both for the Government's general stability and for its Irish policies, Peel was freed from any dependence on the support of a party standing outside the main political groupings and exerting a constant pressure on the formulation and passage of Irish legislation.

O'Connell had now lost the commanding position in politics which he had held since 1835. With only 18 close followers, he had almost lost his parliamentary party.[1] The electoral disaster of 1841, following the long and politically debilitating alliance with the Whigs, was an important factor in determining his next move and in opening up a new phase in the history of the Irish nationalist movement, when the emphasis shifted decisively from the operations of a parliamentary party at Westminster to the revival of mass political agitation in

[1] Duffy, *Young Ireland*, I, 27, 50, estimated the Repeal party in 1841 at less than 12, though he thought that by 1844, they numbered 19 with 7 Federalists.

Ireland. But O'Connell had compelling private as well as political motives for this new departure. His dislike and distrust of Peel, whose smile, he said once, reminded him of 'the silver plate on a coffin', was intense and long-standing. He was no doubt right to suppose that Peel's own contempt for him and for all his works had not been lessened by thirty years of bitter personal conflict and political warfare.[1] O'Connell was convinced, as he had been in November 1834, that Conservative government meant an immediate return to the Protestant Ascendancy and the certain proscription of himself and his movement, and in contrast to the situation in 1835, there was little use in forming an alliance with the official Opposition, which for at least two years after 1841 was in an extremely demoralized condition. 'The party included under that name', Edward Ellice wrote rather bitterly in 1841,

is dispersed and scattered to the winds. Some are indifferent—many thinking the present Government more safe than their radical coadjutors —others unwilling to make any effort to replace particular men in offices, in which they thought them incompetent and dangerous—and the aristocratic minority, neither sufficiently generous, [n]or liberal, to encourage their adherents in adversity, or without a clearer prospect of using them again for their exclusive advantage. Be assured many changes must take place before you see again a united and cordial opposition.[2]

The first short and legislatively unproductive session of the Parliament elected in July and August 1841, which saw the final transfer of power to the Conservatives, postponed a clear demonstration of the weakness of O'Connell's parliamentary position. Indeed Greville, recording in August 1841 that Russell had been dissuaded from attacking O'Connell since this could only split an already weak Opposition, still saw O'Connell as the leader of all the Irish 'left-wing' Members, and for a short time in 1842, according to John O'Connell, the Repealers were actually attending Whig meetings. He thought that 'the getting up of mixed dinners at the Reform Club

[1] Lecky, *Leaders of Public Opinion* (1912), II, 34. See also Gash, *Peel*, 162–7, for the abortive affair of honour between the two men in 1815 and its sequel in 1825. It is remarkable that Peel's correspondence, unlike Graham's, contains very few strong expressions of his antipathy to O'Connell. This is a proof rather of Peel's reserve and self-control than of the absence of such feeling.

[2] Ellice to Joseph Parkes, 25 September 1841, Ellice MSS, N.L.S., pkt. 5. Cf. Clarendon's description in December 1841 of the party as being in a state of 'apathetic acquiescence', quoted by Southgate, *Passing of the Whigs*, 123.

once-a-week, where we shall gradually get some knowledge of each other, and perhaps some little mutual asperities may be softened down', showed that the Whigs were at least trying to '*popularize* themselves'; but while M. Soyer's food was good, the dinners only lasted four or five weeks and John O'Connell concluded that they had been ineffective and 'most pre-eminently stupid affairs'.[1]

Throughout the long and important session of 1842, 'the condition of England question', symptomized by the growth of a militant Chartism bred of unemployment, hunger and distress in the manufacturing districts and fully exploited by the increasingly powerful Anti-Corn Law League, dominated the political scene. For almost the first time since the end of the Reform crisis in 1832, 'the Irish question' (or aspects of it) ceased to be a vital and often decisive factor in domestic politics. It became almost impossible to get up debates on Irish affairs. Sheil (no longer a Repealer) discovered this when he planned to raise 'the popular cause from its abject condition' by opening fire on the Irish Church, but was forced to drop the idea until Peel might be ready to deal more liberally with Irish questions and because O'Connell himself, hoping eventually to draw the Irish Protestants into a strong nationalist party, wanted no revival of a bitter past controversy.[2]

Peel's main reforms in 1842, combining measures of industrial free trade and the income-tax with a liberalization of the degree of agricultural protection, were framed to meet an economic crisis in England and had little relevance to or effect on economic conditions in Ireland, which were scarcely discussed during the Budget debates. The decision to exempt Ireland from income-tax represented at best only an indirect victory for the Irish opposition. Peel, preferring to risk English landlord and capitalist resentment rather than raise an inevitable outcry from the Irish against a new and direct form of taxation, could plead that no machinery existed for its collection since the tax had not been applied to Ireland during the Napoleonic Wars. He took some comfort from the fact that Irish absentees

---

[1] Greville, *Journal*, 12 August 1841, V, 27-8; John O'Connell, *Recollections*, II, 131-2, 137.

[2] Torrens, *Sheil*, II, 319. Cf. Thomas Wyse to George Wyse, 10 June 1846, Wyse MSS, quoted by Auchmuty, *Wyse*, 190, for the unkind view that Sheil's only idea in politics was to cut down Protestant endowments and to increase those of the Catholic Church; and O'Connell's remark about the main obstacle to the success of Repeal: '*The* difficulty . . . is Protestantism', O'Neill Daunt, *Journal*, 4 December 1842, N.L.I., 2040.

in England would at least be affected.[1] O'Connell, a strong critic
of the tax in principle and a firm believer in the view that Ireland
was already heavily over-taxed, could not block Peel's compensatory
proposal to increase the Irish stamp and spirits duties, nor did he put
up an effective fight for the Irish distillers and graziers whose
interests he privately believed to be damaged by the lowering of
duties on foreign provisions and livestock.[2] Indeed in opposing the
Third Reading of the Corn Importation Bill in April, he would allow
no preferential treatment for Irish agriculture (such as that proposed
by Fitzstephen French, the Whig M.P. for Roscommon) and carried
most of his own followers, though by no means all of the Irish
Liberal opposition, in support of Charles Villiers' unsuccessful
motion in July for a total repeal of the Corn Laws.[3]

If Richard Cobden emerged in 1842 as the outstanding opponent
of the Government's economic policies, O'Connell was not far
behind him in his denunciations of the Corn Laws, the instruments
by which, he told a Manchester audience, 'the landlords' venison
was sweetened with widows' tears and their claret dyed with orphans'
blood'.[4] His alliance with the Anti-Corn Law League, a reflection
of his own economic views, was in fact an important part of his
strategy for the Irish nationalist movement. He was convinced,
plausibly but wrongly, that by maintaining agricultural protection in
1842, Peel had 'put himself in the hands of the landlords'. Although
he greatly exaggerated the effects of the re-imposition of the income
tax on Peel's reputation and on the stability of his Government,
O'Connell rightly judged that the League, a new model of his own
political organizations, would soon prove formidable; and he assumed,
not unnaturally in view of his identification of Peel with the landed
interest, that Irish nationalism could only derive advantage from an
alliance with the opponents of the Corn Laws against the great
common enemy. The League, he wrote in 1842, would 'compel the
aristocracy to yield in England and to leave us Ireland to ourselves'.[5]

---

[1] See Goulburn to Peel, 22 July 1841, Parker, *Peel*, II, 490–1; Herries to
Goulburn, 2 March 1842; Peel to Goulburn, 25 March 1842, Peel Papers,
Add. MSS 40443, 143–6, 150. Peel was particularly anxious to 'touch the Con-
tinental Irish non Resident'.

[2] O'Connell to Fitzpatrick, 12, 18 March 1842, *O'Connell Corr.*, II, 283–4, 286.

[3] Hansard, LXII, 63–66, 66–71, 444–50; LXIV, 1365–7, 7, 13 April; 11 July
1842, Divisions and debate on French's and Villiers' motions.

[4] Quoted by Halévy, *History*, IV, 12–13.

[5] O'Connell to Fitzpatrick, 11 February 1842, *O'Connell Corr.*, II, 281.

He can only have been disappointed. Peel was not so much defeated in 1845 as converted, and while the League derived considerable benefits from O'Connell's influence over the Irish in England, notably on the League's home ground of Manchester, its leaders gave no support or encouragement to the nationalist cause, which in England was popular only in a quarter least welcome to O'Connell, with Feargus O'Connor and the Chartists.[1] Cobden later justified his refusal to speak in Parliament on Irish questions, despite his interest in the country, on the grounds of 'a complete antagonism and repulsion' towards the Irish party and its leader, who 'always treated me with friendly attention, but I never shook hands with him or faced his smile without a feeling of insecurity; and as for trusting him on any public question where his vanity or passions might interpose, I should have as soon thought of an alliance with an Ashantee Chief'.[2]

The rise and progress of the Repeal movement in Ireland completely overshadowed the operations of the Repeal party in Parliament, but until the end of 1842 the movement's existence was itself weak and uncertain. O'Connell's election as Lord Mayor of Dublin in November 1841, the first Catholic to hold the position since 1688, may have given him what his son John proudly called 'a legally recognized *lordship* from the *people* utterly unconnected with court

---

[1] See above p. 165; and O'Neill Daunt, *Journal*, 6 January 1843, N.L.I., 2040, for O'Connell's contemptuous comments on O'Connor and the *Northern Star*: '"Let us see what poor Balderdash has to say for himself this week . . . What a notion of the fellow, to set up a newspaper to praise himself!"' This was in fact a fair description of O'Connell's own use of the *Pilot*. The same entry contains an interesting judgement by Daunt, who knew him well, of O'Connor (partly printed in *A Life Spent for Ireland, being selections from the Diary of W. J. O'Neill Daunt*, edited by his daughter (1896): 'much imposing power in the thumping, whacking, thundering sledgehammer energy both of manner and language . . . vast volubility, enormous assurance, an appearance of great enthusiasm, much tact in discerning the feelings and tickling the prepossessions of his hearers, a bold face, a burly figure, and a reckless daredevil air of defiance . . . [with] an insatiable passion for notoriety.'

[2] Cobden to G. Combe, 4 October 1848, in John Morley, *The Life of Richard Cobden* (1903), 491–2. But Cobden had not always felt this. In 1838, he subscribed £5 to the English fund for O'Connell (see above p. 124) and wrote of him as 'the most potent champion that was ever raised up by Heaven to defend the cause of good government against the acts of tyrants and bigots'; to Sir Thomas Potter, 15 August 1838, Cobden Papers, Add. MSS 43667, 20. John Bright's interest in Ireland, his support for schemes of Free Trade in land and Disestablishment began in earnest after the repeal of the Corn Laws.

favour or aristocratic usage—in short a most democratic dignity';
but the pledge of strict political impartiality which O'Connell gave
and on the whole kept during his year of office was clearly incompatible with nationalist agitation.[1] The movement did not begin to
reveal its full potentiality until the appearance and immediate success in October 1842 of the *Nation* under Charles Gavan Duffy,
Thomas Davis and John Blake Dillon, the provincial campaigns in
the autumn and winter conducted by John O'Connell, O'Neill
Daunt, Thomas Steele and Thomas Ray and the impressive three-
day debate in Dublin Corporation in February 1843, when O'Connell, after a speech of four hours and ten minutes—'the finest
oratorical effort' O'Neill Daunt had ever heard—carried a motion
in favour of Repeal by 45 votes to 15.[2] By the summer and autumn
of 1843 a succession of over forty huge, orderly and well-organized
mass meetings in the three provinces outside Ulster demonstrated
that the great pressure-group which had forced the surrender of
Emancipation had been solidly reconstituted behind a programme
in which the cause of legislative independence was coupled with
specific social and political demands, designed to appeal to the
needs and interests both of the peasantry and of the agricultural and
commercial middle class: fixity of tenure with fair rents and compensation for improvements, the reduction of taxation, the abolition
of tithes, the encouragement and protection of native industry and
the introduction of the ballot and of manhood suffrage.

Institutionally, the movement was a modernized replica of the

[1] John O'Connell to Daniel O'Connell [n.d. November 1841], O'Connell
MSS, U.C.D. See W. M. Thackeray, *Paris, Irish and Eastern Sketches* (1875),
550–1, for a vivid description and sketch of O'Connell as Mayor 'in a brilliant
robe of crimson velvet, ornamented with white satin bows and sable collar, in an
enormous cocked-hat, like a slice of an eclipsed moon'. The only lapse into party
politics seems to have been in the Dublin by-election of 1842, when O'Connell
seconded the Whig Lord Morpeth in his unsuccessful contest with William
Gregory. See Sir William Gregory, *An Autobiography* (1894), 58–75.

[2] O'Neill Daunt, *Journal*, 4 March 1843, N.L.I., 2040. See also entries of
26 January; 28 February 1843, for the provincial campaigns and the Corporation
debate, in which O'Connell's principal opponent was Isaac Butt, later the first
leader of the Home Rule party. For the founding of the *Nation*, the personalities
and political aims of the Young Irelanders and a general history of the Repeal
movement after 1841, Charles Gavan Duffy's classic account, *Young Ireland*
1896), is still indispensable. Allowance should always be made for Duffy's political prejudices, which are often most subtly disguised, but his book is of absorbing
interest, accurate, well-written and full of interesting character-judgements.

Catholic Association. The Repeal Association in Dublin, departmentalized and staffed by paid workers under an efficient Secretary, Thomas Matthew Ray, held weekly public meetings at its permanent headquarters after 1843, Conciliation Hall on Burgh Quay, and was officially controlled by a large General and Finance Committee of 150 members. A hierarchy of membership descended from Volunteers and Members subscribing annually £10 and £1 respectively to Associates paying 1/- a year; and provincial branches, the responsibility of Repeal directors and wardens, supervised reading-rooms and acted as local collecting centres for the Repeal rent.[1] 'What a marvellous organization is ours!', O'Neill Daunt wrote with perhaps pardonable exaggeration. 'Every parish in the kingdom is banded with the rest in our great national confederacy, and all are in constant communication with one common centre . . . No government ever possessed a more thoroughly organized administration.'[2] Financial support and sympathy from Irish centres in the United States, notably from New York, Boston, Philadelphia and Baltimore, and in Canada was matched by the increasing interest of the French Liberal press and of prominent Liberals like Ledru-Rollin. O'Connell's energy and powers of endurance rose for the last time to the occasion. Carried away by the success of the mass demonstrations, he became increasingly more extreme in his speeches, interpolating into the familiar doctrine of moral force and constitutionalism rhetorical allusions to the power of Irish numbers, 'a nation of eight millions', and to the possibility of resisting any aggression on the part of the Government.[3]

The Government's attitude, one of contemptuous forbearance in 1841-2 for what Peel, Lord De Grey in Ireland and Graham at the Home Office regarded as a 'failing concern',[4] changed by April and May 1843 to one of increasing anxiety and alarm as the Repeal rent

[1] See John O'Connell, *Recollections*, II, 156-90, 327-31, for the organization of the Association, which included also a Parliamentary Committee and sub-Committees producing reports on specific questions, designed less for use at Westminster than to give the Association the appearance of an Irish Parliament.

[2] O'Neill Daunt, *Journal*, 17 August 1843, N.L.I., 2040.

[3] Duffy, *Young Ireland*, I, 86-98, 105-24, 148-54, who shows clearly that O'Connell fought shy of French Liberal support in July and August 1843. For him French Liberalism was deeply tainted with atheism.

[4] See Peel to Graham, 2, 3 January 1842, Peel Papers, Add. MSS 40446, 284-5, 288; Graham to Peel, 21 October; 6 November 1841; De Grey to Graham, 29 December [1841], Parker, *Graham*, I, 350-3.

leapt from £60 to £700 a week. Most of the Catholic hierarchy and clergy, many of the middle class town councils and increasing numbers of magistrates came out in support of the movement and nationalist M.P.s announced that they could best serve their constituents by remaining in Ireland.[1] Graham reported Sheil's great alarm,

> that he never knew the excitement to be so great or the danger so imminent . . . He said that an immediate increase of the military Force was necessary; that the feebleness of Eliot [the Chief Secretary] was an encouragement to violence; that the Burthens of the Poor Rate and of the Tithe Rent Charge had driven the small, half-ruined Protestant Proprietors into the ranks of the disaffected; and he appeared to think that we were on the Eve of a Convulsion.[2]

Serious private warnings from Ireland of the equally grim possibilities of civil war or social revolution, 'a general combination of the people having for its object the withholding of rents and taxes of all kinds', were supported in June by police reports from Cork and Tipperary. These spoke of a rumour in the countryside 'that a Cabinet Council had declared the intention to grant Repeal of the Union under certain conditions—and the exultation of the People was quickly manifested by the appearance of innumerable bonfires which . . . were suddenly lighted up throughout the country as far as the eye could reach in every direction'.[3] From May to July Graham poured military reinforcements into the country, strengthened barracks and strongpoints and provided large stores of food in depots at Dublin, Belfast, Cork and Limerick.[4] But the Government decided against calling out the yeomanry or, as Wellington and some Irish judges recommended, rushing through emergency legislation to suppress the Association. Stanley, not generally noted for his patience in dealing with Irish affairs, produced a cogent parallel

[1] Graham to De Grey, 24, 28 April 1843, Parker, *Graham*, I, 359–60; De Grey to Peel, 6 May 1843, Parker, *Peel*, III, 46–7.

[2] Graham to Peel, 6 May 1843, Peel Papers, Add. MSS 40448, 290–1.

[3] Mr. Strange to his father, 1 June 1843 (a letter passed on to Graham); Graham to Peel, 4 June 1843, passing on Lord Farnham's alarming reports from Ulster; Police Reports, 17 June 1843, Peel Papers, Add. MSS 40448, 305–6, 309–10; 40530, 120–1.

[4] Graham to Peel, 6 May; 17, 18 June 1843, Peel Papers, Add. MSS 40448, 290–1, 319–20, 325; Graham to General Murray (Master General of Ordnance), 23 June 1843; to Lords Commissioners of the Admiralty, 23 June 1843; to De Grey, 2 July 1843, H.O. Papers, 79/9, 123–4, 125, 129.

with the Anti-Corn Law League, which was 'founded on the model
of the Repeal Association; and if one be suppressed and the other is
left untouched, there will be an appearance of unequal justice; if we
attack both, we shall embark on a Sea of Trouble, and enter on a
course of measures, which may precipitate disastrous events in both
countries at the same moment'.[1]

Instead, at the end of May, after Peel had told the Commons that
like the Whig Althorp in 1834 he could envisage no alternative which
was not preferable to the dismemberment of the Empire, the Irish
Government made its first offensive move by dismissing twenty-four
magistrates from the Commission of the Peace (including O'Connell, four other Repeal M.P.s and Lord Ffrench) for presiding at
Repeal meetings.[2] O'Connell responded promptly to this challenge.
The Repeal Association adopted a plan to by-pass the normal courts
of law by setting up local arbitration courts, and in August, O'Connell proposed to call a Council of Three Hundred which would constitute a National Assembly and a *de facto* Government, whose
delegates, in order to avoid any breach of the Convention Act, would
not be elected but would meet in Dublin as the bearers of the Repeal
rent from their constituencies.[3] This, the most revolutionary of
O'Connell's proposals, could perhaps never have repeated in the
very different conditions of 1843 the *coup* carried out by the Irish

[1] Graham to Peel, 7 May 1843, Peel Papers, Add. MSS 40448, 297–8, giving
Stanley's views. Peel and Graham had much trouble with Wellington at this
time, who showed a most alarming desire to go to Ireland and believed, wrote a
most doubtful Graham, 'that the winds and the waves will obey him and that in
his presence there will be a great calm.' Pressure was successfully brought to
bear on him by Baron Neumann, the Austrian Ambassador, to drop any idea
of a visit to Ireland as offensive to the Queen and to the Austrian as well as the
British Governments: Graham to Peel, 16 September; 19 October 1843, Peel
Papers, Add. MSS 40449, 31–3, 96–7.

[2] Hansard, LXIX, 25, 9 May 1843, Peel; Sir Edward Sugden to Peel, 28 May;
O'Connell to Sugden, 27 May 1843, Parker, *Peel*, II, 49–51; Duffy, *Young
Ireland*, I, 109 ff. The Repeal M.P.s who lost their commissions were Maurice
O'Connell, E. B. Roche, Sir Valentine Blake and Colonel Pierce Butler.

[3] See Duffy, *Young Ireland*, I, 141–7; O'Neill Daunt, *Journal*, 28 August 1843,
N.L.I., 2040. Both the unofficial courts and the *de facto* assembly were important
features of later Sinn Fein policy. Little is known about the working of the
courts, which were copied from those set up by the Canadian colonists in 1837–9;
but see Peel to Graham, 23 December 1844, Peel Papers, Add. MSS 40449, 280,
reporting Lord Monteagle's opinion that they were the greatest blunder made
by the Association. The arbitrator in his neighbourhood in Limerick was a
drunkard, respected by nobody.

Volunteers at Dungannon in 1782. As late as September it was still being seriously considered, although O'Connell had drastically weakened the force of the plan by suggesting unrealistically that the Council might be legally recognized as the Irish Parliament by the simple exercise of the royal prerogative. But by 22 September, Graham, who had been clear a few days earlier that 'we must at all hazards proclaim this Assembly', was writing that O'Connell's abandonment of the scheme was 'conclusive proof of the success of our Policy and of the difficulties to which it has reduced him'.[1]

For over a month the Government had in fact been searching for a cast-iron case against O'Connell. It finally moved by banning the last of the great meetings planned for Clontarf on 8 October. Six days later, O'Connell and eight of his associates, drawn whether by accident or by design from each of the main nationalist groups with the significant exception of the peasantry, were arrested on an indictment of conspiracy to alter the government, laws and constitution of the country 'by intimidation and the demonstration of great physical force'.[2] The State Trial in the Four Courts ended in February 1844 in a verdict for the Crown. In May O'Connell was sentenced by the Court of Queen's Bench to a year's imprisonment and a fine of £2,000 and was ordered to give securities of £5,000 for good behaviour for seven years. But the defendants had clearly not had a fair trial. The law officers, with what Greville called 'a stupid, narrow-minded, short-sighted, professional eagerness to ensure a conviction', had produced a wholly Protestant and largely Conservative jury by making extensive use of the Crown's right to challenge jurors and by illegal manipulation of the jury lists.[3] The defence,

[1] John O'Connell to T. Davis, 20 October 1843, in Duffy, *Young Ireland*, I, 144; Graham to Peel, 16, 22 September 1843, Peel Papers, Add. MSS 40449, 31–3, 47. Graham had a 'confidential Reporter' in constant attendance at all O'Connell's meetings.

[2] See H. Manners-Sutton (Under Secretary, Home Office) to Attorney and Solicitor-General, 31 August; 4, 10 September 1843, H.O. Papers, 79/9, 132–4, requests for legal opinions on the Council of 300, O'Connell's seditious language, especially with reference to the Army, and the Arbitration courts; and Graham to Peel, 23 September 1843, Peel Papers, Add. MSS 40449, 53–4. Two Catholic priests, John O'Connell, T. M. Ray of the Association, Thomas Steele, the Protestant nationalist, Barrett and Dr. John Gray, the editors of the *Pilot* and the *Freeman's Journal*, and Charles Gavan Duffy, editor of the *Nation*, were co-defendants with O'Connell.

[3] Greville, *Journal*, 14 January 1844, V, 222–4. His later view of the Trial (26 January 1844, V, 225) that 'nobody takes much interest in it' was scarcely

which the Home Secretary ruefully called a 'formidable array of legal knowledge and oratorical power' and which included Sheil, Pigot and other leaders of the Irish Bar, had thrown considerable doubt on several counts in the indictment itself before the Law Lords reversed the verdict in September by three votes to two.[1]

The events of 1843 and 1844 in Ireland had several important effects on O'Connell, on his party and on Irish political alignments in general. Throughout 1843 O'Connell remained in Ireland, as also did those of his followers like John and Maurice O'Connell, Dillon Browne and E. B. Roche who were active figures in the Association and in the provincial nationalist organizations; and in 1844 he made only one brief appearance in the Commons, when he delivered a single impressive and remarkably moderate speech before beginning his imprisonment from May to September.[2] With this unplanned and involuntary secession, the initiative in Irish affairs in Parliament passed to Thomas Wyse, Smith O'Brien and the Irish Whig-Liberal party. Peel's initial approach to Irish questions was cautious and relatively uncontroversial, much hampered by acute difficulties between the Lord Lieutenant Earl De Grey, whose family connections and views were strongly Tory and the Chief Secretary, the more liberal Lord Eliot.[3] It was singularly unfortunate that the

true even of English public opinion. See *History of The Times*, II, 8-9, for the paper's elaborate precautions to 'scoop' the news of the verdict, which was published in London less than 29 hours after W. H. Russell, the chief reporter, had left Dublin in a specially chartered steamer, the *Iron Duke*.

[1] Graham to Peel, 2 November 1843, Peel Papers, Add. MSS 40449, 182. See *Campbell*, II, 184-7, for the legal reasons of one of the three Whigs who voted against the verdict. See also Graham to Peel, 25 October 1843; 6, 13 April; 25 May 1844; Peel to Graham, 7 April 1844, Peel Papers, Add. MSS 40449, 136-7, 384-6; 40450, 16-17, 34-5; 40449, 388-91, correspondence revealing the grave doubts of Peel and Graham about the actual conduct of the Trial, which had made it possible, if not probable, that the Law Lords would uphold O'Connell's appeal. But Peel very firmly and sensibly insisted that the final decision should not be taken on a political vote of the whole House of Lords.

[2] Hansard, LXXII, 929, 15 February 1844, recording that he entered the House to the cheers of the Opposition; LXXIII, 185-206, 23 February 1844, O'Connell; Greville, *Journal*, 25 February 1844, V, 237.

[3] The Government's policy largely consisted before 1843 of a successful resistance to attempts by Irish Tories to disrupt the National System of education and of a modification of the Poor Law, much resented by the landed interest, which lightened the tax burdens on smaller ratepayers. See esp. Graham to Brougham, 24 October 1841; to De Grey, 9 November 1842, Parker, *Graham*, I, 338, 356-7; to Peel, 24 November 1841, Peel Papers, Add. MSS 40446, 142-4;

Government's first substantive Irish measure, brought in at the end of May 1843 as the Repeal campaign gathered momentum, should have been a draconian Arms Bill designed to control the import and distribution of firearms, by which all weapons were to be registered and branded, the search powers of the police were extended and the possession of an unlicensed firearm was to constitute an offence punishable by seven years' transportation.[1]

The concerted opposition to this Bill, which took two and a half months to pass, offers the first genuine example of the use of those methods of obstruction by which Parnell and his party later brought parliamentary government to a standstill. Night after night, in debates frequently degenerating into what Hansard called 'confused and stormy discussion' lasting sometimes until 3 a.m. and often far removed from the details of the Bill itself, an organized group of Irish Liberals and moderate nationalists, with little or no help from the official Opposition leadership, fought every clause in the Bill. They denounced it as 'a political measure' and an unwarrantable restriction on the liberty of the subject, treating Ireland, in Sheil's words, as if she were 'a mere provincial appurtenance'.[2] By 3 July eight or nine nights of debate had covered only four or five clauses out of 72 and the Government's majorities of 165 and 154 in May and June had fallen by the middle of July to between 20 and 30.[3] When the Bill at last passed at the end of the session in August, it was to apply for only two years instead of five, and Morgan John O'Connell had succeeded in reducing the possible sentence of

McDowell, *Public Opinion*, 204–9. For the difficulties between De Grey and Eliot, see the correspondence between all parties in Parker, *Graham*, I, 354–5; *Peel*, III, 36–7, 40, 41–5, 53–5, 60–2.

[1] Hansard, LXIX, 996–1010, 29 May 1843, Eliot.

[2] Hansard, LXIX, 1041, 1153, 1578 ff.; LXX, 388–92, 516–4, 29, 31 May; 15, 26 June; 3 July 1843, Sheil, Wyse, Debates and Divisions. The most prominent Liberals in opposition were Smith O'Brien, Pigot, Wyse, More O'Ferrall and Lord Clements supported by Federalists or ex-Repealers like Crawford, O'Conor Don, Barron and M. J. O'Connell. Cf. Lady Holland to Henry Fox, 3 July [1843], Ilchester, *Lady Holland to Her Son*, 209: 'The Parlt. is dragging on. . . . The Irish Arms Bill is tedious; & every clause contested by very tiresome speakers, Lord Clements especially, of whom Serjeant Murphy says, "the penalties are bad enough, but the *Clement*cy worse".'

[3] Hansard, LXIX, 1217–20; LXX, 142–5, 1197, 31 May; 19 June; 14 July 1843, Divisions; LXX, 560, 3 July 1843, Peel. See also Graham to Peel, 15 July 1843, Peel Papers, Add. MSS 40448, 353–4, on a meeting of Irish M.P.s at the Irish Office.

transportation to one year's and three years' imprisonment respectively for the first and second offences.[1]

Smith O'Brien and Wyse were the acknowledged leaders of the Irish opposition. Thomas Davis, the moving spirit of Young Ireland and the *Nation*, naturally wrote to Wyse in July 1843 to recommend pressing motions on a long list of Irish grievances. With youthful optimism and no experience of the House of Commons, Davis thought that

> 2 or 3 nights vigorous debating on each of these [topics] . . . would break down the ministry, give the opposition the fire and progress of an attacking party, accustom the English educated classes to see that we had real grievances the redress of which could not be safely postponed, and the people of Ireland might be induced to consider the propriety of accepting federalism and a full equality instead of that independence which they otherwise can and will conquer for themselves.[2]

But Smith O'Brien had discovered less than a week earlier that the Government was less easily moved. In the thick of the struggle on the Arms Bill, he had initiated a full-dress debate, lasting five days and one of the most remarkable Lord Palmerston had ever heard, on the condition of Ireland. Despite O'Brien's powerful speech, an impressive indictment of British policy and misgovernment ranging from the economic and social consequences of the Union to the deficiencies of recent reforming legislation, the evils of the land system and the deep-seated causes of the nationalist movement, and despite the support of a large section of the Opposition and of the Young England group, his attempt to move the Commons into committee on the state of the country was defeated by a majority of 79 in a House less than two-thirds full.[3]

At the end of the session, an Irish Members of Parliament London Conference of 29 M.P.s, with Wyse as chairman and O'Brien as secretary, drew up an eloquent address of protest to the English people, a 'solemn remonstrance against the fatal policy which has alienated from your Government and your institutions, the minds of a large portion of our fellow countrymen'. The address pointed to the disordered condition of Irish society in which the landlord-tenant relationship had been 'deranged . . . by a long course of vicious legislation', to the 'languishing and neglected' condition of

[1] Hansard, LXX, 1288, 1309, 20, 24 July 1843, M. J. O'Connell, et al.
[2] Davis to Wyse, 10 July 1843, Wyse MSS, in Auchmuty, *Wyse*, 169, n. 1.
[3] Hansard, LXX, 630–77, 1064, 1088–92, 4, 12 July 1843, O'Brien, Palmerston, Division.

Irish commerce, industry and agriculture and to a Church Establishment maintained for the exclusive benefit of one-tenth of the nation. It severely criticized the inadequacy of Irish parliamentary representation and franchises, the lack of real powers of local self-government to compensate for the failure of Parliament to consider Irish local wants and the anti-Catholic and anti-Irish spirit of exclusion which governed the distribution of official appointments. The address ended on a note of warning, that 'we recognize in you no superior title to political rights . . . we warn you that every day's delay increases the difficulty of the task and gives additional strength to those who maintain that there is no hope of good government for Ireland, except in the restoration of her National Parliament'.[1] The signatories of this remarkable Liberal-Unionist document, largely of Smith O'Brien's drafting, included five M.P.s who had been Repealers in 1832; and a large proportion of the rest, like Matthew Corbally, M.P. for Meath, John O'Brien of Limerick City, M. J. O'Connell, Robert Archbold, M.P. for Kildare and Sir Thomas Esmonde, M.P. for County Wexford had been faithful O'Connellite Liberals before 1841.[2]

For Smith O'Brien the rejection of his motion and the failure of his address to bring about any public change in the Government's policy marked the turning-points in his political development. In May 1843, with several other prominent Liberals he had resigned his own commission as a J.P. in protest at the dismissal of the Repeal magistrates; and in October, soon after the news of the arrest and prosecution of O'Connell, he finally joined the Repeal Association, writing in his application for membership that 'the Ministry, instead of applying themselves to remove the causes of complaint, have resolved to deprive us even of the liberty of discontent . . . Slowly, reluctantly convinced that Ireland has nothing to hope from the sagacity, the justice and the generosity of the English Parliament, my reliance shall henceforth be placed upon our own native energy and patriotism.'[3]

[1] Address of Irish M.P.s to the English People [August 1843], O'Connell Papers, N.L.I. uncatalogued; Auchmuty, *Wyse*, 193.

[2] See the much corrected copy of the Address in O'Brien Papers, N.L.I., 433; Pierce Butler, M.P., to O'Brien, 8 August 1843, ibid., 433, refusing to sign because he had voted for Repeal in 1834. Henry Grattan, W. Macnamara, H. Barron, D. Roche and O'Conor Don felt no such scruples.

[3] Smith O'Brien to Repeal Association, 20 October 1843, Gwynn, *Young Ireland and 1848*, 17; see also Duffy, *Young Ireland*, I, 115, 189–90; II, 49–50.

O'Brien's accession was of great value to the nationalist movement. A man of fine presence and romantic good looks, a Protestant of impeccably landed and aristocratic antecedents, claiming descent (of which both he and all nationalists were inordinately proud) from Brian Boroimhe, Smith O'Brien's integrity, conscientiousness and firmness of purpose more than compensated for his lack of humour, the coldness of his manners and for his real deficiencies as a popular orator and leader. Opponents could never regard him, as Tories regarded O'Connell, as a wild beast or a coward, and it was not easy to treat him as a social and political leper.[1] With none of O'Connell's gifts for rapid political improvisation or his capacity for inspiring deep and lasting popular devotion, O'Brien was nonetheless a man of very considerable ability and experience, perhaps the most upright and the least fortunate of all Irish political leaders.

The emerging Young Ireland group found in O'Brien a politician with whom they could work freely and confidently. For O'Connell he was the 'beau idéal' of an Irish nationalist, whose presence in the movement guaranteed the 'due sway and legitimate station' of Protestantism in the future Irish state, and a deputy who assumed the official leadership of the Association during O'Connell's trial and imprisonment.[2] The success of the appeal to the Lords could not conceal the serious weaknesses in O'Connell's position or the real extent of the Government's victory. O'Connell had gambled and lost. The authorities, relying on overwhelming English support, had refused to be stampeded into surrender. By delaying action until the last moment they had risked the possibility of a massacre if O'Connell had been unable to control his followers, but they had won the war of nerves. By trying and imprisoning him they had not only damaged his reputation for infallibility, but, more important, although neither Peel nor Graham seem to have realized this, they had destroyed his will power and self-confidence.

[1] Gregory, *Autobiography*, 67–75. William Gregory's own relations with O'Connell, who deeply impressed him, were good and his evidence on Conservative reactions to O'Connell in 1842 is therefore particularly valuable.

[2] O'Connell to O'Brien, 23 March 1844, O'Brien Papers, N.L.I., 433, conveying 'most emphatically cordial thanks for the manner in which you have conducted the Repeal cause'. See Gwynn, *Young Ireland and 1848*, 19–23, for O'Brien's leadership, with its emphasis on team-work and the production of reports on Irish questions to the Association's Parliamentary Committee, and his encouragement of Davis and the Young Irelanders.

O'Connell's remarkable physique, even at the age of sixty-eight, had been equal to the strenuous demands of the campaign of 1843. But the prolonged strain and anxiety of the State Trial had severely over-taxed his mind, and the restricted, sedentary life in prison, even though the authorities did their best to make it as comfortable as possible, undoubtedly undermined his constitution. In Richmond Bridewell Prison, he had developed a pathetic, old-man's infatuation for the young daughter of a Protestant businessman from Belfast. His alarmed family managed to conceal this from general knowledge but his closest associates were aware, for over two years before his death, that his physical and mental condition was gradually deteriorating.[1] Within a year of his release, progressive congestion of the brain was affecting his walk, handwriting and speech.[2] Rapidly ageing and often in considerable pain, increasingly disillusioned and frequently depressed, he remained for long periods in semi-retirement at Darrynane, while lieutenants, notably John O'Connell, his favourite son and political heir, managed the day-to-day affairs of the Association. But he still remained the official leader of the movement, largely responsible both for its general policies and for the conduct of his party, and although he could still display flashes of his old energy and lucidity, he was certainly in no condition either to deal effectively with the internal difficulties which now plagued his movement or to prevent its gradual disintegration.

The rise of Young Ireland, the most important single feature of the internal history of the last years of the Repeal movement, scarcely falls within the scope of a study concerned principally with the history of the O'Connellite parliamentary party. The personalities,

[1] Duffy, *Young Ireland*, II, 81; Gwynn, *Young Ireland and 1848*, 23–5. See also O'Neill Daunt, *Journal*, 2 November 1846, N.L.I., 2040; and Daunt, *Personal Recollections of O'Connell*, II, 253, 256.

[2] For a full account of O'Connell's medical history, see *The Lancet*, II (1847), 580–1, which contains reports of the diagnoses and prescriptions of two doctors in Paris in March 1847 and of the post-mortem examination carried out by Dr. Lacour, who concluded that death was entirely attributable to *ramollissement*, softening or congestion of the brain 'from which O'Connell had suffered for two years . . . [and] which produced uncertain gait and failing intellect'. But it might be conjectured that the brain changes recorded by Lacour, coupled with the presence of ossifications on the aorta, point to the possibility that O'Connell's condition might have been partly the consequence of syphilis. The evidence is not conclusive. O'Connell's symptoms could have been the product of arteriosclerosis, and the case for syphilis would be stronger if he had died at fifty or younger.

political aims and achievements of the Young Irelanders, the acute differences of temperament, principle and policy which separated them from the main body of the nationalist movement and which led finally to their secession in July 1846 from the Repeal Association and to the formation of the Irish Confederation in January 1847, have received generous treatment from Irish historians.[1] It will be necessary to deal here only with those features of the quarrel which affected or were affected by the operations of the parliamentary party. With the exception of Smith O'Brien, who was not completely identified with the Young Irelanders until the final rupture, this party was wholly O'Connellite before the death of its leader. The Young Irelanders, with their programme of national regeneration, self-reliance and cultural revival were not interested in working through a parliamentary party, and in breaking 'free from the quarrels, the interests, the wrongs and even the gratitude of the past',[2] they implicitly condemned all that O'Connell and his party had stood for (at least between 1835 and 1841) and might stand for in the future. Finally, although the Irish measures of Peel's Government first revealed those divisions between Old and Young Ireland which were brought to a head by O'Connell's decision in 1846 to support the Whigs, the fundamental point at issue—the choice between 'moral force' constitutionalism and a possible final resort to armed rebellion—was far removed from mere personal differences or from disagreements about Government policies and parliamentary tactics.

O'Connell, undeterred by the solid Unionism of the Whig Opposition and of its leaders, had always kept open his lines of communication with them. In September 1843 at the height of his struggle with the Government, he wrote to Lord Campbell, with whom his relations had always been good, to ask why the Whig leaders were 'not up to the level of the times they live in'; why did Russell not imitate Peel's tactics in opposition and come forward with 'a definite plan', for which O'Connell provided some suggestions, for redressing Irish grievances?[3] In January 1844, in response to an overture

[1] See Randall Clarke, 'The relations between O'Connell and the Young Irelanders', *Irish Historical Studies*, III, No. 9 (March 1942), 18–30; R. Dudley Edwards, 'The contribution of Young Ireland to the development of the Irish national idea', *Féilscríbhinn Torna* (1947); Duffy, *Young Ireland*; and *Four Years of Irish History*; Gwynn, *Young Ireland and 1848*; McDowell, *Public Opinion*, 230–59.

[2] Prospectus of the *Nation*, in Gwynn, *Young Ireland and 1848*, 7.

[3] O'Connell to Campbell, 9 September 1843, *Campbell*, II, 179–80.

from the Whig-Radical Charles Buller, O'Connell produced a list of measures which he thought would 'mitigate the present ardent desire for repeal' and on which, in other words, the alliance of 1835–1841 might eventually be rebuilt. His terms—religious equality, the repeal of post-Union landlord legislation and a consideration of fixity of tenure, further municipal reform and an extension of the parliamentary franchises—seemed reasonable to Lord Clarendon, who disliked only the proposal for an absentee income tax.[1]

Russell and the other Whig leaders, doubtless aware that even the suspicion of sympathy with the Irish cause would have been politically fatal in England, had come out strongly in support of the Union. They were still very much against acting openly with O'Connell but they also condemned the Government's treatment of him and of Ireland, a policy which Macaulay summarized in the Commons as 'Soldiers, barracks, a useless State prosecution and an unfair trial . . . An unjust sentence, its infliction and more barracks and more soldiers'. In February 1844, a fortnight after Campbell attended a dinner of the Whig leaders which seemed to show that the party was never 'in a more dilapidated or ruinous condition', the Opposition at last began to show some signs of vigour and a sense of purpose. Russell's motion for a Committee of the whole House to inquire into the state of Ireland was defeated by 99 votes, but it produced a great debate lasting nine nights and when O'Connell entered the House, the Opposition gave him an impressive and generous ovation.[2]

A more serious attempt to revive the Whig alliance followed soon after O'Connell's release from prison. Despite the belligerent tone of his speeches, he plainly did not intend to repeat the agitation of 1843. Alliance with the Opposition seemed to offer the only method of defeating the Conservative Government. To the Prime Minister, it was evident that 'the first and immediate object of O'Connell will be to attempt to make the late Events the instrument of effecting the overthrow of the present Government—and that for

---

[1] O'Connell to Buller [n.d. January 1844], Walpole, *Russell*, I, 395–6. The letter was passed to Russell, who thus read some home-truths about what O'Connell called his 'thorough, contemptuous Whig hatred of the Irish' and his 'conscientious abhorrence of Popery everywhere, but . . . particularly of Irish Popery'.

[2] Hansard, LXXII, 683 ff., 1190; LXXIII, 266–71, 13, 19, 23 February 1844, Russell, Macaulay, Division; *Campbell*, II, 183–4. For the debates, see Greville, *Journal*, 15, 17, 22, 25 February 1844, V, 233–8.

this purpose there will be concert between him and our political opponents'.[1] The fears of the Young Irelanders that 'O'Connell will run no more risks . . . and from the day of his release the cause will be going back and down'[2] were confirmed in October 1844. In a long statement of policy from Darrynane, O'Connell suddenly abandoned 'simple Repeal of the Union' and the restoration of the Irish Parliament, which had been the policy of his movement since 1832, in favour of an indefinite federal scheme by which Ireland would acquire increased representation in the Imperial Parliament and a legislative council with local powers.[3] This egregious 'kite-flying' completely failed to attract the Whigs and Federalists for whom it was intended, dismayed the Young Irelanders who promptly repudiated it and was not popular even with faithful O'Connellites like O'Neill Daunt or with the bulk of the nationalist press. Within a month O'Connell was forced to acknowledge his mistake.[4]

Peel's policy towards Ireland had meanwhile entered its second and constructive phase. It was obvious to the Prime Minister that 'mere force . . . will do nothing as a permanent remedy for the social evils of that Country. We must look beyond the present, must bear in mind that the day may come . . . when this Country may be involved in serious disputes or actual war with other Powers—and when it may be of the first importance that the foundations of a better state of things in Ireland should have been laid.'[5] Between February and April 1844 he and Graham worked out the main lines of their Irish policy. A Royal Commission was set up in November

[1] Peel to Graham, 14 September 1844, Add. MSS 40450, 152-3. Greville, *Journal*, 14 September 1844, V, 260-1, came substantially to the same conclusion; see also Duffy, *Young Ireland*, II, 84.

[2] Davis' remark, quoted by Clarke, 'The relations between O'Connell and the Young Irelanders', *Irish Historical Studies*, III, 22.

[3] O'Connell to Secretary, Repeal Association, 12 October 1844, *O'Connell Corr.*, II, 433-48. See also the draft constitutional scheme in ibid., II, 329-31.

[4] Duffy, *Young Ireland*, II, 107 ff.; *O'Connell Corr.*, II, 334-45; Kennedy, 'Sharman Crawford's Federal Scheme for Ireland', loc. cit., 247-54; O'Connell to Maurice O'Connell, 17 October; Daunt to O'Connell, 29 October 1844, O'Connell Papers, N.L.I., uncatalogued. O'Connell's mistaken belief that the English Whigs would support a federal scheme was probably grounded on an article in the *Edinburgh Review*, LXXIX (1844), 189-266, in which it was tentatively suggested that sessions of Parliament might be held in Dublin.

[5] Peel to Graham, 19 October 1843, Peel Papers, Add. MSS 40449, 105, partly in Parker, *Peel*, III, 65.

1843 under the Earl of Devon to inquire into the land system; the county franchise was to be lowered to £5 freehold; the law relating to charitable bequests, particularly those made by Catholics, was to be reformed; the State grant to Maynooth College, the main educational centre for the priesthood, was to be considerably increased and finally, three provincial Colleges in Cork, Galway and Belfast, open to all denominations and in which no provision was to be made for theological teaching of any kind, would provide much needed facilities for the higher education of the Catholic laity.[1]

In the sessions of 1844 and 1845 the Government carried through most·of this programme. The Charitable Bequests Bill passed easily in August 1844, generally supported by Irish Liberals and opposed only by a small knot of Repealers led by Dillon Browne who could not even find a seconder for his attempt to wreck the Bill.[2] The increased Maynooth grant, violently opposed in and out of Parliament by many English Tories, anti-Establishment Radicals and representatives of the Dissenter interest, was carried through in April and May 1845 by an impromptu coalition of English liberal Conservatives and Whigs and a solid band of Irish Liberals and those Repealers who had not seceded from Parliament.[3] The Colleges Bill, equally abhorrent both to many of the Tories who had opposed the Maynooth grant and to O'Connell, was supported in principle by the Whig Opposition and by Catholic Liberals like Wyse (who had long campaigned for such a scheme) and More O'Ferrall, whose criticism of details of the Bill was very different from O'Connell's general opposition to it.[4]

The Government's Registration Bill incorporating the £5 freehold franchise, which Peel and Graham regarded as giving Ireland equality of civil rights with England and which they were prepared to carry even if it cost the Conservatives several Irish county seats,

[1] See esp. Peel, Cabinet Memos, 11, 17 February 1844, Parker, *Peel*, III, 101-3, 105-7; Graham to Peel, 17 October 1843; Cabinet Papers, 12 April; 26 November 1844, Peel Papers, Add. MSS 40449, 91-3; 40450, 12-13; H.O. Papers, 79/9, 159-82.

[2] Hansard, LXXVI, 1511-15, 1780-1, 29 July; 5 August 1844, Graham, Browne, Division.

[3] Hansard, LXXIX, 108-11, 1042-5; LXXX, 744-8, 3, 18 April; 21 May 1845, Divisions on First, Second and Third Readings.

[4] Hansard, LXXX, 366-74, 9 May 1845, Wyse; LXXXI, 629-30, 1089-98, 16, 23 June 1845, O'Connell; LXXXII, 377-9, 379-81, 10 July 1845, Divisions.

was abandoned in April 1844 because a long struggle on this controversial issue might have endangered the rest of the Government's
programme.¹ Far more serious was the complete failure to carry
through any agrarian legislation. The Government would have
nothing to do with any proposal for fixity of tenure, the legalization
of the Ulster custom of tenant right or even with the Repeal Association's moderate recommendations for increasing the security of
tenants; and the half-hearted attempt in June 1845 to carry out the
principal recommendation of the Devon Commission—compensation for agricultural improvements—was sabotaged by the rooted
opposition of the Whig and Tory landed interest in the Lords.²

Peel had attempted with great parliamentary skill and regardless
of possible effects on the unity of his party or on his own popularity
to satisfy at least some of the demands of the Irish Catholic middle
class, and although he and Graham were under no illusions as to the
real extent of their success or the depth of Irish gratitude, they had
undoubtedly succeeded in driving some deep wedges into the solidarity of the Irish Catholics and of the nationalist movement.³ The
Bequests Act, which O'Connell and Archbishop MacHale tried unsuccessfully to sabotage, produced serious divisions both in the
Catholic hierarchy and among the laity, while the angry public disputes on the Colleges Bill unmistakably revealed the deep gulf
between the Old Ireland, Catholic nationalism of the O'Connells
and Dr. MacHale, for whom the Bill was anti-Catholic and even
anti-Christian, 'a gigantic scheme of godless education', and the
Young Irelanders led by Davis and supported by Smith O'Brien,
who strongly favoured any scheme of mixed, undenominational

¹ Graham to Cabinet, 7 March 1844; Peel to Wellington, 22 March; Wellington to Peel, 23 March [1844], Peel Papers, Add. MSS 40449, 341–4; 40460,
167–72; McDowell, *Public Opinion*, 213. The Duke was most unhappy about the
whole plan and had agreed to it unwillingly.

² Hansard, LXXXI, 211 ff.; 1116–52, 9, 24 June 1845, Stanley, Debate,
Division; Wellington to Peel, 20, 25 June 1845, Peel Papers, Add. MSS 40461,
140; Parker, *Peel*, III, 178, wrongly dated January. O'Connell's grudging attitude towards the Devon Commission, 'all landlords and no tenants', was typical
of Irish opinion generally. See O'Connell to Fitzpatrick, 13 December 1843; to
P. Mahony, 26 April 1845, *O'Connell Corr.*, II, 311, 351–2; McDowell, *Public
Opinion*, 238–9.

³ The aim of killing Repeal by kindness stands out clearly from Ministers'
correspondence. See esp. Graham to Peel, 5 December 1844, Peel Papers, Add.
MSS 40450, 356; Heytesbury to Peel, 19, 20 December 1844; Peel to Gladstone,
2 January 1845; Parker, *Peel*, III, 132–3, 165–6.

education and regarded its opponents as bigoted sectarians intent on the establishment of a Catholic ascendancy.[1]

Furthermore, the Government's policies exposed the lamentable weakness of the Repeal party in Parliament which had been quite unable to throw out or even to amend any of these measures. On the Bequests and Colleges issues, O'Connell was cut off from the 43 Irish Whig, Liberal and Federalist M.P.s[2] many of whom had been his followers before 1841 and who might have been willing but for these issues to serve under him again. He was forced back after March 1844 on a policy of deliberate secession from Parliament, which had been first suggested by Davis during O'Connell's imprisonment and which exactly fitted O'Brien's views.[3] Most of the party and certainly its leaders remained in Ireland until June 1845, when O'Connell wrote to O'Brien from Cork for his advice about the party's tactics on the Colleges Bill, which had already reached its committee stage:

> . . . are *we* to go over [?] Decide for me as well as for yourself and if that decision be in favour of action—I mean of course in favour of going over—I will leave here . . . immediately . . . It will be no small sacrifice to give up my loved mountains but if you *continue* to think that sacrifice necessary I will readily make it.
>
> I am very strongly for throwing out the Colleges Bill this session. If we could do so we should get a better nay a decidedly good one next year—so I think.[4]

O'Connell's realism had deserted him. When he and O'Brien

[1] See Gwynn, *Young Ireland and 1848*, 32–47; and Broderick, 'The Holy See', 163 ff., for the Government's interesting diplomatic moves at Rome designed to produce Papal support for the moderate Irish Catholics.

[2] Duffy's figures, *Young Ireland*, II, 50: 36 Whigs, 7 Federalists.

[3] O'Brien to Wyse, 27 November 1843, Wyse MSS, quoted by Auchmuty, *Wyse*, 193–4: 'I will waste no time in vainly seeking from parliamentary debate measures which I am sure will only be yielded to fear.' Wyse (to O'Brien, 24 November 1843, Smith O'Brien Papers, op. cit., 194) was sure that O'Brien's decision to abstain from Parliament was 'the result of deepest conviction, noblest self-sacrifice, and thorough love of country which few in this jobbing, party-hunting age can appreciate, much less practise'.

[4] O'Connell to O'Brien, 9 June 1845, O'Brien Papers, N.L.I., 434. The Irish leaders had received an appeal from Hume in February 1845: Gwynn, *Young Ireland and 1848*, 60. But they had not gone over for the Maynooth debates in April and May despite appeals from Henry Warburton and others. Fitzpatrick's note, *O'Connell Corr.*, II, 353, is inaccurate, as also is his dating of Warburton's letter (1845, not 1843).

went over they were quite unable to amend the Bill against 'a most overwhelming majority',[1] and were also subjected to a virulent attack by the Radical John Arthur Roebuck, who singled out O'Brien particularly for failing in his duties as an M.P. and attacked him with what O'Brien called 'the accumulated venom' of three months.[2] Roebuck could not simply be dismissed as 'the bitter little gentleman who sits for Bath & snarls . . . at every man who does not bring him flattery or profit', and it was scarcely a sufficient reply to challenge him to a duel, as Patrick Somers, the M.P. for Sligo did, for insulting the Repeal party.[3] Roebuck was a powerful independent figure in the House, strongly opposed both to the nationalist movement and to the Irish landlord class;[4] and his private campaign against the Irish party in the next two years helped to deprive the Irish people of much English sympathy in the disaster which struck Ireland less than three months after the passing of the Colleges Bill.

The disintegration of the Irish party

The sudden failure in the late autumn of 1845 of the greater part of the potato crop immediately confronted Ireland with the certainty of famine. For Peel, moving gradually away from the protectionism of his party, the calamity which swept away the bulk of the Irish food supply also provided a convenient pretext for the lifting of all restrictions on corn imports and the abandonment of agricultural protection. O'Connell too at once grasped the full extent of the disaster. In October he organized the setting up of the Mansion House Committee in Dublin, which included leading Whigs like the Duke of Leinster and Lord Cloncurry as well as Repealers and which was to act as a receiving centre for reports from all parts of the country.[5] On 3 November a deputation from this Committee led by O'Connell and Leinster waited on the Lord Lieutenant, Lord Heytesbury, to demand the immediate stoppage of all exports of corn and provisions, the opening of the ports for the import of food, the setting up of

---

[1] O'Connell to Fitzpatrick, 25 June 1845, *O'Connell Corr.*, II, 359.

[2] Hansard, LXXXI, 488–91, 493–5, 13 June 1845, Roebuck, O'Brien.

[3] Thomas Davis to O'Brien, 17 June 1845, O'Brien Papers, N.L.I., 434; Leader, *Roebuck*, 198–9. Roebuck raised the matter in Parliament and Somers was forced to apologize to him and to the House.

[4] Leader, *Roebuck*, 171–2, 176–9.

[5] *Times*, 30 October 1845; Kevin B. Nowlan, 'The Political Background', in *The Great Famine*, 135–6.

relief machinery and food stores in counties and the provision of employment on useful public works, whose cost was to be met by an income tax of 10 per cent on resident and from 20 per cent to 50 per cent on absentee landlords and by raising a loan of £1,500,000 on Government security. Heytesbury's cold reception of these proposals helped to confirm O'Connell in his belief that the Conservative Government could not be trusted to deal generously with the situation.[1]

Thus during the political crisis in December 1845, when the Whigs attempted and failed to form a Government, he came out openly in their support. It made little difference that since August, in a campaign in the south and west of Ireland, he had been calling for an independent nationalist party of 70 Members who would hold the balance of power in the Commons and prevent the formation of any Ministry 'strong enough to postpone the discussions of the terms on which to found the restoration of the Irish Parliament'.[2] Now he was ready to commit his party both to repeal of the Corn Laws and to alliance with the Whigs.[3] Smith O'Brien, who for over two years had occupied a neutral but increasingly uncomfortable position between the O'Connellites and Young Ireland, for the first time came down decidedly against O'Connell's policy.

Like the Young Irelanders, O'Brien believed strongly in some protection for Irish agriculture. He was certainly not ready, he wrote to O'Connell, 'to change that opinion merely because Lord John Russell finds it convenient for party purposes to abandon the Ground which he formerly occupied and for the sake of rallying a great party to announce himself a convert to the opinions of Mr. Cobden'. The Corn Laws, he insisted, must remain 'an open question' in the nationalist movement. But he was even more horrified by the prospect of alliance with the Whigs and protested that 'If all our exertions—our pledges may I say—our *sacrifices* are to end in placing the Irish nation under the feet of the English Whigs, I own I cannot justify to myself the part which I have acted nor do I think that the Repeal agitation will have conferred upon Ireland anything but injury and disgrace.' He went on to state what later became the classic conception of the role of the Irish party:

[1] Cecil Woodham-Smith, *The Great Hunger* (1962), 48-9.
[2] O'Connell to Repeal Association, 14 August 1845, *Pilot*, 20 August 1845; see also *Times*, 21 October 1845, for his speech in similar terms at Sligo.
[3] *Times*, 17 December; *Nation*, 20 December 1845.

... We shall go to the House of Commons as [or ?] we shall stay at Conciliation Hall with a phalanx of fifty or sixty men ... with such a body acting upon high & independent principles we shall not only command the respect of all parties but we shall hold under our hands and control the destinies of the Empire ... I believe it to be for the interest of Ireland that administration after administration should be shipwrecked until England shall have learnt that it would be wise as well as just on her part to conform to the wish & the determination of Ireland by acceding to our demand for a national legislature. In the mean time ... the alternative which ought to be presented to the Minister is in my opinion not—'if you give us these measures we will support you'—but 'if you do not give us these measures we will oppose you'.[1]

In his reply O'Connell paid lip-service to the idea of independence, but he was already deeply committed to repeal of the Corn Laws, and impending famine seemed to him only to add another and still more urgent argument for free trade. 'How', he asked, 'can we insist upon the Government finding employment and food ... if we vote in favour of the Corn Laws and thereby prevent food being as cheap as it would otherwise be?'[2] In relation to English public opinion and its possible reaction to heavy financial demands for Irish relief, this argument was valid enough. Yet free trade by itself could not possibly have forestalled or prevented famine in a country where the purchasing power of a peasantry immersed in a subsistence economy was as limited as the country's internal marketing facilities. The Corn Laws had not affected the price of potatoes on which most of the Irish mainly lived, and the withdrawal of agricultural protection, as Peel himself realized and as Lord George Bentinck constantly emphasized, might well cause lasting damage to Ireland's only major industry.[3]

There was never any doubt about O'Connell's own position on this issue. In January 1846 the Whig Opposition knew that he would 'support all the *strong* views of the opponents of the corn laws.'[4] But

[1] Smith O'Brien to O'Connell, 18 December 1845, O'Connell Papers, N.L.I., uncatalogued. For the Young Irelanders' support of protection see Black, *Economic Thought*, 143, who does not make it clear that on this issue they were at variance with O'Connell.

[2] O'Connell to Smith O'Brien, 20 December 1845, O'Brien Papers, quoted by Gwynn, *Young Ireland and 1848*, 55-6.

[3] B. Disraeli, *Lord George Bentinck* (1852), 73, 138, 140, 165-71, 218-25. See also Black, *Economic Thought*, 140-4, on the general case for Irish protectionism.

[4] D. R. Pigot, M.P., to Russell, 19 January 1846, Russell Papers, P.R.O. 30/22/5A.

in April, after Smith O'Brien had successfully appealed to Bentinck in the Commons to support a proposal for a temporary suspension of the Corn Laws, it still seemed that many of the Irish might go over to the protectionists.[1] 'They are a very odd and unmanageable set', Cobden told his wife, 'and I fear many of the most Liberal patriots amongst them would if they could find an excuse pick a quarrel with us and vote against us or stay away.'[2] The Irish Repealers and Liberals were indeed deeply divided on the issue. When the Corn Bill finally passed the Commons, its 329 supporters included O'Connell and 34 members of the Repeal-Liberal party, but the abstention of 41 Irish Members, 13 of them Tories, in reality helped the Government more than its opponents.[3]

There was a much greater degree of unanimity among the Irish in their opposition to Peel's Government, in whose downfall the combined Repeal-Liberal party under O'Connell played for the last time a conspicuous, even perhaps a decisive role. Unlike the Whig leaders or Bentinck, O'Connell had decided from the first to oppose the Protection of Life (Ireland) Bill which the Government regarded as an indispensable precautionary measure in famine-stricken Ireland and which it intended to pass concurrently with repeal of the Corn Laws.[4] It was vital if the Government was eventually to be defeated to prolong debates on this Coercion Bill and thus to hold up the Corn Bill, whose passing would certainly only strengthen Peel's general position. From the end of March, O'Connell with a body of about 50 Repealers and Liberals fought a long and successful delaying action against the Coercion Bill, convincing the Prime Minister that 'There is an Irish party, a determined and not insignificant one, for which British indignation has no terrors. Their wish is to disgust

[1] O'Brien to Bentinck, 19 April 1846, O'Brien Papers, quoted by Gwynn, *Young Ireland and 1848*, 67–8; Hansard, LXXXV, 980–4, 985–92, 24 April 1846, O'Brien, Bentinck, who agreed to the proposal for allowing duty-less corn into Ireland even though he thought it would bring no relief to the Irish. He pointed out that Ireland was currently exporting large quantities of grain. The problem was not food, but money to buy food.

[2] Cobden to Mrs. Cobden, 27 April 1846, Morley, *Cobden*, 380. He thought them 'landlords, and like the rest afraid of rent'.

[3] Hansard, LXXXVI, 721–8, 15 May 1846, Division. O'Brien and Maurice O'Connell were among those who abstained.

[4] O'Connell to Martin Crean, 13 February 1846, *O'Connell Corr.*, II, 367–70; Hansard, LXXXV, 333–60, 30 March 1846, Graham. The Bill allowed the proclamation of districts and the imposition of a curfew, breaches of which were to be punished by 15 years' transportation.

England with Irish business and with Irish members, and to induce England . . . to listen to a repeal of the Legislative Union for the purpose of purging the House of a set of troublesome and factious members, who equally obstruct legislation for Ireland and for Great Britain.'[1]

By the first week in June the Whig Opposition had settled its acute differences on the Coercion Bill. O'Connell officially placed his party at Russell's disposal at a meeting where it was decided to move a wrecking motion against the Bill and where O'Connell, in a long speech unusually laudatory of Russell, had said that he was 'only too proud to serve under such a leader'. In another camp Bentinck, Disraeli and 70 to 80 Tory protectionists were now ready to avenge their betrayal.[2] In one of his bitter onslaughts on the Prime Minister, Disraeli saw poetic justice in the fact that Ireland, which had been Peel's 'difficulty' in 1835, was now about to ruin him: 'It is Nemesis that inspires this debate, and dictates this division and seals with the stigma of Parliamentary reprobation the catastrophe of a sinister career.'[3] What Wellington called 'this blackguard combination' had now been formed.[4] Peel had categorically refused in the event of defeat to dissolve and to go to the country on the Bill, which would mean appealing to Great Britain against Ireland, and on 25 June, only a few hours after the Corn Bill had passed the Lords and after six nights of debate on Sir William

[1] Peel to Wellington, 21 June 1846, Parker, *Peel*, III, 363–5. See also Disraeli, *Bentinck*, 148–58, on the 'allowable but very unusual' Irish opposition to the First Reading of a Bill which had already passed the Lords (and would normally have been read for the first time *pro forma*), and for this opposition's important connection with the tactics of the protectionists.

[2] For divisions inside the Whig party on the Coercion Bill, which was actually supported by Irish landlords like Clanricarde, Bessborough and Lansdowne, and for Russell's difficulties, see Clarendon to Russell, 11 March 1846, Russell Papers, P.R.O. 30/22/5A; Greville, *Journal*, 18, 29 March; 23 April 1846, V, 383–4, 387–8, 389–91; Peel to Queen Victoria, 4 April 1846; Arbuthnot to Peel, 5, 22 April; 2 May 1846, Parker, *Peel*, III, 344–7. For the Whig and Irish meeting on 7 June, see Auchmuty, *Wyse*, 190; Arbuthnot to Peel, 7 June 1846, Parker, *Peel*, III, 351.

[3] Hansard, LXXXVII, 537, 15 June 1846, Disraeli. But cf. John Wilson Croker to Graham, 21 February 1846, *Croker Papers*, III, 64, quoted by Monypenny, *Disraeli*, II, 345: 'Ireland has no more to with the grand convulsion than Kamschatka . . .' As Croker correctly saw, Ireland was the occasion, not the cause of Peel's fall.

[4] Wellington to Peel, 8 June 1846, Parker, *Peel*, III, 353.

Somerville's motion to postpone the Coercion Bill, the Government was decisively defeated in the Commons by 73 votes.[1]

The Irish party's alliance with Lord John Russell's Government, which was to form the basis of O'Connell's policy in the last year of his life, had been forged in the parliamentary struggle against Peel and was now rapidly completed in Ireland. O'Connell's active co-operation, notably in ensuring Sheil's unopposed re-election at Dungarvan, allowed Russell to give junior ministerial posts to five Irish M.P.s, two of whom had been Repealers in 1832.[2] But the policy of partnership with the Whigs was also the immediate cause of the final rupture with Smith O'Brien and the Young Irelanders, who regarded a Whig Government, in Thomas Francis Meagher's words, as 'little else than a State Relief Committee for the beggarly politicians that beset the country'.[3] Outmanoeuvred by John O'Connell who acted throughout with his father's approval and even at his instigation, O'Brien and his associates drove themselves out of the Repeal Association and into a position of political isolation and weakness.[4]

[1] Peel to Wellington, 21, 23 June; to Cobden, 24 June 1846, Parker, *Peel*, III, 363–8; Hansard, LXXXVII, 1027–32, 25 June 1846, Division. Forty-eight Irish Members opposed Peel, 31 supported him, but it was the English majority of 56 against the Government which turned the scales decisively.

[2] O'Connell to D. R. Pigot, 8 July 1846, *O'Connell Corr.*, II, 377–9. The ex-Repealers were Sheil (Master of the Mint) and The O'Conor Don (a Lord of the Treasury). Wyse, whose claims to Cabinet rank were pressed unsuccessfully by O'Connell, became Joint Secretary of the (India) Board of Control; see Auchmuty, *Wyse*, 200–1. Richard Moore and J. H. Monahan were brought in as Attorney and Solicitor-General respectively. Thomas Redington, M.P. for Dundalk (1837–46), who had been a member of the Precursor Society in 1838, now resigned his seat to become Under-Secretary in Ireland. The appointment of the Catholic Redington was approved of by O'Connell, even though he was not on speaking terms with him (see letter to Pigot cited above).

[3] *Nation*, 20 June 1846. Smith O'Brien had already been almost completely alienated from the O'Connells by their failure to support him in April and May 1846, when he had been imprisoned by the Commons for refusing to serve on Committees dealing with other than Irish affairs. Gwynn, *Young Ireland and 1848*, 59–66, gives a complete account of this episode, to which it is only necessary to add, as reasons for O'Connell's desertion of O'Brien, that by April 1846 O'Connell was not ready to do anything which might injure his alliance with the Whigs; and secondly, that whatever O'Connell might agree to in Ireland, he had at bottom a profound respect for Parliament. 'It is a foolish thing', he told O'Neill Daunt, 'to run amuck at the house of Commons': O'Neill Daunt, *Journal*, 26 May 1846, N.L.I., 2040, partly printed in *A Life Spent for Ireland*, 50.

[4] Gwynn, *Young Ireland and 1848*, 67–78, et seq.; Nowlan, 'The Political Background', loc. cit., 144–7.

While these bitter disputes were splitting the nationalist movement beyond repair, famine tightened its grip on Ireland. O'Connell
made great and despairing efforts in major speeches in February and
April 1846 to bring home the real extent of the disaster to Parliament.[1]
Disraeli movingly described the second occasion, when O'Connell
sat in the place usually occupied by the leader of the Opposition
and spoke for nearly two hours in a voice audible only to those near
him and to Ministers, as 'a strange and touching spectacle to those
who remembered the form of colossal energy and the clear and
thrilling tones which had once startled, disturbed and controlled
senates . . . To the house generally it was a performance of dumb
show, a feeble old man muttering before a table; but respect for the
great parliamentary personage kept all as orderly as if the fortunes
of a party hung upon his rhetoric.'[2] It was not a party but a people
who depended on his words.

His alliance with the Whig Government did not give O'Connell
the command over policy for which he had hoped. Ministers were
certainly ready to attend to his recommendations for patronage and
appointments. They restored the nationalist magistrates dismissed
by the Conservatives and pleased him by appointing his son-in-law,
Charles O'Connell, to a resident magistracy, by promoting his son
Morgan and by finding a safe billet for the faithful Fitzpatrick.[3]
They listened sympathetically to his complaints about the 'Infidel
Colleges' scheme.[4] But in the all-important sphere of famine policy
his increasingly urgent appeals to Russell in London and to the

---

[1] Hansard, LXXXIII, 1050–68; LXXXV, 493–527, 17 February; 3 April
1846, O'Connell.

[2] Disraeli, *Bentinck*, 159–60. O'Connell, who had quarrelled violently with
Disraeli in 1835 and whose followers had drowned Disraeli's maiden speech in
1837, was now at last reconciled with him. He had been delighted by Disraeli's
'smashing' of Peel, 'one of the ablest speeches I ever heard in the House of
Commons, but for the invective . . . and that made it incomparable': Monypenny, *Disraeli*, I, 295; II, 9–11, 388.

[3] O'Connell to Pigot, 12 July; 4, 13, 14, 15 August 1846, *O'Connell Corr.*,
II, 380–4, 403; Greville, *Journal*, 18 July 1846, V, 415–16. In September 1846,
Maurice O'Connell was made a Deputy Lieutenant of Kerry, O'Connell MSS,
U.C.D.

[4] Bessborough to Russell, 11 September; Russell to Bessborough, 15 September 1846, Russell Papers, P.R.O. 30/22/5C; Bessborough reported an interview
with O'Connell in which he 'expressed the greatest anxiety to assist me'
and asked that one of the new Colleges should be exclusively Catholic.
Russell thought O'Connell 'very fair and reasonable'.

Viceroy, Lord Bessborough and the Chief Secretary, Henry Labouchere in Ireland were met either with evasive acknowledgments or with statements of policies on which the Government had already decided.

Thus in August 1846 he pleaded with Pigot that the Government must feed the people '*no matter at what cost*, and without delay', and wrote to Russell suggesting that the Government ask Parliament for 'extraordinary powers of directing, *without any delay*, the execution of Works of Public Utility and of supplying the immediate means of paying the wages of the Labourers employed at such works'. Russell politely acknowledged 'the sense of public duty which has dictated your letter' and said that he would not 'lose sight of its suggestions'.[1] But the Government's actual policy ran clean contrary to the spirit and even to the letter of O'Connell's advice. Government purchase and importation of food, as laid down by Peel in 1845, was severely curtailed. The Labour Rate Act was passed in August 1846 which allowed only for unproductive public works and threw the whole cost on localities and landlords (Peel had given generous Treasury subsidies), and although pressure from O'Connell, the Irish administration and Irish landlords forced the Government in October to authorize the setting up of useful improvement schemes even if they benefited individual landowners, the financial terms laid down robbed this concession of much of its value and prevented it from reducing the mounting pressure on existing public works schemes.[2] Labouchere dutifully passed on to London O'Connell's suggestion that the Lord Lieutenant should have a fund of at least £1,000,000 for use in emergencies but there was never any question of its being adopted.[3]

When Ireland stood most in need of it, there was no strong and united party to bring pressure to bear on the Government or to plead her cause with the English people, whom Greville described well as torn 'between indignation, resentment, rage and economical

[1] O'Connell to Pigot, 13 August 1846, *O'Connell Corr.*, II, 383; to Russell, 12 August; Russell to O'Connell, 14 August 1846, Russell Papers, P.R.O. 30/22/5B.

[2] Nowlan, 'The Political Background', loc. cit., 148–52; Black, *Economic Thought*, 114–17; O'Connell to Labouchere, 29 September; 4 October; Bessborough to O'Connell, 6 October 1846, *O'Connell Corr.*, II, 385–7.

[3] Labouchere to O'Connell, 8 October 1846, O'Connell Papers, N.L.I., uncatalogued.

fear on the one hand, and pity and generosity on the other'.[1] In January 1847 O'Connell, whose faith in the Whigs had been shattered, presided over the only expression of national unity in the face of the famine when Irish landlords and politicians of all parties met in Dublin and decided to act together in bringing pressure on the Government.[2] Within two months of the meeting of Parliament, this so-called 'Irish party', its unity essentially the product of alarm at steeply rising taxation, had been totally disrupted. Bentinck's generous scheme for a Treasury loan of £16,000,000 for Irish railways was treated by Russell as an issue of confidence. Thirty-seven Irish M.P.s supported Bentinck, 63 voted against him or abstained, and his plan was crushingly defeated.[3] Secondly, the Government's Poor Relief (Ireland) Bill, which sanctioned relief outside the workhouses and was a fundamental part of the Government's new policy of throwing almost the entire cost and responsibility for relief on to the Irish Poor Law, divided O'Connell and his followers (who reluctantly accepted the measure) from the rest of the Irish landed interest, Whig and Tory.[4]

Thus divided, the Irish party was unable to force the Government to carry out its promised programme of agrarian legislation or to shake its determination to reduce Treasury assistance for Ireland to a minimum and to throw the bulk of the costs of famine relief on Ireland and the Irish landlords. In this determination, the Government accurately reflected English public opinion. The reports of T. C. Foster, *The Times*' special correspondent in Ireland, beginning in August 1845 and continuing throughout the early months of the first potato failure, brought fully home to the English upper and middle classes the plight of the Irish people and saddled Irish landlordism with complete responsibility for it.[5] Predictably, O'Connell was the newspaper's principal target. The wretched appearance of

[1] Greville, *Journal*, 23 March 1847, VI, 72. Greville's own comments on the Irish and the famine (see esp. entry of 12 December 1846, V, 443) exactly bear out the truth of his own generalization.

[2] Nowlan, 'The Political Background', loc. cit., 154–7. See McDowell, *Public Opinion*, 258, for O'Connell's advocacy at the meeting of a party which would 'bring to the altar of our country our prejudices and bad passions, and sacrifice them to the object of rescuing Ireland from misery'.

[3] Hansard, XC, 123–6, 15 February 1847, Division. Seventeen Repealers supported Bentinck, 5 abstained and 6 supported the Government.

[4] Nowlan, 'The Political Background', loc. cit., 161–2; see also O'Connell to T. M. Ray, 13 February 1847, *O'Connell Corr.*, II, 405–7'.

[5] *History of The Times*, II, 9–10; *Times*, 21 August to November 1845.

the towns of Cahirciveen and Darrynane Beg and the presence on O'Connell's own lands of a swarming, poverty-stricken tenantry allowed *The Times* to label him as the chief of 'the most neglectful landlords who are a curse to Ireland', a member of 'the vilest class in all Europe'.[1] He and his party were accused of doing nothing and caring nothing for the starving peasantry. 'The braggard leader and mouthpiece of discontent, . . . the King of Tara—the high priest of Irish liberties—the defier of the Saxon—the emancipator of the Celt' was now interested, according to *The Times*, only in collecting his annual Tribute and in securing his 70 Repeal Members or 'a fine Parliament of fine old Irish gentlemen'; and the newspaper went on to say that 'If men are responsible for their actions in proportion to the talent which is committed to them, how fearful must be the responsibility of that man who, having great influence over a people's mind, never used it for their good; and who when they suffered, jested; when they starved, extorted; at once the cutpurse and buffoon of a hideous tragedy.'[2]

The Times both reflected and moulded public opinion. Growing English resentment of Irish landlordism and of its representatives in Parliament, combined with exasperation at Ireland's unceasing troubles and fear of the hordes of destitute Irish pouring into England, contributed powerfully to the demand that Irish property must support Irish poverty. But whatever their sins, the landlords, even under compulsion, could not save the Irish people from the effects of what Russell called 'a famine of the 13th century acting upon a population of the 19th'.[3] In his last speech, O'Connell told the Commons that Ireland 'was in their hands. If they did not save

[1] *Times*, 18 November 1845; 24 May 1847. The exposure of these conditions touched off a furious and much publicized controversy (see esp. *Times*, 26, 28 November; 20 December 1845, for the replies of Daniel and Maurice O'Connell). But while O'Connell was not a model or improving landlord, his main fault seems to have been the indulgence which allowed his tenants to sub-divide their holdings unchecked. Despite the Tributes and like many other landlords, he was habitually short of capital for agricultural investment; hospitable, and careless about money, he had also to meet very large political expenses.

[2] *Times*, leader, 30 October 1845.

[3] Quoted by Woodham-Smith, *The Great Hunger*, 408. Mrs. Woodham-Smith's book is the best general account of the Famine, particularly informative as to the motives and attitudes of Charles Trevelyan at the Treasury and of the Whig Government. But the more specialized and detailed articles in *The Great Famine, Studies in Irish History, 1845–52*, eds. R. Dudley Edwards and T. Desmond Williams (1956), still remain indispensable.

her, she could not save herself.' The knowledge that the generosity of individuals and the activities of voluntary groups like the Quakers and the British Association could not meet the situation, that, as he told Ray in February 1847, 'there will not be sufficient relief given by the Parliament . . . and . . . it will not be until after the decease of hundreds of thousands that the regret will arise that more was not done to save a sinking nation', added greatly to the sufferings of O'Connell's last months.[1] Late in March, an exhausted and grief-stricken old man, he set out from England for Rome accompanied by his confessor and by his youngest son. In Paris, the warm tributes of French Liberals and Catholics headed by Charles de Montalembert—proof of the European reputation which he had acquired but had never attempted to use—can now have meant little to him, and the slow pilgrimage to Rome ended with his death, after great agony of mind and body, at Genoa on 15 May 1847.

O'Connell's party and the political movement which he had created did not long survive him. Nationalist gains in the General Election of August 1847, when 39 Repealers were returned, startled English politicians, most of whom had expected Repeal to be buried with O'Connell.[2] But these successes did not represent any great or organized wave of political feeling in famine-stricken Ireland, still less the re-emergence of a united or independent parliamentary party. The Colleges Bill, tenant-right and the inadequacy of the Government's relief measures were much more important electoral issues than Repeal. John O'Connell, now the official leader of the Repeal Association, made the fullest possible use of his father's name and prestige to whip up enthusiasm and to damage the Young Irelanders of the Irish Confederation; and by refusing to accept the Confederates' demand that Repeal candidates should pledge themselves against placemanship, he fought the Election in tacit alliance with the Whig Government.[3]

[1] Hansard, LXXXIX, 942–5, 8 February 1847, O'Connell; to Ray, 13 February 1847, *O'Connell Corr.*, II, 407.

[2] 'Election Returns of 1841 and 1847', *Westminster Review*, XLVIII (1847–8), 261 ff.; Nowlan, 'The Political Background', loc. cit., 167–8.

[3] Gwynn, *Young Ireland and 1848*, 114–29; Duffy, *Four Years of Irish History*, 413–22. See Auchmuty, *Wyse*, 212–13, for the Waterford City election, when Wyse, despite his support of tenant-right, was defeated largely because of his support of the Colleges Bill and the consequent opposition to him of Bishop Foran and the priesthood. Daniel O'Connell's name also played an important part in this election.

John O'Connell found no great difficulty in defeating his father's Irish opponents, who possessed neither the electoral organization nor the popular appeal to offset the hostility of the priesthood,[1] but he soon demonstrated his own inability either to provide effective leadership for the parliamentary Repeal party or to prevent its rapid and complete disintegration. His authority was at once successfully challenged by his father's old enemy, Feargus O'Connor, now the Chartist M.P. for Nottingham, who insisted on bringing forward in the Commons a motion on Repeal. The debate, which never arose far above the level of a parliamentary farce, exposed the party to the ridicule and contempt of English Members, and the division on the motion, supported by only 23 Repealers, fully revealed the party's weakness.[2] Less than half the party could be brought to oppose the first and least severe of the Government's repressive Irish measures, the Crime and Outrage Bill of November 1847, which the Whigs had been unable to carry in Daniel O'Connell's lifetime.[3] Only Smith O'Brien, disgusted by a party most of whose members he saw 'wallowing in the mire of Whiggery', protested strongly at the Treason-Felony Bill of April 1848.[4] By July, when the Bill suspending Habeas Corpus in Ireland passed almost unopposed through all its stages in one day, the Repeal party had finally disintegrated, most of its members caught up in the scramble for places and patronage which had destroyed the first Repeal party.[5]

The dissolution of the bankrupt and policy-less Repeal Association in June 1848 marked the final collapse of the Repeal movement

[1] Only two Confederates, Smith O'Brien in Co. Limerick and Chisholm Anstey, the English barrister returned for Youghal, were successful in 1847, with two or three other sympathizers.

[2] Hansard, XCV, 752–99, 7 December 1847, Debate, Division.

[3] Hansard, XCV, 748, 7 December 1847, Division. Cf. O'Connell to Pigot, 13 August 1846, *O'Connell Corr.*, II, 383; Greville, *Journal*, 13, 17 August 1846, V, 417, 419; Auchmuty, *Wyse*, 191.

[4] Smith O'Brien to Duffy, 28 February 1848, O'Brien Papers; and his speech in April, much-interrupted by English M.P.s, in Gwynn, *Young Ireland and 1848*, 159, 169–70.

[5] Duffy, *Four Years of Irish History*, 420–1, calculated that of the party of 1847 'nearly twenty . . . accepted places for themselves and more than twenty habitually begged places for others'. See also Whyte, *Independent Irish Party*, 45–6. John O'Connell, a Whig ministerialist after 1848, himself became a place-man in 1857 as Clerk of the Hanaper Office in Ireland, but 'his position in the House of Commons, always insignificant', had long been 'one of obscurity': art., John O'Connell, *D.N.B.*

and the end of the O'Connellite tradition in Irish politics. O'Connellism had nothing to offer a starving and emigrating people, too demoralized to support or even to sympathize strongly with the Young Ireland rising of July 1848. O'Connell's movement, although undeniably nationalist in its origins and appeal, had been evolutionary and reformist in practice, reflecting the pragmatic and flexible genius of its creator and finding characteristic expression in the O'Connellite parliamentary party. Through their concentration on immediate political gains and advantages, O'Connell and his party had been drawn into that alliance with the Whig Government which had led to compromise solutions for Irish problems and which had in the end destroyed the party's independence.

O'Connellism had indeed always tended to subordinate social and economic questions to political demands, and O'Connell and his followers can scarcely be said to have evolved a coherent policy of social reform. As landlords and landholders, they had little interest in a radical reconstruction of Irish society and had certainly never been principally concerned with the vital and increasingly urgent problems of the land system. The Young Irelanders, despite a political failure apparently more complete even than that of O'Connellism, in reality held the key to the future, when the cause of national independence and self-government was to be linked to an equally powerful and well-organized demand for social reform. The ideals of James Fintan Lalor and the personality of John Mitchel connected one section of Young Ireland with the early Fenians and with the Irish revolutionary tradition, while William Smith O'Brien and Charles Gavan Duffy were in different ways the direct links between the first Irish parliamentary party and its successors, from the Irish Brigade (the 'Pope's Brass Band' of the 1850's) to the great party of Isaac Butt, Charles Stewart Parnell and John Redmond, with its firm basis on a programme of Home Rule and agrarian reform and with its political independence ensured by pledges and by the pressure of Irish public opinion.

Although O'Connell as a pioneer of mass political organization had many imitators and successors in England as well as in Ireland, he left no direct political heirs in his own country. The whole political tradition associated with his name died out, overshadowed by the Famine, discredited by failure and rendered obsolete by changes in the direction, methods and ideas of the Irish nationalist movement. In modern Ireland, Wolfe Tone and Robert Emmet (not to speak of later Irish leaders) are perhaps better known and certainly more widely admired than O'Connell. John Mitchel, whose *Jail Journal* constituted one of the most influential texts of the nationalist tradition, described O'Connell as a 'wonderful, mighty, jovial and mean old man' who had led the Irish people 'all wrong for forty years. He was a lawyer, and could never come to the point of denying and defying all British Law. He was a Catholic, sincere and devout; and would not see that the Church had ever been the enemy of Irish Freedom. He was an aristocrat, by position and taste; and the name of a Republic was odious to him.' For Mitchel, the O'Connellite doctrine of moral force in politics was 'the most astounding *organon* of public swindling since first man bethought him of obtaining money by false pretences'.[1]

Against this judgement might be set the verdict of Gladstone who in 1889, when he thought of O'Connell as having become like Chatham and Strafford only a name in history, made what he called 'a small effort at historical justice'. Almost from the beginning of his own career, Gladstone wrote, he had regarded O'Connell as 'the greatest popular leader whom the world had ever seen'. Now he ranked him above Kossuth or Mazzini as a national leader and saw him as the missionary of an idea, bent on restoring the public life of his country which had been ruined by the Union. Although Gladstone was not blind to some of O'Connell's defects and compared the O'Connellite party unfavourably with the party under Parnell, he praised O'Connell as a statesman who 'never for a moment changed his end [and] never hesitated to change his means'. In the light of the Home Rule issue, O'Connell seemed 'a prophet of the coming time'.[2] When his friends placed Parnell's grave near O'Connell's monument in Glasnevin, they did better than perhaps they knew.

The last word might rest with the Irish people. When in 1862 depression struck the Lancashire spinning industry, urgent appeals, some of them in verse, went out to the Irish in Yorkshire and the north of England to send contributions to their countrymen in the Lancashire mill towns. Fifteen years after his death, one aspect of O'Connell's career was still affectionately remembered:[3]

---

[1] John Mitchel, *Jail Journal* (1913), xxxv, 141.

[2] W. E. Gladstone, in *The Nineteenth Century*, XXV (1889), 149–68.

[3] *An Appeal to the English and Irish in Yorkshire on behalf of the Starving in Lancashire* (1862), quoted by J. A. Jackson, *The Irish in Britain*, 178, n. 10.

As t'aingul teuk wing, ah said, 'Fynd if ya can
A curly-wig'd, puddin-cheeked, double-chin'd man;
The name o' that darlin and conjuror's Dan,
An a shamrock he weers fur a badge.
He could squeeas aht o' t'Irish his theesands a year,
An if t'Poap an his Cardinals gate him up thear,
Cut t'tail off a comit an swing him dahn here,
For O'Connell's a jewel to cadge.'

APPENDIX A

IRISH ELECTORAL STATISTICS, 1832–1847

Results of General Elections, 1832–1841:

1. *1832*	Seats	Co. M.P.s	Bor. M.P.s	M.P.s Unopposed Cos.	Bos.		M.P.s Opposed Cos.	Bos.	
Repeal	39	20	19	10	4	(14)	10	15	(25)
Cons.	29[1]	19	10	12	4	(16)	7	6	(13)
Lib.	36	25	11	4	0	(4)	21	11	(32)
2. *1835*									
Repeal	34	20	14	7	4	(11)	13	10	(23)
Cons.	38	23	15	13	8	(21)	10	7	(17)
Lib.	33	21	12	12	4	(16)	9	8	(17)
3. *1837*									
Repeal	32	20	12	12	3	(15)	8	9	(17)
Cons.	34	20	14	16	5	(21)	4	9	(13)
Lib.	39	24	15	14	5	(19)	10	10	(20)
4. *1841*									
Repeal	18	12	6	6	5	(11)	6	1	(7)
Cons.	40	26	14	20	9	(29)	6	5	(11)
Lib.	47	26	21	18	13	(31)	8	8	(16)

5. *Contested Elections, Ireland (66 Constituencies)*

1832	1835	1837	1841	1847
45	36	34	20	26

See Gash, *Politics*, 440–1, for slightly different calculations for 1832, 1835 and 1837, and for a general discussion of the problems involved in establishing exact figures.

[1] Carrickfergus temporarily disfranchised, 1833–5.

6. *Registered Electors in Ireland, 1832–1848*

These figures show the increase of the Irish electorate between 1832 and 1837, the sharp fall in 1841, when the Repeal party suffered its major electoral reverse, the rise again in 1847 and the decline in 1848 with the collapse of the Repeal movement and under the impact of Famine emigration. But these movements, though highly indicative politically, remained almost insignificant in proportion to the total population, over 8,000,000 in 1841. Finally, it may be noted that where the relevant figures are available (as for 1835, 1837 and 1841), the total electorates of the 26 'plain' borough constituencies remained approximately half the size of those of the 8 'counties of cities and towns'.

Years	Counties	Boroughs, Counties of Cities and Towns	Totals
1832[1]	60,607	31,545	92,152
1835[2]	64,666	33,641	98,307
1837	76,046	44,321	120,367
1841[3]	57,103	39,771	96,874
1847	70,884	55,337	126,221
1848	59,309	48,830	108,139

[1] Dod, *Electoral Facts* (1852), 151.
[2] Return of . . . Electors, Ireland, P.P. 1841, XX, 615.
[3] Return of . . . Electors, Ireland, P.P. 1847–8, LVII, 210.

1. *The Repeal Party, 1832*

Name	Constituency	Religion
Baldwin, H.	Cork City	RC
Barron, H. W.	Waterford City	RC
Bellew, R. M.	Co. Louth	RC
Blake, M. J.	Galway Borough	RC
Blackney, W.	Co. Carlow	RC
Butler, Hon. P.	Co. Kilkenny	P
Callaghan, D.	Cork City	P
Finn, W. F.	Co. Kilkenny	RC
Fitzgerald, T.	Co. Louth	RC
Fitzsimon, C.	Co. Dublin	RC
Fitzsimon, N.	King's Co.	RC
Galwey, J. M.	Co. Waterford	RC
Grattan, H.	Co. Meath	P
Lalor, P.	Queen's Co.	RC
Lynch, A.	Galway Borough	RC
Macnamara, F.	Ennis	P
Macnamara, W. N.	Co. Clare	P
Mullins, F. W.	Co. Kerry	P
Nagle, Sir R.	Co. Westmeath	RC
O'Brien, C.	Co. Clare	P
O'Connell, C.	Co. Kerry	RC
O'Connell, D.	Dublin City	RC
O'Connell, J.	Youghal	RC
O'Connell, Maurice	Tralee	RC
O'Connell, Morgan	Co. Meath	RC
O'Connor, F.	Co. Cork	P
O'Conor Don, The	Co. Roscommon	RC
O'Dwyer, A. C.	Drogheda	RC
Roche, D.	Limerick City	P
Roche, W.	Limerick City	RC
Roe, J.	Cashel	RC
Ronayne, D.	Clonmel	RC

Name	Constituency	Religion
Ruthven, E. S.	Dublin City	P
Ruthven, E.	Co. Kildare	P
Sheil, R. L.	Co. Tipperary	RC
Sullivan, R.	Kilkenny City	RC
Talbot, J. H.	New Ross	RC
Vigors, N. A.	Carlow Borough	P
Walker, C.	Wexford Borough	P

2. Biographical Notes on Repeal M.P.s, 1832–1847

BALDWIN, Herbert: M.P. Cork City (1832–7); Catholic; a first cousin of Daniel O'Connell; landowner, with estate of Clohina, Co. Cork, which had been in his family since 1678; in 1875 the family owned 10,000 acres in the county.

BARRON, Henry Winston: M.P. Waterford City (1832–41, 1842–7, 1848–1852); Catholic; D.L. (Co. Waterford), J.P.; landowner, with estates and two seats in Cos. Kilkenny and Waterford, and newspaper-owner. Cr. Baronet (1841). His family was descended from the Fitzgeralds, Barons of Burnchurch; he m. only dau. of Sir Gregory Page Turner Bt.

BELLEW, Richard Montesquieu: M.P. Co. Louth (1832–52); Catholic; D.L. (Louth); landowner; 2nd son of Sir Edward Bellew, 6th Bt., and brother of Sir Patrick Bellew, 7th Bt., M.P. Co. Louth (1831–2, 1835–7), Lord-Lieutenant (Louth), who was cr. Baron Bellew (1848). R. M. Bellew was a Lord of the Treasury (1847–52). The family owned over 5,000 acres, n.a.v. £5,000, in Louth in 1875.

BLACKNEY, Walter: M.P. Co. Carlow (1831–5); Catholic landowner; D.L. (Co. Carlow); J.P. (Cos. Kilkenny and Carlow); known as 'Dr. Doyle's member'.

BLAKE, Martin Joseph: M.P. Galway Borough (1833–52); Catholic landowner; J.P.; head of the Blakes of Ballyglunin and connected with the family of Blake, Baronets, of Langham, Suffolk.

BLAKE, Sir Valentine: M.P. Galway Borough (1812–20, 1841–7); Protestant; 12th Bt., of Menlough or Menlo, succeeding his father in 1834. His heirs held only 2,030 acres, n.a.v. £350, in Galway in 1875.

BRABAZON, Sir William: M.P. Mayo (1835–40); Protestant landowner; succ. his father as 2nd Bt. (1803), of Brabazon Park; High Sheriff, Mayo (1826).

BROWNE, Robert Dillon: M.P. Mayo (1836–50); Protestant; J.P., D.L.; impecunious landowner, connected with family of Lord Kilmaine.

BUTLER, Hon. Pierce Somerset: M.P. Co. Kilkenny (1832–47); Protestant; D.L. (Co. Kilkenny); son of 11th Viscount Mountgarret; a landowner and Colonel in Army. In 1854 he brought an unsuccessful action against the 12th Lord Mountgarret to recover possession of valuable lands in Kilkenny, on grounds of Mountgarret's illegitimacy.

BUTLER, Pierce Somerset; M.P. Co. Kilkenny (1843–52); Protestant; son of Hon. P. S. Butler; Trinity College, Dublin, with highest classical honours; barrister; Captain in Kilkenny Militia.

CALLAGHAN, Daniel: M.P. Cork City (1830–49); Catholic; a Government contractor, merchant and distiller; son of an immensely successful Cork merchant.

FINN, William Francis: M.P. Co. Kilkenny (1832–7); Catholic barrister with commercial and newspaper interests; son of a rich tanner of Carlow; brother-in-law of Daniel O'Connell.

FITZGERALD, Thomas: M.P. Co. Louth (1832–5); Catholic landowner and West India proprietor.

FITZSIMON, Christopher: M.P. Co. Dublin; (1832–7); Catholic; D.L., J.P. (Cos. Wicklow and Dublin); landowner and barrister; m. Ellen, O'Connell's eldest daughter; Clerk of the Hanaper, Crown and Custos Rotulorum in Ireland (1837). His family owned some 2,000 acres, n.a.v. over £1,000, in Wicklow and Dublin in 1875.

FITZSIMON, Nicholas: M.P. King's Co. (1832–41); Catholic landowner in King's Co. and Co. Dublin, with seat at Broughall Castle, King's Co.; m. Katherine, 2nd dau. of Sir John Power, 1st Bt. (1841), the whiskey distiller, whose son James was M.P. for Co. Wexford (1835–47); cr. Kt. Bachelor (1841), and given post of Magistrate in head Police Office at Dublin (Feb. 1841) after taking Chiltern Hundreds. Known for obvious reasons as 'Fat-Simon'.

GALWEY, John Matthew: M.P. Co. Waterford (1832–5); Catholic; J.P., Grand Juror (Co. Waterford); wine-merchant and land-agent, with estate in Co. Cork, m. cousin of Henry Barron.

GRATTAN, Henry: M.P. Dublin City (1826–30), Co. Meath (1832–52); Protestant; second son and biographer of the great Henry Grattan, brother of the Whig James Grattan, M.P. Co. Wicklow (1820–41); J.P., barrister, landowner and owner-editor of *Freeman's Journal* until 1832. His representatives held 926 acres, n.a.v. £810, in Meath in 1875; his co-heiresses married into the Bellew and Esmonde families (Sir Thomas Esmonde, 7th Bt., Liberal M.P. Wexford Borough 1841–7).

LALOR, Patrick: M.P. Queen's Co. (1832–5); Catholic leaseholder and middleman; father of James Fintan Lalor, the revolutionary of 1848 and the theorist of tenant right.

LYNCH, Andrew: M.P. Galway Borough (1832–41); Catholic barrister at English Bar; appointed Master in Chancery in England (1838).

MACNAMARA, Francis: M.P. Ennis (1832–5); Protestant; Captain 8th Hussars, later Lieut.-Col. Clare Militia; D.L., J.P.; High Sheriff, Clare (1839); eldest son of W. N. Macnamara.

MACNAMARA, William Nugent: M.P. Co. Clare (1830–52); Protestant, J.P., High Sheriff, Clare (1798); landowner; Major in Army and seconded O'Connell in his duel with Alderman D'Esterre. His family, which claimed descent from the ancient Admirals of Munster, owned 15,000 acres, n.a.v. £6,932, in Clare in 1875.

MULLINS, Frederick William Beaufort: M.P. Co. Kerry (1831–7), Protestant landowner; eldest son of the Hon. and Rev. Frederick Mullins and grandson of Thomas, 1st Lord Ventry.

NAGLE, Sir Richard: M.P. Co. Westmeath (1832–41); Catholic landowner; 2nd Bt., of Jamestown; D.L. and High Sheriff (Westmeath).

O'BRIEN, Cornelius: M.P. Co. Clare (1832–47, 1852–7); Protestant; J.P.; landowner, solicitor and director of National Bank of Ireland; m. Margaret, dau. of Peter Long of Waterford and niece of William Roche. His family had 4,400 acres in Co. Clare in 1875.

O'BRIEN, William Smith: M.P. Ennis, as Tory Emancipationist (1828–1831), Co. Limerick as Liberal and Repealer (1835–49); Protestant; 2nd son of Sir Edward O'Brien, 4th Bt., of Dromoland, Co. Clare; educated Harrow and Trinity College, Cambridge; the leader of Young Ireland and of the rising of 1848.

O'CONNELL, Charles: M.P. Co. Kerry (1832–5); Catholic landowner, of Bahoss, Kerry; m. Kate, O'Connell's 2nd daughter.

O'CONNELL, Daniel: M.P. Co. Clare (1829–30), Waterford City (1830–1), Co. Kerry (1831–2), Dublin City (1832–6), Kilkenny Borough (1836–7), Dublin City (1837–41), Co. Cork (1841–7); Catholic; J.P., Kerry (1835–43, 1846–7), barrister (K.C. 1831), director (1834) and Governor (1841) of National Bank of Ireland, investor in O'Connell Brewery, leaseholder and landowner in Kerry (the Darrynane estate comprised 17,394 acres, n.a.v. £1,626, in 1875); descended from a family long settled in Kerry, whose first prominent member was Maurice O'Connell of Bally Carbery, High Sheriff of Kerry, who died in 1609; inherited property from his uncles, Maurice O'Connell of Darrynane and Daniel, Count O'Connell.

O'CONNELL, Daniel: M.P. Dundalk (1846–7); Catholic, youngest son of Daniel; succeeded his eldest brother Maurice as M.P. for Tralee (1853), and was later a Commissioner of Inland Revenue at Somerset House.

O'CONNELL, John: M.P. Youghal (1832–7), Athlone (1837–41), Kilkenny Borough (1841–7), Limerick City (1847–51), Clonmel (1853–7); Catholic barrister (Gray's Inn); 3rd and favourite son of Daniel; Clerk of the Hanaper in Ireland (1857–8).

O'CONNELL, Maurice: M.P. Co. Clare (1831–2), Tralee (1832–7, 1838–53); Catholic; eldest son of Daniel; m. Frances, only dau. of Bindon Scott, a landowner, of Cahircon, Co. Clare, a marriage which brought him £6,000 and little domestic happiness; director of National Bank, J.P. (Kerry), barrister.

O'CONNELL, Morgan: M.P. Co. Meath (1832–40); Catholic; 2nd son of Daniel; served with Irish South American Legion under Simon Bolivar and with Austrian Army; retired as Assistant-Registrar of Deeds in Ireland (1840–68) with salary of £1,200 p.a.

O'CONNELL, Morgan John: M.P. Co. Kerry (1835–52); Catholic; son of John O'Connell of Grenagh, Daniel O'Connell's brother; barrister, D. L. Kerry; m. dau. of Charles Bianconi, the Irish transport magnate.

O'CONNOR, Feargus: M.P. Co. Cork (1832–5), Nottingham (1847–52); Protestant; son of Roger O'Connor of Connorville, Co. Cork, the last owner of Dangan Castle, Co. Meath, and nephew of Arthur O'Connor, the rebel of 1798; barrister and landowner of Fort Robert, Co. Cork; unseated in 1835 for lack of property qualification. Later the Chartist leader.

O'CONOR DON, THE, Denis O'Connor: M.P. Co. Roscommon (1831–47); Catholic; J.P.; landowner, succeeding his father as M.P. and connected through his wife with the Whig Lords Charlemont and Leitrin. This well-known aristocratic family, descended from the last two 12th-century High-Kings of Ireland, had consistently maintained its position despite its inflexible Catholicism, and in 1875 owned 12,400 acres in Roscommon, n.a.v. £5,900.

O'DWYER, Andrew Carew; M.P. Drogheda (1832–5); Catholic barrister; unseated in 1835 for lack of property qualification, stood again and though successful, was unseated soon afterwards as being unduly elected; retired as Filacer of the Exchequer (1837) with subsequent pension of £3,000 a year.

POWELL, Caleb: M.P. Co. Limerick (1841–7); Protestant landowner.

ROCHE, David Vandeleur: M.P. Limerick City (1832–44); Protestant landowner in Clare and Limerick; J.P. (Co. Limerick), descended from a family which had produced mayors and M.P.s for Limerick since the early 18th century, and even earlier; cr. Bt. (1841).

ROCHE, Edmund Burke: M.P. Co. Cork (1837–55); Protestant landowner of Trabolgan, Co. Cork, from the same family as Edmund Burke; cr. an Irish peer as Lord Fermoy (1855), a title to which he had some hereditary claim; J.P.; Lord-Lieutenant, Co. Cork (1856–74).

ROCHE, William: M.P. Limerick City (1832–41); Catholic banker and landowner; son of Stephen Roche of Granagh Castle and Limerick, and cousin of David Roche: his family was one of the richest of the Catholic merchant dynasties in Limerick in the second half of the 18th century.

ROE, James: M.P. Cashel (1832–5); Catholic; small landowner, of Roesborough, Co. Tipperary; described by John O'Connell as 'one of the best and truest of our band' but by others as a very poor public speaker.

RONAYNE, Domick: M.P. Clonmel (1832–6); Catholic merchant with considerable interests in Dungarvan and Youghal; distant cousin and close crony of O'Connell. He died in 1836.

RUTHVEN, Edward Southwell: M.P. Downpatrick (1830–2), Dublin City (1832–6); Protestant landowner; m. dau. of Philip Crampton, Whig Solicitor-General (1831–4); known as 'Old Judy'.

RUTHVEN, Edward: M.P. Co. Kildare (1832–7); Protestant; son of E. S. Ruthven.

SHEIL, Richard Lalor: M.P. Milborne Port (1831), Co. Louth (1831–2), Co. Tipperary (1832–41), Dungarvan (1841–50); Catholic barrister (K.C. 1830); son of Edward Sheil, an Irish Cadiz merchant who acquired (1783) an estate in Co. Waterford. Educ. Stonyhurst and Trinity College, Dublin; m. 2nd, Anastasia, dau. and co-heiress of John Lalor of Cranagh and relict of Edmund Power of Gurteen, with estates in Tipperary and Waterford which Sheil administered during the minority of his step-son, John Power, M.P. Dungarvan (1837), Co. Waterford (1837–40). Commissioner of Greenwich Hospital (1838–9), Vice-President of the Board of Trade (1839–41), Judge Advocate-General (1841), Master of the Mint (1846–50), Minister at the Court of Tuscany (1850–1). Brother-in-law of R. M. Bellew.

SOMERS, John Patrick: M.P. Sligo Borough (1837–52 with intervals); Catholic; merchant (?)

SULLIVAN, Richard: M.P. Kilkenny Borough (1832–6); Catholic merchant, taking Chiltern Hundreds in 1836 to renounce his seat in Daniel O'Connell's favour.

TALBOT, John Hyacinth: M.P. New Ross (1832–41, 1847–52); Catholic landowner; formerly held post in Revenue Dept.; 2nd son of Matthew Talbot, by his 2nd wife Jane, Countess D'Arcy and related to family of Earls of Shrewsbury; D.L. (Co. Wexford), J.P.; married into wealthy banking family of Redmond. His 2nd dau. m. James Power, M.P. Co. Wexford (1835–47), the eldest son of Sir John Power, 1st Bt., the Irish whiskey magnate.

VIGORS, Nicholas Aylward: M.P. Carlow Borough (1832–5), Co. Carlow (1837–40); Protestant landowner; D.L. (Co. Carlow); Army officer and first Secretary of the Royal Zoological Society. Died 1840.

WALKER, Charles: M.P. Wexford Borough (1831–41); Protestant land-owner, with large estate near Wexford Town; son of a Master in Irish Chancery.

WHITE, Henry: M.P. Co. Leitrim (1812–24), Co. Longford (1824–32, 1837–47, 1857–61); Protestant landowner in Leitrim; younger brother of Luke White. A Repealer in the 1830's, he later became a steady Whig-Liberal and was cr. an Irish peer as Baron Annally (1854); Lord-Lieutenant, Co. Leitrim (1841–73).

WHITE, Luke: M.P. Co. Longford (1836–7, 1837–42), Protestant; eldest son of Luke White, the Dublin bookseller and lottery-office keeper who was thought to have left the largest fortune ever amassed by trade in Ireland; an extensive landowner in Longford.

In compiling these notes, which are intended as a guide to the social position and economic interests of most Repeal M.P.s, the following works have been consulted: John Burke, *A Genealogical and Heraldic History of the Commoners of Great Britain and Ireland* (1833–8); *Burke's Landed Gentry of Ireland*, ed. L. G. Pine (4th edn. 1958); G.E.C., *Complete Baronetage* (1900); *The Complete Peerage*, ed. Doubleday and Howard de Walden; Charles R. Dod, *Electoral Facts* (1852–3); Dod, *Peerage, Baronetage and Knightage of Great Britain and Ireland* (1842, 1850); Dod, *Parliamentary Pocket Companion* (1833–52); Edward MacLysaght, *Irish Families* (1957); Madden, *Ireland and Its Rulers; O'Connell Corr*; John O'Connell, *Recollections*; Sheil, *Sketches*; A. Webb, *Compendium of Irish Biography* (1878); *Return of Owners of Land . . . in Ireland* (1876); Sir Henry Blackall's Notes, *Irish Historical Studies*, XII, No. 46 (Sept. 1960), 139–43; Maureen Wall, 'The rise of a Catholic middle class in eighteenth-century Ireland', *Irish Historical Studies*, XI, No. 42 (Sept. 1958), 91–115.

In the Hobhouse Papers, British Museum Add. MSS 36467, 38–43, there is an interesting document relating to the Irish party in 1833. This is a letter, dated 9 April 1833 and marked 'Confidential', from one of the Whig whips, C.W. (Charles Wood, Joint Secretary to the Treasury, 1832–4) to Sir John Hobhouse, then Chief Secretary for Ireland. It consists mainly of a list compiled for Hobhouse's use of all the Irish Members, with appropriate comments and recommendations attached to almost all the names. Wood gave O'Connell between 36 and 40 followers, listed 26 M.P.s as 'Orangemen' or 'Conservative Opposition' and reckoned on about 29 fairly firm supporters of the Government. But he frankly admitted that there were very few 'real *steady* friends' of Government, most of the Whigs' supporters being, like Messrs. Fitzgibbon and O'Grady the M.P.s for Co. Limerick (see above, p. 67), members of 'that numerous body of Irish jobbers who support the Government de facto for loaves and fishes'. On the other hand Wood thought that between 15 and 17

Liberals and Repealers, who were believed secretly to detest or fear O'Connell, could be detached by civility, hospitality or jobs. These men were generally the most socially respectable of Irish left-wing M.P.s like the Catholic Liberals Henry Lambert, 'a gentleman', and Richard More O'Ferrall, also 'a gentleman . . . but of extreme opinions, a good deal of weight and an enthusiast', or the Repealers J. H. Talbot, Charles Walker and R. M. Bellew, who was described with Sir Richard Nagle as 'worth trying'; and The O'Conor Don, 'a gentleman, not wise but worth attention and civility'. In most of these cases, Wood's attitude (one common among Whig politicians at this time) was the product of wishful thinking and took far too little account of the extent of O'Connell's influence or the pressure of Irish opinion on M.P.s with popular constituencies. But certainly some men either deeply disapproved of O'Connell or had quarrels with him, for instance Lambert, William O'Reilly, M.P. for Dundalk and J. Talbot, M.P. for Athlone, none of whom enjoyed long careers as M.P.s once they had incurred O'Connell's enmity (see above, p. 54, n. 4).

3. *Occupations and Interests of the Repeal Party, 1832–5*

Land	Commerce	Land/ Commerce	Law	Army/ Land	J.P.	D.L.	Sheriff
31	6	8–9	11	5	15	8	3

The number of barristers, or at least of those who had been called to the English or Irish Bar, was almost certainly somewhat higher than that given in this table, but information on this point is not easily come by. Under the heading of 'Commerce' are included men with interests in trade, industry or finance. Only one member of the party, Francis Macnamara, seems to have been a serving Army Officer at the time of his election.

POLITICS (1830–47) AND LANDOWNERSHIP (1876).

Unfortunately, no statistics for individual landownership in Ireland exist in a convenient form for the period 1830–47. But a sample by families of the first official *Return of Owners of Land . . . in Ireland* (Dublin, 1876) bears out the statement in the text, above p. 76 (figures approximate and generally for land owned only in a single county):

Family	Repealer Acreage	N.a.v. (net annual valuation)
Annally (White)	12,160: Longford	£6,954
Bellew	5,000: Louth	£5,000
Blake (Sir V.)	2,030: Galway	£350
Brabazon	6,857: Mayo	£2,081
Fitzsimon	2,690: Dublin, Wicklow	£1,100
Grattan (reps. of Henry)	926: Meath	£810
Macnamara	15,000: Clare	£6,932
O'Connell (Darrynane)	17,394: Kerry	£1,626
O'Conor Don	12,400: Roscommon	£5,900
	Whig-Liberal	
Crawford (C'sburn)	5,748: Down	£5,943
Evans (Portrane)	1,456: Dublin	£1,427
Fitzwilliam	89,891: Wicklow	£46,444
Keane	8,909: Waterford	£3,237
Kenmare	91,080: Kerry	£25,252
More O'Ferrall	3,210: Kildare	£2,305
Rossmore (Westenra)	14,839: Monaghan	£13,427
Somerville	10,213: Meath	£9,131
	Conservative	
Abercorn (Hamilton)	47,615: Tyrone	£25, 420
Bandon (Bernard)	40,914: Cork	£19,215
Brooke	27,994: Fermanagh	£15,288
Dunsandle (Daly)	33,543: Galway	£11,860
Enniskillen (Cole)	29,635: Fermanagh	£18,795
Granard (Forbes)	14,978: Longford	£6,636
O'Neill	64,163: Antrim	£44,947

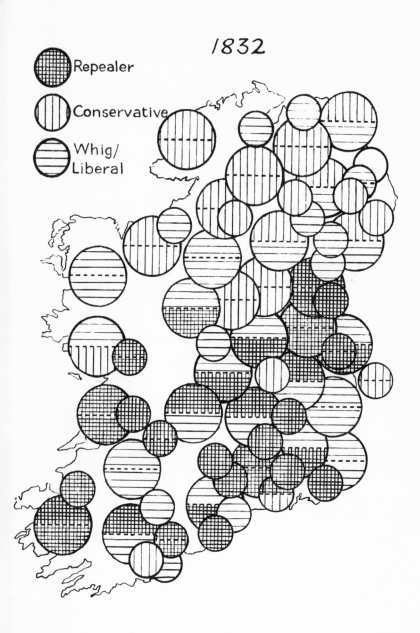

1832

Repealer

Conservative

Whig/
Liberal

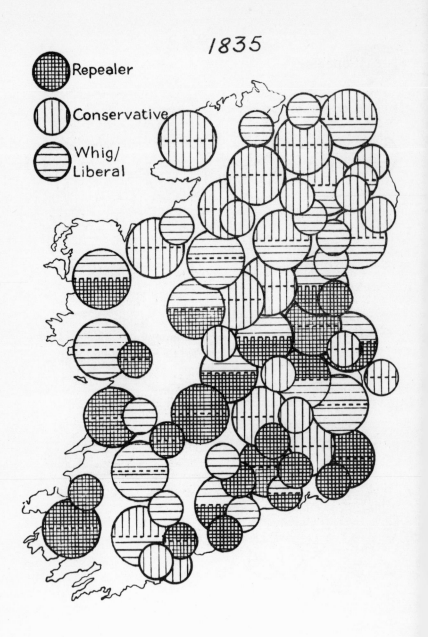

1835

Repealer

Conservative

Whig/
Liberal

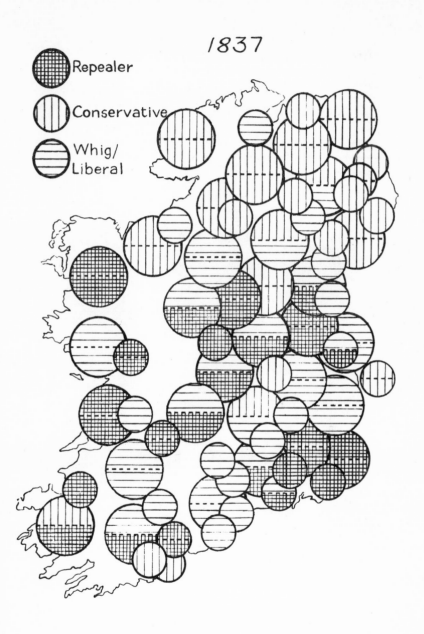

1837

Repealer

Conservative

Whig/
Liberal

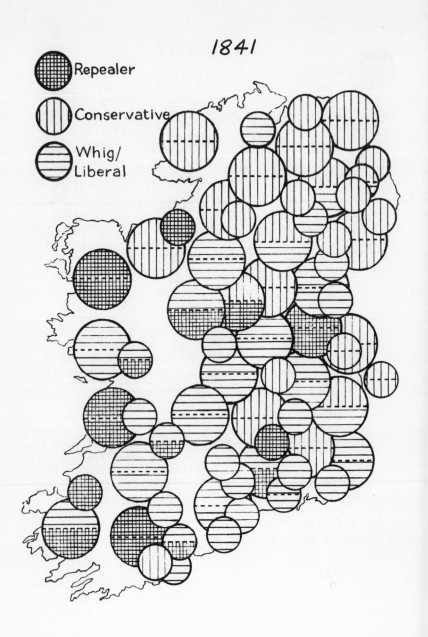

1841

Repealer

Conservative

Whig/
Liberal

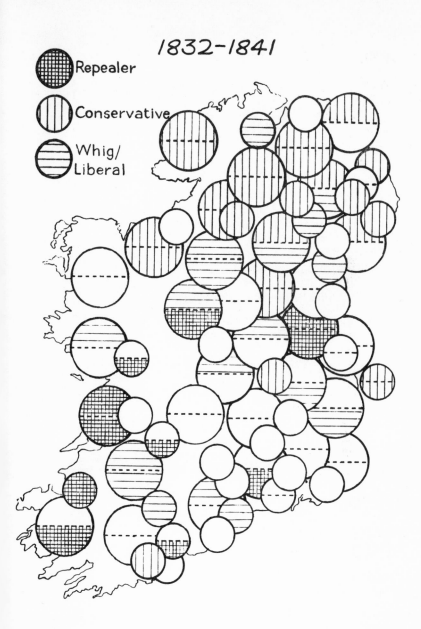

1832-1841

Repealer

Conservative

Whig/
Liberal

Bibliography

A. Manuscript Collections

I. *National Library of Ireland, Dublin*

Beresford-Leslie MSS, 4838:
    Correspondence, 1823–32, of Lord John George Beresford, Arch-
    bishop of Armagh (1773–1862). Typescript.

Drummond Papers, 2149–50:
Correspondence of Thomas Drummond (1797–1840), Under-Secretary for Ireland, 1835–40.

Monteagle Papers, 501–605:
Correspondence and Papers of Thomas Spring Rice, 1st Baron Monteagle (1790–1866).

Newport Papers, 796:
Correspondence of Sir John Newport, Bt. (1756–1843).

O'Brien Papers, 428–30, 433–4, 437:
Correspondence of William Smith O'Brien (1803–64), for years 1836–1846.

O'Connell Papers, 422–3, 696, 2152, 5242–3, 5759, 10523:
Correspondence of Daniel O'Connell (1775–1847), notably with his Constituents and with Richard Barrett, editor of *The Pilot*.

O'Connell Papers, uncatalogued:
This large collection had only recently been deposited in the National Library and had not been sorted or catalogued when I inspected it. It was clearly used in part by W. J. Fitzpatrick for his two-volume edition of the *Correspondence of Daniel O'Connell* (1888), the most important single source for O'Connell's personality and political career. Comparisons between published letters and their originals prove Fitzpatrick to have been an admirable editor, who went to considerable trouble to ensure that his edition should be as comprehensive as possible. He was remarkably accurate as to the transcribing and dating of letters, apparently guiltless of the common Victorian sin of conflating two or more letters into one, and ready, despite his admiration for O'Connell and devotion to his memory (and perhaps also because of a certain *naïveté*), to print material even if it occasionally showed O'Connell in a less than perfect or heroic light.

Fitzpatrick was a respectable historian, the author of several works on Irish history, including full-length lives of Bishop Doyle and Lord Cloncurry. His notes in the *Correspondence* are usually scholarly, informative and often entertaining on obscure Irish political figures. As the nephew of O'Connell's man of business, confidant and political agent, he was able to publish a great number of O'Connell's letters to P. V. Fitzpatrick, which are of the first importance for O'Connell's political career after 1830. But W. J. Fitzpatrick, even in a work running to 976 pages, could not print all the available material, and some of the letters which he omitted were of real importance (see, for example above, pp. 67–8 for letters on the 1841 Election, pp. 116–17 for Father Sheehan's letters on Waterford politics, p. 121 for O'Connell's funds, 1840–5, and pp. 285–6 for Smith O'Brien's important policy letter, 18 Dec. 1845). The main interest of this collection is that it allows several gaps to be filled, while at the same time it enhances the general value of Fitzpatrick's edition.

O'Connell–Drummond Papers, 2152:
Letters of Daniel O'Connell to Thomas Drummond, 1836–40.

O'Neill Daunt Journal, 2040:
Vol. I, 1842–53, of the Journal of William Joseph O'Neill Daunt, most of which was published as *A Life Spent for Ireland, being Selections from the Journals of the late W. J. O'Neill Daunt*, edited by his daughter and with an Introduction by W. H. Lecky (1896).

Pilltown Papers, 635:
Letters and Papers of the Brodigan family, of Pilltown House, Drogheda, relating to tithes in the parish of Colpe, Co. Meath.

Weldon Papers, 486:
Letters and Papers of the Weldon family, relating to tithes owned by Colonel Anthony Weldon in the parishes of Dunleckney and Augha, Co. Carlow.

II. *University College, Dublin*

O'Connell MSS, box-files:
Letters and Papers of Daniel O'Connell. This collection, though smaller than the uncatalogued O'Connell Papers, has similar interest and importance. It contains part of O'Connell's correspondence with Bentham (see above, p. 19 and n. 2) as well as Henry Warburton's letters to O'Connell (see, for example, pp. 59–60).

III. *Public Record Office, Belfast*

George Robert Dawson's Londonderry Election Diary, 1837 (Typescript).

IV. *British Museum, Additional Manuscripts*

Peel Papers:
Correspondence and Papers, official and private, of Sir Robert Peel, 2nd Bt. (1788–1850):
40309–10, 40459–61: Corr., 1830–46, with Arthur Wellesley, Duke of Wellington.
40313–14: Corr., 1822–41, with Sir Henry Hardinge.
40316: Corr., 1827–41, with John Copley, Baron Lyndhurst.
40318, 40446–52: Corr., 1834–50, with Sir James Graham, 2nd Bt.
40323: Corr., 1829–41, with William Vesey-Fitzgerald, Baron Fitzgerald and Vesci.
40333: Corr., 1828–41, with Henry Goulburn.

40340–1: Corr., 1822–41, with Charles Arbuthnot.
40421–9: General Correspondence, 1835–41.
40612: Official Papers, 1831–49.
40616–17: Corr., 1832–59, of F. R. Bonham with Sir James Graham *et al.*

Wellesley Papers:
Official and General Correspondence of Richard Colley Wellesley, 1st Marquis Wellesley (1760–1842):
37306–7: Correspondence, 1832–5.
37311–13: Correspondence, 1831–42.

V. *Public Record Office, London*
Home Office Papers:
H.O. 79/9: Entry Book, Private and Secret, 1830–64.
    100/232–4: Letters and Papers, Ireland, 1830.
    /235: Miscellaneous Correspondence, 1830.
    /236–46: Letters and Papers, 1831–5.
    /251: Miscellaneous Correspondence, 1836–7.
    /257: Miscellaneous Correspondence, 1838–51.
    122/15–19: Letter Books, General, 1830–47.

Russell Papers:
Correspondence, private and official Papers of Lord John Russell, 1st Earl Russell (1792–1878):
P.R.O. 30/22/2 A–F: Correspondence 1836–7.
        /3 A–E: Correspondence 1838–40.
        /4 A–E: Correspondence 1839–45.
        /5 A–C: Correspondence 1846.
Ellenborough Papers, P.R.O. 30/12/28/2–7:
Political Journal, 1830–41, of Edward Law, Earl of Ellenborough (1790–1871).

VI. *Other Manuscript Collections*
Quotations from the Ellice MSS in the National Library of Scotland, the Graham MSS at Netherby, the Salisbury MSS at Hatfield, the Melbourne Papers, the Diary of E. J. Littleton, the first Lord Hatherton, in the Staffordshire Record Office, and the Hughenden MSS, I owe to the kindness of M. G. Brock Esq., Fellow and Tutor of Corpus Christi College, Oxford.

B. *Parliamentary Proceedings, Reports, etc.*

Hansard's Parliamentary Debates, Third Series, I–XCVI (1830–48), cited as Hansard, Vol., cols., date and speaker.

Parliamentary Papers (P.P.): Titles, cited in abbreviated form in footnotes to the text, are here given in full.

I. *Reports of Select Committees and Commissions*

Second Report from the Select Committee on the state of the Poor in Ireland, 1830 (654), VII, 451.

Report from the Select Committee on the Dublin City Election, 1831 (145), IV, 447.

First and Second Reports from the Select Committee, Commons, on Tithes in Ireland, 1831–2 (177, 508), XXI, 1, 245.

First and Second Reports from the Select Committee, Lords, on Tithes in Ireland, 1831–2 (271, 663), XXII, 1, 181.

Report from the Select Committee appointed to inquire into the state of the Municipal Corporations in England and Wales and Ireland, 1833 (344), XIII, 1.

First Report of the Commissioners appointed to inquire into the Municipal Corporations in Ireland, 1835 (23), XXVII, 1; Part II, 1835 (28), XXVIII, 357; Part III, 1836 (29), XXIV, 1.

Report from the Select Committee appointed to inquire into the circumstances of the traffic and agreement alleged to have taken place between Daniel O'Connell and Alexander Raphael, Esquires . . ., County Carlow Election, 1836 (89), XI, 1.

Third Report from the Commissioners for inquiring into the Condition of the Poor in Ireland, 1836 [43], XXX, 1.

Report of the State of the Irish Poor in Great Britain, by G. C. Lewis, Esq., 1836 [40], XXXIV, 427.

Letter from N. W. Senior Esq. to His Majesty's Principal Secretary of State for the Home Department on the Third Report from the Commissioners for inquiring into the Condition of the Poor in Ireland, 1837 [90], LI, 241.

Remarks by G. C. Lewis Esq. on Poor Laws, Ireland, 1837 [91], LI, 253.

First, Second and Third Reports of G. Nicholls Esq. to His Majesty's Principal Secretary of State for the Home Department, on Poor Laws, Ireland, 1837 [69], LI, 201; 1837–8 [104, 126], XXXVIII.

First, Second and Third Reports from the Select Committee appointed to inquire how far the intentions of the Reform Bill are defeated by creating and registering fictitious and improper votes in Ireland, 1837-8 (259, 294, 643), XIII, 1, 339; Parts I and II.

Report from Select Committee on Belfast City Election (1841), 1842, V, 263.

II. *Accounts and Papers, Returns, etc.*

Only the most important sources are listed below; for other Returns consulted, see the relevant footnotes in the text.

Return of all Monies deposited with Sheriffs or Returning Officers, and of the expenditure of the same at the last General Election in Ireland, 1833 (401), XXVII, 255.

Returns of the Electors registered in each County, County of City, County of a Town and Borough in Ireland, entitled to vote under the Act 2 Will. IV c. 88, at the last General Election in Ireland, 1833 (177), XXVII, 289; 1836 (227), XLIII, 469; 1841 (240–II), XX, 615; 1847–8 (691), LVII, 203.

Return of Money advanced to ecclesiastical persons etc., 1833 (480), XXVII, 493.

Return of Arrears of Tithe due in Ireland in the several dioceses [from 1829], 1833 (509), XXVII, 499.

Returns of Amount of Composition for Tithes registered under several Acts; parishes in which tithes remain to be compounded, etc., 1834 (309, 333, 401), XLIII, 265, 311, 317.

Return of Applications for relief, 1831–1833; amount of claims each year, distinguishing clerical from impropriate claims, 1834 (382), XLIII, 321.

Return of Amount of Composition for Tithes in Ireland, distinguishing lay from ecclesiastical, 1835 (405), XLVII, 79.

Returns from the Ecclesiastical Commissioners, relating to Church Temporalities, Ireland, 1835 (460), XLVII, 89.

Proceedings at Armagh in consequence of transactions which took place at Keady between police and people, 1835 (179), XLVII, 99.

Return of the Appropriation of £1,000,000 voted for the Irish clergy; name, residence of and amount borrowed by each person etc., 1836 (355), XL, 51.

Orders issued to police since 1833, as to granting or withholding assistance; correspondence with Government on the subject of assistance for collection of tithes, rent, or execution of law process, 1836 (420), XL, 101.

Returns from clergy in Ireland to whom advances were made under the 3 & 4 Will. IV, c. 100, 1836 (562), XL, 135.

Return of the total number of persons . . . committed to prison since January 1831, in consequence of any proceedings connected with the recovery of Tithes etc., 1837–8 (253), XXXVIII, 319.

Return of Registered Electors, Co. Cavan, 1 January 1833–1 February 1841, State Paper Office, Dublin.

Return of Amount of Tithe Arrears due in Ireland etc., 1844 (305), XLIII, 555.

Return of Owners of Land, Ireland, 1876 (412) LXXX, published separately (Dublin, 1876).

C. *Contemporary Newspapers and Journals*

Annual Register
Dublin Evening Mail
Dublin Evening Post
Edinburgh Review
Freeman's Journal
Journal of the Dublin Statistical Society
Kilkenny Moderator
Lancet
Nation
Northern Whig
Pilot
Quarterly Review
The Times
Westminster Review

D. *Contemporary Pamphlets, Works, etc.*

Anonymous, *State of Ireland Considered, with an Enquiry into the History and Operation of Tithes* (Dublin, 1810).

— *The Belfast Election: Mr. Emerson Tennent's Claims and Conduct* Belfast, 1832).

Beaumont, Gustave de, *L'Irlande Sociale, Politique et Religieuse* (Paris, 1839), 2 vols.; Eng. trans. as *Ireland, Social, Political and Religious*, by W. Cooke Taylor (London, 1839).

Blackstone, Sir William, *Commentaries on the Laws of England* (London, 1811), 4 vols.

Burn, Richard, *The Ecclesiastical Law*, ed. Robert Phillimore (9th edn., London, 1842), 4 vols.

Butt, Isaac, *A Speech in Defence of the City of Dublin* (London, 1840).

— *The Poor Law Bill for Ireland Examined, Its Provisions, and the Report of Mr. Nicholls Contrasted with the Facts Proved by the Poor Inquiry Commission, in a letter to Lord Viscount Morpeth* (London, 1837).

Clements, Lord, *The Present Poverty of Ireland Convertible into the Means of her Improvement, under a well-administered Poor Law* (London, 1838).

Cobbett, W., *Cobbett's Manchester Lectures . . . [and] a Letter to Mr. O'Connell on his Speech made in Dublin, on 4th of January 1831, against the Proposition for the establishing of Poor-Laws in Ireland* (London, 1832).

Cotton, Henry, *Cui Bono? A Letter to the Right Hon. E. C. Stanley* (Dublin, 1838).

Crawford, W. S., *A Defence of the Small Farmers of Ireland* (Belfast, 1839).

Croly, Rev. David, *An Essay on Ecclesiastical Finance as regards the Roman Catholic Church in Ireland* (Cork, 1834).

D'Alton, John, *The History of Tithes, Church Lands and other Ecclesiastical Benefices, with a plan for the abolition of the former and the better distribution of the latter* (Dublin, 1832).

Daly, Thomas, *An Outline of a Plan for the Abolition of Tithes in Ireland* (Dublin, 1834).

Dickens, Charles, *Sketches by Boz* (London, 1890).

[Doyle, John Warren, Bishop of Kildare and Leighlin], *Letters on the State of Ireland; Addressed by J.K.L. to a Friend in England* (Dublin, 1825).

Dwyer, George, *A View of Evidence on the Subject of Tithes in Ireland* (London, 1833).

[Elrington, Thomas, Bishop of Ferns], *An Enquiry whether the Disturbances in Ireland have originated in Tithes or can be suppressed by a commutation of them, by S.N.* (London, 1823).

Finlay, John, *A Treatise on the Law of Tithes in Ireland* (Dublin, 1828).

[Grant, James], *Random Recollections of the House of Commons* (London, 1836).

Hall, Mr. and Mrs. S. C., *Ireland, Its Scenery and Character* (London, 1841–3), 3 vols.

Horton, Sir Robert Wilmot, *The Object and Effect of the Oath in the Roman Catholic Relief Bill* (London, 1838).

Inglis, Henry D., *Ireland in 1834: A Journey throughout Ireland during the Spring, Summer and Autumn of 1834* (3rd edn., London, 1835), 2 vols.

Kane, [Sir] Robert, *The Industrial Resources of Ireland* (2nd edn., Dublin, 1845).

Kinahan, Daniel, *A Digest of the Act for the Abolition of Tithes* (Dublin, 1838).

Lewis, George Cornewall, *On Local Disturbances in Ireland, and on the Irish Church Question* (London, 1836), cited as Lewis, *Disturbances*.

Lewis, S., *A Topographical Dictionary of Ireland* (London, 1837–42), 3 vols.

'Mediensis', *Tithes No Tax* (Dublin, 1823).

Moore, Thomas, *Memoirs of Captain Rock* (London, 1824).
— *Travels of an Irish Gentleman in search of a Religion* (London, 1833), 2 vols.

[Newman, J. H. *et al*], *Tracts for The Times*, by members of the University of Oxford (London, 1840), 5 vols.

O'Brien, William Smith, *Thoughts upon Ecclesiastical Reform [and] the Tithe Question* (Limerick, 1833).

O'Callaghan, John Cornelius, *The Green Book, or Gleanings from the Writing Desk of a Literary Agitator* (Dublin, 1845).

O'Connell, Daniel, *Seven Letters on the Reform Bill and the Law of Elections in Ireland* (Dublin, 1835).
— *A Memoir of Ireland, Native and Saxon, 1172–1660* (Dublin, 1843).

O'Connor, Feargus, *Letter to H.E. the Marquis of Anglesey* (Cork, 1832).

O'Leary, Joseph, *The Law of Statutable Composition for Tithes in Ireland* (Dublin, 1834).

Paley, William, *The Principles of Moral and Political Philosophy* (London, 1811), 2 vols.

Phillimore, Sir Robert, *The Ecclesiastical Law of the Church of England*, ed. Sir W. Phillimore (2nd edn., London, 1895), 2 vols.

Russell, Lord John, *Letter to the Electors of Stroud on the Principles of the Reform Act* (2nd edn., London, 1839).

Scrope, G. Poulett, *Plan of a Poor Law for Ireland, with a Review of the Arguments for and against it* (London, 1833).
— 'Foreign Poor Laws—Irish Poverty', *Quarterly Review*, LV (Dec. 1835).
— *How is Ireland to be Governed? A Question addressed to the New Administration of Lord Melbourne in 1834, with a Postscript, in which the*

same Question is addressed to the Administration of Sir Robert Peel in 1846 (London, 1846).

— *Letters to Lord John Russell on the Expediency of enlarging the Irish Poor-Law to the full extent of the Poor-Law of England* (London, 1846).

— *Remarks on the Irish Poor Relief Bill* (London, 1847).

Senior, William Nassau, *A Letter to Lord Howick on a Legal Provision for the Irish Poor* (London, 1831).

— *Journals, Conversations and Essays Relating to Ireland* (London, 1868), 2 vols., cited as Senior, *Journals*.

Smith, Adam, *An Inquiry into the Nature and Causes of the Wealth of Nations* (Edinburgh, 1828), 4 vols.

Spring Rice, T., *An Inquiry into the Effects of the Irish Grand Jury Laws* (London, 1815).

Tocqueville, Alexis de, *Journeys to England and Ireland*, ed. J. P. Mayer (London, 1958).

Wakefield, Edward, *An Account of Ireland, Statistical and Political* (London, 1812), 2 vols.

Whately, Richard, *Introductory Lectures on Political Economy* (4th edn., London, 1855).

Young, Arthur, *A Tour in Ireland in the Years 1776, 1777 and 1778, and brought down to 1779* (London, 1780).

E. Collections of Printed Correspondence, Memoirs, Diaries and Biographies

Anglesey, Marquess of, *One-Leg, The Life and Letters of Henry William Paget, First Marquess of Anglesey, K.G., 1768–1854* (London, 1961), cited as Anglesey, *One-Leg*.

Aspinall, A., *Lord Brougham and the Whig Party* (Manchester U.P., 1927).

— ed. *Three Early Nineteenth Century Diaries* (London, 1952), cited as Aspinall, *Three Diaries*.

Auchmuty, James Johnston, *Lecky, A Biographical and Critical Essay* (Dublin, 1945).

— *Sir Thomas Wyse, 1791–1862* (London, 1939), cited as Auchmuty, *Wyse*.

Bentham, J., *The Works of Jeremy Bentham*, ed. John Bowring (Edinburgh, 1843–59), 11 vols.

Blackburne, Edward, *Life of the Right Hon. Francis Blackburne* (London, 1874).

Broughton, Lord [John Cam Hobhouse], *Recollections of a Long Life, with Additional Extracts from His Private Diaries*, ed. Lady Dorchester (London, 1909–11), 6 vols., cited as Broughton, *Recollections*.

Buckley, J. K., *Joseph Parkes of Birmingham* (London, 1926).

Campbell, J., *Life of John, Lord Campbell*, ed. The Hon. Mrs. Hardcastle (London, 1881), 2 vols., cited as *Campbell*.

Cloncurry, *Personal Recollections of the Life and Times, with Extracts from the Correspondence of Valentine, Lord Cloncurry* (Dublin, 1849).

Creevey, Thomas, *The Creevey Papers: A Selection from the Correspondence & Diaries of the late Thomas Creevey, M.P.*, ed. Sir Herbert Maxwell (London, 1903), 2 vols.

— *Creevey*, ed. John Gore (London, 1949).

Daunt, W. J. O'Neill, *A Life Spent for Ireland, being Selections from the Journals of the late W. J. O'Neill Daunt*, edited by his daughter and with an Introduction by W. E. H. Lecky (London, 1896).

— *Personal Recollections of the late Daniel O'Connell, M.P.* (London, 1848), 2 vols.

Disraeli, B., *Lord George Bentinck: A Political Biography* (London, 1852), cited as Disraeli, *Bentinck*.

Ellenborough, Edward Law, Earl of, *A Political Journal, 1828–1830*, ed. Lord Colchester (London, 1881), 2 vols.

Fagan, William, *The Life and Times of Daniel O'Connell* (Cork, 1848), 2 vols., cited as Fagan, *O'Connell*.

Fitzpatrick, W. J., *The Life, Times and Contemporaries of Lord Cloncurry* (Dublin, 1855).

— *The Life, Times and Correspondence of the Right Rev. Dr. Doyle, Bishop of Kildare and Leighlin* (Dublin, 1880), 2 vols., cited as Fitzpatrick, *Doyle*.

Gash, Norman, *Mr. Secretary Peel, The Life of Sir Robert Peel to 1830* (London, 1961), cited as Gash, *Peel*.

Gladstone, William Ewart, 'Daniel O'Connell', *The Nineteenth Century*, No. 143, XXV (1889).

Graham, Sir James, *Life and Letters of Sir James Graham, Second Baronet of Netherby, 1792–1861*, ed. C. S. Parker (London, 1907), 2 vols., cited as Parker, *Graham*.

Gregory, Sir William, *An Autobiography*, ed. Lady Gregory (London, 1894).

Greville, *The Greville Memoirs, A Journal of the Reigns of King George IV, King William IV and Queen Victoria*, by Charles Greville, ed. Henry Reeve (London, 1913), 8 vols., cited as Greville, *Journal*.

Grote, Mrs., *The Personal Life of George Grote* (London, 1873).

Guizot, F., *An Embassy to the Court of St. James's in 1840* (London, 1862).

Gwynn, Denis, *Daniel O'Connell, The Irish Liberator* (London, 1929).
— *Daniel O'Connell and Ellen Courtenay* (Blackwell, Oxford, 1930).
— *The O'Gorman Mahon: Duellist, Adventurer and Politician* (London, 1934).

Hamilton, J. A., *Life of Daniel O'Connell* (London, 1888).

Holland, Lady, *Elizabeth, Lady Holland to Her Son, 1821–1845*, ed. Earl of Ilchester (London, 1946).

Ilchester, Earl of, *Chronicles of Holland House, 1820–1900* (London, 1937).

Jones, W. B., *Lord Derby and Victorian Conservatism* (Blackwell, Oxford, 1956).

Knatchbull-Hugessen, Sir Hughe, *A Kentish Family* (London, 1960), cited as *Kentish Family*.

Leader, R. E., ed. *Life and Letters of John Arthur Roebuck* (London, 1897), cited as Leader, *Roebuck*.

MacDonagh, Michael, *Daniel O'Connell and the Story of Catholic Emancipation* (Dublin and Cork, 1929).

Malmesbury, James Harris, 3rd Earl of, *Memoirs of an Ex-Minister* (London, 1884), 2 vols.

McLennan, J. F., *A Memoir of Thomas Drummond* (Edinburgh, 1867).

Melbourne, Lord, *Lord Melbourne's Papers*, ed. Lloyd C. Sanders (London, 1889), cited as *Melbourne Papers*.

Mill, J. S., *Letters of John Stuart Mill*, ed. Hugh Elliott (London, 1910), 2 vols.

Mitchel, John, *Jail Journal* (Dublin, 1913).

Monypenny, W. F. and Buckle, G. E., *The Life of Benjamin Disraeli, Earl of Beaconsfield* (London, 1910–20), 6 vols.

Morgan, Lady, *Lady Morgan's Memoirs*, ed. W. Hepworth Dixon (London, 1862), 2 vols.

Moore, Thomas, *Memoirs, Journal and Correspondence of Thomas Moore*, ed. Lord John Russell (London, 1853–4), 8 vols.

Morley, John, *The Life of Richard Cobden* (London, 1903).

Newman, Henry, *Newman's Apologia pro vita sua: The two versions of 1864 and 1865*, with an Introduction by Wilfrid Ward (O.U.P., 1931).

O'Brien, R. Barry, *Thomas Drummond, Under-Secretary in Ireland, 1835–40: Life and Letters* (London, 1889).

O'Connell, *Daniel O'Connell: His Early Life and Journal, 1795 to 1802*, ed. Arthur Houston (London, 1906).

— *Daniel O'Connell: Nine Centenary Essays*, ed. Michael Tierney (Dublin, 1947).

— *Correspondence of Daniel O'Connell, The Liberator*, ed. W. J. Fitzpatrick (London, 1888), 2 vols., cited as *O'Connell Corr.*

O'Connell, John, *Recollections and Experiences during a Parliamentary Career from 1833 to 1848* (London, 1849), 2 vols., cited as John O'Connell, *Recollections.*

O'Connell, Mrs. Morgan John, *The Last Colonel of the Irish Brigade, Count O'Connell, and Old Irish Life at Home and Abroad, 1745–1833* (London, 1892), 2 vols.

O'Connor, T. P., *Memoirs of an Old Parliamentarian* (London, 1929), 2 vols.

Ó Faoláin, Seán, *King of the Beggars: A Life of Daniel O'Connell* (London, 1938).

O'Reilly, Bernard, *John MacHale, Archbishop of Tuam* (New York, 1890) 2 vols.

O'Rourke, Very Rev. Canon John, *The Centenary Life of O'Connell* (7th edn., Dublin, 1900).

Packe, Michael St. John, *The Life of John Stuart Mill* (London, 1954).

Patterson, M. W., *Sir Francis Burdett and His Times, 1770–1844* (London, 1931), 2 vols.

Peel, *Sir Robert Peel from his Private Papers*, ed. Charles Stuart Parker (London, 1891–9), 3 vols., cited as Parker, *Peel.*

Read, Donald and Glasgow, Eric, *Feargus O'Connor: Irishman and Chartist* (London, 1961).

Russell, Lord John, *The Early Correspondence of Lord John Russell, 1805–1840*, ed. Rollo Russell (London, 1913), 2 vols.

Russell, Earl, *Recollections and Suggestions, 1813–1873* (London, 1875).

Sheil, Richard Lalor, *Sketches Legal and Political*, ed. M. W. Savage (London, 1855), 2 vols.

Smith, Sydney, *The Works of the Rev. Sydney Smith* (London, 1850).

Thackeray, William Makepeace, *The Paris Sketch Book, The Irish Sketch Book, with notes of a Journey from Cornhill to Grand Cairo* (London, 1875).

— *The Book of Snobs* (London, 1889).

Torrens, W. McCullagh, *Memoirs of the Right Honourable Richard Lalor Sheil* (London, 1855), 2 vols., cited as Torrens, *Sheil.*

— *Memoirs of the Right Honourable William, Second Viscount Melbourne* (London, 1898), 2 vols., cited as Torrens, *Melbourne.*

Trevelyan, Sir George Otto, *The Life and Letters of Lord Macaulay* (London, 1908).

Wallas, Graham, *The Life of Francis Place, 1771–1854* (London, 1951).

Walpole, Spencer, *Life of Lord John Russell* (London, 1889), 2 vols., cited as Walpole, *Russell.*

Wellesley, *The Wellesley Papers*, by the Editor of 'The Windham Papers' (London, 1914), 2 vols.

Whately, E. J., *Life and Correspondence of Richard Whately D.D., Late Archbishop of Dublin* (London, 1866), 2 vols.

F. Secondary Sources

I. *General Works*

Aspinall, A., *Politics and the Press, c. 1780–1850* (London, 1949).

Auchmuty, James Johnston, *Irish Education* (London, 1937).

Black, R. D. Collison, *Economic Thought and the Irish Question, 1817–1870* (C.U.P. 1960), cited as Black, *Economic Thought.*

Burke, O. J., *The History of the Catholic Archbishops of Tuam* (Dublin, 1882).

Church, R. W., *The Oxford Movement: Twelve Years, 1833–1845* (London, 1891).

Connell, K. H., *The Population of Ireland, 1750–1845* (O.U.P., 1950).

Daunt, W. J. O'Neill, *Eighty-Five Years of Irish History, 1800–1885* (London, 1896), 2 vols.

Davies, G. C. B., *Henry Phillpotts, Bishop of Exeter, 1778–1869* (London, 1954).

Dolléans, Edouard, *Le Chartisme* (Paris, 1949).

Duffy, Charles Gavan, *Young Ireland: A Fragment of Irish History, 1840–45* (London, 1896), 2 vols., cited as Duffy, *Young Ireland.*
— *Four Years of Irish History, 1845–1849* (London, 1883).

Edwards, R. Dudley and Williams, T. Desmond, eds., *The Great Famine: Studies in Irish History, 1845–52* (Dublin, 1956).

Engels, F., *The Condition of the Working Class in England*, trans. and eds. W. O. Henderson and W. H. Chaloner (Blackwell, Oxford, 1958).

Eversley, C. Shaw-Lefevre, Viscount, *Peel and O'Connell* (London, 1887).

Finlayson, G. B. A. M., *The Municipal Corporations Act, 1835* (unpublished B.Litt. Thesis, Oxford University, 1959).

Freeman, T. W., *Pre-Famine Ireland* (Manchester U.P., 1957).

Gash, Norman, *Politics in the Age of Peel: A Study in the Technique of Parliamentary Representation, 1830–1850* (London, 1953), cited as Gash, *Politics*.
— *Mr. Secretary Peel* (see Section E).

Gwynn, Denis, *Young Ireland and 1848* (Cork U.P., 1949).

Halévy, Elie, *A History of the English People in the Nineteenth Century*, translated by E. I. Watkin (London, 1949–51), 6 vols., cited as Halévy, *History*.

Inglis, Brian, *The Freedom of the Press in Ireland, 1784–1841* (London, 1954).

Jackson, John Archer, *The Irish in Britain* (London, 1963).

Jones, W. B., *Lord Derby and Victorian Conservatism* (see Section E).

Killen, W. D., *Ecclesiastical History of Ireland* (London, 1875), 2 vols.

Kitson Clark, G., *Peel and the Conservative Party, 1832–41* (London, 1929).

Lecky, W. E. H., *Leaders of Public Opinion in Ireland* (London, 1912), 2 vols.

Lynch, Patrick and Vaizey, John, *Guinness's Brewery in the Irish Economy, 1759–1876* (C.U.P., 1960).

Maccoby, S., *English Radicalism, 1832–52* (London, 1935).

Machin, G. I. T., *The Catholic Question in English Politics, 1820 to 1830* (O.U.P., 1964).

Madden, Daniel Owen, *Ireland and Its Rulers Since 1829* (London, 1843), 3 vols.

Martineau, Harriet, *History of England during the Thirty Years Peace* (London, 1849), 2 vols.

Mathieson, William Law, *English Church Reform, 1815–40* (London, 1923).

McCord, Norman, *The Anti-Corn Law League, 1838–46* (London, 1958).

McDowell, R. B., *Public Opinion and Government Policy in Ireland, 1801–1846* (London, 1952), cited as McDowell, *Public Opinion*.
— ed. *Social Life in Ireland, 1800–45* (Dublin, 1957).

Nicholls, George, *A History of the Irish Poor Law* (London, 1856).

O'Brien, George, *The Economic History of Ireland from the Union to the Famine* (London, 1921).

O'Brien, R. Barry, *The Parliamentary History of the Irish Land Question* (London, 1880).
— *Fifty Years of Concessions to Ireland, 1831–1881* (London, 1883), 2 vols.
— *Thomas Drummond* (see Section E).
— ed. *Two Centuries of Irish History, 1691–1870* (London, 1907).

O'Connor, Sir James, *History of Ireland* (London, 1925), 2 vols.

O'Hegarty, P. S., *A History of Ireland under the Union, 1801–1922* (London, 1952).

Reynolds, James, *The Catholic Emancipation Crisis in Ireland, 1823–1829* (Yale U.P., 1954).

Schoyen, A. R., *The Chartist Challenge: A Portrait of George Julian Harney* (London, 1958).

Smellie, K. B., *A Hundred Years of English Government* (2nd edn., London, 1950).

Southgate, Donald, *The Passing of the Whigs, 1832–1886* (London, 1962).

Strauss, E., *Irish Nationalism and British Democracy* (London, 1951).

Times, The History of The Times: Vol. I, *'The Thunderer' in the Making, 1785–1841*; II, *The Tradition Established, 1841–1884* (London, 1935, 1939).

Turberville, A. S., *The House of Lords in the Age of Reform, 1784–1837* (London, 1958).

Venn, J. A., *Foundations of Agricultural Economics* (C.U.P., 1923).

Webb, John J., *Municipal Government in Ireland* (Dublin, 1918).

Whyte, J. H., *The Independent Irish Party, 1850–9* (O.U.P., 1958).

Wilmer, Helen E., *The Property Qualifications of Members of Parliament* (London, 1943).

Woodham-Smith, Cecil, *The Great Hunger: Ireland, 1845–9* (London, 1962).

Woodward, E. L., *The Age of Reform, 1815–1870* (2nd edn., O.U.P., 1962).

II. *Articles in Learned Journals, Periodicals, etc.*

Aspinall, A., 'The Irish Proclamation Fund, 1800–42'; 'The Use of Irish Secret Service Money in subsidising the Irish Press', *English Historical Review*, LVI (April, Oct. 1941), 265–80, 639–46.

Blackall, Sir Henry and J. H. Whyte, 'Correspondence on O'Connell and the repeal party', *Irish Historical Studies*, XII, No. 46 (Sept. 1960), 139–43, cited as Blackall, 'Corr.'.

Brock, M. G., 'Politics at the Accession of Queen Victoria', *History Today*, III, No. 5 (May 1953), 329–38.

Broderick, John F., S.J., 'The Holy See and the Irish Movement for the Repeal of the Act of Union with England, 1829–47', *Analecta Gregoriana* LV (Rome, 1951), cited as Broderick, 'The Holy See'.

Clarke, Randall, 'The relations between O'Connell and the Young Irelanders', *Irish Historical Studies*, III, No. 9 (March 1942), 18–30.

Connell, K. H., 'Some unsettled problems in English and Irish Population History, 1750–1841', *Irish Historical Studies*, VII, No. 28 (Sept. 1951), 225–34.

— 'Peasant Marriage in Ireland after the Great Famine'; 'The Potato in Ireland', *Past and Present*, Nos. 12 and 23 (Nov. 1957, Nov. 1962), 76–91, 57–71.

Edwards, R. D., 'The contribution of Young Ireland to the development of the Irish national idea', in *Féilscríbhínn Torna; Essays and Studies Presented to Professor Taghg Ua Donnchadha*, ed. Séamus Pender (Cork, 1947).

Graham, A. H., 'The Lichfield House Compact, 1835', *Irish Historical Studies*, XII, No. 47 (March 1961), 209–25.

Horgan, John H., 'O'Connell: The Man', in *Daniel O'Connell: Nine Centenary Essays*, ed. Michael Tierney (Dublin, 1949).

Hughes, E., 'The Bishops and Reform, 1831–3: Some Fresh Correspondence', *English Historical Review*, LVI, No. 223 (July 1941), 459–90.

Inglis, Brian, 'O'Connell and the Irish Press, 1800–42', *Irish Historical Studies*, VIII, No. 29 (March 1952), 1–27.

Johnson, D. W. J., 'Sir James Graham and the "Derby Dilly" ', *University of Birmingham Historical Journal*, IV (1953–4), 66–80.

Kemp, Betty, 'The General Election of 1841', *History*, XXXVII (June 1952), 146–57.

Kennedy, B. A., 'Sharman Crawford's Federal Scheme for Ireland', in *Essays in British and Irish History in honour of James Eadie Todd*, eds. H. A. Cronne, T. W. Moody and D. B. Quinn (London, 1949).

Kennedy, David, 'Education and the People', in *Social Life in Ireland, 1800–45*, ed. R. B. McDowell (Dublin, 1957).

Large, David, 'The House of Lords and Ireland in the Age of Peel, 1832–50', *Irish Historical Studies*, IX, No. 36 (Sept. 1955), 367–99, cited as Large, 'House of Lords'.

Lavrosky, V., 'Tithe Commutation as a Factor in the Gradual Decrease of Landownership by the English Peasantry', *Economic History Review*, IV, No. 3 (Oct. 1933), 273–89.

McDowell, R. B., 'The Irish Executive in the Nineteenth Century', *Irish Historical Studies*, IX, No. 35 (March 1955), 264–80.
— 'Ireland on the Eve of the Famine', in *The Great Famine: Studies in Irish History, 1845–52*, eds. R. D. Edwards and T. D. Williams (1956).

Nowlan, Kevin B., 'The Political Background', in *The Great Famine: Studies in Irish History*, eds. Edwards and Williams.

O'Higgins, Rachel, 'Irish Trade Unions and Politics, 1830–50', *The Historical Review*, IV, No. 2 (1961), 208–17.

O'Raifeartaigh, T., 'Mixed Education and the Synod of Ulster, 1831–40', *Irish Historical Studies*, IX, No. 35 (March 1955), 281–99.

Simington, Robert C., 'The Tithe Applotment Books of 1834', *Journal of the Eire Department of Agriculture*, XXXVIII, No. 2 (1941), 289–343.
— 'Note [on Tithe Applotment Books]', *Analecta Hibernica*, X (1941), 293–8.

Thompson, F. M. L., 'Whigs and Liberals in the West Riding, 1830–1860', *English Historical Review*, LXXIV, No. 291 (April 1959), 214–39.

Wall, Maureen, 'The rise of a Catholic middle class in eighteenth-century Ireland', *Irish Historical Studies*, XI, No. 42 (Sept 1958), 91–115.

Whyte, J. H., 'Daniel O'Connell and the repeal party', *Irish Historical Studies*, XI, No. 44 (Sept. 1959), 297–316.
— 'The Influence of the Catholic Clergy on Elections in Nineteenth Century Ireland', *English Historical Review*, LXXV, No. 295 (April 1960), 239–44.

Wilson, J. M., 'Statistics of Crime in Ireland, 1842 to 1856', *Journal of the Dublin Statistical Society* (Nov. 1857).

G. Works of Reference

Burke, John, *A Genealogical and Heraldic History of the Commoners of Great Britain and Ireland* (London, 1833–8), 4 vols.

Burke's Landed Gentry of Ireland, ed. L. G. Pine (4th edn., London, 1958).

G.E.C., *Complete Baronetage* (Exeter, 1900–6), 5 vols.

G.E.C., *The Complete Peerage*, eds. The Hon. Vicary Gibbs, H. A. Doubleday, Lord Howard de Walden and others (London, 1910–40), 13 vols.

Dictionary of National Biography, eds. Leslie Stephen and Sidney Lee (London, 1910–).

Dod, Charles R., *The Peerage, Baronetage and Knightage of Great Britain and Ireland* (London, 1842, 1850).

— *Electoral Facts, 1832–52* (London, 1852, 1853).

— *Parliamentary Pocket Companion* (London, 1833–47, published annually), cited as Dod, *P.P.C.*

MacLysaght, Edward, *Irish Families: Their Names, Arms and Origins* (Dublin, 1957).

Webb, Alfred, *A Compendium of Irish Biography* (Dublin, 1878).

Index

Abercorn, 2nd Marquess of, 104
Abercromby, James, 60, 97 n., 132 and n.; as Speaker, 140, 142, 193, 245 n.
Aberdeen, George Gordon, 4th Earl of, 191
Abrahams, Dr., R.C. Bishop of Waterford, 56 n., 112
Acheson, Viscount, 16, 71, 96, 97 n., 104
Acland, Sir Thomas, 197
Acton, W., 100
Adelaide, Queen, 136 and n.
Althorp, John Charles Spencer, Viscount, uneasy at O'Connell's arrest, 23; meets O'Connell on Irish Reform Bill, 32; and Irish Church, 39–40, 41; and Coercion Bill, 49; in Grey Government, 129, 131, 132; and Grey's resignation, 133, 134 and ns.; as 3rd Earl Spencer, 135, 142; controversy with Sheil, 151; 158, 211; on Lansdowne, 216; n. 270
Alvanley, 2nd Lord, 156 and n.
Anglesey, Henry William Paget, 1st Marquess of, patron of Sheil, 18 and n.; tries to buy off O'Connell, 21 and n.; campaign against O'Connell, 22–3; abused by O'Connell, 25, 39; and state of Ireland, 45–6; and 1832 Dublin election, 119; retires from Ireland, 129 and n.; on Irish tithes, 186; on Poor Law, 210 n.
Anglican Church, in Ireland, and primary education, 28; revenues, membership and position, 36–7, 37 n.; Temporalities Act, 37–42; as

political issue, 129, 131; and tithes, 167, 169, 173–4, 182–3, 186–8, 199–200; Sheil on, 185; Bishop Doyle on, 205 n. See also Appropriation
Annual Register, 62, 70, 220 n.
Anstey, Chisholm, 295 n.
Anti-Corn Law League, xv; O'Connell's support, of 165 and n., 264, 265–6; compared to Repeal Association, 269–70
Anti-Tory Association, 58, 79, 89, 93 n.
Antrim, Co., 32, 97, 104, 105
Appropriation, Lay, in Temporalities Bill, 39–42; divides Grey Government, 129, 131–2; and dismissal of Melbourne, 135–6; and defeat of Peel, 143–4; and Irish party, 188, 191; and tithe question, 192–7, 200; 221, 249, 251
Arbuthnot, Charles, 238, 257–8
Archbold, Robert, 275
Archdale, General Mervyn, 105
Archdale, Captain Mervyn, 105
Armagh, Archbishop of, see Beresford, Lord J. G.
Armagh, borough, 51, 104, 108, 109, 234
Armagh, Co., 97, 104, 178
Arms Bill (Ireland), 273–4
Ashbourne, 1st Lord, 207
Athlone, borough, 58, 61, 106, 108 n., 233 n., 234
Attwood, Thomas, 48, 78, 220

Baldwin, Dr. Herbert, 53–4, 151, App. B, 302

335

Q

F